THE NEW INTERNATIONAL

WEBSTER'S POCKET SPELLING DICTIONARY

OF THE ENGLISH LANGUAGE

◆◆◆

TRIDENT PRESS INTERNATIONAL

Published by

Trident Press International

1998 EDITION

Cover Design Copyright © Trident Press International
Text Copyright © 1997 J. Radcliffe

ISBN 1-888777-51-6

A

aard´vark
aard´wolf
a·back´
ab´a·cus
a·bac·te´ri·al
a·baft´
ab-a-lo´ne
a·ban´don
a·ban´don-a·ble
a·ban´doned
a·ban´don·er
a·ban´don-ment
a·base´
a·based´
a·bas´ed·ly
a·base´ment
a·bas´er
a·bash´
a·bash´ed·ly
a·bash´ment
a·bas´ing
a·bat´a·ble
a·bate´
a·bate´ment
a·bat´er
a·bat´ing
ab-ax´i·al
ab´ba·cy
ab-bé´
ab´bess
ab´bey

ab´bot
ab´bot·cy
ab-bre´vi-ate
ab-bre´vi-at·ed
ab-bre´vi-at-ing
ab-bre-vi-a´tion
ab-bre´vi-a-tor
ab-bre´vi-a-to·ry
ab´di-ca·ble
ab´di-cate
ab´di-cat-ing
ab-di-ca´tion
ab´di-ca-tive
ab´di-ca-tor
ab´do-men
ab-dom´i-nal
ab-dom´i-nal·ly
ab-du´cent
ab-duct´
ab-duc´tion
ab-duc´tor
a·beam´
a·be-ce-dar´i·an
a·bed´
ab-er´rance
ab-er´ran·cy
ab-er´rant
ab-er´rant·ly
ab-er-ra´tion
ab-er-ra´tion-al
a·bet´
a·bet´ment
a·bet´tal

a·bet´ted
a·bet´ting
a·bet´tor
a·bey´ance
a·bey´ant
ab-hor´
ab-horred´
ab-hor´rence
ab-hor´rent
ab-hor´rent·ly
ab-hor´ring
a·bid´ance
a·bide´
a·bid´ing
a·bid´ing·ly
a·bid´ing-ness
a·bil´i-ties
a·bil´i·ty
a·bi-o-gen´e-sis
a·bi-o-ge-net´ic
a·bi-o-gen´ic
a·bi-og´e-nist
a·bi-ot´ic
ab-ject´, ab´ject
ab-jec´tion
ab-ject´ly
ab-ject´ness
ab-ju-ra´tion
ab-jur´a-to·ry
ab-jure´
ab-jur´er
ab-jur´ing
ab-late´

1

ab·la′tion
ab′la·tive
ab′laut
a·blaze′
a′ble
able–bodied
a′bler
a′blest
a·bloom′
ab′lu·ent
ab·lu′tion
ab·lu′tion·ar·y
a′bly
ab′ne·gate
ab·ne·ga′tion
ab′ne·ga·tive
ab′ne·ga·tor
ab·nor′mal
ab·nor·mal′i·ties
ab·nor·mal′i·ty
ab·nor′mal·ly
ab·nor′mal-ness
ab·nor′mi·ty
a·board′
a·bode′
a·boil′
a·bol′ish
a·bol′ish-a·ble
a·bol′ish·er
a·bol′ish-ment
ab-o-li′tion
ab-o-li′tion-ism
ab-o-li′tion-ist

a·bom′i-na·ble
a·bom′i-na·ble-ness
a·bom′i-na·bly
a·bom′i-nate
a·bom′i-nat·ed
a·bom-i-na′tion
ab-o-rig′i-nal
ab-o-rig-i-nal′i·ty
ab-o-rig′i-nal·ly
ab-o-rig′i·ne
a·bort′
a·bor′ti-cide
a·bor′ti-fa′cient
a·bor′tion
a·bor′tion-ist
a·bort′ive
a·bor′tive·ly
a·bor′tive-ness
a·bound′
a·bound′ing
a·bound′ing·ly
a·bout′
about–face
a·bove′
a·bove′board
a·bove′ground
a·bove′men-tioned
ab-ra-ca-dab′ra
a-brad′a-ble
a·brad′ant
a·brade′
a·brad′ed
a·brad′er

a·brad′ing
a·bran′chi·an
a·bran′chi-ate
a·bra-si-om′e-ter
a·bra′sion
a·bra′sive
a·bra′sive·ly
a·bra′sive-ness
ab-re-act′
ab-re-ac′tion
ab-re-ac′tive
a·breast′
a·bridge′
a·bridge′a·ble
a·bridg′er
a·bridg′ing
a·bridg′ment
a·bris′tle
a·broach′
a·broad′
ab′ro-ga-ble
ab′ro-gate
ab′ro-gat·ed
ab′ro-gat-ing
ab-ro-ga′tion
ab′ro-ga-tive
ab′ro-ga-tor
ab-rupt′
ab-rup′tion
ab-rupt′ly
ab-rupt′ness
ab′scess
ab′scessed

ab-scise´
ab-scis´sa
ab-scis´sion
ab-scond´
ab-scond´ed
ab-scond´ence
ab-scond´er
ab´sence
ab´sent *(adj.)*
ab-sent´ *(v.)*
ab-sen-ta´tion
ab-sen-tee´
ab-sen-tee´ism
ab´sent·ly
ab´sent-mind·ed
ab´sent-ness
ab´sinthe
ab-sin´thi·an
ab´so-lute
ab´so-lute´ly
ab-so-lute´ness
ab´so-lu´tion
ab´so-lut-ism
ab´so-lut-ist
ab´so-lu-tis´tic
ab´so-lu-tive
ab´so-lut-ize
ab-sol´u-to·ry
ab-solv´a·ble
ab-solve´
ab-solved´
ab-sol´vent
ab-solv´er

ab-solv´ing
ab-sorb´
ab-sorb´a·ble
ab-sorb-a-bil´i·ty
ab-sorb´ance
ab-sorbed´
ab-sorb´ed·ly
ab-sorb´ed-ness
ab-sor-be-fa´cient
ab-sorb´en·cy
ab-sorb´ent
ab-sorb´er
ab-sorb´ing
ab-sorb´ing·ly
ab-sorp´tance
ab-sorp´tion
ab-sorp´tive
ab-stain´
ab-stained´
ab-stain´er
ab-ste´mi-ous
ab-ste´mi-ous·ly
ab-sten´tion
ab-sten´tious
ab-ster´gent
ab-ster´sion
ab´sti-nence
ab´sti-nent
ab´sti-nent·ly
ab´stract *(n., adj.)*
ab-stract´ *(v.)*
ab-stract´ed
ab-stract´ed·ly

ab-stract´ed-ness
ab-stract´er
ab-strac´tion
ab-strac´tion-al
ab-strac´tion-ism
ab-strac´tive
ab-strac´tive·ly
ab´stract·ly
ab´stract-ness
ab-stric´tion
ab-struse´
ab-struse´ly
ab-struse´ness
ab-surd´
ab-surd´ism
ab-surd´i·ty
ab-surd´ly
ab-surd´ness
a·bub´ble
a·bu´li·a
a·bu´lic
a·bun´dance
a·bun´dant
a·bun´dant·ly
a·bus´a·ble
a·buse´
a·bused´
a·bus´er
a·bus´ing
a·bu´sive
a·bu´sive·ly
a·bu´sive-ness
a·but´

3

a·but´ment
a·but´tal
a·but´ted
a·but´ter
a·but´ting
a·buzz´
a·bysm´
a·bys´mal
a·bys´mal·ly
a·byss´
a·byss´al
a·ca´cia
ac´a-deme
ac-a-de´mi·a
ac-a-dem´ic
ac-a-dem´i-cal
ac-a-dem´i-cal·ly
ac-a-de-mi´cian
ac-a-dem´ics
a·cad´e·my
a·cap-pel´la
a·cau´dal
a·cau´date
a·cau-les´cent
a·cau´line
a·caus´al
a·cau-sal´i·ty
ac-cede´
ac-ced´ence
ac-ce-le-ran´do
ac-cel´er-ant
ac-cel´er-ate
ac-cel-er-a´tion

ac-cel´er-a-tive
ac-cel´er-a-tor
ac-cel´er-a-to·ry
ac´cent *(n., v.)*
ac-cent´ *(v.)*
ac-cen´tu-ate
ac-cen-tu-a´tion
ac-cept´
ac-cept-a-bil´i·ty
ac-cept´a·ble
ac-cept´a·bly
ac-cept´ance
ac-cept´ant
ac-cep-ta´tion
ac-cept´ed
ac-cept´er
ac-cep´tor
ac´cess
ac-ces´sa·ry
ac-ces-si-bil´i·ty
ac-ces´si·ble
ac-ces´si·bly
ac-ces´sion
ac-ces-so´ri·al
ac-ces´so-ri·ly
ac-ces´so-rize
ac-ces´so·ry
ac´ci-dence
ac´ci-dent
ac-ci-den´tal
ac-ci-den´tal·ly
ac-cip´i-tral
ac-claim´

ac-claim´ing
ac-cla-ma´tion
ac-clam´a-to·ry
ac-cli´mat-a·ble
ac-cli´mate
ac-cli-ma´tion
ac-cli-ma-ti-za´tion
ac-cli´ma-tize
ac-cliv´i·ty
ac-cli´vous
ac-co-lade´
ac´co-lade
ac-com´mo-date
ac-com´mo-dat-ing
ac-com-mo-da´tion
ac-com-mo-da´-
   tion·al
ac-com´mo-da-tive
ac-com´pa-nied
ac-com´pa-nies
ac-com´pa-ni-ment
ac-com´pa-nist
ac-com´pa·ny
ac-com´plice
ac-com´plish
ac-com´plished
ac-com´plish-ment
ac-compt´
ac-cord´
ac-cord´a·ble
ac-cord´ance
ac-cord´ant

ac-cord´ed
ac-cord´ing
ac-cord´ing·ly
ac-cor´di·on
ac-cor´di-on-ist
ac-cost´
ac-couche-ment´
ac-cou-cheur´
ac-count´
ac-count-a·bil´i·ty
ac-count´a·ble
ac-count´a·bly
ac-count´an·cy
ac-count´ant
ac-count´ing
ac-cou´ter
ac-cou´ter-ment
ac-cred´it
ac-cres´cence
ac-crete´
ac-cre´tion
ac-cre´tive
ac-cru´al
ac-crue´
ac-crue´ment
ac-cru´ing
ac-cul-tur-a´tion
ac-cum´ben·cy
ac-cum´bent
ac-cu´mu-late
ac-cu´mu-lat-ing
ac-cu´mu-la´tion
ac-cu´mu-la-tive

ac-cu´mu-la-tor
ac´cu-ra·cy
ac´cu-rate
ac´cu-rate·ly
ac´cu-rate-ness
ac-curs´ed
ac-curs´ed·ly
ac-cus´al
ac-cu-sa´tion
ac-cu´sa-tive
ac-cu´sa-tive·ly
ac-cus´a-to·ry
ac-cuse´
ac-cused´
ac-cus´er
ac-cus´ing
ac-cus´ing·ly
ac-cus´tom
ac-cus´tomed
ace
ac´er-bate
a·cer´bic
a·cer´bi·ty
ac´er-ose
ache
ached
a·che´ni·al
a·chiev´a·ble
a·chieve´
a·chieved´
a·chieve´ment
a·chiev´ing
ach´i·ness

ach´ing·ly
ach-ro-mat´ic
ach-ro-mat´i-cal·ly
a·chro´ma-tism
a·chro´ma-tize
a·chro´ma-tous
ach´y
ac´id
a·cid´ic
a-cid´i-fi-a·ble
a·cid-i-fi-ca´tion
a·cid´i-fied
a·cid´i·fy
a·cid´i·ty
ac-i-doph´i-lus
a·cid´u-late
a·cid-u-la´tion
a·cid´u-lous
acid--washed
ac-knowl´edge
ac-knowl´edge-
   a·ble
ac-knowl´edged
ac-knowl´edg-ing
ac-knowl´edg-ment
a·clin´ic
ac´me
ac´ne
ac´o-lyte
a´corn
a·cous´tic
a·cous´ti-cal
a·cous´ti-cal·ly

ac-ous-ti´cian
ac-quaint´
ac-quaint´ance
ac-quaint´ance-
  ship
ac-quaint´ed
ac-qui-esce´
ac-qui-es´cence
ac-qui-es´cent
ac-qui-es´cent·ly
ac-qui-esc´ing
ac-qui-esc´ing·ly
ac-quir-a-bil´i·ty
ac-quir´a·ble
ac-quire´
ac-quire´ment
ac-quir´er
ac-quir´ing
ac-qui-si´tion
ac-qui-si´tion·al
ac-quis´i-tive
ac-quis´i-tor
ac-quit´
ac-quit´tal
ac-quit´ted
ac-quit´ting
a´cre
a´cre-age
ac´rid
a·crid´i·ty
ac´rid·ly
ac´rid-ness
ac-ri-mo´ni-ous

ac´ri-mo·ny
ac´ro-bat
ac´ro-bat´ic
ac´ro-nym
ac-ro-pho´bi·a
ac-ro-pho´bic
a·cross´
a·cryl´ic
act
act´able
act´ing
ac´tion
ac´tion-a·ble
ac´tion-less
ac´ti-vate
ac-ti-va´tion
ac-ti-va-tor
ac´tive
ac´tive·ly
ac´tive-ness
ac´tiv-ism
ac´tiv-ist
ac-tiv´i-ties
ac-tiv´i·ty
ac´tor
ac´tress
ac´tu-al
ac-tu-al´i·ty
ac-tu-al-i-za´tion
ac´tu-al-ize
ac´tu-al·ly
ac´tu-al-ness
ac-tu-ar´i·al

ac´tu-ar-ies
ac´tu-ar·y
ac´tu-ate
ac´tu-at-ing
ac-tu-a´tion
ac´tu-a-tor
ac´u-ate
a·cu´i·ty
a·cu´men
ac´u-pres-sure
ac´u-punc-ture
ac´u-punc-tur-ist
a·cute´
a·cute´ly
a·cute´ness
ad´age
ad´a-man·cy
ad´a-mant
ad-a-man´tine
ad´a-mant·ly
a·dapt´
a·dapt-a-bil´i·ty
a·dapt´a·ble
ad-ap-ta´tion
ad-ap-ta´tion·al
ad-ap-ta´tion-al·ly
a·dapt´er
a·dapt´ive
a·dap´tive·ly
a·dap´tive-ness
ad-ap-tiv´i·ty
a·dap´tor
ad-ax´i·al

add´a·ble
add´ed
ad´dend
ad-den´da
ad-den´dum
ad´dict *(n.)*
ad-dict´ *(v.)*
ad-dict´ed
ad-dic´tion
ad-dic´tive
ad-di´tion
ad-di´tion·al
ad-di´tion-al·ly
ad´di-tive
ad´dle
ad´dled
add–on
ad-dress´
ad-dress´a·ble
ad-dress-ee´
ad-dress´er
ad-dress´ing
ad-dres´sor
ad-duce´
ad-du´cent
ad-duc´i·ble
ad-duc´ing
ad-duct´ *(v.)*
ad´duct *(n.)*
ad-duc´tion
ad-duc´tor
a·dept´ *(adj.)*
ad´ept *(n.)*

a·dept´ly
a·dept´ness
ad´e-qua·cy
ad´e-quate
ad´e-quate·ly
ad´e-quate-ness
ad-here´
ad-her´ence
ad-her´ent
ad-her´ent·ly
ad-her´ing
ad-he´sion
ad-he´sive
ad hoc
a·dieu´
ad in-fi-ni´tum
ad in´ter·im
a·dios´
ad-ja´cen·cy
ad-ja´cent
ad-ja´cent·ly
ad-jec-ti´val
ad´jec-tive
ad-join´
ad-joined´
ad-join´ing
ad-journ´
ad-journed´
ad-journ´ment
ad-judge´
ad-judg´ing
ad-ju´di-cate
ad-ju´di-cat-ing

ad-ju-di-ca´tion
ad-ju´di-ca-tive
ad-ju´di-ca-tor
ad-ju´di-ca-to·ry
ad´junct
ad-junc´tion
ad-junc´tive
ad-junct´ly
ad-ju-ra´tion
ad-jur´a-to·ry
ad-jure´
ad-ju´ror
ad-just´
ad-just-a-bil´i·ty
ad-just´a·ble
ad-just´er
ad-just´ment
ad-jus´tor
ad´ju-tant
ad´ju-vant
ad–lib *(v., adj.)*
ad lib´i-tum
ad-min´is-ter
ad-min´is-trate
ad-min-is-tra´tion
ad-min´is-tra-tive
ad-min´is-tra-
   tive·ly
ad-min´is-tra-tor
ad´mi-ra·ble
ad´mi-ra·bly
ad´mi-ral
ad´mi-ral·ty

ad-mi-ra´tion
ad-mire´
ad-mired´
ad-mir´er
ad-mir´ing
ad-mir´ing·ly
ad-mis-si-bil´i·ty
ad-mis´si·ble
ad-mis´sion
ad-mis´sive
ad-mit´
ad-mit´tance
ad-mit´ted
ad-mit´ted·ly
ad-mit´ting
ad-mix´
ad-mix´ture
ad-mon´ish
ad-mon´ish-ing·ly
ad-mon´ish-ment
ad-mo-ni´tion
ad-mon´i-to·ry
a·do´
a·do´be
ad-o-les´cence
ad-o-les´cent
ad-o-les´cent·ly
a·dopt´
a·dopt´a·ble
a·dopt´er
a·dop´tion
a·dop´tive
a·dop´tive·ly

a·dor´a·ble
a·dor´a·bly
ad-o-ra´tion
a·dore´
a·dored´
a·dor´er
a·dor´ing
a·dor´ing·ly
a·dorn´
a·dorned´
a·dorn´ing
a·dorn´ment
a·down´
ad-ren´a-lin
a·drift´
a·droit´
a·droit´ly
a·droit´ness
ad-sorb´
ad-sorb´ent
ad-sorp´tion
ad-sorp´tive
ad´u-late
ad-u-la´tion
ad´u-la-to·ry
a·dult´
a·dul´ter-ant
a·dul´ter-ate
a·dul-ter-a´tion
a·dul´ter-a-tor
a·dul´ter·er
a·dul´ter-ess
a·dul´ter-ous

a·dul´ter·y
a·dult´hood
ad va-lo´rem
ad-vance´
ad-vanced´
ad-vance´ment
ad-vanc´ing
ad-van´tage
ad-van´taged
ad-van-ta´geous
ad-van-ta´geous·ly
ad-van-ta´geous-
   ness
ad´vent
ad-ven-ti´tious
ad-ven-ti´tious·ly
ad-ven´ture
ad-ven´tur·er
ad-ven´ture-some
ad-ven´tur-ous
ad´verb
ad-verb´i·al
ad´ver-sar-ies
ad´ver-sar·y
ad´verse
ad´verse·ly
ad-verse´ness
ad-ver´si·ty
ad-vert´
ad-vert´ence
ad-vert´en·cy
ad-vert´ent
ad-vert´ent·ly

ad´ver-tise
ad-ver-tise´ment
ad´ver-tis·er
ad´ver-tis-ing
ad-vice´
ad-vis-a-bil´i·ty
ad-vis´a·ble
ad-vis´a·ble-ness
ad-vis´a·bly
ad-vise´
ad-vised´
ad-vis´ed·ly
ad-vise´ment
ad-vis´er
ad-vis´ing
ad-vi´sor
ad-vis´o·ry
ad´vo-ca·cy
ad´vo-cate
ad´vo-ca´tion
ad´vo-ca-tor
ad-voc´a-to·ry
adz, adze
aer´ate
aer-a´tion
aer´a-tor
aer´i·al
aer´i-al-ist
ae´rie
aer-o-bat´ics
aer-o´bic
aer·o-dy-nam´ic
aer´o-naut

aer·o-nau´ti-cal
aer·o-nau´ti-cal·ly
aer-o-pho´bi·a
aer´o-plane
aer´o-sol
aer´o-space
a´er·y
aes´thete
aes-thet´ic
aes-thet´i-cal
aes-thet´i-cal·ly
aes-thet´ics
ae´ther
a·far´
af-fa-bil´i·ty
af´fa-ble
af´fa-bly
af-fair´
af-fect´
af-fec-ta´tion
af-fect´ed
af-fect´ing
af-fect´ing·ly
af-fec´tion
af-fec´tion·al
af-fec´tion-ate
af-fec´tion-ate·ly
af´fer-ent
af-fi´ance
af-fi´anced
af-fil´i-ate
af-fil´i-at·ed
af-fil-i-a´tion

af-fin´i-ties
af-fin´i-tive
af-fin´i·ty
af-firm´
af-firm´a·ble
af-firm´a·bly
af-fir-ma´tion
af-firm´a-tive
af-firm´a-tive·ly
af-firm´ing·ly
affix´ (v.)
af´fix (n.)
af-flict´
af-flic´tion
af-flict´ive
af´flu-ence
af´flu-en·cy
af´flu-ent
af´flu-ent·ly
af-ford´
af-ford-a-bil´i·ty
af-ford´a·ble
af-ford´a·bly
af-fray´
af-fright´
af-front´
af-front´ive
a·fi-cio-na´do
a·field´
a·fire´
a·flame´
a·float´
a·flut´ter

a·foot´

a·fore´men-tioned

a·fore´said

a·fore´thought

a-fore´time

a·foul´

a·fraid´

A´–frame

a·fresh´

af´ter

af´ter-birth

af´ter-burn·er

af´ter-care

af´ter-deck

af´ter-ef-fect

af´ter-glow

after–hours

af´ter-im-age

af´ter-life

af´ter-math

af-ter-noon´

af´ter-shave

af´ter-shock

af´ter-taste

af´ter-thought

af´ter-ward

af´ter-wards

a·gain´

a·gainst´

a·gape´ *(ajar)*

a·ga´pe *(love feast)*

a-gaze´

age

aged, ag´ed

age´less

a´gen-cies

a´gen·cy

a·gen´da

a·gen´dum

a´gent

ag-glom´er-ate

ag-glom-er-a´tion

ag-grade

ag-gran´dize

ag-gran´dize-ment

ag´gra-vate

ag´gra-vat·ed

ag´gra-vat-ing

ag-gra-va´tion

ag´gra-va-tor

ag´gre-gate

ag´gre-gate·ly

ag´gre-gat-ing

ag-gre-ga´tion

ag´gre-ga-tive

ag´gre-ga-to·ry

ag-gress´

ag-gres´sion

ag-gres´sive

ag-gres´sive·ly

ag-gres´sive-ness

ag-gres´sor

ag-griev´ance

ag-grieve´

ag-grieved´

ag-grieve´ment

a·ghast´

ag´ile

ag´ile·ly

ag´ile-ness

a·gil´i·ty

ag´ing

ag´i-tate

ag´i-tated

ag´i-tat-ed·ly

ag´i-tat-ing

ag´i-ta´tion

ag´i-ta-tive

ag´i-ta-tor

a·gleam´

a·glow´

ag-nos´tic

ag-nos´ti-cal

ag-nos´ti-cism

a·go´

a·gog´

ag´o-nist

ag-o-nis´tic

ag´o-nize

ag´o-niz-ing

ag´o·ny

ag-o-ra-pho´bi·a

a·grar´i·an

a·gree´

a·gree-a-bil´i·ty

a·gree´a·ble

a·gree´a·bly

a·greed´

a·gree´ing

a·gree′ment
ag′ri-bus·i-ness
ag-ri-cul′tur·al
ag′ri-cul-ture
ag-ri-cul′tur-ist
a·gron′o-mist
a·gron′o·my
a·ground′
a′gue
a′gue-weed
a′gu-ish
a·head′
a·hoy′
aide–de–camp
ail′ment
aim′less
aim′less·ly
aim′less-ness
air′brush
air′craft
air′field
air′flow
air′foil
air force
air′freight
air′i·ly
air′i-ness
air′ing
air′less
air′lin·er
air′ lock
air′mail
air′man

air′ mat-tress
air′plane
air pock′et
air′port
air pres′sure
air′show
air′sickness
air′speed
air′stream
air′strip
air′tight
air′ traf-fic
air′waves
air′way
air′wor·thy
air′y
aisle
a·jar′
a·kim′bo
a·kin′
al′a-bas-ter
à la carte
a·lac′ri·ty
à la king
à la mode
a·larm′
a·larm′ing
a·larm′ing·ly
a· larm′ist
a·las′
al′ba-tross
al-bi′no
al′bum

al-bu′men *(egg white)*
al-bu′min *(protein)*
al′che-mist
al′che·my
al′co-hol
al-co-hol′ic
al-co-hol-ic′i·ty
al′co-hol-ism
al′cove
al-co-vi-nom′e-ter
al den′te
al′der
al′der-man
al-der-man′ic
ale
ale′house
a·lert′
a·lert′ly
a·lert′ness
al-fres′co
al′ga, al′gae
al′ge-bra
al-ge-bra′ic
al-ge-bra′i-cal
al-ge-bra′i-cal·ly
al′go-rithm
a′li·as
al′i·bi
al′i-bi-ing
al′ien
al′ien-a·ble
al′ien-ate

11

al′ien-at-ing
al′ien-a′tion
al′ien-ist
a·light′
a·lign′
a·lign′ment
a·like′
al′i-ment
al-i-men′ta·ry
al-i-men-ta′tion
al′i-mo·ny
a·line′
a·line′ment
a·live′
al′ka·li
al′ka-line
al-ka-lin′i·ty
al′ka-loid
all–American
all–around
al-lay′
al-lay′ing
all clear
all–day
al-le-ga′tion
al-lege′
al-lege′a·ble
al-leged′
al-leg′ed·ly
al-le′giance
al-leg′ing
al-le-gor′ic
al-le-gor′i-cal

al-le-gor′i-cal·ly
al′le-go-ries
al′le-go-rist
al′le-go-rize
al′le·go·ry
al′ler-gen
al-ler-gen′ic
al-ler′gic
al′ler-gist
al′ler·gy
al-le′vi-ate
al-le′vi-at-ing
al-le-vi-a′tion
al-le′vi-a-tive
al′ley
al′leys
al′ley-way
al-li′ance
al-lied′
al-lies′
al′li-ga-tor
all–important
al-lit′er-ate
al-lit-er-a′tion
al-lit′er-a-tive
all–night
al′lo-cate
al′lo-cat-ing
al-lo-ca′tion
al-lot′
al-lot′ment
al-lot′ted
al-lot′ting

all–out
all–over
al-low′
al-low′a·ble
al-low′ance
al-lowed′
al′loy
all–powerful
all–purpose
all right
all–round
all-spice
all–star
al-lude′
al-lure
al-lured′
al-lure′ment
al-lur′ing
al-lu′sion
al-lu′sive
al-lu′sive·ly
al-lu′sive-ness
al′ly *(n.)*
al·ly′ *(v.)*
al·ly′ing
al′ma-nac
al-might′y
al′mond
al′mo-ner
al′most
a·loft′
a·lone′
a·long′

a·long·side´
a·loof´
a·loof´ness
a·loud´
al´pha
al´pha·bet
al-pha-bet´ic
al-pha-bet´i-cal
al´pha·bet-ize
al·read´y
al·right´
al´tar
al´tar-piece
al´ter
al-ter-a-bil´i·ty
al´ter-a-ble
al-ter-a´tion
al´ter-cate
al-ter-ca´tion
al´ter-nate
al´ter-nat·ed
al´ter-nate·ly
al´ter-nat-ing
al-ter-na´tion
al-ter´na-tive
al´ter-na-tor
al-though´
al´ti-tude
al´to
al´to-geth·er
al´tru-ism
al´tru-ist
al-tru-is´ti-cal·ly

al-u-min´i·um
a·lum´ni
a·lum´nus
al´ways
a·mal´ga-mate
a·mal-ga-ma´tion
a·mal´ga-ma-tor
a·man-u-en´sis
am-a-ret´to
a·mass´
a·mass´a·ble
a·mass´ment
am´a-teur
am´a-teur-ish
am´a-teur-ism
am´a-to·ry
a·maze´
a·mazed´
a·maz´ed·ly
a·maze´ment
a·maz´ing
a·maz´ing·ly
am-bas´sa-dor
am-bas-sa-do´ri·al
am´bi-ance
am-bi-dex´trous
am´bi-ence
am´bi-ent
am-bi-gu´i·ty
am-big´u-ous
am-bi´tion
am-bi´tious
am-biv´a-lence

am-biv´a-lent
am´ble
am´bled
am´bling
am´bling·ly
am-bro´si·a
am´bu-lance
am´bu-la-to·ry
am´bush
am´bushed
am´bush·er
a·me´lio-rate
a·me-lio-ra´tion
a·me´lio-ra-tive
a·me´lio-ra-tor
a´men´
a·me-na-bil´i·ty
a·me´na·ble
a·mend´
a·mend´a·ble
a·mend´a-to·ry
a·mend´ed
a·mend´ment
a·mends´
a·men´i-ties
a·men´i·ty
a·mi-a-bil´i·ty
a´mi-a·ble
a´mi-a·bly
am-i-ca-bil´i·ty
am´i-ca·ble
am´i-ca·bly
a·mid´

a·midst´
a·miss´
am´i·ty
am·ne´sia
am·ne´si·ac
am´nes·ty
a·moe´ba
a·mong´
a·mongst´
a·mor´al
a·mo·ral´i·ty
a·mor´al·ly
am·o·ret´to
am´o·rous
a·mor´phous
am´or·tize
am´or·tiz·ing
a·mount´
am´per·age
am´pere
am´per·sand
am·phet´a·mine
am·phib´i·an
am·phib´i·ous
am·phib´i·ous·ly
am´phi·the·a·ter
am´ple
am´ple·ness
am·pli·fi·ca´tion
am´pli·fied
am´pli·fi·er
am´pli·fy
am´pli·fy·ing

am´pli·tude
am´ply
am´pu·tate
am´pu·tat·ing
am·pu·ta´tion
am´pu·tee´
a·muck´
am´u·let
a·muse´
a·muse´ment
a·mus´ing
a·nach´ro·nism
a·nach·ro·nis´tic
a·nae´mi·a (Br.)
an·al·ge´sic
an´a·log
a·nal´o·gies
a·nal´o·gize
a·nal´o·gous
a·nal´o·gous·ly
an´a·logue
a·nal´o·gy
an´a·lyse (Br.)
a·nal´y·ses
a·nal´y·sis
an´a·lyst
an·a·lyt´ic
an·a·lyt´i·cal
an·a·lyt´i·cal·ly
an´a·lyze
an´a·lyz·ing
an´ar·chism
an´ar·chist

an·ar·chis´tic
an´ar·chy
a·nath´e·ma
an·a·tom´i·cal
a·nat´o·mist
a·nat´o·mize
a·nat´o·my
an´ces·tor
an·ces´tral
an´ces·try
an´chor
an´chor·age
an´cho·ret
an´cho·vies, an-
  cho´vies
an´cho·vy
an·cho´vy
an´cient
an´cil·lar·y
and´i·ron
an´droid
an´ec·dot·al
an´ec·dote
a·ne´mi·a
a·ne´mic
an·es·the´sia
an·es·the·si·ol´o-
  gist
an·es·thet´ic
a·nes´the·tist
a·nes´the·tize
an´eu·rysm
a·new´

an´gel
an´gel-fish
an-gel´ic
an´ger
an-gi´na
an-gi´na pec´to-ris
an-gi-os´to·my
an´gle
an´gler
an´gle-worm
an´gling
an´gri·ly
an´gri-ness
an´gry
an´guish
an´guished
an´gu-lar
an-gu-lar´i·ty
an´i-mal
an´i-mal-ism
an´i-mate
an´i-mat·ed
an´i-mat-ed·ly
an´i-mat-ing
an-i-ma´tion
an´i-ma-tor
an-i-mos´i·ty
an´i-mus
an´ise
an´i-seed
an-i-sette´
an´kle
an´klet

an´nal
an-neal´
an-nealed´
an-nex´ *(v.)*
an´nex *(n.)*
an-nex-a´tion
an-ni´hi-late
an-ni-hi-la´tion
an-ni´hi-la-tor
an-ni-ver´sa-ries
an-ni-ver´sa·ry
an´no-tate
an-no-ta´tion
an´no-ta-tor
an-nounce´
an-nounce´ment
an-nounc´er
an-nounc´ing
an-noy´
an-noy´ance
an-noyed´
an-noy´ing
an´nu·al
an´nu-al-ize
an´nu-al·ly
an-nu´i·ty
an-nul´
an-nulled´
an-nul´ling
an-nul´ment
an´num
an-nun´ci-ate
an-nun-ci-a´tion

an-nun´ci-a-tor
a·noint´
a·noint´ed
a·noint´er
a·noint´ment
a·nom-a-lis´tic
a·nom´a-lous
a·nom´a-lous·ly
a·nom´a·ly
an-o-nym´i·ty
a·non´y-mous
a·non´y-mous·ly
an-o-rex´i·a
an-o-rex´ic
an-oth´er
an´swer
an´swer-a·ble
an´swered
an´swer-ing
an-tag´o-nism
an-tag´o-nist
an-tag-o-nis´tic
an-tag´o-nize
an´te
an´te-bel´lum
an-te-cede´
an-te-ced´ence
an-te-ced´ent
an´te-cham-ber
an´te-date
an-ten´na
an-te´ri·or
an´te-room

15

an´them
an-thol´o·gy
an´thro-poid
an-thro-po-log´i-
    cal
an-thro-pol´o-gist
an-thro-pol´o·gy
an-thro-po-
    morph´ic
an-thro-po-mor´-
    phize
an´ti
an-ti-bi-ot´ic
an´ti-bod-ies
an´ti-bod·y
an´tic
an-tic´i-pate
an-tic´i-pat·ed
an-tic´i-pat-ing
an-tic-i-pa´tion
an-tic´i-pa-tive
an-tic´i-pa-to·ry
an-ti-cli´max
an´ti-dote
an´ti-freeze
an-ti-grav´i·ty
an-ti-his´ta-mine
an´ti-mat-ter
an-ti-pas´to
an-tip´a-thy
an´ti-quate
an´ti-quat·ed
an´ti-quat-ing

an-tique´
an-tiq´ui·ty
an-ti-sep´tic
an-ti-so´cial
an-tith´e-sis
an-ti-thet´ic
an-ti-thet´i-cal
an-ti-thet´i-cal·ly
an-ti-trust´
an´to-nym
an´vil
anx-i´e·ty
anx´ious
anx´ious·ly
an´y
an´y-bod·y
an´y-how
an-y-more´
an´y-one
an´y-place
an´y-thing
an´y-time
any-way
an´y-where
a·part´
a·part´heid
a·part´ment
ap-a-thet´ic
ap-a-thet´i-cal·ly
ap´a-thy
a ·pér-i-tif´
ap´er-ture
a´pex

aph´o-rism
aph-o-ris´tic
a´pi-ar·y
a·piece´
a·poc´a-lypse
a·poc-a-lyp´tic
a·poc´ry-phal
a-po-lit´i-cal
a·pol-o-get´ic
a·pol-o-get´i-cal
a·pol-o-get´i-cal·ly
ap-o-lo´gi·a
a·pol´o-gies
a·pol´o-gise (Br.)
a·pol´o-gist
a·pol´o-gize
a·pol´o-giz-ing
a·pol´o·gy
ap-os-tol´ic
ap-os-tol´i-cal
a·pos´tro-phe
a·poth´e-car·y
ap-pal´ (Br.)
ap-pall´
ap-pall´ing
ap-pall´ing·ly
ap-pa-rat´us
ap-par´el
ap-par´ent
ap-par´ent·ly
ap-pa-ri´tion
ap-peal´
ap-pealed´

ap-peal´er
ap-peal´ing
ap-peal´ing·ly
ap-pear´
ap-pear´ance
ap-peared´
ap-pear´ing
ap-pease´
ap-pease´ment
ap-peas´er
ap-peas´ing
ap-peas´ing·ly
ap-pel´lant
ap-pel´late
ap-pel-la´tion
ap-pend´
ap-pend´age
ap-pend´aged
ap-pend´ed
ap´pe-tite
ap´pe-tiz·er
ap´pe-tiz-ing
ap-plaud´
ap-plaud´er
ap-plaud´ing
ap-plause´
ap´ple
ap´ple-jack
ap´ple-sauce
ap-pli´ance
ap-pli-ca-bil´i·ty
ap´pli-ca·ble
ap´pli-ca·bly

ap´pli-cant
ap-pli-ca´tion
ap´pli-ca-tive
ap´pli-ca-tor
ap´pli-ca-to·ry
ap-plied´
ap-pli´er
ap-pli-que´
ap-ply´
ap-ply´ing
ap-point´
ap-point´ed
ap-poin-tee´
ap-point´er
ap-point´ing
ap-point´ment
ap-por´tion
ap-por´tioned
ap-por´tion·er
ap-por´tion-ment
ap-pos´a·ble
ap-pose´
ap´po-site
ap-po-si´tion
ap-pos´i-tive
ap-prais´al
ap-praise´
ap-praised´
ap-prais´er
ap-prais´ing
ap-pre´cia·ble
ap-pre´ci-ate
ap-pre´ci-at·ed

ap-pre´ci-at-ing
ap-pre-ci-a´tion
ap-pre´cia-tive
ap-pre´cia-tive·ly
ap-pre´cia-to·ry
ap-pre-hend´
ap-pre-hend´ed
ap-pre-hend´ing
ap-pre-hen´si·ble
ap-pre-hen´sion
ap-pre-hen´sive
ap-pre-hen´sive·ly
ap-pren´tice
ap-pren´ticed
ap-pren´tice-ship
ap-prise´
ap-prised´
ap-pris´ing
ap-prize´
ap-proach´
ap-proach-a-bil´i·ty
ap-proach´a·ble
ap-proached´
ap-proach´ing
ap-pro-ba´tion
ap-pro´pri-ate
ap-pro´pri-at·ed
ap-pro´pri-at·ly
ap-pro´pri-ate-ness
ap-pro´pri-at-ing
ap-pro-pri-a´tion
ap-prov´al
ap-prove´

ap-proved
ap-prov´ing
ap-prov´ing·ly
ap-prox´i-mate
ap-prox´i-mat·ed
ap-prox´i-mate·ly
ap-prox´i-mat´ing
ap-prox-i-ma´tion
ap-pur´te-nance
ap-pur´te-nant
a´pron
ap´ro-pos
apse
ap´ti-tude
apt´ly
apt´ness
aq´ua
aq´ua-cade
aq´ua-cul-ture
aq´ua-lung
aq-ua-ma-rine´
aq´ua-plane
a·quar´i·um
a·quat´ic
a·quat´i-cal·ly
aq´ue-duct
a´que-ous
aq´ui-fer
a-quiv´er
ar´a·ble
ar´bi-ter
ar´bi-trage
ar´bi-trag·er

ar´bi-trar-i·ly
ar´bi-trar·y
ar´bi-trate
ar´bi-trat-ing
ar-bi-tra´tion
ar´bi-tra-tive
ar´bi-tra-tor
ar´bi-tress
ar´bor
ar-bo´re·al
ar´bour (Br.)
ar-cade´
ar-cane´
ar-chae-ol´o-gist
ar-chae-ol´o·gy
ar-cha´ic
ar-cha´i-cal·ly
ar-che-o-log´ic
ar-che-o-log´i-cal
ar-che-ol´o-gist
ar-che-ol´o·gy
arch´er
ar´cher-fish
arch´er·y
ar´che-type
ar´chi-tect
ar-chi-tec´tur·al
ar´chi-tec-ture
ar-chi´val
ar´chive
ar´chi-vist
arch´way
arc´ing

ar´dent
ar´dent·ly
ar´dor
ar´du-ous
ar´du-ous·ly
ar´e·a-way
a·re´na
ar´go·sy
ar´gu-a·ble
ar´gue
ar´gued
ar´gu-ing
ar´gu-ment
ar-gu-men-ta´tion
ar-gu-men´ta-tive
a´ri·a
ar´id
a·rid´i·ty
ar´id-ness
a·right´
a´ri-ose
a·rise´
a·ris´en
a·ris´ing
ar-is-toc´ra·cy
a·ris´to-crat
a·ris-to-crat´ic
a·rith´me-tic (n.)
ar-ith-met´ic (adj.)
ar-ith-met´i-cal
ar-ma´da
ar´ma-ment
ar´ma-ture

18

arm´band	ar-ray´	ar´ti-fice
arm´chair	ar-rayed´	ar-ti-fi´cial
armed	ar-ray´ing	ar-ti-fi-ci-al´i·ty
arm´ful	ar-rear´	ar-ti-fi´cial·ly
ar´mies	ar-rear´age	ar´ti-san
ar´mil-lar·y	ar-rest´	art´ist
ar´mi-stice	ar-rest´ed	ar-tiste´
ar-moire´	ar-rest´er	ar-tis´tic
ar´mor	ar-rest´ing	ar-tis´ti-cal
ar´mored	ar-res´tive	ar-tis´ti-cal·ly
ar-mo´ri·al	ar-riv´al	ar´tist·ry
armor–plated	ar-rive´	art´less
ar´mo·ry	ar-riv´ing	art´work
ar´mour (Br.)	ar´ro-gance	art´y
arm´pit	ar´ro-gant	as-cend´
arm´rest	ar´ro-gate	as-cend´a·ble
ar´my	ar´ro-gat-ing	as-cend´an·cy
a·ro´ma	ar-ro-ga´tion	as-cend´ant
ar-o-mat´ic	ar´se-nal	as-cend´ing
ar-o-mat´i-cal·ly	ar´se-nate	as-cen´sion
a·ro´ma-tize	ar´se-nic (n.)	as-cent´
a·rose´	ar-sen´ic (adj.)	as-cer-tain´
a·round´	ar´son	as-cer-tain´a·ble
a·rous´al	ar´son-ist	as-cet´ic
a·rouse´	art´ful	as-cet´i-cism
a·rous´ing	art´ful·ly	as-crib´a·ble
ar-raign´	ar´ti-cle	as-cribe´
ar-raign´ment	ar´ti-cled	as-crip´tive
ar-range´	ar-tic´u-late	as-crip´tion
ar-range´a·ble	ar-tic´u-lat-ed	a·sex´u-al
ar-range´ment	ar-tic-u-la´tion	a·shamed´
ar-rang´er	ar-tic´u-la-tor	a·sham´ed·ly
ar-rang´ing	ar´ti-fact	ash´en

a·shore´
ash´tray
ash´y
a·side´
as´i-nine
as-i-nin´i·ty
a·skance´
a·skew´
a·slant´
a·sleep´
a-so´cial
as´pect
as´per-ate
as-per´i·ty
as-perse´
as-per´sion
as-phyx´i·a
as-phyx´i-ate
as´pic
as´pi-rant
as´pi-rate
as-pi-ra´tion
as´pi-ra-tor
as-pir´a-to·ry
as-pire´
as´pi-rin
as-pir´ing
as-pir´ing·ly
as-sail´
as-sail´a·ble
as-sail´ant
as-sas´sin
as-sas´si-nate

as-sas-si-na´tion
as-sas´si-na-tor
as-sault´
as-sault´er
as´say (n.)
as-say´ (v.)
as-say´er
as-sem´blage
as-sem´ble
as-sem´bler
as-sem´bling
as-sem´bly
as-sent´
as-sert´
as-ser´tion
as-ser´tive
as-sess´
as-sess´ment
as´ses´sor
as´set
as-sid´u-ous
as-sid´u-ous·ly
as-sign´
as-sign-a-bil´i·ty
as-sign´a·ble
as-sig-na´tion
as-sign·ee´
as-sign´er
as-sign´ment
as-sign´or
as-sim´i-late
as-sim´i-lat-ing
as-sim-i-la´tion

as-sim´i-la-tive
as-sim´i-la-tor
as-sist´
as-sist´ance
as-sist´ant
as-sist´ed
as-sist´er
as-sist´ing
as-so´ci-ate
as-so´ci-at-ing
as-so-ci-a´tion
as-sort´
as-sort´ed
as-sort´ment
as-suage´
as-suag´ing
as-sum´a·ble
as-sum´a·bly
as-sume´
as-sumed´
as-sum´er
as-sum´ing
as-sump´tion
as-sump´tive
as-sur´ance
as-sure´
as-sured´
as-sur´ed·ly
as-sur´ed-ness
as-sur´ing
as´ter-isk
a·stern´
as´ter-oid

a·stir´
as-ton´ish
as-ton´ished
as-ton´ish·ing
as-ton´ish·ing·ly
as-ton´ish-ment
as-tound´
as-tound´ed
as-tound´ing·ly
as´tral
a·stray´
a·stride´
as-trin´gen·cy
as-trin´gent
as´tro-dome
as´tro-labe
as-trol´o-ger
as-tro-log´i-cal·ly
as-trol´o·gy
as´tro-naut
as-tron´o-mer
as-tro-nom´ic
as-tro-nom´i-cal·ly
as-tron´o·my
as-tro-phys´i-cal
as-tro-phys´i-cist
as-tro-phys´ics
as-tute´
as-tute´ly
as-tute´ness
a·sun´der
a·sy´lum
a·sym-met´ric

a·sym-met´ri-cal
a·sym´me-try
a·te-lier´
a´the-ism
a´the-ist
a·the-is´tic
a·the-is´ti-cal·ly
ath´lete
ath-let´ic
ath-let´i-cal·ly
a·tin´gle
at´mo-sphere
at-mo-spher´ic
at´oll
at´om
a·tom´ic
at´om-iz·er
a·ton´al
a·ton-al-is´tic
a·to-nal´i·ty
a·tone´
a·tone´ment
a·ton´ing
a·top´
a-trem´ble
a´tri·um
a·tro´cious
a·tro´cious·ly
a·troc´i·ty
at-tach´
at-tach´a·ble
at-ta-ché´
at-tached´

at-tach´ment
at-tack´
at-tacked´
at-tack´er
at-tack´ing
at-tain´
at-tain-a·bil´i·ty
at-tain´a·ble
at-tain´a·ble-ness
at-tain´ment
at-tempt´
at-tend´
at-tend´ance
at-tend´ant
at-tend´ing
at-ten´tion
at-ten´tive
at-ten´tive·ly
at-ten´u-ate
at-ten-u-a´tion
at-test´
at´tic
at-tire´
at´ti-tude
at-ti-tu´di-nize
at-tor´ney
at-tract´
at-trac´tion
at-tract´ive·ly
at-tract´ive-ness
at-trib´ut-a·ble
at´tri-bute *(n.)*
at-trib´ute *(v.)*

at-tri-bu′tion
at-trib′u-tive
at-tri′tion
at-tri′tus
at-tune′
a·typ′i-cal
au′burn
auc′tion
auc-tion-eer′
au-da′cious
au-dac′i·ty
au-di-bil′i·ty
au′di·ble
au′di·bly
au′di-ence
au′di·o
au-di-o-vis′u·al
au′dit
au-di′tion
au′di-tor
au-di-to′ri·um
au′di-to·ry
au′ger
aug-ment′ *(v.)*
aug′ment *(n.)*
aug-ment′a·ble
aug-men-ta′tion
aug-men′ta-tive
au′gu·ry
au-gust′
au′ra
au′re-ole
au′ri-cle

au-ric′u-lar
au-ro′ra
aus′cul-tate
aus-cul-ta′tion
aus-pi′cial
aus-pi′cious
aus-pi′cious·ly
aus-tere′
aus-tere′ly
aus-ter′i·ty
au-then′tic
au-then′ti-cal·ly
au-then′ti-cate
au-then-ti-ca′tion
au-then-tic′i·ty
au′thor
au-thor-i-tar′i·an
au-thor′i-ta-tive
au-thor′i·ty
au-tho-ri-za′tion
au′tho-rize
au′tho-rized
au′tho-riz-ing
au′thor-ship
au′tism
au′to
au-to-bi-og′ra-phy
au-toc′ra·cy
au′to-crat
au-to-crat′ic
au-to-crat′i-cal·ly
au′to-graph
au-to-im-mune′

au′to-mate
au-to-mat′ic
au-to-mat′i-cal·ly
au-to-ma′tion
au-tom′a-ton
au-to-mo-bile′
au-to-mo′tive
au-ton′o-mist
au-ton′o-mous
au-ton′o·my
au′top·sy
au′tumn
au-tum′nal
aux-il′ia·ry
a·vail′
a·vail-a·bil′i·ty
a·vail′a·ble
a·vailed′
av′a-lanche
av′a-rice
av-a-ri′cious
a·venge′
a·venged′
a·veng′er
a·veng′ing
av′e-nue
a·ver′
av′er-age
a·verse′
a·ver′sion
a·vert′
a·vert′ed
a′vi-ar·y

a´vi-ate
a·vi-a´tion
a´vi-a-tor
a·vi-a´trix
av´id
a·vid´i·ty
av´id·ly
av-o-ca´tion
a·void´
a·void´a·ble
a·void´a·bly
a·void´ance
a·void´ed
a·vow´
a·vow´al
a·vowed´
a·vow´ed·ly
a·vul´sion
a·vun´cu-lar
a´wait´
a·wake´
a·wak´en-ing
a·wak´ing
a·ward´
a·ward´ed
a·ware´
a·ware´ness
a·wash´
a·way´
awe
a·weigh´
awe´some
awe´stricken

awe´struck
aw´ful
aw´ful·ly
a·while´
a·whirl´
awk´ward
awk´ward·ly
awk´ward-ness
aw´ning
a·woke´
a·wry´
ax´i·om
ax-i-o-mat´ic
ax-i-o-mat´i-cal·ly
ax´is
ax´le
az´i-muth
az´ure

B

bab´ble
bab´bler
bab´bling
babe
ba´bied
ba´bies
ba´by
ba´by-ish
baby–sit
bac-ca-lau´re-ate
bac´cha-nal
bac-cha-na´lia
bac-cha-na´lian

bach´e-lor
back´ache
back´bend
back´bite
back´bit-ing
back´board
back´bone
back´break-ing
back´date
back´drop
backed
back´er
back´field
back´fire
back´flip
back´gam-mon
back´ground
back´hand-ed
back´ing
back´lash
back´list
back´log
back´pack
back–pedal
back´rest
back´slap-ping
back´slash
back´slid-ing
back´stage´
back´stop
back´stretch
back´stroke
back´swing

back′talk
back′track
back′up
back′ward
back′ward-ness
back-woods′
back-yard′
ba′con
bac-te′ri·a
bac-te′ri·al
bad′ly
bad′min-ton
bad–mouth
bad–tem-pered
baf′fle
baf′fling
bag′a-telle′
ba′gel
bag′ful
bag′gage
bagged
bag′ger
bag′ging
bag′gy
bag′pipe
ba-guette′
bail
bailed
bai′liff
bai′li-wick
bail′ment
bail′or
bail′out

bake
bak′er
bak′er·y
bak′ing
bal′ance
bal′anc·er
bal′anc-ing
bal′co-nies
bal′co·ny
bal′der-dash
bald′head·ed
bald′ness
bale′ful
bal′er
bal′ing
balk′i·er
balk′ing
balk′y
bal′lad
bal′lad·ry
bal′last
bal-le-ri′na
bal′let
bal-loon′
bal-loon′ist
bal′lot
ball′room
bal′ly-hoo
balm′i-ness
balm′y
ba-lo′ney
bal′us-ter
bal-us-trade′

bam-boo′
bam-boo′zle
ba′nal
ba-nal′i·ty
ban′dage
ban′dag-ing
ban-dan′na
band′box
band′ed
band′er
ban′dit
ban′dit·ry
band′stand
band′wag·on
ban′dy
ban′dy-ing
handy–legged
ban′gle
ban′ish
ban′ish-ment
ban′is-ter
ban′jo
ban′jos
bank
bank′a·ble
bank′er
bank′ing
bank′rupt
bank′rupt·cy
ban′ner
ban′quet
ban′tam
ban′ter

ban´ter-ing·ly

bap´tism

bap´tis´mal

bap-tize´

bap-tized´

bap-tiz´ing

bar

bar-bar´i·an

bar-bar´ic

bar-bar´i-cal·ly

bar´ba-rism

bar´ba-rous

bar´be-cue

bar´bell

bar´ber

bar´ber-shop

bare

bare´back

bared

bare´faced

bare´foot

bare–handed

bare´head·ed

bare´leg-ged

bare´ly

bar´gain

bar´gain·er

barge

bar´keep

bark´er

bark´ing

bar´maid

bar´man

bar mitz´vah

bar´na-cle

barn´dance

barn´storm

barn´yard

ba-rom´e-ter

bar-o-met´ric

ba-roque´

bar´rack

bar-rage´

barred

bar´rel

bar´ren

bar´ren-ness

bar-rette´

bar´ri-cade

bar´ri-cad´ing

bar´ri·er

bar´ring

bar´ris-ter

bar´room

bar´tender

bar´ter

ba´sal

base´ball

base´board

base´less

base´ly

base´ment

base´ness

bash´ful

bash´ful·ly

bash´ful-ness

bash´ing

ba´sic

ba´si-cal·ly

ba-sil´i·ca

ba´sin

ba´sin-like

ba´sis

bas´ket

bas´ket-ball

bas´ket-ful

bas´ket·ry

bas´ket-work

bas-si-net´

bas´tion

bath (n.)

bathe (v.)

bath´er

bath´house

bath´ing

bath´robe

bath´room

bath´tub

ba-ton´

bat-tal´ion

bat´ten

bat´ter

bat´ter-ies

bat´ter-ing

bat´ter·y

bat´ting

bat´tle

bat´tle-field

bat´tle-ground

bat´tle-ment	bear´able	beck´on-ing
battle–scarred	bear´a·bly	be-cloud´
bat´tle-ship	beard	be-come´
bat´ty	beard´ed	be-com´ing
bau´ble	beard´less	be-daub´
bawd´i-ness	bear´er	be-daz´zle
bawd´y	bear´ing	be-daz´zle-ment
bay´o-net	bear´ish	be-daz´zling
bay´ou	bear´skin	bed´bug
ba-zaar´	beast	bed´clothes
ba-zoo´ka	beast´li-ness	bed´ded
beach´ball	beast´ly	bed´ding
beach´comb·er	beat	be-dev´il
beach´front	beat´en	bed´fel-low
beach´head	beat´er	bed´jack·et
beach´wear	be-at-i-fi-ca´tion	bed´lam
bea´con	be-at´i-fied	bed´post
bead´ed	be-at´i·fy	be-drag´gle
bead´ing	beat´ing	bed´rid-den
bead´work	be-at´i-tude	bed´rock
bead´y	beau´te-ous	bed´roll
beak	beau-ti´cian	bed´room
beaked	beau´ties	bed´sheet
beak´er	beau´ti-fi-ca´tion	bed´side
beam	beau´ti-fied	bed´sore
beamed	beau´ti-fi·er	bed´spread
beam´ing	beau´ti-ful·ly	bed´spring
bean	beau´ti-fy-ing	bed´stead
bean´bag	beau´ty	bed´time
bean´ie	be-calm´	beef
bean´pole	be-came´	beef´i-ness
bean´stalk	be-cause´	beef´steak
bear	beck´on	beef·y

bee´hive
bee´keep·er
bee´keep-ing
bee´line
beep
beep´er
bees´wax
be-fall´
be-fall´en
be-fell´
be-fit´
be-fit´ting·ly
be-fog´
be-fogged´
be-fog´ging
be-fore´
be-fore´hand
be-fore´time
be-friend´
be-fud´dle
beg
be-gan´
beg´gar
beg´gar-li-ness
beg´gar·ly
beg´ging
be-gin´
be-gin´ner
be-gin´ning
be-grudge´
be-grudg´ing·ly
be-guile´ment
be-guil´er

be-guil´ing·ly
be-gun´
be-half´
be-hav´ior
be-hav´ior-al
be-hav´ior-al·ly
be-hav´ior-ism
be-head´
be-head´ed
be-held´
be-he´moth
be-hest´
be-hind´
be-hind´hand
be-hold´
be-hold´en
be-hold´er
be-hold´ing
be´ing
be-jew´el
be-jew´eled
be-la´bor
be-lat´ed
be-lat´ed·ly
be-lat´ed-ness
be-lay´
belch
be-lea´guer
be-lea´guered
be-lea´guer-ment
bel´fry
be-lie
belief´

be-li´er
be-liev-a·bil´i·ty
be-liev´a·ble
be-liev´a·bly
be-lieve´
be-lieved´
be-liev´er
be-liev´ing
be-lit´tle
be-lit´tle-ment
be-lit´tling
bel´li-cose
bel´li-cose·ly
bel´li-cose-ness
bel-li-cos´i·ty
bel-lig´er-ence
bel-lig´er-en·cy
bel-lig´er-ent
bel´low
bell–shaped
bell´tow·er
bell´weth·er
bel´ly
bel´ly-ache
bel´ly-but-ton
bel´ly-ful
be-long´
be-longed´
be-long´ing
be-long´ings
be-loved´
be-low´
belt

belt´ed	be-quest´	be-tray´al
belt´ing	be-rate´	be-tray´er
be-ly´ing	be-rat´ed	be-troth´
be-moan´	be-rat´ing	be-troth´al
be-moaned´	be-reave´	be-throthed´
be-moan´ing	be-reaved´	bet´ter
be-muse´	be-reave´ment	bet´ter–off
be-mused´	be-reav´ing	bet´ter-ment
be-mus´ed·ly	be-reft´	bet´ting
be-muse´ment	ber´ries	be-tween´
be-mus´ing	ber´ry	be-twixt´
bend´a·ble	ber´ry-like	bev´el
bend´ed	ber-serk´	bev´eled
bend´er	berth	bev´el-ing
bend´ing	berth´ing	bev´er-age
be-neath´	be-seech´	bev´ies
ben-e-dic´tion	be-seeched´	bev´y
ben-e-dic´to·ry	be-seech´er	be-wail´
ben´e-fac-tor	be-seech´ing·ly	be-wail´ing
ben´e-fice	be-set´	be-ware´
ben-e-fi´cial	be-side´	be-wil´der
ben-e-fi´cial·ly	be-smirch´	be-wil´dered
ben-e-fi´cia-ries	be-smirch´er	be-wil´der-ing·ly
ben-e-fi´cia·ry	best–known	be-wil´der-ment
ben´e-fit	best–liked	be-witch´
ben´e-fit·ed	be-stow´	be-witch´ing·ly
ben´e-fit-ing	be-stow´al	be-yond´
be-nev´o-lence	best–paid	bi-an´nu·al
be-nev´o-lent	be-stride´	bi-an´nu-al·ly
be-nign´	best–selling	bi´as
be-nign´ly	be-tide´	bi´ased
be-numb´	be-times´	bi´as-ing
be-queath´	be-tray´	bib-li-og´ra-phy

bib′li-o-phile
bi-cam′er-al
bi-cen-ten′a-ry
bi-cen-ten′ni-al
bick′er
bick′er-ing
bi′cy-cle
bi′cy-cler
bi′cy-clist
bid
bid′den
bid′der
bid′ding
bid′dy
bide
bid′ing
bi-di-rec′tion-al
bi-en′ni-al-ly
bi-fo′cals
bi′fur-cate
bi′fur-cat-ed
bi′fur-ca′tion
big′a-mist
big′a-mous
big′a-my
big′ger
big′heart-ed
big′heart-ed-ly
big′heart-ed-ness
big′ness
big′ot
big′ot-ed
big′ot-ry

big′wig
bike
bik′er
bi-ki′ni
bi-lat′er-al
bi-lat′er-al-ly
bi-lin′e-ar
bi-lin′gual
bil′ious
bil′ious-ly
bil′ious-ness
bill′board
bil′liards
bill′ing
bil′lion
bil′lion-aire
bil′lionth
bill of sale
bil′low
bil′low-y
bi-month′ly
bi′na-ry
bind
bind′er
bind′er-y
bind′ing
bin-oc′u-lars
bi-o-de-grad′a-ble
bi-o-feed′back
bi-o-gen′e-sis
bi-o-ge-net′ic
bi-og′ra-pher
bi-o-graph′ic

bi-o-graph′i-cal
bi-og′ra-phy
bi-o-log′i-cal-ly
bi-ol′o-gist
bi-ol′o-gy
bi-on′ic
bi-on′i-cal-ly
bi′o-rhythm
bi′o-sphere
bi-par′ti-san
bird′bath
bird′cage
bird′house
bird′seed
bird's–eye
birth′day
birth′place
birth′rate
birth′right
birth′stone
bis′cuit
bi-sect′
bi-sec′tion
bish′op
bish′op-ric
bite
bit′er
bit′ing
bit′ten
bit′ter
bit′ter-ness
bit′ter-sweet
biv′ouac

biv´ouacked
biv´ouack-ing
bi-week´ly
bizarre´
blab
blab´ber
black–eyed pea
black´mail
black´out
black´smith
blam´a·ble
blam´a·bly
blame
blamed
blame´ful·ly
blame´ful-ness
blame´less·ly
blame´less-ness
blame´wor-thy
blam´ing
blanch
blanch´er
blanch´ing
bland
blan´dish-ment
bland´ly
bland´ness
blank
blan´ket
blank´ly
blank´ness
blar´ney
bla-sé´

blas´pheme
blas´phem·er
blas´phem-ing
blas´phe-mous·ly
blas´phe·my
blast
blast´ed
blast´er
bla´tant
bla´tant·ly
blath´er
blath´er-ing
blaze
blazed
blaz´er
blaz´ing
bla´zon
bleak
bleak´ly
blear´i·ly
blear´i-ness
blear´y
blear´y–eyed
bleed
bleed´er
bleed´ing
blem´ish
blend
blend´er
blend´ing
bless
bless´ed·ly
bless´ing

blind´ing
blind´ing·ly
blind´ly
blind´ness
blink
blink´er
blink´ing
bliss
bliss´ful·ly
bliss´ful-ness
blis´ter
blis´ter-ing
blis´ter·y
bliz´zard
bloat
bloat´ed
bloat´er
block
block-ade´
block-ad´ed
block-ad´er
block-ad´ing
block´age
block´buster
block´head
blond, blonde
blood
blood´cur-dling
blood´hound
blood´i-est
blood´less
blood´let-ting
blood´shed

blood´stain
blood´suck·er
blood´thirst·y
blood´y
bloom
bloom´ers
bloom´ing
bloop´er
blos´som
blot
blotch
blotch´y
blot´ted
blot´ter
blot´ting
blouse
blow
blow–dry
blow–dryer
blow´er
blown
blow´out
blow´torch
bludg´eon
blue´berry
blue´bird
blue–black
blue–blooded
blue–collar
blue–eyed
blue´grass
blue–pencil
blue´print

bluff
bluff´er
bluff´ing
blun´der
blun´der·er
blun´der-ing·ly
blunt
blunt´ly
blunt´ness
blur
blurred
blur´red-ness
blur´ring
blur´ry
blurt
blurt´ed
blush
blushed
blush´er
blush´ing·ly
blus´ter
blus´ter-ing·ly
blus´ter-ous
blus´ter·y
board´er
board´ing-house
board´walk
boast
boast´er
boast´ful
boast´ing·ly
boat´house
boat´ing

bob´bin
bob´bing
bob´ble
bob´sled
bo-da´cious
bod´ice
bod´i·ly
bod´y
bod´y-build·er
bod´y-guard
body–search
bod´y-work
bog´gle
bo´gus
bo´gy
boil
boil´er
boil´ing
bois´ter-ous
bois´ter-ous·ly
bois´ter-ous-ness
bold
bold´face
bold–faced
bold´ly
bold´ness
bol´ster
bom-bard´
bom-bard´ment
bom-bas´tic
bom-bas´ti-cal·ly
bo´na fide
bo-nan´za

bond´age	boot´ed	bot´tle–fed
bond´ed	boot´ie	bot´tle-neck
bond´ing	boot´leg	bot´tler
bon´fire	boot´leg-ger	bot´tling
bon´net	boot´leg-ging	bot´tom
bon´ny	boot´strap	bot´tom-less
bo´nus	boo´ty	bought
bon´y	booze	boul´der
book	booz´er	bou´le-vard
book´bind-ing	booz´y	bounce
book´case	bop	bounc´er
book´end	bor´der	bounc´ing
book´ie	bor´dered	bounc´y
book´ing	bor´der·er	bound
book´ish-ness	bor´der-line	bound´a-ries
book´keep·er	bore´dom	bound´a·ry
book´keep-ing	bor´er	bound´ed
book´let	bor´ing	bound´er
book´mak·er	born	bound´less-ness
book´mark	borne	boun´te-ous·ly
book´sell·er	bor´ough	boun´te-ous-ness
book´sell-ing	bor´row	boun´ti-ful·ly
book´shelf	bor´row·er	boun´ti-ful-ness
book´store	bor´row-ing	boun´ty
book´worm	boss´i-ness	bou-quet´
boor	boss´y	bour´bon
boor´ish	bo-tan´i-cal	bour´geois,
boor´ish·ly	bo-tan´i-cal·ly	bour´geoise
boor´ish-ness	bot´a-nist	bour´geoi-sie´
boost	bot´a·ny	bourne
boost´er	both´er	bou-tique´
boot	both´er-some	bou´ton-niere´
boot´black	bot´tle	bow´er

bow´er·y	brain´less	brawn´i·er
bow´ing	brain´pow·er	brawn´i-est
bow´leg-ged	brain´storm	brawn´i-ness
bowl´er	brain´storm-ing	brawn´y
bowl´ing	brain´teas·er	bra´zen
box´car	brain´wash	bra´zen·ly
box´er	brain´wash-ing	bra´zen-ness
box´ing	brain´y	braz´er
box´y	braise	bra´zier
boy´cott	braised	braz´ing
boy´friend	brais´ing	bread
boy´ish	bram´ble	bread´bas-ket
boy´ish-ness	bram´bly	bread´board
brace´let	bran´died	bread´box
brac´ing·ly	bran´dish	bread´crumb
brac´ing-ness	brand–new	bread´pan
brac´ing	bran´dy	breadth
brack´et	brash	bread´win-ner
brack´ish	brash´ly	break
brag	brash´ness	break´a·ble
brag-ga-do´ci·o	bras-siere´	break´age
brag´gart	brass´i-ness	break´a-way
bragged	brass´y	break´down
brag´ger	brave	break´er
brag´ging	brave´heart·ed	break–e´ven
braid	brave´ly	break´fast
braid´ing	brav´er·y	break–in
brain	brav´est	break´ing
brain´child	bra´vo	break´through
brain–dead	bra-vu´ra	break´up
brain´i·er	brawl	breath
brain´i·ly	brawl´er	breath´a·ble
brain´i-ness	brawn	breathe

breath´er
breath´ing
breath´less·ly
breath´less-ness
breath´tak-ing·ly
breed
breed´er
breed´ing
breeze
breeze´way
breez´i·ly
breez´i-ness
breez´y
breth´ren
brev´i·ty
brew
brew´er
brew´er·y
brew´ing
bribe
bribed
brib´er
brib´er·y
brib´ing
bric–a–brac
brick
brick´lay·er
brick´laying
brick´work
brick´yard
brid´al
bride´groom
brides´maid

bridge
bridge´a·ble
bridge´head
bridge´work
bridg´ing
brief
brief´case
brief´ing
brief´ly
bright
bright´en
bright´en·er
bright–eyed
bright´ly
bright´ness
bril´liance
bril´lian·cy
bril´liant
bril´liant·ly
bril´liant-ness
brim
brim´ful
brim´less
brimmed
brim´ming
bring
bring´ing
brin´y
brisk
brisk´ly
brisk´ness
bris´tle
bris´tling

bris´tly
brit´tle
brit´tle-ness
broad´cast
broad´cast-ing
broad´en
broad´ly
broad–mind·ed
broad–spectrum
bro-cade´
bro-cad´ed
bro-chure´
broil
broil´er
broke
bro´ken
broken–down
bro´ken-heart·ed
bro´ker
bro´ker-age
broth´el
broth´er-hood
brother–in–law
broth´er-li-ness
broth´er·ly
brou´ha-ha
brow´beat
brow´beat·er
brow´beat-ing
brown–bag
brown´out
brown´stone
browse

brows´er
brows´ing
bruise
bruised
bruis´er
bruis´ing
brush
brushed
brush–off
brush´work
brusque
brusque´ly
brusque´ness
bru´tal
bru-tal´i·ty
bru´tal-ize
bru´tal·ly
brute
brut´ish·ly
brut´ish-ness
bub´ble
bub´ble-gum
bub´ble-top
bub´bli-ness
bub´bling
bub´bly
buc´ca-neer
buck´et
buck´le
buck´ler
buck´ling
buck´shot
buck´skin

buck´tooth
bu-col´ic
bu-col´i-cal·ly
bud´ding
bud´dy
bud´get
bud´get-ar·y
bud´get·ed
bud´get·er
bud´get-ing
buff´er
buf´fet *(strike)*
buf-fet´ *(food)*
buf-foon´
buf-foon´er·y
buf-foon´ish
bug´a-boo
bug–eyed
bug´gy
bu´gle
bu´gler
bu´gling
build
build´er
build´ing
build´up
built
built–in
built–up
bul´bous
bul´bous·ly
bulge
bulg´i-ness

bulg´ing
bulg´y
bulk´i·er
bulk´i-ness
bulk´y
bull´doze
bull´doz·er
bull´doz-ing
bul´le-tin
bul´let-proof
bull´fight
bull´fight·er
bull´fight-ing
bull´head·ed
bull´head-ed-ness
bull´horn
bul´lied
bull´ish
bull´ish-ness
bull´pen
bull´s–eye
bul´ly
bul´ly-ing
bum´ble
bum´bler
bum´bling
bum´mer
bump´er
bumper–to–
   bumper
bump´i·er
bump´i·ly
bump´i-ness

bump´kin
bump´tious
bump´y
bun´dle
bun´dling
bun´ga-low
bun´gee
bun´gle
bun´gled
bun´gler
bun´gling
bunk´house
bunt´ing (cloth)
buoy´an·cy
buoy´ant
bur´den
bur´dened
bur´den-some
bu´reau
bu-reauc´ra·cy
bu´reau-crat
bu-reau-crat´ic
bur´geon
burg´er
bur´glar
bur´gla-ries
bur´glar-ize
bur´glar-proof
bur´gla·ry
bur´i·al
bur´ied
bur´ies
bur´lap

bur´lesque´
bur´li-ness
bur´ly
burn
burned
burn´er
burn´ish
burnt
bur´row
bur´row·er
burst
burst´ing
bur´y
bur´y-ing
bus´boy
bush
bushed
bush´el
bush´i·er
bush´i-ness
bush´y
bus´ied
bus´i·er
bus´i-est
bus´i·ly
bus´i-ness
bus´i-ness-like
bus´i-ness-man
bus´tle
bus´tled
bus´tler
bus´tling
bus´y

bus´y-bod·y
butch´er
butch´er·y
but´ler
butt
butte
but´ter (spread)
butt´er (one who
  butts)
but´ter-ball
but´ter-fat
but´ter-fin-gers
but´ter-i-ness
but´ter·y
but´ton
button–down
but´ton-hole
but´tress
bux´om
bux´om·ly
bux´om-ness
buy
buy´back
buy´er
buy´ing
buy´off
buy´out
buzz´er
buzz´ing
buzz´word
by
by–and–by
bye

by´gone
by´law
by–line
by´pass
by–product
by´stand·er
byte
by´way
by´word

C

ca-bal´
cab´a·la
cab-a-lis´tic
cab-a-ret´
cab´by
cab´driv·er
cab´in
cab´i-net
cab´i-net-mak·er
cab´i-net·ry
cab´i-net-work
ca´ble
ca´ble-cast
ca´ble-gram
ca´ble-vi-sion
ca´bling
ca-boose´
cab´o-tage
cab´stand
cache
cached
ca-chet´

cack´le
cack´ling
ca-coph´o-nous
ca-coph´o-nous·ly
ca-coph´o·ny
ca-dav´er
ca-dav´er-ous
cad´dy
ca´dence
ca´denced
ca-det´
ca-det´ship
cadge
cad´re
ca-fé´
caf-e-te´ri·a
caf´fein-at·ed
caf´feine
caf´tan
cage´ling
ca´gey
ca´gi·er
ca´gi·ly
cag´i-ness
ca-jole´
ca-jol´er·y
ca-jol´ing·ly
ca-lam´i-tous·ly
ca-lam´i-tous-ness
ca-lam´i·ty
cal´cu-la-ble
cal´cu-la-bly
cal´cu-late

cal´cu-lat·ed
cal´cu-lat-ed·ly
cal´cu-lat-ed-ness
cal´cu-lat-ing
cal´cu-lat-ing·ly
cal-cu-la´tion
cal´cu-la-tor
cal´cu-li
cal´cu-lous
cal´cu-lus
cal´en-dar
calf´skin
cal´i-ber
cal´i-brate
cal-i-bra´tion
cal´i-bra-tor
cal´i·co
cal´i-per
ca´liph
ca´liph-ate
cal-is-then´ics
calk
calk´ing
call
call´able
call´er
cal-lig´ra-pher
cal-lig´ra-phy
call´ing
cal-li´o·pe
cal´low
cal´low-ness
calm´ing·ly

calm´ly
calm´ness
ca-lor´ic
ca-lor´i-cal·ly
cal´o-rie
cal-o-rif´ic
ca-lum´ni-ate
ca-lum-ni-a´tion
ca-lum´ni-a-tor
cal´um-nies
cal´um·ny
ca-lyp´so
ca-ma-ra´de-rie
cam´bric
cam´cord·er
cam´er·a
cam´er·a-man
camera–ready
camera–shy
cam´i-sole
cam´ou-flage
cam-paign´
cam-paign´er
camp´er
camp´fire
camp´ground
camp´i-ness
camp´site
cam´pus
camp´y
ca-nal´
ca´na-pé
ca-nard´

can´cel
can´cel-a·ble
can´celed
can´cel·er
can´cel-ing
can-cel-la´tion
can´cer
can´cer-ous
can-de-la´bra
can-de-la´brum
can´did
can´di-da·cy
can´di-date
can´did·ly
can´did-ness
can´died
can´dies
can´dle
can´dle-light
can´dle-pow·er
can´dler
can´dle-shade
can´dle-stick
can´dor
can´dy
cane´brake
ca´nine
can´is-ter
can´ker
canned
can´ner
can´ner·y
can´ni-bal

can´ni-bal-ism
can-ni-bal-is´tic
can´ni-bal-ize
can´ni·ly
can´ni-ness
can´ning
can´non
can´non-ade´
can´non-ball
can´non-eer
can´not
can´ny
ca-noe´
ca-noe´ing
ca-noe´ist
ca-noes´
can´o·la
ca-non´i-cal
can-on-i-za´tion
can´on-ize
can´o-pies
can´o·py
can-tan´ker-ous
can-ta´ta
can-teen´
can´vas
can´vas-back
can´vass
can´vass·er
can´yon
ca-pa·bil´i-ties
ca-pa·bil´i·ty
ca´pa·ble

38

ca´pa·bly
ca-pa´cious
ca-pac´i-tate
ca-pac´i·ty
cap´ful
cap´i·ta
cap´i-tal
cap´i-tal-ism
cap´i-tal-ist
cap-i-tal-is´tic
cap´i-tal-ize
cap´i-tol
ca-pit´u-late
ca-pit-u-la´tion
cap-puc-ci´no
ca-price´
ca-pri´cious·ly
ca-pri´cious-ness
cap´size
cap´siz-ing
cap´su-lar
cap´sule
cap´tain
cap´tion
cap´tious
cap´tious·ly
cap´tious-ness
cap´ti-vate
cap´ti-vat-ing·ly
cap-ti-va´tion
cap´tive
cap-tiv´i·ty
cap´tor

cap´ture
cap´tur·er
cap´tur-ing
ca-rafe´
car´a-mel
car´a-mel-ize
car´at
car´a-van
car-a-van´sa·ry
car´barn
car-bo-hy´drate
car´bon
car-bon-a´tion
car´bun-cle
car´cass
card´board
card–carrying
card´case
car´di-nal
card´sharp
ca-reen´
ca-reer´
care´free
care´ful·ly
care´giv·er
care´less·ly
care´less-ness
ca-ress´
ca-ress´ing·ly
car´et
care´tak·er
care´worn
car´fare

car´go
car´goes
car´i-ca-ture
car´i-ca-tur-ist
car´il-lon
car´nage
car´nal
car´nal·ly
car-na´tion
car´ni-val
car´ni-vore
car-niv´o-rous
car´ol
car´ol·er
car´om
ca-rous´al
ca-rouse´
car-ou-sel´
ca-rous´ing
ca-rous´ing·ly
car´pen-ter
car´pen-try
car´pet
car´pet-ing
carp´ing
car´pool
car´port
car´riage
car´ri·er
car-rou-sel´
car´ried
car´ry
car´ry-all

car´ry–on
car´sick
cart´age
car-tel´
car-tog´ra-pher
car-tog´ra-phy
car´ton
car-toon´
car-toon´ist
car´tridge
cart´wheel
carve
carv´er
carv´ing
cas-cade´
case´book
case´ment
cash–and–carry
cash-ier´
cash´mere
cas´ing
cas´ket
cas´se-role
cas-sette´
cas-ta-net´
cast´a-way
cas´ti-gate
cas-ti-ga´tion
cas-ti-ga´tor
cast´ing
ca´su-al
ca´su-al·ly
ca´su-al-ness

ca´su-al·ty
cat´a-comb
cat´a-log, cat´a-
   logue
cat´a-log·er, cat´a-
   logu·er
cat´a-log-ing, cat´a-
   logu-ing
cat´a-lyst
cat-a-lyt´ic
cat-a-ma-ran´
cat´a-pult
ca-tas´tro-phe
cat-a-stroph´ic
cat-a-stroph´i-cal
catch´all
catch´er
catch´i·er
catch´ing
catch´word
catch´y
cat-e-gor´i-cal
cat-e-gor´i-cal·ly
cat-e-go-ri-za´tion
cat´e-go-rize
cat´e-go-ry
cat´e-nate
ca´ter
ca´ter·er
ca-the´dral
cath´ode
cat´nap
cat´nip

cat´sup
cat´ty
cau´cus
caul´dron
caulk´ing
caus´al
caus´al·ly
cau-sa´tion
caus´a-tive
cause
caus´er
cause´way
caus´ing
caus´tic
caus´ti-cal·ly
cau´tion
cau´tion-ar·y
cau´tious·ly
cau´tious-ness
cav´al-cade´
cav´a-lier´
cav-a-lier´ly
cav´al·ry
ca´ve·at
cave–in
cave´man
cav´ern
cav´ern-ous
cav´il
cav´i·ty
cavort´
ca-vort´ing
cease´less

cease´less·ly
ceas´ing
cede
ced´ed
ced´ing
ceil´ing
ceil´inged
cel´e-brate
cel´e-brat·ed
cel-e-bra´tion
cal´e-bra-tive
cel´e-bra-tor
cel´e-bra-to·ry
ce-leb´ri·ty
ce-ler´i·ty
ce-les´tial
cel´i-ba·cy
cel´i-bate
cel´lar
cell´mate
cel´lo
cel´lo-phane
cel´lu-lar
cel´lu-lite
ce-ment´
cem´e-ter-ies
cem´e-ter·y
cen´sor
cen´sor-a·ble
cen-so´ri·al
cen-so´ri-ous·ly
cen´sor-ship
cen´sur-a·ble

cen´sure
cen´sured
cen´sur-ing
cen´sus
cen-te-nar´i·an
cen-ten´ni·al
cen´ter
cen´ter-fold
cen´ter-line
cen´ter-piece
cen´ti-grade
cen´ti-gram
cen´ti-me-ter
cen´tral
cen-tral-i-za´tion
cen´tral-ize
cen´tral·ly
cen´tre (Br.)
cen´tric
cen-tric´i·ty
cen-trif´u-gal
cen´tri-fuge
cen´trist
cen´tu·ry
ce-ram´ic
ce´re-al
cer-e-mo´ni-al
cer-e-mo´ni-al·ly
cer´e-mo-nies
cer-e-mo´ni-ous
cer-e-mo´ni-ous·ly
cer´e-mo·ny
cer´tain

cer´tain·ly
cer´tain·ty
cer´ti-fi-a·ble
cer´ti-fi-a·bly
cer-tif´i-cate
cer-ti-fi-ca´tion
cer´ti-fied
cer´ti-fies
cer´ti·fy
cer´ti-fy-ing
ces-sa´tion
cess´pool
cha-grin´
cha-grined´
chair
chair´lift
chair´per-son
chaise
chal-ced´o·ny
chal´dron
cha´let
chal´ice
chalk
chalk´y
chal´lenge
chal´leng·er
chal´leng-ing
cham´ber
cham´ber-maid
cham´ois
cham´o-mile
cham-pagne´
cham´pi·on

cham´pi-on-ship
chan´cel
chan´cel-lor
chanc´i-ness
chanc´y
chan´de-lier´
change´a·ble
change´a·ble-ness
change´a·bly
changed
change´less·ly
change´less-ness
change´ling
chang´er
chang´ing
chan´nel
chan´neled
chan´nel-ing
chant
chant´er
cha´os
cha-ot´ic
cha-ot´i-cal·ly
chap´el
chap´er·on
chap´lain
chap´lain·cy
chap´ter
char´ac-ter
char-ac-ter-is´tic
char-ac-ter-i-
  za´tion
char´ac-ter-ize

cha-rade´
char´coal
charge´a·ble
charge´a·bly
charged
charg´er
charg´ing
cha-ris´ma
char´is-mat´ic
char´i-ta·ble
char´i-ta·ble-ness
char´i-ta·bly
char-i-ties
char´i·ty
char´la-tan
charm
charmed
charm´er
charm´ing·ly
char´ter *(grant)*
chart´er *(planner)*
chartreuse´
chase
chased
chas´er
chas´ing
chasm
chas´sis
chaste
chaste´ly
chaste´ness
chas´ten
chas-tise´ment

chas-tis´er
chas´ti·ty
châ-teau´
cha-teaux´ *(pl.)*
chat´tel
chat´ter
chat´ter-box
chat´ter-er
chat´ti·ly
chat´ti-ness
chat´ting
chat´ty
chauf´feur
chau´vin-ism
chau´vin-ist
chau-vin-is´ti-cal·ly
cheap
cheap´en
cheap´ened
cheap´ly
cheap´skate
cheat
cheat´er
check´book
checked
cheek´er
check´er-board
check´ered
check´ers
check´list
check–out
check´point
check´up

42

cheek´bone
cheek´y
cheer´ful
cheer´ful·ly
cheer´ful-ness
cheer´i·ly
cheer´i-ness
cheer´lead·er
cheer´less
cheer´y
chees´y
chem´i-cal
chem´i-cal·ly
che-mise´
chem´ist
chem´is-try
cher´ish
cher´ish-a·ble
cher´ish·er
cher´ish-ing·ly
cher´ub
che-ru´bic
cher´u-bim (pl.)
chest
chest´ed
chest´ful
chest´i·ly
chest´nut
chest´y
chev´ron
chew´a·ble
chew´ing
chew´y

chew´i-ness
chi-ca´ner·y
chi´cle
chide
chid´ing·ly
chief
chief´ly
chief of state
chief´tain
chif-fon´
chif-fo-nade´
chi´gnon
child
child´bear-ing
child´birth
child´hood
child´ish·ly
child´ish-ness
child´like
chil´dren
chill´i-ness
chill´ing·ly
chill´y
chime
chimed
chim´er
chi-me´ra
chi-mer´i-cal
chim´ing
chim´ney
chi´na-ware
chintz
chintz´y

chip´board
chip´per
chis´el
chis´el·er
chis´el-ing
chit´chat
chi-val´ric
chiv´al-rous·ly
chiv´al-rous-ness
chiv´al·ry
choc´o-late
choice
choic´est
choir
choir´boy
choir´mas-ter
choke
choked
chok´er
chok´ing
chol´er
cho-les´ter-ol
cho´line
choose
choos´y
choos´ing
chop
chop´per
chop´pi-ness
chop´ping
chop´py
chop´stick
cho´ral

cho-rale´
cho´re-o-graph
cho-re-og´ra-pher
cho-re-o-graph´ic
cho-re-og´ra-phy
cho´ris-ter
chor´tle
chor´tling
cho´rus
chose
cho´sen
chow´der
chris´ten
chris´ten-ing
chron´ic
chron´i-cal·ly
chron´i-cle
chron´i-cler
chron´i-cling
chron-o-log´ic
chron-o-log´i-cal
chro-nol´o·gy
chro-nom´e-ter
chub´by
chuck´le
chuck´led
chuckle-head
chuck´ling
chum´mi·ly
chum´mi-ness
chum´my
chunk´i·ly
chunk´i-ness

chunk´y
church
church´go·er
church´ly
church´yard
churl
churl´ish
churl´ish·ly
churl´ish-ness
churn
churn´er
chutz´pa
ci-gar´
cig-a-rette´,
   cig-a-ret´
cigar–shaped
cinc´ture
cin´der
cin´e·ma
cin-e-ma-theque´
cin-e-mat´ic
cin-e-mat´i-cal·ly
ci´pher
ci´pher-a·ble
cir´cle
cir´cled
cir´clet
cir´cling
cir´cuit·ry
cir-cu´i·ty
cir-cu´i-tous
cir´cu-lar
cir-cu-lar´i·ty

cir´cu-lar-ize
cir´cu-late
cir´cu-la´tion
cir´cu-la-tor
cir´cu-la-to·ry
cir-cum´fer-ence
cir-cum-fer-en´tial
cir-cum-lo-cu´tion
cir-cum-nav´i-gate
cir´cum-scribe
cir-cum-scrip-tion
cir´cum-spect
cir-cum-spec´tion
cir-cum-spec´tive
cir´cum-stance
cir´cum-stanced
cir´cum-stan´tial
cir´cum-stan´tial·ly
cir´cum-stan´ti-ate
cir´cum-vent
cir-cum-ven´tion
cir´cus
cis´tern
cit´a-del
ci-ta´tion
ci-ta´tion·al
cit´ies
cit´ied
cit´i-fied
cit´i·fy
cit´i-ng
cit´i-zen
cit´i-zen·ry

cit'i-zen-ship
cit'y
cit'y-scape
city–state
cit'y-wide
civic–minded
civ'ics
civ'il
ci-vil'ian
ci-vil'i·ty
civ-i-li-za'tion
civ'i-lize
civ'i-lized
civ'i-liz-ing
civ'il·ly
claim
claim'ant
claim'er
clair-voy'ance
clair-voy'ant
clair-voy'ant·ly
clam'ber
clam'mi-ly
clam'mi-ness
clam'my
clam'or
clam'or·er
clam'or-ous
clam'or-ous·ly
clam'or-ous-ness
clamp
clan-des'tine
clan-des'tine·ly

clan-des'tine-ness
clang
clang'er
clang'or-ous
clan'nish
clans'man
clap
clapped
clap'per
clap'ping
clap'trap
clar-i-fi-ca'tion
clar'i-fied
clar'i-fy
clar'i-fy-ing
clar'i-on
clar'i-ty
clasp
clasp'er
clas'sic
clas'si-cal·ly
clas'si-fi-a·ble
clas-si-fi-ca'tion
clas'si-fied
clas'si-fi·er
clas'si·fy
clas'si-fy-ing
class'mate
class'room
class'y
clat'ter
clat'tered
clat'ter·er

clat'ter-ing
clau-di-ca'tion
claus'al
clause
claus-tro-pho'bi·a
claus-tro-pho'bic
cla-vier'
clay
clay'ey
clean
clean–cut
clean'er
clean–handed
clean'li-ness
clean'ly
clean'ness
cleanse
cleansed
cleans'er
clean–shaven
cleans'ing
clean'up
clear'ance
clear–cut
clear–eyed
clear'head·ed
clear'head-ed-ness
clear'ing-house
clear'ly
clear–sight'ed
clear'wing
cleav'age
cleave

cleaved
cleav´er
cleav´ing
clem´en·cy
clem´ent
clem´ent·ly
cler´gy
cler´gy-man
cler´ic
cler´i-cal
clev´er
clev´er·ly
clev´er-ness
cli-che´
cli-ched´
click
click´er
cli´ent
cli´en-tele´
cliff
cliff´hang·er
cliff´y
cli-mac´tic
cli-mac´ti-cal·ly
cli´mate
cli-mat´ic
cli´ma-tize
cli-ma-tol´o·gy
cli´max
climb
climb´a·ble
climbed
climb´er

climb´ing
clinch
clinch´er
cling
cling´er
cling´i-ness
cling´ing
cling´y
clin´ic
clin´i-cal·ly
cli-ni´cian
clink
clink´er
clip
clip´board
clip–on
clipped
clip´per
clip´ping
clique
cli´quish
cli´quish-ness
cloak
cloak–and–dagger
clob´ber
cloche
clock´mak·er
clock´mak-ing
clock´wise
clock´work
clod
clod´hopper
clod´dish

clois´ter
clois´tered
clois´tral
close
close–by
close call
closed
closed–circuit
closed–door
close–fisted
close–fitting
close–knit
close´ly
close´mouthed
close´ness
close´out
clos´est
clos´et
clos´et-ful
close–up
clos´ing
clo´sure
cloth
clothe
clothes´horse
clothes´line
clothes´pin
cloth´ier
cloth´ing
clo´ture
cloud´burst
cloud´i-ness
cloud´less

cloud´y

clo´ver-leaf

clown

clown´ish

clown´ish·ly

cloy´ing·ly

club

clubbed

club´ber

club´bi-ness

club´bing

club´by

club´house

clum´si·er

clum´si·ly

clum´si-ness

clum´sy

clunk

clunk´er

clunk´y

clus´ter

clus´ter·y

clutch

clut´ter

co-ag´u-lant

co-ag´u-late

co-ag-u-la´tion

co-a-lesce´

co-a-les´cence

co-a-les´cent

co-a-lesc´ing

co-a-li´tion

co-an´chor

co´apt

coarse´ly

coars´en

coarse´ness

coast´al

coast´er

coast´line

coast–to–coast

coat

coat´ed

coat´ing

coat´rack

coat´room

coat´tail

co-au´thor,

  co–au´thor

coax

co-ax´i·al

coax´ing

coax´ing·ly

cob´bler

cob´ble-stone

cob´web

cock´eyed

cock´i·ly

cock´i-ness

cock´tail

cock´y

co-coon´

cod´dle

code

cod´ed

co-de-fend´ant

co-de-pend´ence

co-de-pend´en·cy

co-de-pend´ent

codg´er

cod´i-cil

cod-i-fi-ca´tion

cod´i-fied

cod´i·fy

cod´ling

co´ed

co-ed-u-ca´tion·al

co´ef-fi´cient

co-erce´

co-erc´i·ble

co-erc´ing

co-er´cion

co-er´cive·ly

co-er´cive-ness

co-ex-ist´

co-ex-is´tence

cof´fee-cake

cof´fee-house

cof´fee-pot

cof´fer

cof´fin

co´gent

cog´i-tate

cog´i-tat-ing

cog-i-ta´tion

cog´i-ta-tor

cog-ni´tion

cog´ni-tive

co-hab´it

co-hab´i-tate
co-hab-i-ta´tion
co-here´
co-her´ence
co-her´ent·ly
co-he´sion
co-he´sive·ly
co-he´sive-ness
co´hort
co–host´
coin´age
co-in-cide´
co-in´ci-dence
co-in´ci-dent
co-in-ci-den´tal
co-in-ci-den´tal·ly
co-in-cid´ing
coin–operated
co-in-sur´ance
co-in-sure´
col´an-der
cold´–blood´ed
cold´heart´ed
cold´ly
cold´ness
col´ic
col´ick·y
col-i-se´um
col-lab´o-rate
col-lab´o-rat-ing
col-lab-o-ra´tion
col-lab´o-ra-tive
col-lab´o-ra-tor

col-lage´
col-lapse´
col-lapsed´
col-laps´i·ble
col-laps´ing
col´lar-bone
col´lar but-ton
col-late´
col-lat´er·al
col-lat´er-al-ize
col-lat´ing
col-la´tion
col-la´tor
col´league
col-lect´
col-lect´ed
col-lect´i·ble
col-lec´tion
col-lec´tive·ly
col-lec´tor
col´leen
col´lege
col-le´gi·al
col-le´gian
col-le´giate
col-lide´
col-lid´ing
col-li´sion
col-lo´qui·al
col-lo´qui-al-ism
col-lo´qui-al·ly
col´lo-quy
col-lude´

col-lud´ing
col-lu´sion
col-lu´sive
co-logne´
co´lon
col´o-nel
co-lo´ni·al
co-lo´ni-al-ism
col-o-ni-za´tion
col´o-nize
col-on-nade´
col´o-phon
col´or
col´or-ant
col-or-a´tion
col´or-bear·er
color–blind
color–code
col´ored
col´or-fast
col´or-ful
col´or-ist
col´or-ize
col-or-i-za´tion
col´or-less
co-los´sal
co-los´sus
col´our (Br.)
colt´ish
col´umn
co-lum´nar
col´um-nist
co´ma

co´ma-tose
com´bat (n., v.)
com-bat´ (v.)
com-bat´ant
com-bat´ing
com-bat´ive
comb´er
com-bin´a-ble
com-bin-a-bil´i-ty
com-bi-na´tion
com-bine´ (to join)
com´bine (n.
   harvester)
com-bin´ing
com´bo
com-bust´
com-bus´ti-ble
com-bus´tion
come´back
co-me´di-an
co-me´dic
com´e-dies
com´e-dy
come–hither
come´li-ness
come·ly
come–on
co-mes´ti-ble
com´et
come-up´pance
com´fit
com´fort
com´fort-a·ble

com´fort-a·bly
com´fort·er
com´fy
com´ic
com´i-cal·ly
com´ing
coming–out
com´ma
com-mand´
com´man-dant
com´man-deer´
com-mand´er
com-mand´ing
com-mand´ing·ly
com-mand´ment
com-man´do
com-man´dos
com-mem´o-rate
com-mem´o-rat-ing
com-mem-o-ra´tion
com-mem´o-ra-tive
com-mem´o-ra-
   to·ry
com-mence´
com-mence´ment
com-menc´ing
com-mend´a·ble
com-mend´a·bly
com-men-da´tion
com-men´su-rate
com´ment
com´men-tar·y
com´men-ta-tor

com´merce
com-mer´cial
com-mer´cial-ism
com-mer-ci-al´i·ty
com-mer-cial-i-
   za´tion
com-mer´cial-ize
com-mer´cial-ized
com-mer´cial·ly
com-min´gle
com-min´gling
com-mis´er-ate
com-mis-er-a´tion
com´mis-sar·y
com-mis´sion
com-mis´sion-a·ble
com-mis´sioned
com-mis´sion-er
com-mit´ment
com-mit´ted
com-mit´tee
com-mit´ting
com-mo´di-ous
com-mo´di-ous·ly
com-mod´i-ties
com-mod´i·ty
com´mo-dore
com´mon
com-mon-al´i·ty
com´mon-al·ty
com´mon·er
com´mon·ly
com´mon-place

com´mon-weal
com´mon-wealth
com-mo´tion
com-mu´nal
com-mu´nal·ly
com-mu-nal-is´tic
com-mu-nal´i·ty
com-mu´nal-ize
com-mune´ (v.)
com´mune (n.)
com-mu´ni-ca·ble
com-mu´ni-cate
com-mu´ni-cat-ing
com-mu´ni-ca´tion
com-mu´ni-ca´-
  tion·al
com-mu´ni-ca-tive
com-mu´ni-ca-tor
com-mu´nion
com´mu-nism
com´mu-nist
com´mu-nis´tic
com-mu´ni-ties
com-mu´ni·ty
com-mu-ta´tion
com-mute´
com-mut´er
com-mut´ing
com´pact (n.)
com-pact´ (adj., v.)
com-pact´ed
com-pact´ly
com-pact´ness

com-pac´tor
com´pa-nies
com-pan´ion
com-pan´ion-ship
com´pa·ny
com-pa-ra-bil´i·ty
com´pa-ra·ble
com´pa-ra·bly
com-par´a-tive·ly
com-pare´
com-par´ing
com-par´i-son
com-par´i-son–
  shop
com-part´ment
com-part-men´tal
com-part-men´tal-
  ize
com´pass
com´pass·es
com-pas´sion
com-pas´sion-ate
com-pat-i·bil´i·ty
com-pat´i·ble
com-pat´i·bly
com-pa´tri·ot
com-pel´
com-pel´la·bly
com-pelled´
com-pel´ling
com-pel´ling·ly
com-pen´di-ous
com-pen´di-ous·ly

com-pen´di·um
com´pen-sate
com´pen-sat-ing
com-pen-sa´tion
com-pen-sa´tion·al
com-pen´sa-to·ry
com-pete´
com´pe-tence
com´pe-ten·cy
com´pe-tent
com´pe-tent·ly
com-pet´ing
com-pe-ti´tion
com-pet´i-tive
com-pet´i-tive·ly
com-pet´i-tive-ness
com-pet´i-tor
com-pi-la´tion
com-pile´
com-pil´er
com-pil´ing
com-pla´cence
com-pla´cen-cy
com-pla´cent·ly
com-plain´
com-plain´ant
com-plain´ing·ly
com-plaint´
com-plai´sance
com-plai´sant·ly
com-plect´ed
com´ple-ment
com-ple-men´ta·ry

com-plete
com-plet´ed
com-plete´ly
com-plete´ness
com-ple´tion
com´plex
com-plex´ion
com-plex´ioned
com-plex´i·ty
com-plex´ness
com-pli´a·ble
com-pli´ance
com-pli´ant
com´pli-cate
com´pli-cat·ed
com-pli-ca´tion
com-plic´i·ty
com-plied´
com´pli-ment
com-pli-men´ta·ry
com-ply´ing
com-po´nent
com-port´ment
com-pos´a·ble
com-pose´
com-posed´
com-pos´er
com-pos´ite
com-po-si´tion
com-pos´i-tor
com´post
com-po´sure
com´pote

com´pound (n.,
    adj.)
com-pound´ (v.,
    adj.)
com-pre-hend´
com-pre-hend´i·ble
com-pre-hen´si·ble
com-pre-hen´sion
com-pre-hen´sive
com´press (n.)
com-press´ (v.)
com-pressed´
com-press´i·ble
com-pres´sion
com-prise´
com-pris´ing
comp-trol´ler
comp-trol´ler-ship
com-pul´sion
com-pul´sive·ly
com-pul´sive-ness
com-pul´so·ry
com-punc´tion
com-punc´tious
com-pu-ta´tion
com-put´a·ble
com-put´a·bly
com-put-a·bil´i·ty
com-pute´
com-put´er
com-put´er-ize
com-put-er-i-za´-
    tion

com-put´ing
com´rade
com´rade·ly
com´rade-ship
con-cat´e-nate
con-cat-e-na´tion
con´cave
con-cave´ly
con-cave´ness
con-cav´i·ty
con-ceal´a·ble
con-ceal-a·bil´i·ty
con-ceal´ment
con-cede´
con-ced´ed·ly
con-ced´er
con-ced´ing
con-ceit´
con-ceit´ed
con-ceiv-a·bil´i·ty
con-ceiv´a·ble
con-ceiv´a·bly
con-ceive´
con-ceiv´ing
con´cen-trate
con´cen-trat·ed
con´cen-trating
con-cen-tra´tion
con-cen-tra-tive
con-cen´tric
con-cen´tri-cal·ly
con-cen-tric´i·ty
con´cept

con-cep´tive
con-cep´tu-al
con-cep´tu-al-ize
con-cep-tu-al-i-za´-
  tion
con-cep´tu-al·ly
con-cern´
con-cerned´
con-cern´ing
con´cert (n.)
con-cert´ (v.)
con-cert´ed
con-cer´to
con-ces´sion
con-ces´sion-aire´
con-cierge´
con-cil´i-ate
con-cil´i-at-ing
con-cil-i-a´tion
con-cil´i-a-tor
con-cil´ia-to·ry
con-cise´ly
con-cise´ness
con´clave
con-clude´
con-clud´ing
con-clu´sion
con-clu´sive·ly
con-clu´sive-ness
con-coct´
con-coc´tion
con-com´i-tance
con-com´i-tan·cy

con-com´i-tant
con´cord (n.)
con-cord´ (v.)
con-cor´dance
con-cor´dant
con´course
con´crete,
  con-crete´
con-crete´ly
con-crete´ness
con´cu-bine
con-cur´
con-curred´
con-cur´rence
con-cur´ren·cy
con-cur´rent·ly
con-cur´ring·ly
con-cus´sion
con-demn´
con-dem´na·ble
con-dem-na´tion
con-demned´
con-demn´er
con-demn´ing
con-dens´a·ble
con-den´sate
con-den-sa´tion
con-dense´
con-densed´
con-dens´er
con-dens´ing
con-de-scend´
con-de-scend´ence

con-de-scend´ing·ly
con-de-scen´sion
con´di-ment
con-di´tion-al
con-di´tion-al·ly
con-di´tioned
con-di´tion-er
con-di´tion-ing
con-do´lence
con-dol´ing
con´dom
con-do-min´i·um
con-don´a·ble
con-done´
con-duce´
con-du´cive
con´duct (n.)
con-duct´ (v.)
con-duct´ed
con-duc´tion
con-duc-tiv´i·ty
con-duc´tor
con´duit
con-fab´u-late
con-fab-u-la´tion
con-fec´tion-ar·y
con-fec´tion·er
con-fec´tion-er·y
con-fed´er-a·cy
con-fed´er-ate
con-fed-er-a´tion
con-fer´
con´fer·ee´

con´fer-ence
con-fer´ment
con-ferred´
con-fer´ring
con-fess´
con-fessed´
con-fess´ed·ly
con-fes´sion
con-fes´sion-al
con-fes´sor
con´fi-dant
con-fide´
con-fid´ed
con´fi-dence
con´fi-dent
con-fi-den´tial
con-fi-den-ti-al´i·ty
con-fi-den´tial·ly
con´fi-dent·ly
con-fid´ing·ly
con-fig-u-ra´tion
con-fig-u-ra´tive
con-fig´ure
con-fin´a·ble
con-fine´ (v.)
con´fine (n.)
con-fined´
con-fine´a·ble
con-fin´ed-ness
con-fine´ment
con-fin´er
con-fin´ing
con-firm´

con-firm´a·ble
con-firm-a·bil´i·ty
con-fir-ma´tion
con-fis´ca·ble
con´fis-cate
con-fis-ca´tion
con-fis´ca-to·ry
con-fla-gra´tion
con´flict (n.)
con-flict´ (v.)
con-flict´ing
con-flic´tive
con-flic´to·ry
con´flu-ence
con´flu´ent
con-form´
con-form´a·ble
con-form´ance
con-for-ma´tion
con-for-ma´tion·al
con-form´ist
con-form´i·ty
con-found´
con-found´a·ble
con-found´ed
con-fra-ter´ni·ty
con-front´
con-fron-ta´tion·al
con-fus´a·ble
con-fus´a·bly
con-fuse´
con-fused´
con-fus´ing·ly

con-fu´sion
con-fu-ta´tion
con-fute´
con-geal´
con-geal´a·ble
con´ge-ner
con-ge-ner´ic
con-ge´nial
con-ge-ni-al´i·ty
con-gen´i-tal
con-gen´i-tal·ly
con-gest´
con-gest´ed
con-ges´tion
con-ges´tive
con-glom´er-ate
con-glom-er-a´tion
con-grat´u-late
con-grat´u-lat-ing
con-grat-u-la´tion
con-grat´u-la-to·ry
con´gre-gate
con-gre-ga´tion·al
con´gress
con-gres´sio-nal
con´gress-man
con´gress-per-son
con´gress-wom·an
con-gru´ence
con-gru´en-cy
con-gru´ent·ly
con-gru´i·ty
con´gru-ous·ly

con´ic
con´i-cal
con-jec´tur-a·bly
con-jec´tur-al
con-jec´ture
con-join´
con´ju-gal
con´ju-gal·ly
con-junc´tion
con-junc´tive
con-junc´ture
con´jure, con-jure´
con´jur·er
con-nect´
con-nect-a·bil´i·ty
con-nect´a·ble
con-nect´ed
con-nect´er
con-nect-i·bil´i·ty
con-nect´i·ble
con-nec´tion
con-nec´tive
con-nec-tiv´i·ty
con-nec´tor
con-nip´tion
con-niv´ance
con-nive´
con-niv´er·y
con´nois-seur´
con´no-ta´tion
con´no-ta-tive
con´no-ta-tive·ly
con-note´

con-not´ing
con-nu´bi·al
con´quer
con´quer-a·ble
con´quered
con´quer-ing
con´quer·or
con´quest
con-quis´ta-dor
con-san-guin´e·ous
con-san-guin´-
   e·ous·ly
con-san-guin´i·ty
con´science
con-sci-en´tious
con-sci-en´tious·ly
con-sci-en´tious-
   ness
con´scion-a·ble
con´scion-a·bly
con´scious·ly
con´scious-ness
con-scribe´
con´script (n.)
con-script´ (v.)
con-scrip´tion
con´se-crate
con´se-crat-ing
con-se-cra´tion
con´se-cra-tor
con-sec´u-tive·ly
con-sen´su-al·ly
con-sen´sus

con-sent´ing·ly
con-sent´er
con-sen´tient·ly
con´se-quence
con´se-quent
con-se-quen´tial
con-se-quen´tial·ly
con´se-quent·ly
con-serv´an·cy
con-ser-va´tion·al
con-serv´a-tism
con-serv´a-tive·ly
con-serv´a-tive-
   ness
con´ser-va-tor
con-serv´a-to·ry
con-serve´
con-serv´ing
con-sid´er
con-sid´er-a·ble
con-sid´er-a·bly
con-sid´er-ate·ly
con-sid-er-a´tion
con-sid´ered
con-sid´er-ing
con-sign´
con-sign´a·ble
con-sig-na´tion
con´sign·ee´
con-sign´ment
con-sign´or
con-sist´
con-sist´ence

con-sist´en·cy
con-sist´ent·ly
con-sis´to·ry
con-sol´a·ble
con-so-la´tion
con-sole´ (v.)
con´sole (n.)
con-sol´i-date
con-sol´i-dat-ing
con-sol-i-da´tion
con-sol´ing
con-sol´ing·ly
con´so-nance
con´so-nant
con-sort´ (v.)
con´sort (n.)
con-sor´ti·al
con-sor´ti·um
con-spic´u-ous
con-spic´u-ous·ly
con-spic´u-ous-ness
con-spir´a·cy
con-spir´a-tive
con-spir´a-tor
con-spir´a-to´ri-
  al·ly
con-spire´
con-spir´ing
con´sta·ble
con-stab´u-lar·y
con´stan·cy
con´stant
con´stant·ly

con-stel-la´tion
con´ster-nate
con-ster-na´tion
con´sti-pate
con´sti-pat·ed
con-sti-pa´tion
con-stit´u-en·cy
con-stit´u-ent
con´sti-tute
con-sti-tu´tion
con-sti-tu´tion·al
con -sti-tu´-tion-
  al·ly
con-strain´
con-strain´a·ble
con-strained´
con-strain´ing
con-straint´
con-strict´
con-stric´tion
con-stric´tive
con-stric´tor
con-strin´gen·cy
con-strin´gent
con-stru´a·ble
con-stru´al
con-struct´ (v.)
con´struct (n.)
con-struct´i·ble
con-struc´tion
con-struc´tive
con-struc´tive·ly
con-struc´tor

con-strue´
con-strued´
con-stru´ing
con´sul
con´sul·ar
con´sul-ate
con-sult´
con-sult´an·cy
con-sult´ant
con-sul-ta´tion
con-sult´ing
con-sul´tor
con-sum´a·ble
con-sume´
con-sumed´
con-sum´er
con-sum´er-ism
con-sum´ing
con-sum´mate
  (adj.)
con´sum-mate
  (v., adj.)
con-sum-ma´tion
con-sump´tion
con´tact
con-ta´gion
con-ta´gious
con-ta´gious-ness
con-tain´
con-tain´a·ble
con-tained´
con-tain´er-ize
con-tain´ing

con-tain´ment
con-tam´i-na-ble
con-tam´i-nant
con-tam´i-nate
con-tam´i-nat-ed
con-tam´i-nat-ing
con-tam-i-na´tion
con-tam´i-na-tive
con-tam´i-na-tor
con-temn´
con-temn´er
con-tem´pla-ble
con´tem-plate
con´tem-plat-ing
con-tem-pla´tion
con-tem´pla-tive
con-tem-po-ra-ne´-
   i-ty
con-tem-po-ra´ne-
   ous
con-tem-po-ra´ne-
   ous-ly
con-tem-po-ra´ne-
   ous-ness
con-tem´po-rar-y
con-tem´po-rize
con-tempt´
con-tempt-i-bil´i-ty
con-tempt´i-ble
con-tempt´i-ble-
   ness
con-temp´tu-ous
con-temp´tu-ous-ly

con-tend´
con-tend´er
con-tent´ *(adj., v.,*
   n.)
con´tent *(n.)*
con-tent´ed
con-tent´ed-ly
con-tent´ed-ness
con-ten´tion
con-ten´tious-ly
con-ten´tious-ness
con-tent´ly
con-tent´ment
con-tent´ness
con´tents
con-ter´mi-nous
con-ter´mi-nous-ly
con-ter´mi-nous-
   ness
con´test *(n.)*
con-test´ *(v.)*
con-test´a-ble
con-test´a-bly
con-tes´tant
con´text
con-tex´tu-al
con-tex´tu-al-ly
con-ti-gu´i-ty
con-tig´u-ous
con-tig´u-ous-ly
con-tig´u-ous-ness
con´ti-nence
con´ti-nent

con-ti-nen´tal
con-ti-nen´tal-ly
con´ti-nent-ly
con-tin´gence
con-tin´gen-cy
con-tin´gent-ly
con-tin´u-a-ble
con-tin´u-al
con-tin´u-al-ly
con-tin´u-ance
con-tin-u-a´tion
con-tin´ue
con-tin´u-ing
con-ti-nu´i-ty
con-tin´u-ous-ly
con-tin´u-ous-ness
con-tin´u-um
con-tort´
con-tort´ed
con-tor´tion
con-tor´tion-ist
con´tour
con´tra
con´tra-band
con´tra-cep´tion
con´tra-cep´tive
con´tract *(n., v.)*
con-tract´ *(v.)*
con-tract´ed
con-tract-i-bil´i-ty
con-tract´i-ble
con-trac´tion
con´trac-tor

con-trac´tu·al
con-trac´tu-al·ly
con-tra-dict´a·ble
con-tra-dict´
con-tra-dic´tion
con-tra-dic´tive·ly
con-tra-dic´tive-
　ness
con-tra-dic´to·ry
con-tra-dis-tinc´-
　tion
con-tra-dis-tinc´-
　tive
con-tral´to
con-trap´tion
con´trar-i-ness
con´trar·i-wise
con´trar·y
con-trast´ (v.)
con´trast (n.)
con-trast´a·bly
con-trast´ing·ly
con-trast´y
con-tra-vene´
con-tra-ven´tion
con´tre-temps
con-trib´ut-a·ble
con-trib´ute
con-trib´ut-ing
con-tri-bu´tion
con-trib´u-tive
con-trib´u-tor
con-trib´u-to·ry

con-trite´
con-trite´ly
con-trite´ness
con-tri´tion
con-triv´a·ble
con-triv´ance
con-trive´
con-trived´
con-triv´er
con-triv´ing
con-trol´
con-trol´la·ble
con-trol´la·bly
con-trol-led´
con-trol´ler
con-trol´ling
con-tro-ver´sial
con-tro-ver´sial·ly
con´tro-ver·sy
con´tro-vert
con-tro-vert´i·ble
con-tro-vert´i·bly
con-tu-ma´cious
con-tu-ma´cious·ly
con-tu-ma´cious-
　ness
con-tu´ma·cy
con-tu-me´li-ous
con-tu-me´li-ous·ly
con-tu´me·ly
con-tu´sion
co-nun´drum
con-va-lesce´

con-va-les´cence
con-va-les´cent
con-va-lesc´ing
con-vect´
con-vec´tion
con-vec´tion·al
con-vene´
con-ve´nience
con-ve´nient
con-ve´nient·ly
con-ven´ing
con´vent
con-ven´tion
con-ven´tion·al
con-ven´tion-al´i·ty
con-ven´tion-al·ly
con-ven-tion-eer´
con-verge´
con-ver´gence
con-ver´gen·cy
con-ver´gent
con-verg´ing
con-ver´sance
con-ver´sant
con-ver-sa´tion
con-ver-sa´tion·al
con-ver-sa´tion-al-
　ist
con´verse
　(reversed)
con-verse´ (speak)
con-verse´ly
con-vers´ing

con-ver´sion
con´vert (n.)
con-vert´ (v.)
con-vert´i·ble
con´vex
con-vex´i·ty
con-vey´
con-vey´a·ble
con-vey´ance
con-vey´ing
con-vey´or
con´vict (n.)
con-vict´ (v.)
con-vict´a·ble
con-vic´tion
con-vince´
con-vinc´i·ble
con-vinc´ing·ly
con-viv´i·al
con-viv-i-al´i·ty
con-viv´i-al·ly
con-vo-ca´tion
con-vo-ca´tion·al
con-voke´
con-vok´ing
con´vo-lute
con´vo-lut·ed
con´vo-lute·ly
con-vo-lu´tion
con-vo-lu´tion·al
con´voy
con-vulse´
con-vul´sion

con-vul´sive
con-vul´sive·ly
cook´book
cook´er
cook´er·y
cook´ie
cook´ing
cook´off
cook´out
cook´stove
cook´ware
cool´ant
cool´er
coo´lie
cool´ly
cool´ness
coop´er-age
co-op´er-ate
co-op-er-a´tion
co-op´er-a-tive·ly
co-or´di-nate
co-or-di-na´tion
co-or´di-na-tor
cop´i·er
cop´ies
co´pi´lot
cop´ing
co´pi-ous
co´pi-ous·ly
co´pi-ous-ness
cop–out
cop´per-plate
copse

cop´ter
cop´u-late
cop-u-la´tion
cop´y
cop´y-cat
cop´y-ed-i-tor
cop´y-ing
cop´y-right
cop´y-right·ed
cor´dial
cor-dial´i·ty
cor´dial·ly
cord´less
cor´du-roy
co-re-la´tion
co-re-spon´dent
cork´age
cork´board
cork´screw
cork´y
cor´ner
cor´nered
cor´ner-stone
cor-net´
corn´fed
corn´field
cor´nice
corn´stalk
cor-nu-co´pi·a
corn´y
cor´o-nar·y
cor-o-na´tion
cor´o-ner

cor-o-net′   cor-rod′i·ble   cos′mos
cor′po-rate   cor-rod′ing   cost′li-ness
cor′po-rate·ly   cor-ro′sion   cost′ly
cor-po-ra′tion   cor-ro′sive   cos′tume
cor-po′re·al   cor-ro′sive·ly   cos′tum·er
corps   cor-ro′sive-ness   co-ten′an·cy
corpse   cor′ru-gate   co-ten′ant
cor′pu-lence   cor′ru-gat·ed   co′te-rie
cor′pu-lent   cor-ru-ga′tion   co-ter′mi-nous
cor-ral′   cor-rupt′   co-ter′mi-nous·ly
cor-rect′   cor-rupt′er   co-til′lion
cor-rect′a·ble   cr-rupt′i·ble   cot′tage
cor-rec′tion   cor-rup′tion   cot′ter
cor-rec′tion-al   cor-rup′tive   cot′ton
cor-rec′tive   cor-rupt′ly   cot′ton-seed
cor-rect′ly   cor-rupt′ness   cough
cor-rect′ness   cor-sage′   could
cor′re-late   cor′set   cou′lee
cor-re-la′tion-al   cor′tege   coun′cil
cor-rel′a-tive   cor′us-cate   coun′sel
cor-re-spond′   cor-us-ca′tion   coun′sel-lor (Br.)
cor-re-spon′dence   co′sign   coun′sel·or
cor-re-spon′dent   co-sig′na-to·ry   coun′te-nance
cor-re-spond′ing   co′sign·er   coun′ter (contra)
cor-re-spon′sive   cos-met′ic   count′er (ledge)
cor′ri-dor   cos-met′i-cal·ly   coun-ter-act′
cor-ri-gi-bil′i·ty cos-me-tol′o·gy   coun′ter-bal-ance
cor′ri-gi·ble   cos′mic   coun′ter-claim
cor-rob′o-rate   cos′mi-cal·ly   coun′ter-clock′wise
cor-rob-o-ra′tion   cos-mo-log′i-cal   coun′ter-cul-ture
cor-rob′o-ra-tive   cos-mol′o·gy   coun′ter-feit·er
cor-rob′o-ra-tor   cos′mo-naut   coun′ter-mand
cor-rode′   cos-mo-pol′i-tan   coun′ter-mine

coun´ter-of-fer
coun´ter-part
coun´ter-point
coun-ter-pro-duc´-
  tive
coun´ter-sign
coun´ter-suit
count´er-top
count´ess
coun´ties
count´less
coun´tries
coun´tri-fied
coun´try
coun´try-man
coun´try-side
coun´ty
cou´ple
cou´pler
cou´plet
cou´pling
cou´pon
cour´age
cou-ra´geous·ly
cou-ra´geous-ness
cou´ri·er
course
cours·er
cours´ing
court
cour´te-ous
cour´te-ous·ly
cour´te-ous-ness

cour´te-san
cour´te·sy
court´house
cour´tier
court´li-ness
court´ly
court´room
court´ship
court´yard
cous´in
cov´en
cov´e-nant
cov´er
cov´er-age
cov´er-all
cov´ered
cov´er-ing
cov´er-let
cov´ert
co´vert·ly
co´vert-ness
cov´er–up
cov´et
cov´e-tous·ly
cov´e-tous-ness
cov´ey
cow´ard
cow´ard-ice
cow´ard·ly
cow´er
cowl
cowl´ing
co–worker

coy
coy´ly
coy´ness
co´zi-est
co´zi·ly
co´zi-ness
co´zy
crab´bi-ness
crab´by
crack´down
cracked
crack´er
cracker–barrel
crack´ing
crack´le
crack´ling
crack´pot
crack–up
cra´dle
craft
craft´i·ly
craft´i-ness
crafts´man-ship
craft´y
crag´gi-ness
crag´gy
cram
crammed
cram´ming
cramp
cramped
crane
craned

cran´ing
crank
crank´case
crank´i-ness
crank´shaft
crank´y
cran´ny
crash´ing
crash–land
crass´ly
crass´ness
crater (chasm)
crat´ing
cra-vat´
crave
cra´ven
crav´ing
craw
craw´dad
craw´fish
crawl
crawl´ing
crawl´space
crawl´y
cray´fish
cray´on
craze
crazed
cra´zi-ly
cra´zi-ness
cra´zy
creak
creak´i-ly

creak´i-ness
creak´y
cream
cream–colored
cream´er
cream´er-y
cream´i-ness
cream´y
cre-ate´
cre-at´ing
cre-a´tion-ism
cre-a´tive
cre-a´tive-ly
cre-a-tiv´i-ty
cre-a´tor
crea´ture
cre´dence
cre-den´tial
cre-den´za
cred-i-bil´i-ty
cred´i-ble
cred´it
cred´it-a-ble
cred´i-tor
cre´do
cre-du´li-ty
cred´u-lous
cred´u-lous-ly
creed
creel
creek
creep
creep´er

creep´i-ness
creep´ing
creep´y
cre´mate
cre-ma´tion
cre-ma-to´ri-um
cre´o-sote
crêpe
cre-scen´do
cres´cent
crest
crest´ed
crest´fall-en
crest´ing
crev´ice
crev´iced
crew´el-work
crew´man
crib´bage
crib´bing
crick´et
crick´et-er
cried
cri´er
crime
crim´i-nal
crim-i-nal´i-ty
crim´i-nal-ly
crim-i-nol´o-gist
crim-i-nol´o-gy
crimp
crim´son
cringe

cringed
cring'ing
crin'kle
crin'kly
crin'o·line
crip'ple
crip'pled
crip'pler
crip'pling
cri'sis
crisp'er
crisp'i·ness
crisp'ly
crisp'ness
crisp'y
criss'cross
cri·te'ri·on
crit'ic
crit'i·cal
crit'i·cal·ly
crit'i·cism
crit'i·ciz·a·ble
crit'i·cize
crit'i·ciz·ing
cri·tique'
crit'ter
cro·chet'
cro·cheted'
cro·chet'er
cro·chet'ing
crock'er·y
crock'et
cro'cus

crois-sant'
cro'ny
cro'ny-ism
crook'ed (v.)
crooked (adj.)
croon'er
cross
cross'bar
cross'bow
cross'–coun'try
cross'cur-rent
cross'–ex-am'ine
cross'hatch
cross'ing
cross'–leg'ged
cross'ness
cross'o·ver
cross'patch
cross'–pol-li-na'-
   tion
cross'–pur'pose
cross'–ref'er-ence
cross'walk
crotch'et
crow'bar
crowd'ed
crowned
crow's–nest
cru'cial
cru'ci·ble
cru'ci-fix
cru'ci·fy
crude

crude'ly
cru'el
cru'el·ly
cru'el·ty
cru'et
cruise
cruised
cruis'er
cruis'ing
crumb
crum'ble
crum'bling
crum'bly
crumb'y
crum'my
crum'ple
crum'pling
crunch
crunch'ing
cru-sade'
cru-sad'er
cru-sad'ing
crush
crush'a·ble
crus-ta'cean
crust'ed
crust'i·ly
crust'i-ness
crust'y
crutch
crux
cry'ba·by
cry'ing

62

cry-o-gen'ics
cry-on'ics
crypt
cryp'tic
cryp'to-gram
cryp-tog'ra-pher
cryp-tog'ra-phy
crys'tal
crys'tal-line
crys-tal-li-za'tion
crys'tal-lize
cub'by-hole
cube
cubed
cu'bic
cu'bi-cal (adj.)
cu'bi-cle (n.)
cub'ism
cub'ist
cud'dle
cud'dled
cud'dling
cud'dly
cud'gel
cui-sine'
cul'–de–sac
cul'i-nar·y
cul'mi-nate
cul-mi-na'tion
cu-lotte'
cul-pa·bil'i·ty
cul'pa·ble
cul'pa·bly

cul'prit
cult
cul'ti-vate
cul'ti-vat·ed
cul-ti-va'tion
cul'ti-va-tor
cul'tur·al
cul'ture
cul'tured
cul'vert
cum'ber-some
cu'mu-la-tive
cu'mu-la-tive·ly
cup'ful
cu-pid'i·ty
cu'po·la
cupped
cup'ping
cur'a·ble
cu'ra-tive
cu-ra'tor
curb'ing
curb'side
curb'stone
curd
cur'dle
cur'dling
cure–all
cur'few
cu'ri·o
cu-ri-os'i·ty
cu'ri-ous
cu'ri-ous·ly

curl'er
cur'li-cue
curl'i-ness
curl'ing
curl'y
cur-mud'geon
cur'ren·cy
cur'rent
cur'rent·ly
curse
cursed
curs'ing
cur'sive
cur'sive·ly
cur'sive-ness
cur'sor
cur'so·ry
curt
cur-tail'
cur-tail'ment
cur'tain
curt'ly
curt'ness
curt'sy, curt'sey
cur-va'ceous
cur-va'ceous-ness
cur'va-ture
curve
curved
curv'ing
cush'ion
cush'y
cuss'ed-ness

cus-to´di·al
cus-to´di·an
cus´to·dy
cus´tom
cus´tom-ar´i·ly
cus´tom-ar·y
cus´tom–built´
cus´tom·er
cus´tom-ize
cus´tom–made´
cut´a·way
cut´back
cut´down
cute
cute´ly
cute´ness
cute´sy
cu´ti-cle
cut´ie
cut´ler·y
cut´off
cut´–rate´
cut´ter
cut´throat
cut´ting
cut´up
cy-ber-net´ics
cy´ber-space
cy´cle
cy´clic, cy´cli-cal
cy´cling
cy´clist
cy´clone

cyl´in-der
cy-lin´dri-cal·ly
cym´bal
cyn´ic
cyn´i-cal·ly
cyn´i-cism

D

dab´ble
dab´bling
dad´dy
daf´fo-dil
daf´fy
dag´ger
dai´lies
dai´ly
dain´ti·ly
dain´ti-ness
dain´ty
dai´qui·ri
dair´ies
dair´y
dair´y-man
dai-shi´ki
dal´li-ance
dal´lied
dal´li·er
dal´ly
dal´ly-ing
dam´age
dam´age-a·ble
dam´ag-ing
dam´ask

dam-na´tion
damned
damn´ing
damp´en
damp´en·er
damp´er
damp´ing
damp´ish
damp´ness
dam´sel
dance´a·ble
danced
danc´er
danc´er-cise
danc´ing
dan´der
dan´di-fied
dan´di·fy
dan´druff
dan´dy
dan´ger
dan´ger-ous·ly
dan´gle
dan´gled
dan´gling
dank´ness
dap´per
dap´ple
dare´dev·il
dare´say
dar´ing
dar´ing·ly
dark´en

dark′ly

dark′ness

dark′room

dar′ling

darn

darned

darn′ing

dash′board

dashed

dash′er

da-shi′ki

dash′ing

das′tard·ly

da′ta

da′ta-base

date

date′book

dat′ed

date′line

dat′ing

da′tum

daub′er

daugh′ter

daugh′ter–in–law

daunt

daunt′ing·ly

daunt′less·ly

daunt′less-ness

dav′en-port

daw′dle

daw′dler

daw′dling

dawn

day′bed

day′break

day′dream

day′light

day′time

day–to–day

dazed

daz′ed·ly

daz′zle

daz′zling

daz′zling·ly

dea′con

dea′con-ess

de-ac′ti-vate

de-ac′ti-va′tion

de-ac′ti-va-tor

dead′beat

dead′bolt

dead′en

dead′en-ing

dead′li·er

dead′line

dead′li-ness

dead′lock

dead′ly

dead′pan

deaf′en

deaf′en-ing

deaf′ness

deal′er

deal′er-ship

deal′ing

dealt

dear′ie

dear′ly

death′bed

death–dealing

death′less

death′ly

death′trap

de-ba′cle

de-bar′

de-bark′

de-bar-ka′tion

de-based′

de-bas′ing

de-bat′a·ble

de-bate′

de-bat′er

de-bat′ing

de-bauch′

de-bauched′

de-bauch′er

de-bauch′er·y

de-ben′ture

de-bil′i-tate

de-bil′i-tat-ed

de-bil-i-ta′tion

deb′it

deb′o-nair′

de-bone′

debt′or

de-bug′

de′but

deb′u-tante

dec′ade

dec´a-dence
dec´a-dent
de-caf´fein-ate
de´cal
de-cant´
de-cant´er
de-cap´i-tate
de-cap-i-ta´tion
de-cay´
de-cayed´
de-cay´ing
de-ceased´
de-ce´dent
de-ceit´
de-ceit´ful·ly
de-ceit´ful-ness
de-ceiv´a·ble
de-ceiv´a·bly
de-ceive´
de-ceiv´er
de-cel´er-ate
de-cel-er-a´tion
de´cen·cy
de´cent
de´cent·ly
de-cen-tral-i-za´-
   tion
de-cen´tral-ize
de-cep´tion
de-cep´tive·ly
de-cer´ti·fy
dec´i-bel
de-cide´

de-cid´ed·ly
de-cid´ing
de-cid´u-ous
de-cid´u-ous·ly
dec´i-mal
dec´i-mate
dec-i-ma´tion
de-ci´pher
de-ci´pher-a·ble
de-ci´sion
de-ci´sive·ly
de-ci´sive-ness
deck´le
de-claim´
dec-la-ma´tion
de-clam´a-to·ry
dec-la-ra´tion
de-clare´
de-clas´si·fy
de-claw´
de-cline´
de-clined´
de-clin´ing
de-cliv´i·ty
de-code´
de-cod´er
de-cod´ing
dé-col-le-tage´
de-com-mis´sion
de-com-pose´
de-com-press´
de-com-pres´sion
de-con-tam´i-nate

de-cor´
dec´o-rate
dec-o-ra´tion
dec´o-ra-tive·ly
dec´o-ra-tor
dec´o-rous·ly
de-co´rum
dé-cou-page´
de´-coy
de´coyed
de´crease (n.)
de-crease´ (v.)
de-creas´ing·ly
de-cree´
de-creed´
de-cree´ing
de-crep´it
de-cried´
de-crim´i-nal-ize
de-cry´
ded´i-cate
ded´i-cat·ed
ded-i-ca´tion
ded´i-ca-to·ry
de-duce´
de-duced´
de-duc´i·ble
de-duc´i·bly
de-duc´ing
de-duct´
de-duct-i·bil´i·ty
de-duct´i·ble
de-duc´tion

de-duc'tive
de-duc'tive-ly
deed
deem
de–em'pha-size
de–em'pha-sis
deep'en
deep–freeze
deep–fry
deep–rooted
deep–seated
deer'skin
de-face'
de-faced'
de-face'ment
de-fac'ing
de fac'to
def-a-ma'tion
de-fam'a-to-ry
de-fame'
de-fault'
de-fault'er
de-feat'ed
de-feat'ist
def'e-cate
def-e-ca'tion
de'fect (n.)
de-fect' (v.)
de-fect'ed
de-fec'tion
de-fec'tive
de-fec'tor
de-fend'

de-fend'a-ble
de-fend'ant
de-fend'er
de-fense'
de-fense'less
de-fen'si-ble
de-fen'si-bly
de-fen'sive
de-fen'sive-ly
de-fer'
def'er-ence
def'er-ent
def-er-en'tial
def-er-en'tial-ly
de-fer'ment
de-ferred'
de-fi'ance
de-fi'ant-ly
de-fi'cien-cy
de-fi'cient
de-fi'cient-ly
def'i-cit
de-fied'
de-fi'er
de-file'
de-file'ment
de-fil'er
de-fil'ing
de-fin'a-ble
de-fin'a-bly
de-fine'
de-fin'ing
def'i-nite

def'i-nite-ly
def-i-ni'tion
de-fin'i-tive
de-fin'i-tive-ly
de-flate'
de-fla'tion
de-fla'tion-ar-y
de-fla'tor
de-flect'
de-flect'a-ble
de-flec'tion
de-flec'tive
de-flec'tor
de-fog'ger
de-fo'li-ant
de-fo'li-ate
de-for-est-a'tion
de-form'
de-for-ma'tion
de-formed'
de-for'mi-ty
de-fraud'
de-fraud'ed
de-fray'
de-frayed'
de-fray'ing
de-frock'
de-frost'er
deft'ly
deft'ness
de-funct'
de-fuse'
de-fy'

de-fy′ing
de-gen′er-a·cy
de-gen′er-ate
de-gen-er-a′tion
de-gen′er-a-tive
de-glaze′
deg-ra-da′tion
de-grade′
de-grad′ed
de-grad′ing
de-grease′
de-gree′
de-hu′man-ize
de-hu-mid′i-fi·er
de-hy′drate
de-hy-dra′tion
de-ice′
de-ic′er
de-i-fi-ca′tion
de′i-fied
de′i·fy
deign
de′i-ties
de′i·ty
de-ject′
de-ject′ed
de-ject′ed·ly
de-jec′tion
de-lam′i-nate
de-lam-i-na′tion
de-lay′
de-layed′
de-lay′ing

de-lec′ta·ble
de-lec′ta·bly
del′e-ga·cy
del′e-gate
del-e-ga′tion
de-lete′
de-let′ed
del-e-te′ri-ous
de-le′tion
del′i
de-lib′er-ate·ly
de-lib-er-a′tion
de-lib′er-a-tive
del′i-ca-cies
del′i-ca·cy
del′i-cate
del′i-cate·ly
del′i-cate-ness
del-i-ca-tes′sen
de-li′cious
de-li′cious·ly
de-light′ed·ly
de-light′ful·ly
de-lim′it
de-lim′it·er
de-lin′e-ate
de-lin-e-a′tion
de-lin′e-a-tor
de-lin′quen·cy
de-lin′quent
de-lin′quent·ly
de-lir′i-ous
de-lir′i-ous·ly

de-lir′i·um
de-liv′er
de-liv′er-ance
de-liv′er·er
de-liv′er-ies
de-liv′er·y
de-louse′
de-lude′
de-lud′ed
de-lud′ing
del′uge
del′uged
de-lu′sion
de-lu′sion-al
de-luxe′
delved
delv′er
delv′ing
de-mag′net-ize
dem′a-gog′ic
dem′a-gogue
de-mand′
de-mand′ed
de-mand′ing
de-mar-ca′tion
de-ma-te′ri-al-ize
de-mean′
de-mean′or
de-ment′ed
de-men′tia
de-mer′it
de-mil′i-ta-rize
de-mise′

dem´i-tasse
dem´o
de-mo´bi-lize
de-moc´ra·cy
dem´o-crat
dem´o-crat´ic
dem´o-crat´i-cal·ly
de-moc´ra-tize
de-mod´u-late
de-mod-u-la´tion
de-mod´u-la-tor
de´mo-graph´ics
de-mol´ish
dem-o-li´tion
de´mon
de-mon´ic
de-mon-ol´o·gy
de-mon´stra·ble
de-mon´stra·bly
dem´on-strate
dem´on-strat-ing
dem-on-stra´tion
de-mon´stra-tive
dem´on-stra-tor
de-mor-al-i·za´tion
de-mor´al-ize
de-mor´al-iz-ing
de´mos
de-mote´
de-mot´ed
de-mo´tion
de-mur´ *(v.)*
de-mure´ *(adj.)*

de-mure´ly
de-mys´ti·fy
de-my-thol´o-gize
de-na´tion-al-ize
de-nat´u-ral-ize
de-na´tured
de-ni´a·ble
de-ni´al
de-nied´
de-nies´
den´i-grate
den-i-gra´tion
den´i-gra-tor
den´im
den´i-zen
de-nom-i-na´tion
de-nom-i-na´tion·al
de-nom´i-na-tor
de-note´
de-not´ing
de-no´tive
de-noue-ment´
de-nounced´
de-nounc´ing
dense´ly
dense´ness
den´si·ty
den´tal
den´tist
den´tis-try
den´ture
de-nude´
de-nun´ci-ate

de-nun-ci-a´tion
de-ny´ing
de-o´dor-ant
de-o´dor-ize
de-o´dor-iz·er
de-part´ed
de-part´ment
de-part-men´tal-ize
de-par´ture
de-pend´
de-pend-a·bil´i·ty
de-pend´a·ble
de-pen´dence
de-pen´dent
de-per-son-a-li-za´-
   tion
de-per´son-al-ize
de-pict´
de-pic´tion
de-pil´a-to·ry
de-ple´tion
de-plor´a·ble
de-plor´a·bly
de-plore´
de-plored´
de-plor´ing·ly
de-ploy´ment
de-po´lar-ize
de-pop´u-late
de-pop-u-la´tion
de-port´
de-por-ta´tion
de-port´ed

de-port-ee´
de-port´ment
de-pose´
de-posed´
de-pos´ing
de-pos´it
de-pos´it·ed
dep-o-si´tion
de-pos´i-to·ry
de´pot
dep-ra-va´tion
de-praved´
de-prav´i·ty
dep´re-cate
dep´re-cat-ing
dep-re-ca´tion
de-pre´cia·ble
de-pre´ci-ate
de-pre-ci-a´tion
de-press´
de-pres´sant
de-pressed´
de-press´ing
de-pres´sion
de-pres´sur-ize
de-pres´sur-i-za´-
   tion
dep-ri-va´tion
de-prive´
de-prived´
de-priv´ing
depth
dep-u-ta´tion

dep´u-ties
dep´u-tize
dep´u·ty
de-rail´ment
de-range´ment
de-rang´ing
der´by
de-reg´u-late
der´e-lict
der-e-lic´tion
de-ride´
de-rid´ing
de-ri´sion
de-ri´sive
de-ri´sive·ly
de-ri´sive-ness
der-i-va´tion
de-riv´a-tive
de-rive´
de-rived´
de-riv´ing
der-ma-tol´o-gist
der-ma-tol´o·gy
der´o-gate
der-o-ga´tion
de-rog´a-tive
de-rog´a-tive·ly
de-rog´a-to·ry
der´rick
der´ring·do
de-scend´ed
de-scend´ent
de-scend´er

de-scrib´a·ble
de-scribe´
de-scribed´
de-scrip´tion
de-scrip´tive
de-scrip´tor
des-cry´
des-cry´ing
des´e-crate
des-e-cra´tion
des´e-cra-tor
de-seg´re-gate
de-seg-re-ga´tion
de-se-lect´
de-sen-si-ti´za-tion
de-sen´si-tize
des´ert *(wasteland)*
de-sert´ *(foresake)*
de-sert´er
de-sert-i-fi-ca´tion
de-ser´tion
de-served´
de-serv´ed·ly
de-serv´ing
de-sign´
des´ig-nate
des-ig-na´tion
des´ig-na-tor
de-sign´er
de-sign´ing
de-sir-a·bil´i·ty
de-sir´a·ble
de-sir´a·bly

de-sire´
de-sir´ous
de-sist´
desk´top
des´o-late
des´o-late-ness
des-o-la´tion
de-sorb´
de-spaired´
de-spair´ing
de-spair´ing·ly
des-per-a´do
des-per-a´does
des´per-ate
des´per-ate·ly
des´per-ate-ness
des-per-a´tion
de-spic´a·ble-ness
de-spic´a·bly
de-spis´a·ble
de-spised´
de-spis´er
de-spis´ing
de-spite´
de-spoil´er
de-spoil´ing
de-spond´
de-spon´dence
de-spon´den·cy
de-spon´dent
des´pot
des-pot´ic
des´po-tism

des-sert´
de-sta´bi-lize
des-ti-na´tion
des´tined
des´ti-nies
des´ti-ny
des´ti-tute
des-ti-tu´tion
de-stroyed´
de-stroy´er
de-struct´
de-struc´ti·ble
de-struc´tion
de-struc´tive·ly
de-struc´tive-ness
des´ul-to·ry
de-tach´
de-tach´a·ble
de-tached´
de-tach´ment
de-tail´, de´tail
de-tailed´
de´tail-ing
de-tain´
de-tain´ment
de-tect´
de-tect´a·ble
de-tec´tion
de-tec´tive
de-tec´tor
dé-tente
de-ten´tion
de-ter´

de-ter´gent
de-te´ri-o-rate
de-te-ri-o-ra´tion
de-ter´ment
de-ter´min-a·ble
de-ter´mi-nant
de-ter-mi-na´tion
de-ter´mined
de-terred´
de-ter´rence
de-ter´rent
de-test´
de-test´a·ble
de-test´a·bly
de-tes-ta´tion
de-throne´
det´o-nate
det-o-na´tion
det´o-na-tor
de´tour
de-tox-i-fi-ca´tion
de-tox´i·fy
de-tract´
de-trac´tion
de-trac´tor
de-train´
det´ri-ment
det-ri-men´tal
deuce
deuc´ed
deuc´ed·ly
de-val´u-ate
de-val-u-a´tion

71

de-val´ue
dev´as-tate
dev´as-tat·ed
dev´as-tat-ing
dev´as-tat-ing·ly
dev-as-ta´tion
de-vel´op
de-vel´oped
de-vel´op·er
de-vel´op-ing
de-vel´op-ment
de-vel´op-men´tal
de´vi-ance
de´vi-ant
de´vi-ate
de-vi-a´tion
de-vice´
dev´il
dev´il-ish·ly
dev´il-ment
dev´il-try
de´vi-ous·ly
de´vi-ous-ness
de-vise´
de-vi-tal-i·za´tion
de-vi´tal-ize
de-void´
de-vote´
de-vot´ed
de-vot´ed·ly
de-vot´ed-ness
dev´o-tee´
de-vo´tion

de-vo´tion-al
de-vour´
de-vout´
de-vout´ly
de-vout´ness
dew´i-ness
dew´lap
dew´point
dew´y
dew´y–eyed
dex-ter´i·ty
dex´ter-ous
dex´ter-ous·ly
dex´ter-ous-ness
dex´trous
di-a-bol´ic
di-a-bol´i-cal
di-a-bol´i-cal·ly
di´ag-nose
di-ag-no´sis
di-ag-nos-ti´cian
di´ag-nos-tics
di-ag´o-nal
di-ag´o-nal·ly
di´a-gram
di´a-gram-mat´ic
di´al
di´a-lect
di´aled
di´al·er
di´al-ing
di´a-logue
di-am´e-ter

di-a-met´ric
di-a-met´ri-cal·ly
di´a-per
di-aph´a-nous
di´a-ries
di´a-rist
di´a·ry
di-as´po·ra
di´a-spore
di´a-tribe
dic´ey
di-chot´o·my
dick´er
dick´ey
dic´tate
dic´tat-ing
dic-ta´tion
dic´ta-tor
dic-ta-to´ri·al
dic-ta´tor-ship
dic´tion
dic´tio-nar-ies
dic´tio-nar·y
dic´tum
di-dac´tic
di-dac´ti-cal·ly
die´sel
di´et
di´e-tar·y
di´et·er
di-e-tet´ic
di-e-ti´tian
dif´fered

dif´fer-ence	dig´ni-fy-ing	dined
dif´fer-ent	dig´ni-tar-ies	din´er
dif-fer-en´tia·ble	dig´ni-tar·y	di-nette´
dif-fer-en´tial	dig´ni-ties	din´gi-ness
dif-fer-en´ti-ate	dig´ni·ty	din´gy
dif´fer-ent·ly	di-gress´	din´ing
dif´fi-cult	di-gres´sion	din´ner
dif´fi-cul-ties	di-gres´sive	din´ner-time
dif´fi-cult·ly	di-lap´i-date	din´ner-ware
dif´fi-cul·ty	di-lap´i-dat·ed	di´no-saur
dif´fi-dence	di-late´	di´o-cese
dif´fi-dent	di-lat´ing	di´ode
dif´fi-dent·ly	di-la´tion	di-o-ram´a
dif-fract´	di-lem´ma	diph´thong
dif-frac´tion	dil-et-tante´	di-plo´ma
dif-fuse´	dil´i-gence	di-plo´ma·cy
dif-fus´i·ble	dil´i-gent	dip´lo-mat
dif-fu´sion	dil´i-gent·ly	dip-lo-mat´ic
dif-fu´sive	dil´ly-dal·ly	dip-lo-mat´i-cal·ly
di´gest (n.)	di-lute´	dipped
di-gest´ (v.)	di-lut´ing	dip´per
di-gest-i·bil´i·ty	di-lu´tion	dip-so-ma´ni·a
di-gest´i·ble	di-men´sion·al	dip-so-ma´ni·ac
di-ges´tion	di-min´ish	dip´stick
di-ges´tive	dim-i-nu´tion	di-rect´
dig´ger	dim´ly	di-rect´ed
dig´gings	dimmed	di-rec´tion
dig´it	dim´mer	di-rec´tive
dig´i-tal	dim´ming	di-rect´ly
dig´it-al·ly	dim´ness	di-rect´ness
dig´i-tize	dim´ple	di-rec´tor
dig´ni-fied	dim´pling	di-rec´tor-ate
dig´ni·fy	dim´wit	di-rec´to·ry

dire´ly
dirge
dir´i·gi·ble
dirt´i·er
dirt´i·ness
dirt´–poor´
dirt´y
dis-a·bil´i·ty
dis-a´ble
dis-a´bled
dis-a´bling
dis´a·buse´
dis-ad-van´taged
dis-ad-van-ta´geous
dis-af-fect´ed
dis-af-fil-i-a´tion
dis-af-firm´
dis-a·gree´
dis-a·gree-a·bil´i·ty
dis-a·gree´a·ble
dis-a·gree´a·bly
dis-a·gree´ment
dis-al-low´
dis-al-low´ance
dis-ap-pear´
dis-ap-pear´ance
dis-ap-peared´
dis-ap-point´
dis-ap-point´ed·ly
dis-ap-point´ing
dis-ap-point´ment
dis-ap-pro-ba´tion
dis-ap-prov´al

dis´ap-prove´
dis´ap-prov´ing
dis´ap-prov´ing·ly
dis-arm´
dis-ar´ma-ment
dis-arm´ing
dis-arm´ing·ly
dis-ar-ray´
dis-as-so´ci-ate
di-sas´ter
di-sas´trous·ly
dis-a·vow´
dis-a·vow´al
dis-a·vow´ed·ly
dis-band´
dis-bar´
dis-bar´ment
dis-be-lief´
dis-be-lieve´
dis-be-liev´er
dis-burs´a·ble
dis-burse´
dis-burse´ment
dis-burs´ing
dis´card (n.)
dis-card´ (v.)
dis-cern´i·ble
dis-cern´i·bly
dis-cern´ing
dis-cern´ment
dis´charge (n.)
dis-charge´ (n., v.)
dis-ci´ple

dis-ci-pli-nar´i·an
dis´ci-pli-nar·y
dis´ci-pline
dis-claim´er
dis-close´
dis-clos´ing
dis-clo´sure
dis´co
dis-col-or-a´tion
dis-com-bob´u-late
dis-com´fit
dis-com´fi-ture
dis-com´fort
dis-con-cert´
dis-con-cert´ed
dis-con-cert´ing
dis-con-nect´ed
dis-con´so-late
dis-con-so-la´tion
dis-con-tent´
dis-con-tent´ed
dis-con-tent´ment
dis-con-tin-u-a´tion
dis-con-tin´ue
dis´cord
dis-cor´dance
dis-cor´dant·ly
dis´co-theque
dis´count
dis-cour´age
dis-cour´age-ment
dis-cour´ag-ing
dis-cour´ag-ing·ly

dis´course *(n.)*
dis-course´ *(v.)*
dis-cour´te-ous·ly
dis-cour´te-ous-
   ness
dis-cour´te·sy
dis-cov´er
dis-cov´er·er
dis-cov´er-ies
dis-cov´er·y
dis-cred´it
dis-cred´it-a·ble
dis-creet´ *(prudent)*
dis-creet´ly
dis-creet´ness
dis-crep´an·cy
dis-crete´ *(distinct)*
dis-cre´tion
dis-cre´tion-ar·y
dis-crim´i-nate
dis-crim´i-nat-ing
dis-crim-i-na´tion
dis-cuss´
dis-cussed´
dis-cus´sion
dis-dain´ful·ly
dis-dain´ful-ness
dis-eased´
dis-em-bark´
dis-em-bar-ka´tion
dis-em-bod´y
dis-en-chant´
dis-en-chant´ing

dis-en-chant´ment
dis-en-fran´chise
dis-en-gage´
dis-en-gage´ment
dis-en-tan´gle
dis-fa´vor
dis-fig-u-ra´tion
dis-fig´ure
disfig´ur-ing
dis-gorge´
dis-grace´
dis-grace´ful·ly
dis-grun´tled
dis-guise´
dis-gust´ed
dis-gust´ed·ly
dis-gust´ing·ly
dis-ha-bille´
dis-har´mo·ny
dish´cloth
dis-heart´en
dis-heart´en-ing
dished
di-shev´eled
di-shev´el-ment
dish´mop
dis-hon´est
dis-hon´est·ly
dis-hon´es·ty
dis-hon´or
dis-hon´or-a·ble
dis-hon´or-a·bly
dish´pan

dish´wash·er
dish´wa´ter
dis-il-lu´sion
dis-in-cli-na´tion
dis-in-cline´
dis-in-clined´
dis-in-fect´
dis-in-fec´tant
dis-in-gen´u-ous
dis-in-her´it
dis-in´te-grate
dis-in-te-gra´tion
dis-in-ter´
dis-in´ter-est
dis-in´ter-est-ed
dis-join´
dis-joint´ed
disk
disk-ette´
dis-like´
dis´lo-cate
dis-lo-ca´tion
dis-lodge´
dis-loy´al
dis-loy´al·ly
dis-loy´al·ty
dis´mal
dis´mal·ly
dis-man´tle
dis-man´tling
dis-may´
dis-mem´ber-ment
dis-miss´

dis-mis´sal
dis-miss´ive
dis-mount´
dis-o·be´di-ence
dis-o·be´di-ent·ly
dis-o·bey´
dis-o·beyed´
dis-or´der
dis-or´dered
dis-or´der·ly
dis-or-ga-ni-za´tion
dis-or´ga-nize
dis-o´ri-ent
dis-o-ri-en-ta´tion
dis-own´
dis-par´age-ment
dis-par´ag-ing·ly
dis-par´i·ty
dis-patch´er
dis-pel´
dispelled´
dis-pel´ling
dis-pens´a·ble
dis-pen´sa·ry
dis-pen-sa´tion
dis-pense´
dis-pens´er
dis-per´sal
dis-per´sant
dis-perse´
dis-per´sion
di-spir´it·ed
dis-place´

dis-placed´
dis-place´ment
dis-play´
dis-please´
dis-pleas´ing
dis-plea´sure
dis-pos´a·ble
dis-pos´al
dis-pose´
dis-posed
dis-po-si´tion
dis-pos-sessed´
dis-proof´
dis-pro-por´tion
dis-pro-por´tion·al
dis-pro-por´tion-
    al·ly
dis-pro-por´tion-
    ate·ly
dis-prove´
dis-put´a·ble
dis-put´a·bly
dis-pu´tant
dis-pu-ta´tion
dis-pute´
dis-qual-i-fi-ca´tion
dis-qual´i-fied
dis-qual´i·fy
dis-qui´et
dis-re-gard´
dis-re-pair´
dis-rep´u-ta·ble
dis-re-pute´

dis-re-spect´
dis-re-spect´ful
dis-robe´
dis-rupt´
dis-rup´tion
dis-rup´tive
dis-sat-is-fac´tion
dis-sat´is-fied
dis-sat´is·fy
dis-sect´
dis-sect´ed
dis-sec´tion
dis-sem´blance
dis-sem´ble
dis-sem´i-nate
dis-sem-i-na´tion
dis-sen´sion
dis-sent´er
dis-sen´tious
dis-ser-ta´tion
dis-serv´ice
dis´si-dence
dis´si-dent
dis-sim´i-lar
dis-sim-i-lar´i·ty
dis-sim´i-lar·ly
dis´si-pate
dis´si-pat·ed
dis-si-pa´tion
dis-so´ci-ate
dis-so-ci-a´tion
dis´so-lute
dis´so-lute·ly

dis-so-lu´tion
dis-solv´a·ble
dis-solve´
dis-solv´ing
dis´so-nance
dis´so-nant
dis-suade´
dis-sua´sion
dis-sua´sive
dis´taff
dis´tance
dis´tant·ly
dis-taste´ful
dis-tem´per
dis-tend´ed
dis-tend´er
dis-till´
dis´til-late
dis-til-la´tion
dis-till´er
dis-till´er·y
dis-till´ing
dis-tinct´
dis-tinc´tion
dis-tinc´tive·ly
dis-tinc´tive-ness
dis-tinct´ly
dis-tinct´ness
dis-tin´guish
dis-tin´guish-a·ble
dis-tin´guished
dis-tort´ed
dis-tor´tion

dis-tract´
dis-tract´ed
dis-tract´ed·ly
dis-tract´ed-ness
dis-tract´ing·ly
dis-trac´tion
dis-trac´tive
dis-traught´
dis-tressed´
dis-tress´ful
dis-tress´ing
dis-tress´ing·ly
dis-trib´ute
dis-tri-bu´tion
dis-trib´u-tor
dis´trict
dis-trust´ful
dis-turb´
dis-tur´bance
dis-turbed´
dis-turb´er
dis-use´
ditch
dit´to
dit´ty
di´va
di-van´
dive
div´er
di-verge´
di-ver´gence
di-ver´gent
di-ver´gent·ly

di´vers (*disparate*)
di-verse´
di-ver´si-fied
di-ver´sion
di-ver´sion-ar·y
di-ver´si·ty
di-vert´
di-vert´ing
di-vest´
di-vest´i-ture
di-vide´
di-vid´ed
div´i-dend
di-vid´er
div-i-na´tion
di-vine´
di-vine´ly
div´ing
di-vin´i·ty
di-vis´i·ble
di-vi´sion
di-vi´sive
di-vi´sive·ly
di-vi´sive-ness
di-vorce´
div´ot
di-vulge´
di-vulg´ing
diz´zi·ly
diz´zi-ness
diz´zy
do´a·ble
doc´ile

doc´ile·ly
dock´et
dock´side
dock´yard
doc´tor
doc´tor·al
doc´tor-ate
doc´tri-naire´
doc´tri-nal
doc´trine
doc´u-dra·ma
doc´u-ment
doc´u-men´ta·ry
doc-u-men-ta´tion
dod´der
dod´dered
dod´der-ing
dodge
dodg´er
dodg´ing
doe
do´er
doe´skin
does´n't
doff
dog´bite
dog´catch·er
dog´–eared
dog´ged·ly
dog´ged-ness
dog´ger·el
dog´gy
dog´house

dog´leg
dog´ma
dog-mat´ic
dog´ma-tism
doi´lies
doi´ly
do´ing
do–it–yourself
dole´ful·ly
dole´ful-ness
dol´lar
dol´lop
dol´ ly
do´lo-rous·ly
do´lo-rous-ness
do-main´
domed
do-mes´tic
do-mes´ti-cate
do-mes´ti-cal·ly
do-mes-tic´i·ty
dom´i-cile
dom´i-nance
dom´i-nant
dom´i-nate
dom-i-na´tion
dom´i-neer´ing
do-min´ion
do-nate´
do-nat´ing
do-na´tion
done
done´ness

don´ny-brook
do´nor
do–nothing
don't
doo´dad
doo´dle
doo´dling
doo´fus
doo´hick·ey
doom
doom´say·er
dooms´day
door´bell
do–or–die
door´frame
door´jamb
door´keep·er
door´mat
door´stop
door–to–door
door´way
doo´zie
dop´ey
dork´y
dor´man·cy
dor´mant
dor´mi-to-ries
dor´mi-to·ry
dos´age
dosed
dos´ing
dos´sier
dot´age

dote
dot´ed
dot´ing
dot´ish
dot´ted
dot´ty
dou´ble
dou´ble–deck´er
dou´ble–head´er
dou´bly
doubt´ful
doubt´ful·ly
doubt´less
dough´nut
dough´ti·ly
dough´ty
dough´y
dour´ly
doused
dous´ing
dove´tail
dow´a-ger
dowd´y
dow´el
dow´er
down–and–out
down´beat
down´cast
down´draft
down´er
down´fall
down´grade
down´heart·ed

down´hill´
down´pour
down´right
down´size
down´stairs´
down´time
down–to–earth
down´town´
down´trod´den
down´turn
down´ward
down´y
dow´ries
dow´ry
dowse
dows´er
dox-ol´o·gy
doze
doz´en
doz´er
doz´ing
drab´ness
draft´i-ness
draft´y
drag
dragged
drag´ging
drag´net
drag´on
drain´age
drain´er
dra´ma
dra-mat´ic

dra-mat´i-cal·ly
dram´a-tist
dram´a-tize
dram´shop
drap´er·y
drap´ing
dras´tic
dras´ti-cal·ly
draw´back
draw´bridge
draw´er
draw´ing
drawl´er
drawl´ing
drawn
draw´string
dray´age
dread´ful
dread´ful·ly
dread´ful-ness
dread´locks
dread´nought
dream´er
dream´i·ly
dream´i-ness
dream´ing
dreamt
dream´y
drear´i·ly
drear´i-ness
drear´i-some
drear´y
dredge

dredg´er
dredg´ing
drench
dress´er
dress´ing
dress´mak·er
dress´mak-ing
dress´y
drib´bled
drib´let
drift´er
drift´ing
drift´wood
dri´ly
drink´a·ble
drink´er
drink´ing
dripped
drip´ping
drip´py
drive
driv´el
driv´en
driv´er
drive´way
driv´ing
driz´zle
driz´zling
driz´zly
droll´er·y
drone
dron´ing
drool

droop´i-ness
droop´ing
droop´y
drop´let
drop´out
dropped
drop´per
drop´ping
dross
drowse
drows´i·ly
drows´i-ness
drows´y
drub´bing
drudge
drudg´er·y
drug
drugged
drug´gist
drug´store
drum´beat
drummed
drum´mer
drum´ming
drum´stick
drunk´ard
drunk´en
drunk´en-ness
dry´er
dry´goods
dry´ing
dry´ly
dry´ness

du´al
du-al´i·ty
du´al·ly
dub´bing
du´bi-ous
duck´ling
duck´y
dud´geon
du´el
du-et´
duf´fer
duf´fle
dug´out
dul´cet
dull
dul´lard
dull´ish
du´ly
dumb´bell
dumb´found
dumb´ly
dumb´struck
dum´found
dum·my
dump´i-ness
dump´ling
dump´y
dunce
dun´der-head
dun-ga-ree´
dun´geon
dun´nage
dunned

dun´ning
duped
dup´ing
du´plex
du´pli-cate
du-pli-ca´tion
du´pli-ca-tor
du-plic´i-tous
du-plic´i·ty
du-ra·bil´i·ty
du´ra·ble
du´ra·bly
du-ra´tion
dur´ing
dusk´i-ness
dusk´y
dust´bin
dust´cloth
dust´er
dust´i-ness
dust´pan
dust´y
du´ties
du´ti-ful
du´ti-ful·ly
du´ty
dut´y–free´
dwarf
dwarf´ish
dwell´er
dwell´ing
dwelt
dwin´dle

dwin´dling
dye
dyed
dye´ing
dye´stuff
dy´ing
dy-nam´ic
dy-nam´i-cal·ly
dy´na-mism
dy´na-mite
dy´na-mit·ed
dy´na-mit·er
dy´na-mo
dy-nas´tic
dy´nas·ty

E

each
each other
ea´ger
ea´ger·ly
ea´ger-ness
ear
ear´ache
ear´drop
ear´drum
eared
ear´flap
ear´ful
ear´li·er
ear´li-est
ear´li-ness
ear´lobe

ear´ly
ear´mark
ear´muff
earn
earn´er
ear´nest
ear´nest·ly
ear´nest-ness
earn´ing
ear´piece
ear´phone
ear´plug
ear´ring
ear´shot
ear´split-ting
earth
earth´born
earth´bound
earth´en
earth´en-ware
earth´i·er
earth´i·ly
earth´i-ness
earth´li-ness
earth´ling
earth´ly
earth´mov·er
earth´mov-ing
earth´quake
earth´rise
earth´shak-ing
earth´y
ease

eased
ease'ful
ease'ful·ly
ease'ful-ness
ea'sel
ease'ment
eas'i·er
eas'i-est
eas'i·ly
eas'i-ness
eas'ing
east
east'bound
east'er·ly
east'ern
east'ern·er
east'ern-most
east'ward
east'ward·ly
eas'y
eas'y chair
eas'y-go-ing
eat
eat'a·ble
eat'en
eat'er
eat'er·y
eat'ing
eave
eaves
eaves'drop
eaves'drop-per
eaves'drop-ing

ebb
ebbed
ebb'ing
ebb tide
eb'o·ny
e·bul'lience
e·bul'lien·cy
e·bul'lient
e·bul'lient·ly
ec-cen'tric
ec-cen'tri-cal
ec-cen'tri-cal·ly
ec-cen-tric'i·ty
ec-cle-si-as'tic
ec-cle-si-as'ti-cal
ech'o
ech'oed
ech'oes
ech'o-ing
ech-o-lo-ca'tion
é'clair
e·clat'
ec-lec'tic
ec-lec'ti-cal
ec-lec'ti-cal·ly
e·clipse'
e·clips'ing
ec-o-log'ic
ec-o-log'i-cal
e·col'o·gy
ec-o-nom'ic
ec-o-nom'i-cal
ec-o-nom'i-cal·ly

ec-o-nom'ics
e·con'o-mies
e·con'o-mist
e·con'o-mize
e·con'o-miz·er
e·con'o-miz-ing
e·con'o-my
ec'o-sphere
ec'o-sys-tem
ec'ru
ec'sta-sies
ec'sta·sy
ec-stat'ic
ec-stat'i-cal·ly
ec-u-men'i-cal
ec-u-men'i-cal·ly
ed'died
ed'dies
ed'dy
ed'dy-ing
e·de'ma
edge
edged
edge'less
edg'er
edge'ways
edge'wise
edg'i·ly
edg'i-ness
edg'ing
edg'y
ed'i·ble
e'dict

ed-i-fi-ca´tion
ed´i-fice
ed´i-fy
ed´i-fy-ing
ed´it
ed´it-a-ble
e-di´tion
ed´i-tor
ed-i-to´ri-al
ed-i-to´ri-al-ize
ed-i-to´ri-al-ly
ed´u-ca-ble
ed´u-cate
ed´u-cat-ed
ed´u-cat-ing
ed-u-ca´tion
ed-u-ca´tion-al
ed´u-ca-tor
e-duce´
e-duc´i-ble
e-duc´tion
e-duc´tive
e-duc´tor
e´duct
eel´grass
ee´rie
ee´ri-ly
ee´ri-ness
ef´fa-ble
ef-face´
ef-face´a-ble
ef-face´ment
ef-fac´ing

ef-fect´
ef-fect´i-ble
ef-fec´tive
ef-fec´tive-ly
ef-fec´tive-ness
ef-fec´tor
ef-fects´
ef-fec´tu-al
ef-fec´tu-al-ly
ef-fec´tu-ate
ef-fem´i-na-cy
ef-fem´i-nate
ef-fem´i-nate-ly
ef´fer-ent
ef-fer-vesce´
ef-fer-ves´cence
ef-fer-ves´cent
ef-fer-vesc´ing
ef-fete´
ef-fete´ly
ef-fete´ness
ef-fi-ca´cious
ef-fi-ca´cious-ly
ef´fi-ca-cy
ef-fi´cien-cy
ef-fi´cient
ef-fi´cient-ly
ef´fi-gy
ef´flu-ence
ef´flu-ent
ef-flu´vi-al
ef-flu´vi-um
ef´flux

ef´fort
ef´fort-less
ef´fort-less-ly
ef-fron´ter-y
ef-ful´gent
ef-fuse´
ef-fu´sion
ef-fu´sive
ef-fu´sive-ly
ef-fu´sive-ness
e-gal-i-tar´i-an
egg´beat-er
egg´cup
egg´head
egg´shaped
egg´shell
e´go
e´go-cen´tric
ego ideal
e´go-ism
e´go-ist
e´go-is´tic
e´go-is´ti-cal-ly
e-go-ma´ni-a
e-go-ma´ni-ac
e´go-tism
e´go-tist
e´go-tis´tic
e´go-tis´ti-cal
e´go-tis´ti-cal-ly
e-gre´gious
e-gre´gious-ly
e-gre´gious-ness

e´gress
eight
eight´ball
eigh-teen´
eigh-teenth´
eighth
eighth rest
eight´i-eth
eight´y
ei´ther
e·jac-u-la´tion
e·jac´u-la-to·ry
e·ject´
e·jec´tion
eke
eked
ek´ing
e·lab´o-rate
e·lab´o-rate·ly
e·lab´o-rate-ness
e·lab´o-rat-ing
e·lab·o-ra´tion
e·lab´o-ra-tive
e·lapse´
e·laps´ing
e·las´tic
e·las´ti-cal·ly
e·las-tic´i·ty
e·las´ti-cize
e·late´
e·lat´ed
e·lat´ed·ly
e·lat´ed-ness

e·la´tion
el´bow
el´bow-room
el´der
el´der-ber·ry
el´der-ly
el´dest
e·lect´
e·lec-tee´
e·lec´tion
e·lec´tion-eer´
e·lec´tive
e·lec´tor
e·lec´tor·al
e·lec´tor-ate
e·lec´tric
e·lec´tri-cal
e·lec´tri-cal·ly
e·lec-tri´cian
e·lec-tric´i·ty
e·lec-tri-fi-ca´tion
e·lec´tri-fied
e·lec´tri·fy
e·lec´tro-cute
e·lec-tro-cu´tion
e·lec´trode
e·lec-trol´y-sis
e·lec´tro-lyte
e·lec´tron
e·lec-tron´ic
e·lec-tron´i-cal·ly
e·lec-tron´ics
el-ee-mos´y-nar·y

el´e-gance
el´e-gant
el´e-gant·ly
el´e-gize
el´e·gy
el´e-ment
el-e-men´tal·ly
el-e-men´ta·ry
el´e-phan´tine
el´e-vate
el´e-vat·ed
el-e-va´tion
el´e-va-tor
e·lev´en
e·lev´enth
elf´in
elf´ish
e·lic´it
e·lic´i-tor
e·lide´
e·lid´i·ble
e·lid´ing
el-i-gi-bil´i·ty
el´i-gi·ble
el´i-gi·bly
e·lim´i-nate
e·lim-i-na´tion
e·lim´i-na-tor
e·lite´
e·lit´ism
e·lit´ist
e·lix´ir
el-lipse´

el·lip´tic
el·lip´ti·cal
el·o·cu´tion
el·o·cu´tion·ar·y
e·loge´
e·lon´gate
e·lon´gat·ed
e·lon·ga´tion
e·lope´
e·lope´ment
e·lop´ing
el´o·quence
el´o·quent·ly
else´where
e·lu´ci·date
e·lu·ci·da´tion
e·lu´ci·da·tive
e·lude´
e·lud´er
e·lu´sive
e·lu´sive·ly
e·lu´so·ry
e·lu´vi·al
e·lu´vi·ate
e·lu·vi·a´tion
e·lu´vi·um
e·ma´ci·ate
e·ma´ci·at·ed
E´–mail
em´a·nate
em·a·na´tion
em·a·na´tion·al
em´a·na·tive

em´a·na·tor
e·man´ci·pate
e·man´ci·pat·ed
e·man·ci·pa´tion
e·man´ci·pa·tor
e·mas´cu·late
e·mas·cu·la´tion
em·balm´
em·balm´er
em·bank´
em·bank´ment
em·bar´go
em·bar´goes
em·bark´
em·bar·ka´tion
em·bar´rass
em·bar´rassed
em·bar´rass·es
em·bar´rass·ing·ly
em·bar´rass·ment
em´bas·sies
em´bas·sy
em·bat´tle
em·bed´ded
em·bel´lish
em·bel´lish·ment
em´ber
em·bez´zle
em·bez´zled
em·bez´zle·ment
em·bez´zler
em·bit´ter
em·blaze´

em·bla´zon
em´blem
em´blem·at´ic
em´blem·at´i·cal
em·bod´i·er
em·bod´i·ment
em·bod´y
em·bold´en
em·boss´
em·bossed´
em·boss´ing
em·bow´el
em·brace´
em·brace´a·ble
em·brac´er
em·brac´ing
em·bra´sure
em·broi´der
em·broi´der·y
em·broil´
em´cee
e·mend´
e·mend´er
e·merge´
e·mer´gence
e·mer´gen·cies
e·mer´gen·cy
e·mer´gent
e·mer´gent·ly
e·merg´ing
e·mer´i·tus
e·mersed´
e·mer´sion

em´er·y
em´i-grant
em´i-grate
em´i-grat-ing
em-i-gra´tion
em-i-gra´tion·al
em´i-gra-tive
e·mi-gre´
em´i-nence
em´i-nen·cy
em´i-nent
em´i-nent·ly
em´is-sar-ies
em´is-sar·y
e·mis´sion
e·mis´sive
e·mis-siv´i·ty
e·mit´
e·mit´ted
e·mit´ter
e·mit´ting
e·mol´lience
e·mol´lient
e·mol´u-ment
e·mote´
e·mot´er
e·mot´ing
e·mo´tion
e·mo´tion-al
e·mo´tion-al·ly
e·mo´tive
em-pan´el
em-pan´el-ing

em-path´ic
em-path´i-cal·ly
em-pa-thet´i-cal·ly
em´pa-thize
em´pa-thy
em´per·or
em´pha-ses
em´pha-sis
em´pha-size
em´pha-siz-ing
em-phat´ic
em-phat´i-cal·ly
em´pire
em-pir´i-cal
em-pir´i-cism
em-place´ment
em-ploy´
em-ploy-a·bil´i·ty
em-ploy´a·ble
em-ploy·ee´
em-ploy´er
em-ploy´ment
em-po´ri·um
em-pow´er
em-pow´er-ment
em´press
emp´tied
emp´ti·er
emp´ties
emp´ti·ly
emp´ti-ness
emp´ty
emp´ty—hand´ed

emp´ty-ing
em´u-late
em-u-la´tion
em´u-la-tor
e·mul-si-fi-ca´tion
e·mul´si-fied
e·mul´si-fi·er
e·mul´si·fy
e·mul´sion
en-a´ble
en-a´bler
en-a´bling
en-act´
en-ac´tor
en-am´el
en-am´eled
en-am´el-ware
en-am´or
en-am´ored
en-camp´
en-cap´su-late
en-case´
en-chant´
en-chant´er
en-chant´ing
en-chant´ing·ly
en-chant´ment
en-chant´ress
en-cir´cle
en-cir´cling
en´clave
en-close´
en-clo´sure

en-code′
en-co′mi·um
en-com′pass
en′core
en-coun′ter
en-cour′age
en-cour′age-ment
en-cour′ag-ing
en-croach′
en-crust′
en-crus-ta′tion
en-crypt′
en-cum′ber
en-cum′brance
en-cy-clo-pae′di·a (Br.)
en-cy-clo-pe′di·a
en-cy-clo-pe′dic
end
en-dan′gered
en-dan′ger-ment
en-dear′
en-dear′ing
en-dear′ment
en-deav′or
en-deav′our (Br.)
en-dem′ic
en-dem′i-cal·ly
end′ing
end′less·ly
end′most
en-dorse′
en-dors·ee′
en-dorse′ment

en-dors′er
en-dors′ing
en-dow′
en-dow′er
en-dow′ment
en-due′
en-dur′a·ble
en-dur′a·bly
en-dur′ance
en-dure′
en-dur′ing
end′ways
end′wise
en′e-mies
en′e-my
en-er-get′ic
en′er-gize
en′er-giz·er
en′er-gy
en′er-vate
en-er-va′tion
en-fee′ble
en-fee′bling
en-fold′
en-force′
en-force′a·ble
en-force′ment
en-forc′er
en-forc′ing
en-fran′chise
en-gage′
en-gaged′
en-gage′ment

en-gag′er
en-gag′ing
en-gag′ing·ly
en-gen′der
en′gine
en-gi-neer′ing
en-gorge′
en-grain′
en-grave′
en-grav′er
en-grav′ing
en-gross′
en-gross′ed·ly
en-gross′er
en-gross′ing
en-gulf′
en-hance′
en-hance′ment
en-hanc′ing
e·nig′ma
e·nig-mat′ic
en-join′
en-join′der
en-join′er
en-joy′
en-joy′a·ble
en-joy′a·bly
en-joy′ment
en-large′
en-large′a·ble
en-large-ment
en-light′en
en-light′en·er

87

en-light´en-ment
en-list´
en-list´ed
en-list´ment
en-liv´en
en-liv´en·er
en-liv´en-ing
en-mesh´
en´mi-ties
en´mi·ty
en-no´ble
en-no´bler
en-no´bling
en-nui´
e·nor´mi·ty
e·nor´mous·ly
e·nough´
en-rage´
en-rapt´
en-rap´ture
en-rich´
en-rich´ment
en-robe´
en-roll´
en-rolled´
en-roll·ee´
en-roll´ing
en-roll´ment
en-rol´ment
en-sem´ble
en-shrine´
en-shrine´ment
en-slave´

en-snare´
en-sue´
en-su´ing
en-tail´ment
en-tan´gle
en-tan´gle-ment
en-tan´gling
en-tente´
en´ter
en-ter´ic
en-ter-i´tis
en´ter-prise
en´ter-pris-ing
en´ter-pris-ing·ly
en-ter-tain´
en-ter-tain´er
en-ter-tain´ing
en-ter-tain´ment
en-thrall´er
en-thrall´ing·ly
en-throne´ment
en-thuse´
en-thu´si-asm
en-thu´si-ast
en-thu-si-as´tic
en-tice´ment
en-tic´ing
en-tic´ing·ly
en-tic´ing-ness
en-tire´ly
en-tire´ty
en-ti´tle
en-ti´tle-ment

en´ti·ty
en-tomb´ment
en-to-mo-log´ic
en-to-mo-log´i-cal
en-to-mol´o-gist
en-to-mol´o·gy
en´tou-rage´
en´trance (n.)
en-trance´ (v.)
en-tranc´ing
en´trant
en-trap´ment
en´tre
en-treat´
en-treat´ies
en-treat´ing
en-treat´y
en´trée
en´tre-pre-neur´
en-tre-pre-neur´i·al
en´tries
en-trust´
en´try
en´try—lev´el
en´try-way
en-twine´
e·nu´mer-ate
e·nu-mer-a´tion
e·nun´ci-ate
e·nun-ci-a´tion
en-ure´
en-vel´op
en´ve-lope

88

en-vel´oped
en-vel´op-ing
en-vel´op-ment
en´vi-a-ble
en´vi-a-bly
en´vied
en´vi-er
en´vies
en´vi-ous
en´vi-ous-ly
en-vi´ron
en-vi´ron-ment
en-vi´ron-men´-
    tal-ly
en-vi´ron-men´tal-
    ist
en-vi´rons
en-vis´age
en-vi´sion
en´voy
en´vy
en´vy-ing
e´on
e-phem´er-al
e-phem´er-al-ly
ep´ic
ep´i-cen´ter
ep´i-cure
ep´i-cu-re´an
ep´i-dem´ic
ep´i-gram
ep´i-logue
ep´i-sode

ep-i-sod´ic
e-pis´tle
ep´i-taph
ep´i-thet
e-pit´o-me
e-pit-o-mize
ep´och
ep´och-al
ep-ox´y
eq´ua-ble
eq´ua-bly
e´qual
e´qualed
e´qual-ing
e´qual-i-ty
e´qual-ize
e´qual-iz-er
e´qual-ly
e-qua-nim´i-ty
e-qua´tion
e-qua´tor
e-qua-to´ri-al
e-ques´tri-an
e´qui-dis´tant
e´quine
e-quip´ment
e-quipped´
e-quip´ping
eq´ui-ta-ble
eq´ui-ta-bly
eq´ui-ty
e-quiv´a-lence
e-quiv´a-len-cy

e-quiv´a-lent-ly
e-quiv´o-ca-cy
e-quiv´o-cal
e-quiv´o-cal-ly
e-quiv´o-cate
e-quiv´o-ca´tion
e-quiv´o-ca-tor
e-rad´i-cate
e-rad-i-ca´tion
e-rase´
e-rased
e-ras´er
e-ras´ing
e-ra´sure
e-rect´
e-rec´tion
ere-now´
er-go-nom´ic
er-go-nom´i-cal-ly
er-go-nom´ics
e-rode´
e-rod´i-ble
e-rog´e-nous
e-ro´sion
e-ro´sive
e-rot´ic
e-rot´i-ca
e-rot´i-cism
er´ran-cy
er´rand
er´rant
er´rant-ly
er-rat´ic

err´ing
err´ing·ly
er-ro´ne-ous
er-ro´ne-ous·ly
er-ro´ne-ous-ness
er´ror
er´satz
erst´while´
er´u-dite
er-u-di´tion
e·rupt´
e·rup´tion
e·rup´tive
es´ca-late
es-ca-la´tion
es´ca-la-tor
es´ca-pade
es-cape´
es-caped´
es-cap·ee´
es-cap´ing
es-cap´ist
es-chew´
es´cort *(n.)*
es-cort´ *(v.)*
es´crow
es´o-ter´ic
es-o-ter´i-cal·ly
es-pe´cial
es-pe´cial·ly
es´pi-o-nage
es´pla-nade
es-pous´al

es-pouse´
es-pous´er
es-pous´ing
es´quire
es´say *(n.)*
es-say´ *(v.)*
es-say´er
es´say-ist
es´sence
es-sen´tial
es-sen´tial·ly
es-tab´lish
es-tab´lish-a·ble
es-tab´lished
es-tab´lish-ment
es-tate´
es-teem´
es´ti-ma·ble
es´ti-mate
es-ti-ma´tion
es´ti-ma-tor
es-trange´
es-trange´ment
es-trang´ing
es´tu-ar·y
etch´ing
e·ter´nal·ly
e·ter´ni·ty
e·the´re-al
e·the´re-al·ly
eth´ic
eth´i-cal·ly
eth´ics

eth´nic
eth´ni-cal·ly
eth-nic´i·ty
eth´no-cen´tric
et´i-quette
e´tude
et-y-mol´o·gy
eu´lo·gy
eu´phe-mis´tic
eu´phe-mize
eu·pho´ri·a
eu-phor´ic
eu-tha-na´sia
e·vac´u-ate
e·vac-u-a´tion
e·vade´
e·vad´ing
e·val´u-ate
e·val-u-a´tion
e´van-gel´ic
e´van-gel´i-cal
e·van´ge-lism
e·van´ge-list
e·van´ge -lis´tic
e·vap´o-rate
e·vap´o-rat-ing
e·vap-o-ra´tion
e·vap´o-ra-tor
e·va´sion
e·va´sive
e·va´sive·ly
e·va´sive-ness
e´ven-hand·ed

e·ven-ing *(equating)*
eve´ning *(night)*
e´ven·ly
e´ven-ness
e·vent´
e·ven–temp´ered
e·vent´ful
e·ven´tu·al
e·ven´tu·al´i·ty
e·ven´tu·al·ly
e·ven´tu-ate
ev´er-green
ev-er-last´ing
ev-er-more´
e·vert´
ev´er·y-bod·y
ev´er·y-day
ev´er·y-one
ev´er·y-thing
ev´er·y-where
e·vic´tion
ev´i-dence
ev´i-denc-ing
ev´i-dent
ev´i-den´tial
ev-i-den´ti-a·ry
ev´i-dent·ly
ev´i-dent-ness
e´vil
e´vil-do·er
e´vil-do-ing
e´vil·ly
e´vil–mind´ed

e·vince´
e·vinc´ing
e·vis´cer-ate
e·vis-cer-a´tion
ev´i-ta·ble
e·voke´
e·vok´ing
ev-o-lu´tion
ev-o-lu´tion-ar·y
ev-o-lu´tion-ist
e·volve´
e·volv´ing
e·vul´sion
ex-ac´er-bate
ex-ac´er-bat-ing
ex-act´
ex-act´ing
ex-ac´ti-tude
ex-act´ly
ex-act´ness
ex-ac´tor
ex-ag´ger-ate
ex-ag´ger-at·ed
ex-ag-ger-a´tion
ex-alt´
ex-al-ta´tion
ex-alt´ed
ex-alt´ed·ly
ex-am´
ex-am-i-na´tion
ex-am´ine
ex-am´in·er
ex-am´ple

ex-as´per-ate
ex-as´per-at-ing
ex-as-per-a´tion
ex´ca-vate
ex´ca-va´tion
ex´ca-va-tor
ex-ceed´
ex-ceed´ing·ly
ex-cel´
ex-celled´
ex´cel-lence
ex´cel-lent
ex-cel´ling
ex-cept´a·ble
ex-cept´ing
ex-cep´tion
ex-cep´tion-al
ex´cerpt *(n.)*
ex-cerpt´ *(v.)*
ex-cess´ *(n.)*
ex´cess *(adj.)*
ex-ces´sive·ly
ex-change´
ex-change´a·ble
ex-chang´ing
ex´che-quer
ex´cise *(n. tax)*
ex-cise´ *(v. cut out)*
ex-ci´sion
ex-cit´a·ble
ex-ci-ta´tion
ex-cite´
ex-cit´ed·ly

ex-cite′ment
ex-cit′er
ex-cit′ing
ex-claim′
ex-claim′er
ex-cla-ma′tion-al
ex-clam′a-to-ry
ex-clude′
ex-clud′ing
ex-clu′sion-ar-y
ex-clu′sive-ly
ex-clu-siv′i-ty
ex-com-mu′ni-cate
ex-com-mu-ni-ca′-
  tion
ex-co′ri-ate
ex-co-ri-a′tion
ex′cre-ment
ex-crete′
ex-cru′ci-at-ing-ly
ex′cul-pate
ex-cul′pa-to-ry
ex-cur′sion
ex-cus′a-ble
ex-cus′a-bly
ex-cuse′
ex-cus′ing
ex-ec′
ex′e-crate
ex-e-cra′tion
ex′e-cute
ex-e-cu′tion
ex-ec′u-tive

ex-ec′u-tor
ex-em′pla-ry
ex-em′pli-fy
ex-empt′
ex-emp′tion
ex′er-cise
ex′er-cis-er
ex-ert′
ex-er′tion
ex-ert′ive
ex-fo′li-ate
ex′hal′ant
ex-ha-la′tion
ex′hale
ex-haust′ed
ex-haust′i-ble
ex-haus′tion
ex-hib′it
ex-hi-bi′tion-ism
ex-hi-bi′tion-ist
ex-hib′i-tor
ex-hil′a-rate
ex-hil-a-ra′tion
ex-hil′a-ra-tor
ex-hort′
ex-hor-ta′tion
ex-hu-ma′tion
ex-hume′
ex′i-gen-cies
ex′i-gen-cy
ex-ig′u-ous
ex′ile
ex-ist′

ex-is′tence
ex-is′tent
ex-is-ten′tial
ex-is-ten′tial-ism
ex′o-dus
ex-on′er-ate
ex-on-er-a′tion
ex-or′bi-tance
ex-or′bi-tant
ex-or′bi-tant-ly
ex′or-cise
ex′or-cism
ex′or-cist
ex-ot′ic
ex-ot′i-ca
ex-pand′
ex-pand′a-ble
ex-pand′ed
ex-panse′
ex-pan′sion
ex-pan′sion-ar-y
ex-pan′sive-ly
ex-pa′tri-ate
ex-pa-tri-a′tion
ex-pect′an-cy
ex-pect′ant-ly
ex-pec-ta′tion
ex-pec′to-rant
ex-pec′to-rate
ex-pe′di-ence
ex-pe′di-en-cy
ex-pe′di-ent
ex-pe′di-ent-ly

ex´pe-dite
ex´pe-dit·er
ex´pe-dit-ing
ex-pe-di´tion
ex-pe-di´tion-ar·y
ex-pe-di´tious·ly
ex-pel´
ex-pelled´
ex-pel´ling
ex-pend´
ex-pend´a·ble
ex-pend´i-ture
ex-pense´
ex-pen´sive·ly
ex-pe´ri-ence
ex-pe´ri-enced
ex-pe´ri-enc-ing
ex-per´i-ment
ex-per´i-men´tal
ex-per´i-men´tal·ly
ex-per-i-men-ta´-
  tion
ex-pert´ (adj.)
ex´pert (n., adj.)
ex-per-tise´
ex´pert·ly
ex´pi-ate
ex-pi-ra´tion
ex-pire´
ex-pired´
ex-pir´ing
ex-plain´
ex-pla-na´tion

ex-plan´a-to·ry
ex´ple-tive
ex-plic´a·ble
ex´pli´ca·bly
ex´pli-cate
ex-pli-ca´tion
ex-plic´it
ex-plic´it·ly
ex-plode´
ex-plod´ing
ex-ploit´ (v.)
ex´ploit (n.)
ex-ploit´a·ble
ex-ploi-ta´tion
ex-ploit´er
ex-ploit´ive
ex-plo-ra´tion
ex-plor´a·tive
ex-plor´a-to·ry
ex-plore´
ex-plor´er
ex-plor´ing
ex-plo´sion
ex-plo´sive
ex-po´nent
ex-po-nen´tial
ex-po-nen´tial·ly
ex´port (n., v.)
ex-port´ (v.)
ex-por-ta´tion
ex-port´er
ex-pose´
ex-po-sé´

ex-posed´
ex-pos´ing
ex-pos´tu-late
ex-po´sure
ex-press´
ex-press´ing
ex-pres´sion
ex-pres´sion-ism
ex-pres´sion-less
ex-pres´sive·ly
ex-press´ly
ex-press´way
ex-pro´pri-ate
ex-pro-pri-a´tion
ex-pul´sion
ex-punge´
ex´pur-gate
ex-pur-ga´tion
ex-quis´ite·ly
ex´tant
ex-tem-po-ra´ne-
  ous
ex-tem-po-ra´ne-
  ous·ly
ex-tem´po-rar·y
ex-tem´po-rize
ex-tend´ed
ex-tend´er
ex-ten´si·ble
ex-ten´sion
ex-ten´sive·ly
ex-tent´
ex-ten´u-ate

ex-ten´u-at-ing
ex-ten-u-a´tion
ex-te´ri·or
ex-ter´mi-nate
ex-ter-mi-na´tion
ex-ter´mi-na-tor
ex-ter´nal
ex-ter´nal-ize
ex-ter´nal·ly
ex-tinct´
ex-tinc´tion
ex-tin´guish
ex-tin´guish-a·ble
ex-tin´guish·er
ex´tir-pate
ex-tol´
ex-tolled´
ex-tol´ling
ex-tort´
ex-tort´ed
ex-tor´tion
ex-tor´tion·er
ex-tor´tion-ist
ex´tra
ex´tract *(n.)*
ex-tract´ *(v.)*
ex-trac´tion
ex´tra-cur-ric´u-lar
ex´tra-dite
ex-tra-di´tion
ex´tra-le´gal
ex´tra-mar´i-tal
ex-tra´ne-ous

ex-tra´ne-ous·ly
ex-traor´di-nar´i·ly
ex-traor´di-nar·y
ex-trap´o-late
ex-trap-o-la´tion
ex-tra-sen´so·ry
ex-tra-ter-res´tri·al
ex-trav´a-gance
ex-trav´a-gant·ly
ex-trav-a-gan´za
ex-treme´ly
ex-trem´ist
ex-trem´i·ty
ex-tric´a·ble
ex´tri-cate
ex´tri-ca´tion
ex´tro-vert
ex-trude´
ex-trud´er
ex-trud´ing
ex-tru´sion
ex-tru´sive
ex-ude´
ex-ult´
ex-ul-ta´tion
ex´urb
ex-ur´ban-ite
ex-ur´bi·a
eye´ball
eye´brow
eye´ful
eye´glass
eye´ing

eye´lash
eye´let
eye´lid
eye´lin·er
eye´o-pen·er
eye´sight
eye´sore

F

fa´ble
fa´bled
fab´ric
fab´ri-cate
fab-ri-ca´tion
fab´u-list
fab´u-lous
fab´u-lous·ly
fab´u-lous-ness
fa-çade´
face´less
face´lift
face´–off
face´plate
fac´et
fac´et·ed
fa-ce´tious
fa-ce´tious·ly
fa-ce´tious-ness
face´–to–face´
fa´cial
fac´ile
fa-cil´i-tate
fa-cil´i-ties

fa-cil´i-ty

fac´ing

fac-sim´i-le

fact´find-ing

fac´tion

fac´tion-al

fac´tious

fac´tious-ly

fac-ti´tious

fac´tor

fac´to-ries

fac-tor´ing

fac´to-ry

fac-to´tum

fac´tu-al

fac´ul-ties

fac´ul-ty

fad´dish

fad´er

fail´ing

fail´ure

faint´ed

faint´heart-ed

faint´ly

fair´ground

fair´ies

fair´ly

fair–mind´ed

fair´ness

fair´way

fair´y

fair´y-land

fair´y tale

faith´ful-ly

faith´ful-ness

faith´less

faith´less-ly

fake

fak´er

fak´er-y

fal´la-cies

fal-la´cious

fal´la-cy

fall´ing

fall´out

fal´low

false´hood

false´ly

fal-si-fi-ca´tion

fal´si-fied

fal´si-fy

fal´ter

fal´ter-ing

fame

famed

fa-mil´ial

fa-mil´iar

fa-mil-iar´i-ty

fa-mil-iar-i-za´tion

fa-mil´iar-ize

fa-mil´iar-ly

fam´i-lies

fam´i-ly

fam´ine

fam´ish

fam´ished

fa´mous

fa´mous-ly

fa-nat´ic

fa-nat´i-cal-ly

fa-nat´i-cism

fan´cied

fan´ci-er

fan´cies

fan´ci-ful

fan´cy

fan´fare

fan´fold

fang

fanged

fan´gled

fanned

fan´ning

fan´ta-size

fan-tas´tic

fan´ta-sy

far´ci-cal

fare-well´

far´fetched

farm´er

farm´hand

farm´house

farm´ing

farm´land

farm´yard

far´sight-ed

far´ther

far´thest

fas´ci-a

fas´ci-nate
fas´ci-nat·ed
fas´ci-nat-ing
fas-ci-na´tion
fash´ion
fash´ion-a·ble
fash´ion-a·bly
fast´ten
fas´ten·er
fas´ten-ing
fas-tid´i-ous
fas-tid´i-ous·ly
fast´ing
fa´tal-ist
fa-tal-is´tic
fa-tal-is´ti-cal·ly
fa-tal´i·ty
fa´tal·ly
fate´ful
fat´head
fa´ther
fa´ther-land
fa´ther-less
fa´ther·ly
fath´om
fath´om-a·ble
fath´om-less
fa-tigue´
fa-tigued´
fa-tigu´ing
fat´ten
fat´ten·er
fat´ty

fa-tu´i·ty
fat´u-ous
fat´u-ous·ly
fau´cet
fault´find-ing
fault´i·er
fault´i·ly
fault´less·ly
fault´y
fau´na
fa´vor
fa´vor-a·ble
fa´vor-a·bly
fa´vor-ite
fa´vor-it-ism
fa´vour (Br.)
fawn´ing·ly
fe´al·ty
fear´ful
fear´less·ly
fea´sance
fea-si·bil´i·ty
fea´si·ble
fea´si·bly
feast
feath´er
feath´er-bed-ding
feath´er-brain
feath´ered
feath´er-weight
feath´er·y
fea´ture
fea´tured

feb´rile
feck´less
feck´less·ly
fed´er-al
fed´er-al-ist
fed-er-a´tion
fe-do´ra
fee´ble
fee´ble-ness
feed´back
feed´er
feed´ing
feed´stuff
feel´er
feel´ing
feet´first´
feign
feigned
feign´ing
feint
feist´i-ness
feist´y
fe-lic-i-ta´tion
fe-lic´i-tous·ly
fe-lic´i·ty
fe´line
fel´low
fel´low-ship
fel´on
fe-lo´ni-ous·ly
fel´o·ny
fe´male
fem´i-na·cy

fem´i-nine·ly
fem-i-nin´i·ty
fem´i-nism
fem´i-nist
fem´i-nize
fenc´ing
fend´er
fe´ral
fer-ment´
fer-men-ta´tion
fe-ro´cious·ly
fe-roc´i·ty
fer´ried
fer´ries
fer´ry
fer´ry-boat
fer´ry-ing
fer´tile
fer-til´i·ty
fer-til-i·za´tion
fer-til-i·za´tion·al
fer´til-ize
fer´til-iz·er
fer´vent
fer´vent·ly
fer´vid
fer´vid·ly
fer´vor
fes´ter
fes´ti-val
fes´tive
fes-tiv´i·ty
fes-toon´

fe´tal
fetch´ing
fet´id
fet´ish
fet´ter
fet´tle
fe´tus
feud
feu´dal
feu-dal-is´tic
fe´ver
fe´ver-ish
fe´ver-ish·ly
few´er
fi-as´co
fi´at
fib´bing
fi´brous
fick´le
fic´tion-al-ize
fic-ti´tious·ly
fid´dle
fid´dler
fid´dle-sticks
fid´dling
fi-del´i·ty
fid´get
fi-du´ci-ar·y
fief´dom
field´er
field´stone
fiend´ish·ly
fierce´ly

fi´er·y
fi-es´ta
fif-teen´
fif-teenth´
fifth
fif´ti-eth
fif´ty
fight´er
fight´ing
fig´ment
fig´ure
fig´ured
fig´ure-head
fil´a-ment
filch´er
fi-let´
fil´i·al
fil´i-bus-ter
fil´i-gree
fill
fill´er
fil´let
fill´ing
fil´ly
film´i·er
film´i·ly
film´i-ness
film´y
fil´ter
filth
filth´i·er
filth´i-ness
filth-y

fil´trate
fil-tra´tion
fi-na´gle
fi-na´gler
fi-na´gling
fi´nal
fi´nal´e
fi´nal-ist
fi-nal´i·ty
fi´na-lize
fi-na-li-za´tion
fi´nal·ly
fi-nance´
fi-nan´cial·ly
fin-an-cier´
fi-nanc´ing
find´er
find´ing
fine´ly
fine´ness
fin´er·y
fi-nesse´
fin´ger
fin´gered
fin´ger-ing
fin´ger-ling
fin´ger-nail
fin´ger-print
fin´i·al
fin´ick·y
fin´is
fin´ish
fin´ished

fin´ish·er
fi´nite
fin´nick·y
fire´arm
fire´brand
fire´crack·er
fire´fight
fire´fly
fire´man
fire´place
fire´proof
fire´side
fire´works
fir´ing
fir´ma-ment
firm´er
firm´ly
fir´ry
first´born
first´ly
fis´cal·ly
fish´bowl
fish´er-man
fish´er·y
fish´hook
fish´ing
fish´mon-ger
fish´net
fish´y
fis´sion
fis´sion-a·ble
fis´sure
fist´fight

fist´ful
fit´ful·ly
fit´ness
fit´ted
fit´ting·ly
fiv´er
fix´ate
fix-a´tion
fix´a-tive
fixed
fix´ing
fix´ture
fiz´zle
fiz´zling
fizz´y
flab´ber-gast
flab´bi-ness
flab´by
flac´cid
flac-cid´i·ty
flag´el-late
flagged
flag´ging
flag´on
fla´grance
fla´gran·cy
fla´grant
fla´grant·ly
flake
flaked
flak´i·er
flak´i-ness
flak´ing

flak´y
flam-boy´ant
flam-boy´ant-ly
flame
flamed
flam´ing
flam´ma·ble
flange
flanged
flank
flank´er
flan´nel
flap´jack
flap´pa·ble
flapped
flap´per
flap´ping
flare
flare´–up
flar´ing
flash
flash´back
flash´bulb
flash´ing
flash´light
flash´y
flat´car
flat´foot
flat–footed
flat´ly
flat´ten
flat´ter
flat´ter·er

flat´ter-ing
flat´ter·y
flat´top
flat´ware
flaunt´ing
fla´vor
fla´vor-ful
fla´vour (Br.)
flaw´less·ly
flea´bag
flea´bite
flea´–bit-ten
fledged
flee´ing
fleet–foot´ed
fleet´ing·ly
fleet´ness
flesh´i-ness
flesh´y
flex-i·bil´i·ty
flex´i·ble
flex´i·bly
flex´time
flick´er·y
fli´er
flight´i-ness
flight´less
flight´y
flim´flam
flim´si·ly
flim´si-ness
flim´sy
flinch´ing

fling´ing
flip´pant
flipped
flip´per
flip´ping
flirt
flir-ta´tion
flir-ta´tious·ly
flirt´er
flirt´y
flit´ting
fliv´ver
float´er
float´ing
flocked
flock´ing
flog´ging
flood´light
floor´board
floor´ing
floor´walk·er
flop´house
flop´pier
flop´ping
flop´py
flo´ra
flo´ral
flo-res´cence
flo-res´cent
flor´id
flor´id·ly
flo´rist
flo-ta´tion

flo-til′la
flot′sam
flounced
flounc′ing
flounc′y
flour′ish
flour′ished
flour′ish-ing
flour′y
flout′ed
flout′ing
flow′ered
flow′er·et
flow′er-ing
flow′er-pot
flow′er·y
flow′ing
flown
fluc′tu-ate
fluc′tu-at·ed
fluc′tu-at-ing
fluc-tu-a′tion
flu′en·cy
flu′ent·ly
fluff′i·er
fluff′i-ness
fluff′y
flu′id
fluke
fluk′y
flum′mer·y
flunk′out
flu-o-res′cence

flu-o-res′cent
flu-o-resc′ing
flu-o-ri-da′tion
flu′o-ride
flur′ry
flus′ter
flut′ed
flut′ing
flut′ist
flut′tered
flut′ter-ing
flut′ter·y
fly′–by–night
fly′catcher
fly′er
fly′ing
fly′wheel
foam′i·er
foam′i-ness
foam′ing
foam′y
fo′cal
fo′cus
fo′cused
fo′cus-ing
fod′der
fog′bound
fog′gi·er
fog′gi-ness
fog′gy
fog′horn
fo′gy
foi′ble

foiled
foil′ing
foist′ed
fold′ed
fold′er
fold′ing
fold′out
fo′li-age
fo-li-a′tion
folk′lore
folk′lor·ic
folks·y
folk′way
fol′low
fol′lowed
fol′low·er
fol′low-ing
fol′low–through
fol′low–up
fo-ment′
fon′dled
fon′dler
fon′dling
fond′ly
fond′ness
food′stuff
fool′er·y
fool′har·dy
fool′ing
fool′ish·ly
fool′ish-ness
fool′proof
foot′age

foot´ed

foot´er

foot´fall

foot´hill

foot´hold

foot´ing

foot´light

foot´print

foot´sie

foot´step

fop´per·y

fop´pish

for´age

for´aged

for´ag·er

for´ag·ing

for´ay

for-bear´

for-bear´ance

for-bid´den

for-bid´ding

forced

force´ful

forc´i·bly

forc´ing

fore´arm

fore-bod´ing

fore´cast

fore´cast·er

fore-close´

fore-clo´sure

fore´fa-ther

fore´go

fore´go-ing

fore´gone´

fore´ground

fore´head

for´eign

for´eign·er

fore´knowl-edge

fore´most

fo-ren´sic

fore-or-dain´

fore´run-ner

fore-see´a·ble

fore-seen´

fore-shad´ow-ing

fore-short´en

fore´sight·ed

fore´sight-ed-ness

for´est

for-est-a´tion

for´est·ed

for´est·ry

fore-tell´

for-ev´er

fore-warn´

fore´word

for´feit

for´fei-ture

forg´er

for´ger·y

for-get´ful

for-get´ful-ness

for-get´ta·ble

for-get´ting

forg´ing

for-give´

for-giv´en

for-give´ness

for-giv´ing

for-go´ing

for-got´ten

fork´ful

for-lorn´ly

for´mal

for-mal´i·ty

for´mal-ize

for´mal-wear

for´mat

for-ma´tion

form´a-tive·ly

for´mer *(bygone)*

for´mer·ly

for´mi-da·ble

for´mi-da·bly

form´less

for´mu·la

for´mu-late

for-mu-la´tion

for´ni-cate

for-sake´

for-sak´en

for-sook´

for-swear´

forth´com-ing

forth´right

for´ti-eth

for-ti-fi-ca´tion

for´ti-fied
for´ti-fi·er
for´ti-fy
for´ti-tude
for´tress
for-tu´i-tous·ly
for-tu´i·ty
for´tu-nate·ly
for´tune
for´ty
fo´rum
for´ward
for´ward·er
fos´sil
fos´sil-ize
fos´ter
foul´ly
foun-da´tion
found´er *(n.)*
foun´der *(v.)*
found´ling
found´ries
found´ry
foun´tain
foun´tain-head
four´flush·er
four´fold
four´some
four-teen´
four-teenth´
fourth
fowl´er
fox´i-ness

fox´y
foy´er
fra´cas
frac´tal
frac´tion
frac´tious·ly
frac´ture
frag´ile
fra-gil´i·ty
frag´ment
frag´men-tar·y
frag´ment·ed
fra´grance
fra´gran·cy
fra´grant
fra´grant·ly
frail´ties
frail´ty
frame´a·ble
frame´a·ble-ness
framed
fram´er
frame´work
fram´ing
fran´chise
fran-chi-see´
fran´chis·er
fran´gi·ble
fran´gi·ble-ness
frank´ly
frank´ness
fran´tic
fran´ti-cal·ly

fran´tic·ly
fra-ter´nal-ism
fra-ter´nal·ly
fra-ter´ni·ty
frat´er-nize
frat´ri-ci-dal
frat´ri-cide
fraud´u-lence
fraud´u-len·cy
fraud´u-lent·ly
fraught
frayed
fraz´zle
freak´ish
freak´y
freck´led
free´bie
free´dom
free´ly
fre´er
free´stand·ing
free´think·er
free-wheel´ing
free´will
freez´er
freez´ing
freight´er
fre-net´ic
fren´zied
fren´zy
fre´quen·cy
fre´quent
fre´quent·er

fre′quent·ly

fre′quent-ness

fres′co

fres′coes

fresh′en

fresh′ly

fresh′man

fresh′man-ship

fret′ful

fret′ful-ness

fri-a·bil′i·ty

fri′a·ble

fri′ar

fri′ar·y

fric′tion

friend′less

friend′li·er

friend′li-ness

friend′ly

fright′en

fright′ened

fright′en-ing

fright′ful·ly

frig′id

fri-gid′i·ty

frill′i-ness

frill′y

fringed

frisk′i·er

frisk′i-ness

frisk′y

frit′ter

fri-vol′i·ty

friv′o-lous·ly

friz′zle

friz′zly

frol′ic

frol′icked

frol′ick-ing

frol′ic-some

front′age

fron′tal

front′al·ly

fron-tier′

fron′tis-piece

frost′bite

frost′bit-ten

frost′ed

frost′i·ly

frost′ing

frost′y

froth′i·er

froth′i-ness

froth′y

frowned

frown′ing

frow′zy

fro′zen

fru′gal

fru-gal′i·ty

fru′gal-ness

fruit′cake

fruit′ful

fruit′i-ness

fru-i′tion

fruit·y

frump′y

frus′trate

frus′trat-ed

frus′trat-ing

frus-tra′tion

fu′el

fu′gi-tive

fugue

ful′crum

ful-fill′ing

ful-fill′ment

ful′gent

full′ness

ful′ly

ful′mi-nate

ful-mi-na′tion

ful′some

fum′ble

fum′bling

fu′mi-gant

fu′mi-gate

fu′mi-gat-ing

fu-mi-ga′tion

fu′mi-ga-tor

fum′ing

func′tion

func′tion·al

func′tion-al·ly

func′tion-ar·y

fun-da-men′tal

fun-da-men′tal·ly

fu′ner-al

fu′ner-ar·y

fu-ne´re·al

fun´gi-cide

fun´gus

fun´neled

fun´nel-ing

fun´ny

fu´ri-ous

fu´ri-ous·ly

fu´ri-ous-ness

fur´lough

fur´nace

fur´nish-ings

fur´ni-ture

fu´ror

fur´row

fur´ry

fur´ther-ance

fur´ther-more

fur´thest

fur´tive·ly

fu´ry

fu´se-lage

fu´si·ble

fu´sion

fuss´budg·et

fuss´i·ly

fuss´i-ness

fuss´y

fu´tile·ly

fu´tile-ness

fu-til´i·ty

fu´ton

fu´ture

fu-tur-is´tic

fuzz´y

G

gab´ar-dine

gab´bing

gab´ble

gab´by

ga´bled

ga´bling

gad´a·bout

gad´fly

gad´get

gad´get·ry

gaffe

gag

ga´ga

gagged

gag´ging

gag´gle

gai´e·ty

gai´ly

gain´a·ble

gai´ner *(dive)*

gain´ful·ly

gain´ly

gain´say·er

gait´ed

ga´la

ga-lac´tic

ga-lax´i·al

gal´ax·y

gal´lant

gal´lant·ly

gal´lant·ry

gal´le·on

gal-le-ri´a

gal´ler·y

gal´ley

gall´ing

gal´li-vant

gal´lon

gal´loped

gal´lop·er

gal´lop-ing

gal´lows

gall´stone

ga-loot´

ga-lore´

gal-va-ni-za´tion

gal´va-nize

gam´bler

gam´bling

gam´bol

gam´boled

gam´bol-ing

game´keep·er

game´ly

games´man-ship

gam´ey

gam´i·ly

gam´y

gan´der

gang´bust·ers

gan´gly

gang´ster

gang´way
ga-rage´
gar´bage
gar´ble
gar´bled
gar´den
gar´den·er
gar-gan´tu·an
gar´gled
gar´gling
gar´goyle
gar´ish·ly
gar´ish-ness
gar´land
gar´lic
gar´lick·y
gar´ment
gar´ner
gar´nish
gar´nish·ee´
gar´nish·er
gar´nish-ment
gar´ret
gar´ri-son
gar´ru-lous
gar´ru-lous-ness
gar´ter
gas´e-ous
gas-o-line´
gasp´ing
gas´tric
gate´house
gate´keep·er

gath´ered
gath´er-ing
gauche
gaud´i·ly
gaud´y
gauged
gaug´ing
gaunt´let
gaunt´ness
gauze
gav´el·er
gay´ly
gazed
ga-zette´
gaz´et-teer´
gaz´ing
gear´box
gear´shift
gee´zer
gel´a-tin
gel´a-tine
ge-lat´i-nous
gel´id
gelled
gel´ling
gen-e-al´o·gy
gen´er-al
gen-er-al´i·ty
gen-er-al-i·za´tion
gen´er-al-ize
gen´er-al·ly
gen´er-ate
gen´er-at-ing

gen-er-a´tion
gen´er-a-tive
gen´er-a-tor
ge-ner´ic
ge-ner´i-cal·ly
gen-er-os´i·ty
gen´er-ous·ly
ge-net´ic
ge-net´i-cal·ly
ge´nial
ge-ni-al´i·ty
ge´nie
ge´nius
gen´o-cide
gen´re
gen-teel´ly
gen´tile
gen-til´i·ty
gen´tle
gen´tle-man·ly
gen´tle-wom·an
gen´tlest
gent´ly
gen-tri-fi-ca´tion
gen´try
gen´u-flect
gen-u-flec´tion
gen´u-ine·ly
ge´ode
ge-o-graph´ic
ge-o-graph´i-cal·ly
ge-og´ra-phy
ge-o-log´ic

ge-o-log´i-cal
ge-ol´o-gist
ge-ol´o-gy
ge-o-met´ric
ge-o-met´ri-cal·ly
ge-om´e-try
ge-o-po-lit´i-cal
ger-i-at´rics
ger-mane´
ger´mi-cide
ger´mi-nate
ges´tur·al
ges´ture
ges´tur·er
ges´tur-ing
get´a·way
get´ter
get´ting
gey´ser
ghast´li-ness
ghast´ly
gher´kin
ghet´to
ghost´li-ness
ghost´ly
ghost´writ·er
ghoul´ish
gi´ant
gib´ber-ish
gibe
gib´ing
gid´di·ly
gid´di-ness

gid´dy
gift´ed
gig´a-byte
gi-gan´tic
gi-gan´ti-cal·ly
gig´gle
gig´gling
gig´gly
gild´ing
gim´let
gim´mick·ry
gim´mick·y
gin´ger
gin´ger-bread
gin´ger·ly
gin´ger-snap
gird´er
gird´ing
gir´dle
girl´friend
gis´mo
give´a·way
giv´en
giv´er
giv´ing
gla´cial
gla´cier
glad´den
glade
glad´i-a-tor
glad´i-a-to´ri·al
glad´ly
glad´ness

glam´or-ize
glam´o-rous·ly
glam´our
glance
glanc´ing
glan´du-lar
glar´ing
glass´es
glass´mak-ing
glass´ware
glass´y
gleam´ing
glee´ful·ly
glib´ly
glid´er
glid´ing
glim´mer-ing
glimpse
glimps´ing
glis´ten
glitch
glit´ter
glit-te-ra´ti
glit´ter-ing
glit´ter´y
glitz´y
gloat´ing
glob´al-ism
glob-al-i-za´tion
glob´al·ly
glob´u-lar
glob´ule
gloom´i·ly

gloom´i-ness

gloom´y

glo-ri-fi-ca´tion

glo´ri-fied

glo´ri-fi·er

glo´ri·fy

glo´ri-fy-ing

glo´ri-ous·ly

glo´ry

glos´sa·ry

glos´si-ness

gloss´y

gloved

glow´er-ing

glow´ing·ly

glued

glum´ly

glut´ted

glut´ton-ous

glut´ton·y

gnarl

gnarled

gnarl´y

gnaw´er

gnaw´ing

gnome

gnos´tic

goad´ed

goal´keep·er

goal´tend·er

goal´tend-ing

gob´ble-dy-gook

gob´bler

gob´bling

gob´let

gob´lin

god´dess

god´fa-ther

god´less

god´like

god´li-ness

god´ly

god´moth·er

god´par-ent

god´send

gold´en

golf´er

gol´ly

gon´do·la

gon-do-lier´

gone

gon´er

good–by´

good-bye´

good–bye´

good´heart´ed

good´ies

good´ness

good´y

goo´ey

goof´i-ness

goof´y

goon´y

gorge

gor´geous·ly

gor´geous-ness

gor´mand-ize

gor´y

gos´pel

gos´sa-mer

gos´sip-ing

gos´sip-mon-ger

gos´sip·y

goth´ic

goth´i-cal·ly

got´ten

gouge

goug´er

goug´ing

gour´mand

gour´man-dise´

gour´met

gout´y

gov´ern-a·ble

gov´ern-ance

gov´er-ness

gov´ern-ment

gov´er-nor

grab´ber

grab´bing

grab´by

grace´ful·ly

grace´ful-ness

grace´less

gra´cious·ly

gra´cious-ness

gra-da´tion

grad´ed

grad´er

gra´di-ent
grad´ing
grad´u-al·ly
grad´u-at·ed
grad´u-at-ing
grad-u-a´tion
graf-fi´ti
graf-fi´to
graft´ing
grain´i-ness
grain´y
gram-mat´i-cal·ly
gra´na·ry
grand-child
grand´chil-dren
grand´dad
grand-daugh-ter
gran-dee´
gran´deur
grand´fa-ther
gran-dil´o-quence
gran-dil´o-quent
gran´di-ose
grand´ly
grand´ma
grand´moth·er
grand´neph·ew
grand´niece
grand´pa
grand´par-ent
grand´son
grand´stand
grang´er

gran´ny
grant´er
grant´or
gran´u-lar
gran-u-lar´i·ty
gran´u-lat·ed
gran-u-la´tion
gran´ule
grape´vine
graph´ic
graph´i-cal·ly
grap´ple
grasped
grasp´ing
grass´i-ness
grass´land
grass´y
grate´ful·ly
grate´ful-ness
grat´er
grat-i-fi-ca´tion
grat´i-fied
grat´i·fy
grat´i-fy-ing
grat´ing
gra´tis
grat´i-tude
gra-tu´i-ties
gra-tu´i-tous·ly
gra-tu´i·ty
grav´el
grav´el·ly
grave´ly

grav´en
grav´i-tate
grav´i-tat-ing
grav-i-ta´tion·al
grav´i·ty
gra-vure´
gra´vy
gray´beard
gray´ish
gray´ness
graz´er
graz´ing
grease´less
greas´y
great´en
great´ly
great´ness
greed´i·ly
greed´i-ness
greed´y
green´er·y
green´gro-cer
green´ish
greet´ing
gre-gar´i-ous
grid´dle
grid´lock
grief´strick·en
griev´ance
grieve
griev´er
griev´ing
griev´ous·ly

grim´ace	group´ie	guid´ance
grime	grov´el	guide´book
grim´y	grov´eled	guide´post
grind´er	grov´el·er	guile´ful
grind´ing	grov´el-ing	guile´less
grind´stone	grow´er	guilt´i·ly
gripe	grow´ing	guilt´less
grip´er	grown	guilt´y
grip´ing	growth	guise
grippe	grub´by	gull´i·ble
gris´ly	grudg´ing·ly	gull´i·bly
grist	grue´some	gum´mi-ness
gris´tle	grum´bler	gum´my
grit´ty	grum´bling	gump´tion
griz´zled	grum´bly	gun´fight·er
groaned	grump´i·ly	gun´fire
groan´ing	grump´i-ness	gun´ner·y
gro´cer	grump´ish	gun´ny-sack
gro´cer-ies	grump´y	gun´shot
gro´cer·y	grun´gy	gur´gle
grog´gy	guar´an-tee´	gur´gling
grooms´man	guar´an-ties	gush´er
gros´grained	guar´an-tor	gush´i-ness
gross´ly	guar´an·ty	gush´ing·ly
gross´ness	guard´ed·ly	gush´y
gro-tesque´ly	guard´i·an	gust´i·ly
grouch´i-ness	guard´i-an-ship	gust·to
grouch´y	guess´er	gust´y
ground´break·er	guess´ing	gut´less
ground´break-ing	guess´ti-mate	guts´y
ground´less	guess´work	gut´ted
grounds´keep·er	guest´house	gut´ter
ground´swell	guf-faw´	gut´tur·al

guz´zle
guz´zling
gym-na´si·um
gym´nast
gym-nas´tics
gy-ne-col´o-gist
gy-ne-col´o·gy
gyp´sy
gy´rate
gy-ra´tion
gy´rat-ing
gy´ro-scope
gy -ro-scop´ic

H

ha-bil-i-ta´tion
hab´it
hab´i-tat
hab-i-ta´tion
ha-bit´u-al·ly
ha-bit´u-ate
ha-bit-u-a´tion
ha-bit´u·é
hab´it·us
hack´er
hack´le
hack´neyed
hag´gard
hag´gle
hair´do
hair´line
hairs´breadth
hair´spring

hair´style
hair´y
half´heart·ed
half´way
hal-i-to´sis
hal-le-lu´jah
hal´lowed
hal-lu-ci-na´tion
hal-lu´ci-na-to·ry
ham´let
ham´per
hand´bas-ket
hand´ful
hand´i-cap
hand´i-capped
hand´i-cap-per
hand´i-craft
hand´i·ly
hand´i-ness
hand´ker-chief
han´dle
han´dler
han´dling
hand´rail
hand´shake
hand´some·ly
hand´stand
hand´wo´ven
hand´writ-ing
hand´y
hang´ing
hang´o·ver
hang´–up

han´ker-ing
han´ky
hap-haz´ard·ly
hap´less
hap´pen-ing
hap´pen-stance
hap´pi·ly
hap´pi-ness
hap´py
ha-rangue´
ha-rangu´ing
ha-rass´
ha-rassed´
ha-rass´ing
ha-rass´ment
har´bin-ger
hard´en
hard´ened
hard´en·er
hard´en-ing
hard´head·ed
har´di·ly
har´di-ness
hard´ly
hard´ness
hard´ship
har´dy
harm´ful
harm´ful-ness
harm´less·ly
harm´less-ness
har-mon´ic
har-mon´i·ca

har-mon´i-cal·ly
har-mo´ni-ous·ly
har´mo-nize
har´mo-niz-ing
har´mo-ny
harp´si-chord
har´ri-dan
harsh´ly
harsh´ness
har´vest
har´vester
has´sle
has´sled
haste
has´ten
hast´i·ly
hast´y
hate´ful
hate´mon-ger
ha´tred
haugh´ti·ly
haugh´ti-ness
haugh´ty
haunt´ed
haunt´ing
hav´oc
hawk´er
hawk´ish
haw´ser
hay´mow
hay´ride
haz´ard
haz´ard-ous

ha´zel-nut
haz´ing
ha´zy
head´ache
head´ach·y
head´dress
head´er
head´hunt·er
head´ing
head´quar-ters
head´strong
head´wait´er
head´y
heal´er
heal´ing
health´ful
health´i·er
health´i-est
health´i-ness
health´y
hear´ing
hark´en
hear´say
hearse
heart´ache
heart´beat
heart´bro-ken
heart´burn
heart´en
heart´felt
heart´less
heart´sick
heart´warm-ing

heart´y
heat´ed
heat´ed·ly
heat´er
hea´then
heat´stroke
heav´en·ly
heaven–sent
heav´en-ward
heav´i·er
heav´i·ly
heav´y
heav´y-set
heck´le
heck´ler
heck´ling
hec´tic
hedg´er
hedg´ing
he´do-nism
he´do-nist
heed´ful
heed´less
heft´i·er
heft´i-est
heft´i·ly
heft´y
heif´er
height´en
hei´nous
heir´loom
heist
hel´i-cop-ter

he´li·um
he´lix
hel´lion
hell´ish
hel·lo´
hel´met·ed
helms´man
help´er
help´ful
help´ing
help´less·ly
help´less-ness
hem´i-sphere
hem´line
hem´lock
hence´forth´
hench´man
her´ald
he-ral´dic
her´ald·ry
her-ba´ceous
herb´al
her´bi-cide
her´biv-ore
here-af´ter
here´by
he-red´i-tar·y
he-red´i·ty
here´in-af´ter
here-of´
her´e·sy
her´e-tic
here´to-fore´

her´i-tage
her-maph´ro-dite
her´mit-age
her´ni·a
her´ni-ate
he´ro
he´roes
he-ro´ic
he-ro´i-cal·ly
her´o-ism
her-self´
hes´i-tan·cy
hes´i-tant
hes´i-tant·ly
hes´i-tate
hes´i-tat-ing·ly
hes-i-ta´tion
het-er-o-sex´u·al
heu-ris´tic
heu-ris´ti-cal·ly
hex-a-dec´i-mal
hex´a-gon
hex-ag´o-nal
hi-a´tus
hi´ber-nate
hi´ber-nat-ing
hi-ber-na´tion
hic´cough
hic´cup
hid´den
hide´a-way
hide´bound
hid´e-ous·ly

hid´ing
hi´er-ar´chal
hi´er-ar´chi-cal·ly
hi´er-ar-chy
hi´er-o-glyph´ic
high´born
high´bred
high´brow
high´lev´el
high´life
high´light
high´way
hik´er
hik´ing
hi-lar´i-ous·ly
hi-lar´i·ty
hill´i-ness
hill´side
hill´top
hill´y
him-self´
hind´most
hin´drance
hind´sight
hip´po-drome
hire´ling
hir´sute
his-to´ri·an
his-tor´ic
his-tor´i-cal
his-tor´i-cal·ly
his´to-ries
his´to·ry

his-tri-on´ics
hitch´hike
hitch´hik·er
hoa´gy
hoard´ing
hoarse·ly
hoarse-ness
hoar´y
hoax
hob´ble
hob´by
hob´by-ist
hob´nob-bing
hock´ey
hodge´podge
hoist´ed
hold´ing
hold´out
hol´i-day
ho´li-ness
ho-lis´tic
ho-lis´ti-cal·ly
hol´low
hol´o-caust
hol´o-gram
hol´o-graph
ho-log´ra-phy
hol´ster
ho´ly
hom´age
home´bod·y
home´buy·er
home´com-ing

home´less
home´li-ness
home´ly
home´mak·er
ho´me·o-path´ic
home´sick-ness
home´stretch
home´ward
hom´ey-ness
hom´i-ci-dal
hom´i-cide
hom´i-lies
hom´i·ly
hom´i·ny
ho-mo-ge´ne·ous
ho-mog´e-nize
ho-mo-sex´u·al
hon´est·ly
hon´es·ty
hon´ey-moon
hon´or-a·ble
hon´or-a·bly
hon-o-rar´i·um
hon´or-ar·y
hon´our (Br.)
hood´ed
hood´lum
hood´wink
hoofed
hoof´er
hook´ed
hook´y
hoo´li-gan

hoop´la
hoo-ray´
hoose´gow
hoot´en-an·ny
hoot´er
hope´ful·ly
hope´less·ly
hope´less-ness
hop´per
hop´ping
ho-ri´zon
hor´i-zon´tal·ly
hor´mone
hor´o-scope
hor-ren´dous·ly
hor´ri·ble
hor´ri·bly
hor´rid
hor-rif´ic
hor-rif´i-cal·ly
hor´ri-fied
hor´ri·fy
hor´ror
hors d'oeuvre
horse´pow·er
hors´y
hor-ti-cul´tur·al
hor´ti-cul-ture
hor´ti-cul´tur-ist
ho´sier·y
hos´pice
hos-pit´a·ble-ness
hos-pit´a·bly

hos´pi-tal

hos-pi-tal´i·ty

hos´pi-tal-ize

hos´tage

hos´tel

host´ess

hos´tile·ly

hos-til´i·ty

hos´tler

hot´bed

ho-tel´

hot´head·ed

hot´house

hot´ly

hot´shot

hound´er

hour´glass

hour´ly

house´bro-ken

house´clean´ing

house´ful

house´keep·er

house´top

house´wares

house´warm-ing

house´work

hous´ing

hov´el

hov´er

hov´er-ing

how´dy

how-ev´er

howl´ing

hub´bub

hu´bris

huck´ster

hud´dle

huff´i-ness

huff´y

huge´ly

hug´ging

hulk´ing

hu´man

hu-mane´ly

hu-man-i-tar´i·an

hu-man´i·ty

hu´man-ize

hu´man·ly

hu´man-oid

hum´ble

hum´bling

hum´bly

hum´bug

hum´ding´er

hum´drum

hu´mid

hu-mid´i-fi·er

hu-mid´i·fy

hu-mid´i·ty

hu´mi-dor

hu-mil´i-ate

hu-mil´i-at-ing

hu-mil-i-a´tion

hu-mil´i·ty

hum´ming

hu´mor

hu´mor-ist

hu´mor-less

hu´mor-ous·ly

hu´mour (Br.)

hump´backed

hunch´back

hun´dred

hun´dred-fold

hun´dredth

hun´ger-ing

hun´gri·er

hun´gri·ly

hun´gry

hunt´er

hunt´ing

hur´dle

hurl´er

hurl´ing

hur-rah´

hur´ri-cane

hur´ried·ly

hur´ry

hur´ry-ing·ly

hurt´ful·ly

hurt´ful-ness

hurt´ing

hur´tle

hur´tling

hus´band

hus´band·ly

hus´band·ry

husk´i·ly

husk´i-ness

husk´y
hus´sy
hus´tler
hus´tling
hy´brid
hy´drant
hy´drate
hy-dra´tion
hy-drau´lic
hy-drau´li-cal·ly
hy-dro-e·lec´tric
hy´dro-foil
hy´dro-gen
hy´giene
hy´gien´ist
hymn
hym´nal
hype
hyp´er
hy´per-link
hy-per-sen´si-tive
hy´per-text
hy´phen
hy´phen-ate
hy´phen-at·ed
hy-phen-a´tion
hyp-no´sis
hyp-no-ther´a·py
hyp-not´ic
hyp´no-tism
hyp´no-tist
hyp´no-tize
hy-po-chon´dri·ac

hy-poc´ri·sy
hyp-o-crit´i-cal
hy-poth´e-ses
hy-poth´e-sis
hy-poth´e-size
hy-po-thet´i-cal·ly
hys-ter´i-cal·ly
hys-ter´ics

I

i-bu-pro´fen
ice´berg
ice´break·er
ice´mak·er
ic´i-cle
ic´i·ly
ic´ing
ick´y
i´con
i·con´o-clast
ic´y
i·de´a
i·de´al
i·de´al-ism
i·de´al-ist
i·de´al-is´tic
i·de-al-is´ti-cal·ly
i·de´al·ly
i´de-ate
i·de-a´tion
i·den´ti-cal·ly
i·den´ti-fi-a·ble
i·den-ti-fi-ca´tion

i·den´ti-fied
i·den´ti-fies
i·den´ti·fy
i·den´ti·ty
i·de-o-log´ic
i·de-o-log´i-cal
i·de-ol´o·gy
id´i-o·cy
id´i·om
id´i-o-mat´ic
id-i-o-syn´cra·sy
id´i-ot
id-i-ot´ic
i´dled
i´dle-ness
i´dler
i´dling
i´dly
i´dol
i·dol´a-ter
i·dol´a-trous
i·dol´a-try
i´dol-ize
i´dyll
i·dyl´lic
if´fy
ig-nite´
lg-nit´ing
ig-ni´tion
ig-no´ble
ig-no´bly
ig-no-min´i-ous·ly
ig-no-ra´mus

ig´no-rance
ig´no-rant
ig-nore´
ill´–ad-vised´
il-le´gal
il-le-gal´i·ty
il-le´gal·ly
il-leg´i·ble
il-le-git´i-ma·cy
il-le-git´i-mate
il-lic´it
il-lic´it·ly
il-lit´er-a·cy
il-lit´er-ate
ill´ness
il´log´i-cal
il-lu´mi-nate
il-lu-mi-na´ti
il-lu-mi-na´tion
il-lu´mi-nat-ing
il-lu-mi-na´tion
il-lu´sion·al
il-lu´sion-ar·y
il-lu´sion-ist
il-lu´sive-ly
il-lu´so·ry
il´lus-trate
il´lus-trat-ing
il´lus-tra´tion
il-lus´tra-tive
il´lus-tra-tor
il-lus´tri-ous·ly
im´age

im´ag-e·ry
im-ag´i-nar·y
im-ag´i-na´tion
im-ag´i-na-tive·ly
im-ag´ine
im-ag´ing
im-ag´in-ing
im-bal´ance
im´be-cile
im-be-cil´ic
im-bibe´
im-bib´er
im-bro´glio
im-bue´
im-bu´ing
im´i-tate
im-i-ta´tion
im´i-ta-tive
im-mac´u-late·ly
im-ma-te´ri·al
im-ma-ture´
lm-ma-tur´i·ty
im-mea´sur-a·ble
im-mea´sur-a·bly
im-me´di-a·cy
im-me´di-ate·ly
im-mense´ly
im-mersed´
im-mers´i·ble
im-mers´ing
im-mer´sion
im´mi-grant
im-mi-gra´tion

im´mi-nent
im-mo´bile
im-mo´bi-lize
im-mod´er-a·cy
im-mod´er-ate
im-mod´er-ate·ly
im-mod´est·ly
im-mod´es·ty
im´mo-la´tion
im-mor´al
im-mo-ral´i·ty
im-mor´al·ly
im-mor´tal
im-mor-tal´i·ty
im-mor´tal-ize
im-mov´a-ble
im-mune´
im-mu-ni-za´tion
im´mu-nize
im-mu-nol´o-gist
im-mu-nol´o·gy
im-mu´ta-ble
im´pact
im-pact´ed
im-pair´ment
im-pale´
im-part´
im-par´tial
im-par-ti-al´i·ty
im-par´tial·ly
im-pass´a·ble
im´passe
im-pas´sioned

im-pas´sive·ly
im-pa´tience
im-pa´tient·ly
im-peach´a·ble
iin-peach´ment
im-pec´ca·ble
im-pec´ca·bly
im-pe-cu´ni·ous
im-ped´ance
im-pede´
im-ped´i-ment
im-ped´ing
im-pel´
im-pend´ing
im-pen´e-tra·ble
im-pen´e-tra·bly
im-pen´i-tent
im-per´a-tive
im-per-cep´ti·ble
im-per-cep´ti·bly
im-per-cep´tive
im-per´fect
im-per-fec´tion
im-pe´ri-al-ist
im-pe´ri-al-is´tic
im-pe´ri-al·ly
im-per´il
im-pe´ri-ous·ly
im-per´ish-a·ble
im-per´ma-nent
im-per´me-a·ble
im-per´son-al
im-per´son-ate

im-per-son-a´tion
im-per´son-a-tor
im-per´ti-nence
im-per´ti-nen·cy
im-per´ti-nent
im-per´ti-nent·ly
im-per-turb´a·ble
im-per´vi-ous·ly
im-pet´u-ous·ly
im-pi´e·ty
im-pinge´
im´pi-ous·ly
imp´ish·ly
im-plac·a·bil´i·ty
im-plac´a·ble
im-plac´a·bly
im-plau´si·ble
im´ple-ment
im-ple-men´ta-tion
im´pli-cate
im-pli-ca´tion
im-plic´it·ly
im-plic´i·ty
im-plied´
im-plore´
im-plor´ing
im-ply´
im-po-lite´
im-pon´der-a·ble
im-port´ (v.)
im´port (n., v.)
im-por´tance
im-por´tant·ly

im-por-ta´tion
im-port´er
im-por´tu-nate
im´por-tune´ly
im-pose´
im-pos´ing
im-po-si´tion
im-pos´si·ble
im-pos´si·bly
im´po-tence
im´po-ten·cy
im´po-tent
im-pound´ment
im-pov´er-ished
im-prac´ti-cal
im-prac-ti-cal´i·ty
im´pre-cate
im-pre-ca´tion
im-pre-cise´ly
im-pre-ci´sion
im-preg-na-bil´i·ty
im-preg´na·ble
im-preg´nate
im-preg-na´tion
im-pre-sar´i·o
im-press´ (v.)
im´press (n.)
im-pres´sion
im-pres´sion-a·ble
im-pres´sion-ist
im-pres´sive·ly
im-pri-ma´tur
im-pri´mis

im´print *(n.)*
im-print´ *(v.)*
im-pris´on
im-pris´on-ment
im-prob´a·ble
im-prop´er·ly
im-pro-pri´e·ty
im-prove´ment
im-prov´i-dent·ly
im-prov´ing
im-prov·i-sa´tion
im´pro-vise
im-pru´dent·ly
im´pu-dent·ly
im-pugn´
im´pulse
im-pul´sive·ly
im-pu´ni·ty
im-pure´
im-pute´
in-a-bil´i·ty
in-ac-ces-si·bil´i·ty
in-ac-ces´si·ble
in-ac-ces´si·bly
in-ac´cu-ra·cy
in-ac´cu-rate·ly
in-ac´tion
in-ac´tive·ly
in-ad´e-qua·cy
in-ad´e-quate·ly
in-ad-mis´si·ble
in-ad-mis´si·bly
in-ad-ver´tent·ly

in-ad-vis´a·ble
in-a´lien-a·ble
in-al´ter-a·ble
in-al´ter-a·bly
in-ane´ly
in-an´i-mate·ly
in-an´i·ty
in-ap´pli-ca·ble
in-ap-pre´cia·ble
in-ap-proach´a·ble
in-ap-pro´pri-ate
in-apt´ness
in-as-much´
in-at-ten´tive
in-au´di·ble
in-au´di·bly
in-au´gu-ral
in-au´gu-rate
in-au´gu-rat-ing
in-au-gu-ra´tion
in-aus-pi´cious·ly
in´breed-ing
in-cal´cu-la·ble
in-can-desce´
in-can-des´cence
in-can-des´cent
in-can-ta´tion
in-ca´pa·ble
in-ca-pac´i-tate
in-ca-pac-i-ta´tion
in-ca-pac´i·ty
in-car´cer-ate
in-car-cer-a´tion

in-car´nate
in-car-na´tion
in-cau´tious·ly
in-cen´di-ar·y
in´cense *(n.)*
in-cense´ *(v.)*
in-cen´tive
in-cep´tion
in-ces´sant·ly
in´cest
in-ces´tu-ous
in-ci-dent
in-ci-den´tal·ly
in-cin´er-ate
in-cin-er-a´tion
in-cin´er-a-tor
in-cip´i-ent
in-cise´
in-ci´sion
in-ci´sive
in-cite´
in-cit´er
in-cit´ing
in-clem´ent
in-cli-na´tion
in-cline´ *(v., n.)*
in´cline *(n.)*
in-clined´
in-clin´ing
in-clude´
in-clud´ed
in-clud´ing
in-clu´sion

in-clu´sive·ly
in-cog-ni´to
in-co-her´ence
in-co-her´ent·ly
in-com-bus´ti·ble
in´come
in´com-ing
in-com-mo´di-ous
in-com-mu-ni-
  ca´do
in-com´pa-ra·ble
in-com´pa-ra·bly
in-com-pat´i·ble
in-com´pe-tence
in-com´pe-ten·cy
in-com´pe-tent·ly
in-com-plete´
in-com-pli´ant
in-com-pre-hen´-
  si·ble
in-con-ceiv´a·ble
in-con-clu´sive
in-con´gru-ent·ly
in-con-gru´i·ty
in-con´gru-ous
in-con-se-quen´tial
in-con-sid´er-a·ble
in-con-sid´er-ate
in-con-sist´en·cy
in-con-sist´ent·ly
in-con-sol´a·ble
in-con-spic´u-ous
in-con-test´a·ble

in-con´ti-nence
in-con-trol´la·ble
in-con-tro-vert´-
  i·ble
in-con-ve´nience
in-con-ven´ient·ly
in-cor´po-rate
in-cor´po-rat·ed
in-cor-po-ra´tion
in-cor-po´re·al
in-cor-rect´ly
in-cor´ri-gi·ble
in-cor-rupt´i·ble
in-crease´ (v.)
in´crease (n.)
in-creas´ing·ly
in-cred´i·ble
in-cred´i·bly
in-cre-du´li·ty
in-cred´u-lous·ly
in´cre-ment
in´cre-men´tal·ly
in-crim´i-nate
in-crim-i-na´tion
in-crim´i-na-to·ry
in-crus-ta´tion
in´cu-bate
in´cu-ba´tion
in´cu-bus
in-cul´cate
in-cul-ca´tion
in-cul´pate
in-cul-pa´tion

in-cul´pa-to·ry
in-cum´ben·cy
in-cum´bent·ly
in-cur´
in-cur´a·ble
in-cur´sion
in-debt´ed-ness
in-de´cen·cy
in-de´cent
in-de-ci´pher-a·ble
in-de-ci´sion
in-de-ci´sive·ly
in-dec´o-rous·ly
in-deed´
in-de-fen´si·ble
in-de-fin´a·ble
in-def´i-nite·ly
in-del´i·ble
in-del´i·bly
in-del´i-cate·ly
in-del´i-cate-ness
in-dem-ni-fi-ca´tion
in-dem´ni-fied
in-dem´ni-fies
in-dem´ni-fy
in-dem´ni-ty
in-dent´
in-den-ta´tion
in-dent´ed
in-den´ture
in-de-pen´dence
in-de-pen´dent·ly
in-de-scrib´a·ble

in-de-struc´ti·ble
in-de-ter´mi-na·cy
in-de-ter´mi-nate
in´dex·er
in´dex·es
in´di-cate
in-di-ca´tion
in-dic´a-tive
in-dic´a-to·ry
in-di´cia
in-dict´a·ble
in-dict´er
in-dif´fer-ence
in-dif´fer-ent·ly
in´di-gence
in-dig´e-nous
in´di-gent
in-di-gest´i·ble
in-di-ges´tion
in-dig´nant·ly
in-dig-na´tion
in-di-rect´ly
in-dis-cern´i·ble
in-dis-creet´
in´dis-crete´
in-dis-cre´tion
in-dis-crim´i-nate
in-dis-pens´a·ble
in-dis-posed´
in-dis-put´a·ble
in-dis-tinct´
in-dis-tin´guish-
  a·ble

in-dite´ment
in-di-vid´u·al
in-di-vid-u-al´i·ty
in-di-vid´u-al·ly
in-di-vis´i·ble
in-doc´tri-nate
in-doc-tri-na´tion
in´do-lence
in´do-lent·ly
in-dom´i-ta·ble
in´doors´
in-du´bi-ta·ble
in-du´bi-ta·bly
in-duce´ment
in-duc´ing
in-dulge´
in-dul´gent
in-dulg´ing
in-dus´tri-al-ist
in-dus-tri-al-i·za´-
  tion
in-dus´tri-al-ize
in´dus-tries
in-dus´tri-ous·ly
in´dus-try
in-e´bri-ant
in-e´bri-ate
in-e-bri-a´tion
in-ed´i·ble
in-ef-fec´tive·ly
in-ef-fec´tu-al·ly
in-ef-fi´cient·ly
in-el´e-gant·ly

in-el´i-gi·ble
in-ept´
in-ep´ti-tude
in-e-qual´i·ty
in-eq´ui-ta·ble
in-eq´ui·ty
in-ert´
in-er´tia
in-es-cap´a·ble
in-es´ti-ma·ble
in-ev´i-ta·ble
in-ex-act´
in-ex-ac´ti-tude
in-ex-act´ly
in-ex-cus´a·ble
in-ex-haust´i·ble
in-ex´o-ra·ble
in-ex-pen´sive·ly
in-ex-pe´ri-enced
in-ex´pert·ly
in-ex´pert-ness
in-ex-plain´a·ble
in-ex-plic´a·ble
in-ex-tric´a·ble
in-ex-tric´a·bly
in-fal-li·bil´i·ty
in-fal´li·ble
in-fal´li·bly
in´fa-mous·ly
in´fa·my
in´fan·cy
in´fant
in´fan-tile

in´fan-try
in-fat´u-ate
in-fat´u-at-ed
in-fat-u-a´tion
in-fect´ant
in-fec´tion
in-fec´tious-ly
in-fer´
in´fer-ence
in-fe´ri-or
in-fe-ri-or´i-ty
in-fer´nal
in-fer´no
in-ferred´
in-fer´ring
in-fer-til´i-ty
in-fest´
in-fes-ta´tion
in´fi-del
in-fi-del´i-ty
in-fil´trate
in-fil-tra´tion
in´fi-nite-ly
in-fin-i-tes´i-mal
in-firm´
in-fir´ma-ry
in-fir´mi-ty
in-flame´
in-flam´ma-ble
in-flam-ma´tion
in-flam´ma-to-ry
in-flat´a-ble
in-flate´

in-flat´ed
in-flat´ing
in-fla´tion
in-fla´tion-ar-y
in-flec-tion
in-flex´i-ble
in-flict´
in´flu-ence
in´flu-en´tial
in-flu-en´za
in-fo-mer´cial
in-form´
in-for´mal
in-for-mal´i-ty
in-for´mant
in-for-ma´tion
in-form´a-tive
in-formed´
in-form´er
in-frac´tion
in´fra-struc-ture
in-fre´quent-ly
in-fringe´ment
in-fu´ri-ate
in-fu´ri-at-ing
in-fuse´
in-fu´sion
in-ge´nious
in-gen´ious-ly
in-ge-nu´i-ty
in-gen´u-ous
in-gest´
in-grained´

in-gra´ti-ate
in-gra´ti-at-ing-ly
in-grat´i-tude
in-gre´di-ent
in´grown
in-hab´i-tant
in-hab´it-ed
in-hal´ant
in-ha-la´tion
in-hale´
in-hal´er
in-hal´ing
in-har-mo´ni-ous
in-her´ent
in-her´it
in-her´i-tance
in-hib´it
in-hib´it-ed
in-hib´it-er
in-hi-bi´tion
in-hos-pit´a-ble
in-hu´man
in-hu-mane´
in-hu-man´i-ty
in-hu´man-ly
in-im´i-cal
in-im´i-ta-ble
in-iq´ui-tous
in-iq´ui-ty
in-i´tial-ize
in-i´tial-ly
in-i´ti-ate
in-i-ti-a´tion

in-ject´
in-jec´tion
in-ju-di´cious
in-junc´tion
in´jure
in´ju-ries
in-ju´ri-ous
in´ju-ry
in-jus´tice
in´kling
ink´well
ink´y
in´laid
in´lay
in-nate´ly
in´ner
in´ner-most
in´no-cence
in´no-cent-ly
in-noc´u-ous-ly
in´no-va´tion
in´no-va-tive
in-nu-en´do
in-nu-en´does
in-nu´mer-a-ble
in-of-fen´sive-ly
in-op´er-a-ble
in-op-por-tune´
in-or´di-nate-ly
in-or´di-nate-ness
in-or-gan´ic
in-or-gan´i-cal-ly
in´put

in´quest
in-quire´
in-quir´er
in´quir-ies
in-quir´ing
in-quir´ing-ly
in´quir-y
in-qui-si´tion
in-quis´i-tive
in´road
in-sane´ly
in-san´i-ty
in-sa´tia-ble
in-scribe´
in-scrib´er
in-scrib´ing
in-scrip´tion
in-scru´ta-ble
in´seam
in´sect
in-sec´ti-cide
in-se-cure´
in-se-cur´i-ty
in-sen´si-tive
in-sen-si-tiv´i-ty
in-sep´a-ra-ble
in-sep´a-ra-bly
in-sert´ *(v.)*
in´sert *(n.)*
in-ser´tion
in-sid´i-ous
in´sight
in´sight-ful-ness

in-sig´ni-a
in-sig-nif´i-cant-ly
in-sin-cere´
in-sin-cer´i-ty
in-sin´u-ate
in-sin´u-at-ing-ly
in-sin-u-a´tion
in-sip´id
insist´
in-sis´tence
in-sis´tent-ly
in´so-lence
in´so-lent-ly
in-sol´u-ble
in-solv´a-ble
in-sol´ven-cy
in-sol´vent
in-som´ni-ac
in-spect´
in-spec´tion
in-spec´tor
in-spi-ra´tion-al
in-spire´
in-spir´ing
in-sta-bil´i-ty
in-stall´
in-stal-la´tion
in-stalled´
in-stall´ing
in-stall´ment
in´stance
in´stant
in-stan-ta´ne-ous

in´step
in´sti-gate
in´sti-gat-ing
in´sti-ga-tor
in-stil´ (Br.)
in-still´
in-stil-la´tion
in-still´ing
in´stinct (n.)
in-stinc´tive-ly
in-stinc´tu-al-ly
in´sti-tute
in-sti-tu´tion-al
in-struct´ed
in-struc´tion-al
in-struc´tive-ly
in-struc´tor
in´stru-ment
in-stru-men´tal
in-stru-men-ta´tion
in-sub-or´di-nate
in-sub-or-di-na´-
  tion
in-sub-stan´tial
in-suf´fer-a-ble
in-suf-fi´cient
in-suf-fi´cient-ly
in´su-lar
in-su-lar´i-ty
in´su-late
in´su-la´tion
in´sult (n.)
in-sult´ (v.)

in-sult´ing-ly
in-sup-port´a-ble
in-sur´a-ble
in-sur´ance
in-sure´
in-sured´
in-sur´er
in-sur´gence
in-sur´gen-cy
in-sur´gent
in-sur´ing
in-sur-mount´a-ble
in-sur-rec´tion
in-sus-cep´ti-ble
in-tact´

in´take
in-tan´gi-ble
in´te-ger
in´te-gral
in´te-grate
in-te-gra´tion
in-teg´ri-ty
in´tel-lect
in-tel-lec´tu-al
in-tel´li-gence
in-tel´li-gent-ly
in-tel-li-gen´tsi-a
in-tem´per-ance
in-tem´per-ate
in-tend´ing
in-tense´
in-tense´ly

in-ten´si-fied
in-ten´si-fi-er
in-ten´si-fies
in-ten´si-fy
in-ten´si-ty
in-tent´
in-ten´tion-al
in-tent´ly
in-ter´
in-ter-act´
in-ter-ac´tion
in-ter-ac´tive
in-ter-cede´
in-ter-ced´ing
in-ter-cept´ (v.)
in-ter-cep´tion
in-ter-col-le´giate
in-ter-con-nect´ed
in´ter-course
in-ter-de-nom-i-
  na´tion-al
in-ter-de-part-
  men´tal
in-ter-dict´
in-ter-dic´tion
in´ter-est-ed
in´ter-est-ing
in´ter-face
in´ter-faith
in-ter-fere´
in-ter-fer´ence
in-ter-fer´ing
in´ter-im

in-te´ri·or
in-ter-ject´
in-ter-jec´tion
in´ter-leaf´
in-ter-leav´ing
in´ter-lop·er
in´ter-lude
in-ter-me´di-ate
in-ter´ment
in-ter´mi-na·ble
in-ter-min´gle
in-ter-min´gling
in-ter-mis´sion
in-ter-mit´tent·ly
in-ter-mix´
in´tern
in-ter´nal
in-ter´nal-ize
in-ter-na´tion·al
in-terned´
In´ter-net
in-tern´ment
in-ter´nist
in-ter-o-cep´tor
in-ter-per´son·al
in-ter-plan´e-tar·y
in´ter-play
in-ter´po-late
in-ter-po-la´tion
in-ter´pret
in-ter-pre-ta´tion
in-ter´pret·er
in-ter´pre-tive

in-ter-ra´cial
in-ter-re-late´
in-ter-re-lat´ed
in-ter´ro-bang
in-ter´ro-gate
in-ter-ro-ga´tion
in-ter-rog´a-tive
in-ter´ro-ga-tor
in-ter-rupt´ed
in-ter-rupt´ing
in-ter-rup´tion
in-ter-rup´tive
in-ter-sec´tion
in´ter-state´
in-ter-stel´lar
in´ter-val
in-ter-vene´
in-ter-ven´tion
in´ter-view·er
in-tes´tate
in-tes´ti-nal
in-tes´tine
in´ti-ma·cy
in´ti-mate·ly
in-ti-ma´tion
in-tim´i-date
in-tim-i-da´tion
in´to
in-tol´er-a·ble
in-tol´er-ance
in-tol´er-ant
in´to-nate
in-to-na´tion

in-tone´
in-tox´i-cant
in-tox´i-cate
in-tox´i-cat-ing
in-tox-i-ca´tion
in-trac´ta·ble
in-tra-ga-lac´tic
in-tra-mu´ral·ly
in-tran´si-gence
in-tran´si-gent
in-tra-pre-neur´i·al
in-tra-state´
in-trep´id·ly
in´tri-ca·cy
in´tri-cate·ly
in-trigued´
in-tri´guing
in-tro-duce´
in-tro-duc´tion
in-tro-duc´to·ry
in-tro-spec´tion
in-tro-spec´tive
in-tro-ver´sion
in´tro-vert
in-trude´
in-trud´er
in-tru´sion
in-tru´sive
in-tu-i´tion
in-tu´i-tive
in´un-date
in-un-da´tion
in-ure´

in-vade´	in-vis´i·ble	ir-ra´di-ant
in-vad´er	in-vi-ta´tion·al	ir-ra´di-ate
in-vad´ing	in-vite´	ir-ra´tion·al
in-val´id *(void)*	in-vit´ing	ir-rec´on-cil-a·ble
in´va-lid *(disabled)*	in-vo-ca´tion	ir-re-cov´er-a·ble
in-val´i-date	in´voice	ir-re-deem´a·ble
in-val-i-da´tion	in´voic-ing	ir-re-fut´a·ble
in-val´u-a·ble	invoke´	ir-reg´u-lar
in-var´i-a·ble	in-vok´ing	ir-reg-u-lar´i·ty
in-var´i-a·bly	in-vol´un-tar·y	ir-rel´e-vant
in-va´sion	in-volved´	ir-rep´a-ra·ble
in-va´sive	in-volve´ment	ir-re-press´i·ble
in-vec´tive	in-volv´ing	ir-re-proach´a·ble
in-vent´	in-vul´ner-a·ble	ir-re-sist´i·ble
in-ven´tion	in´ward·ly	ir-res´o-lute·ly
in-ven´tive	i´o-dine	ir-re-spon´si·ble
in-ven´tor	i´on	ir-re-triev´a·ble
in´ven-to-ries	i·on-i·za´tion	ir-rev´er-ence
in´ven-to·ry	i´on-ize	ir-rev´er-ent·ly
in-verse´ly	i·on´o-sphere	ir-re-vers´i·ble
in-ver´sion	i·o´ta	ir-rev´o-ca·ble
in-vest´	i·ras´ci·ble	ir´ri-ga·ble
in-ves´ti-gate	i·rate´ly	ir´ri-gate
in-ves-ti-ga´tion	ir-i-des´cence	ir-ri-ga´tion
in-ves´ti-ga-tor	ir-i-des´cent·ly	ir´ri-ta·ble
in-ves´ti-ga-to·ry	irk´some	ir´ri-tant
in-vest´ment	i´ron	ir´ri-tate
in-ves´tor	i·ron´ic	ir´ri-tat-ing
in-vet´er-ate	i·ron´i-cal·ly	ir-ri-ta´tion
in-vig´o-rate	i´ron-ing	is´land·er
in-vig´o-rat-ing	i´ron-mon-ger	is´let
in-vin´ci·ble	i´ron-work·er	i´so-late
in-vi´o-la·ble	i´ro·ny *(satire)*	i·so-la´ting

i·so-la´tion-ist
i·so-met´ric
i´so-ton´ic
is´sue
is´su-ing
isth´mus
i·tal´ic
i·tal-i-ci-za´tion
i·tal´i-cize
itch´i-ness
itch´y
i´tem-i·za´tion
i´tem-ize
it´er-ate
it-er-a´tion
i·tin´er-ant
i·tin´er-ar·y
its *(possessive)*
it´s *(it is)*
it-self´
i´vied
i´vo·ry
i´vy

J

jab
jabbed
jab´ber
jab´bing
jack´al
jack´ass
jack´et-ed
jack´pot

jad´ed
jag´ged
jail´bird
jail´break
jail´er
ja-la-pe´ño
ja-lop´y
jal´ou-sie
jam´ming
jan´gle
jan´gling
jan´gly
jan´i-tor
jan-i-to´ri·al
jar´gon
jar´ring
jaun´diced
jaunt
jaun´ti·ly
jaun´ti-ness
jaun´ty
jav´e-lin
jaw´bone
jawed
jazz´er-cize
jazz´y
jeal´ous·ly
jeal´ou·sy
jeer´ing·ly
je-june´
jel´lied
jel´ly
jeop´ar-dize

jeop´ar·dy
jerk´y *(shaky)*
jer´ky *(meat)*
jer´sey
jest´er
jet´sam
jet´ti-son
jet´ty
jew´eled
jew´el·er
jew´el·ry
jif´fy
jig´ger
jig´gle
jig´gly
jilt´ed
jin´gle
jin´gling
jin´gly
jit´ney
jit´ter-bug
jit´ters
jit´ter·y
job´ber
job´less
jock´ey
joc´u-lar
joc-u-lar´i·ty
jog´ging
join´er
joint´ed
joint´er
joint´ly

joist
joked
jok´er
joke´ster
jok´ing·ly
jol´li·ty
jol´ly
josh´er
josh´ing·ly
jos´tle
jos´tled
jos´tling
jounce
jounc´ing
jour´nal
jour´nal-ism
jour´nal-ist
jour´nal-ize
jour´ney
jo´vi·al·ly
joy´ful·ly
joy´ful-ness
joy´less
joy´ous·ly
joy´ous-ness
joy´ride
ju´bi-lance
ju´bi-lant·ly
ju-bi-la´tion
judge´ship
judg´ing
judg´ment
judg-men´tal

ju´di-ca-to·ry
ju-di´cial·ly
ju-di´ciar·y
ju-di´cious·ly
jug´gler
jug´gling
jug´u-lar
juice
juic´er
juic´i-ness
juic´y
ju-li·enne´
jum´bled
jum´bling
jump´er
jump´i-ness
jump´ing
jump´y
junc´tion
junc´ture
jun´gle
jun´ior
jun´ket
junk´ie
ju´ried
ju´ries
ju-ris-dic´tion·al
ju-ris-pru´dence
ju´rist
ju´ror
ju´ry
jus´tice
jus´ti-fi-a·ble

jus-ti-fi-ca´tion
jus´ti-fied
jus´ti-fi·er
jus´ti-fy
ius´ti-fy-ing
just´ly
just´ness
jut´ting
ju´ve-nile
jux-ta-po-si´tion

K

ka-lei´do-scope
ka-lei´do-scop´ic
ka´pok
kar´ma
kay´ak
keen´ly
keen´mess
keep´er
keep´ing
keep´sake
ken´nel
ker´a-tin
ker´chief
kerned
ker´nel
ke´tone
ket´tle-drum
key´board
key´hole
key´note
khak´i

kib´itz-er
kick´back
kid´ded
kid´ding
kid´nap
kid´naped
kid´nap-er
kid´nap-ing
kid´napped
kid´nap-per
kid´nap-ping
kid´ney
kill´er
kill´ing
kill´joy
kiln
ki´lo
kil´o-cy-cle
kil´o-gram
ki-lom´e-ter
kil´o-watt
kil´o-watt–hour
kilt´ed
ki-mo´no
ki-mo´nos
kin´der-gar-ten
kind´heart-ed
kin´dle
kind´li-ness
kin´dling
kind´ly
kind´ness
kin´dred

ki-net´ic
kin´folk
king´dom
king´li-ness
king´ly
king´pin
kink´y
kin´ship
ki´osk
kis´met
kiss´a·ble
kitch´en-ette´
kit´ten
kit´ten-ish
kit´ty
klep-to-ma´ni·a
klep-to-ma´ni-ac
knap´sack
knav´er·y
knead
knee´cap
knee´–deep´
knee´–high´
kneel´ing
knick´knack
knife
knight–er´rant
knight´hood
knight´ly
knit´ter
knit´ting
knives
knobbed

knob´by
knock´a·bout
knock´out
knoll
knot´hole
knot´ted
knot´ting
knot´ty
know´–how
know´ing-ly
knowl´edge
knowl´edge-a·ble
knuck´led
knuck´ling
knurl´y
koi-no-ni´a
ko´sher
kow´tow
kum´quat
ky´ack

L

la´bel
la´beled
la´bel-ing
la´bor
lab´o-ra-to-ry
la´bored
la´bor-er
la-bo´ri-ous
la-bo´ri-ous-ly
la´bour (Br.)
lab´y-rinth

lab-y-rin´thi-an
lab-y-rin´thine
lac´er-ate
lac´er-at-ing
lac-er-a´tion
lace´work
lac´ing
lack-a-dai´si-cal
lack´ey
lack´ing
lack´lus-ter
la-con´ic
la-con´i-cal-ly
lac´quer
lac´tate
lac-ta´tion
lac´tose
lac´y
lad´der
lad´die
lad´en
lad´en-ing
la´dies
lad´ing
la´dle
la´dle-ful
la´dler
la´dy
la´dy-bird
la´dy-bug
la´dy-fin-ger
la´dy–kill-er
la´dy-like

la´ger
lag´gard
lag´ging
la-goon´
la´ic
lais´sez–faire
la´i-ty
lake´side
lam-baste´
la-mé´
lame´ly
lame´ness
la-ment´
lam´en-ta-ble
lam´en-ta-bly
lam-en-ta´tion
la-ment´ed
lam´i-na
lam´i-nal
lam´i-nar
lam´i-nate
lam-i-na´tion
lamp´black
lamp´light
lam-poon´
lamp´post
lanc´er
lan´dau
land´ed
land´fall
land´hold-er
land´ing
land´la-dy

land´locked
land´lord
land´mark
land´own-er
land´–poor
land´scape
land´slide
lan´guage
lan´guid-ly
lan´guish
lan´guished
lan´guish-ing
lan´guor
lan´guor-ous
lank´i-er
lank´y
lan´tern
lan´yard
la-pel´
lap´ping
lapsed
lar´ce-nist
lar´ce-nous
lar´ce-ny
lar´der
large´ly
large´ness
larg´er
lar-gess´
larg´est
lar´go
lar´i-at
lar´va

lar'vae
lar'val
lar-yn-gi'tis
lar'ynx
las-civ'i-ous
la'ser
lash'ing
las'sie
las'si-tude
las'so
las'so-er
last'ing
last'ly
latch'et
late'ly
late'ness
la'tent-ly
lat'er
lat'er-al
lat'er-al-ly
lat'est
la'tex
lath
lathe
lath'er
lath'er-ing
lath'ing
lat'i-ces
lat'ish
lat'i-tude
la-trine'
lat'ter
lat'tice-work

laud'a·ble
lau'da-to-ry
laugh'a·ble
laugh'ing
laugh'ter
launched
launch'er
laun'der
laun'dries
laun'dry
lau'rel
la'va
lav'a-to-ry
lav'en-der
lav'ish
law'–a·bid'ing
law'break-er
law'ful
law'giv-er
law'less
law'suit
law'yer
lax'a-tive
lax'i-ty
lay'er
lay-ette'
lay'man
la'zi-er
la'zi-ly
la'zi-ness
la'zy
lead'en
lead'er-ship

leaf'less
leaf'y
league
leak'y
lean'ing
lean'ness
lean'–to
leap'frog
leap'ing
learned *(detected)*
learn'ed *(smart)*
learn'er
learn'ing
leased
lease'hold
leas'ing
leath'er
leath'er·y
leav'en
leav'ing
lech'er-ous
lech'er·y
lec'i-thin
lec'tern
lec'ture
lec'tured
lec'tur-er
lec'tur-ing
ledg'er
leer'ing
leer'ing-ly
leer'y
lee'way

left´o·ver
leg´a-cies
leg´a-cy
le´gal
le-gal´i-ty
le-gal-i·za´tion
le´gal-ize
le´gal-ly
leg´ate *(delegate)*
le-gate´ *(bequeath)*
leg´a-tee´
le-ga´tion
leg´end-ar·y
leg´er-de-main´
leg´ged
leg´gings
leg-i-bil´i-ty
leg´i-ble
le´gion
leg´is-late
leg-is-la´tion
leg´is-la-tive
leg´is-la-tor
leg´is-la-ture
le-git´i-ma-cy
le-git´i-mate
le-git´i-mize
lei´sure-ly
lem´on-ade´
lend´er
lend´ing
length´en
length´wise

length´y
le´nience
le´nien-cy
le´nient
le´nient-ly
len´til
le´o-nine
le´o-tard
lep´er
lep´re-chaun
lep´ro-sy
lep´rous
le´sion
les-see´
less´en
less´er
les´son
le´thal
le-thar´gic
le-thar´gi-cal-ly
leth´ar-gy
let´ter
let´rered
let´ter-head
let´ter–per´fect
let´ter-press
let´tuce
leu-ke´mi·a
lev´el
lev´eled
lev´el-er
lev´el-ing
lev´er-age

le-vi´a-than
lev´i-tate
lev´i-tat-ing
lev-i-ta´tion
lev´i-ty
lev´y-ing
lewd´ness
lex-i-cog´ra-pher
lex-i-cog´ra-phy
lex´i-con
li-a-bil´i-ty
li´a·ble
li´ai-son
li´ar
li-ba´tion
li´bel
li´beled
li´bel-er
li´bel-ing
li´bel-ous
lib´er-al
lib´er-al-ism
lib´er-al-ize
lib´er-al-ly
lib´er-ate
lib-er-a´tion
lib´er-a-tor
lib-er-tar´i-an
lib´er-tine
lib´er-ty
li-bi´do
li-brar´i-an
li´brar·y

li-bret´tist
li-bret´to
li´cens-a·ble
li´cense
li´censed
li´cens-ee´
li´cens-er
li´cens-ing
li-cen´tious
lic´it
lien
lieu-ten´ant
life´blood
life´boat
life´guard
life´less
life´like
life´line
life´long
life´sav-er
life´time
lift´er
lig´a-ment
li-ga´tion
lig´a-ture
light´ed
light´en
light´ened
light´en-ing
light´er
light´–fin-gered
light´heart-ed
light´house

light´ing
light´ning *(adj., n.)*
light´weight
like´li-hood
like´ly
lik´en
like-ness
like´wise
lik´ing
lim´ber
lim´bo
lime´ade
lime´kiln
lime´light
lim´er-ick
lime´stone
lim´it
lim-i-ta´tion
lim´it-ed
lim´it-less
lim´ou-sine
lim´pid
limp´ly
lin´e·age
lin´e·ar
line´man
lin´en
lin´er
lin´ger
lin-ge-rie´
lin´gua
lin´gual
lin´guist

lin-guis´tic
lin-guis´ti-cal-ly
lin-guis´tics
lin´i-ment
lin´ing
link´age
link´ing
li-no´le-um
lin´seed
lin´tel
li´on-ess
li´on-heart-ed
li´on-ize
lip´stick
liq´ue-fied
liq´ue-fy-ing
li-queur´
liq´uid
liq´ui-date
liq´ui-da´tion
liq´ui-da-tor
li-quid´i-ty
li´quor
lisp´ing
lis´some
lis´ten-er
list´er
list´less-ness
lit´a-ny
li´ter
lit´er-a-cy
lit´er-al
lit´er-al-ly

lit´er-ar·y
lit´er-ate
lit-e-ra´ti
lit´er-a-ture
lithe´some
lith´i-um
li-thog´ra-pher
lith´o-graph´ic
li-thog´ra-phy
lit´i-gant
lit´i-gate
lit-i-ga´tion
lit´i-ga-tor
li-ti´gious
lit´mus
li´tre (Br.)
lit´ter
lit´tle
li-tur´gi-cal
lit´ur-gy
liv´a·ble
live´li-hood
live´li-ness
live´long
live´ly
liv´er-ied
liv´er·y
live´stock
liv´id
liv´ing
lla´ma
load´er
loaf´er

loam´y
loath (adj.)
loathe (v.)
loath´ing
loath´some
loaves
lobbed
lob´bied
lob´bing
lob´by-ing
lob´by-ist
lo-bot´o-my
lo´cal
lo-cale´
lo-cal´i-ty
lo-cal-i·za´tion
lo´cal-ize
lo´cal-ly
lo´cate
lo-cat´er
lo-cat´ing
lo-ca´tion
lock´er
lock´et
lock´jaw
lock´smith
lock´stitch
lo´co
lo-co-mo´tion
lo-co-mo´tive
lo´cust
lodg´er
lodg´ing

loft´i-ly
loft´i-ness
loft´y
log´a-rithm
log´book
log´ger-head
log´ging
log´ic
log´i-cal-ly
lo-gis´tic
lo-gis´tics
log´o-type
loin´cloth
loi´ter-er
loll´ing
lol´li-pop
lone´li-ness
lone´ly
lone´some
long´er
long´est
lon-gev´i-ty
long´–haired
long´hand
long´ing
lon´gi-tude
lon-gi-tu´di-nal
long´–lived´
long´–suf´fer-ing
long´–term
long´–wind-ed
look´er
look´ing

look´out
loop´hole
loose´–leaf
loose´ly
loos´en
loot´er
lop´sid-ed
lo-qua´cious
lo-quac´i-ty
lord´li-ness
lor-gnette´
los´er
los´ing
lo´tion
lot´ter·y
lo´tus
loud´ness
loud´speak-er
lounged
loung´er
loung´ing
louse
lous´i-ness
lous´y
lout´ish
lou´ver
lov´a·ble
love´less
love´li-er
love´li-ness
love´lorn
love´ly
lov´er

love´sick
lov´ing–kind´ness
low´boy
low´brow
low´–cut´
low´er
low´er-ing
low´land
low´li-ness
low´ly
loy´al
loy´al-ist
loy´al-ly
loy´al-ty
lu´bri-cant
lu´bri-cate
lu-bri-ca´tion
lu´cent
lu´cid
lu-cid´i-ty
lu´cid-ness
lu´ci-fer
luck´i-er
luck´i-est
luck´i-ly
luck´y
lu´cra-tive
lu´cre
lu´di-crous
lu´di-crous-ness
lug´gage
lug´ger
lug´ging

lu-gu´bri-ous
luke´warm
lull´a-by
lum-ba´go
lum´ber-jack
lum´ber-yard
lu´men
lu´mi-nar·y
lu-mi-nes´cence
lu-mi-nes´cent
lu´mi-nous
lum´mox
lump´i-er
lump´ish
lump´y
lu´na-cy
lu´nar
lunch´eon-ette´
lunch´room
lunged´
lung´er
lung´ing
lurched
lurch´ing
lured
lu´rid-ly
lur´ing
lurk´er
lurk´ing
lus´cious
lush´ly
lus´ter
lust´ful

lust´i-er
lust´i-ly
lus´trous
lust´y
lux-u´ri-ance
lux-u´ri-ant
lux-u´ri-ate
lux-u´ri-at-ing
lux´u-ries
lux-u´ri-ous
lux´u-ry
ly´can-throp´ic
ly-can´thro-py
ly´ing
lymph
lym-phat´ic
lynch´ing
lyr´ic
lyr´i-cal

M

ma-ca´bre
mac-ad´am
mac-ad´am-ize
mac´er-ate
ma-chet´e
mach-i-a-vel´li-an
mach-i-na´tion
mach´i-na-tor
ma-chine´
ma-chin´er·y
ma-chin´ist
mack´i-naw

mack´in-tosh
mac´ra-me´
mac´ro-cosm
mac´ro-scop´ic
mad´am
ma-dame´
mad´cap
mad´den-ing
mad´der
mad´dest
ma-de-moi-selle´
mad´house
mad´ly
mad´man
mad´ness
ma-dras´
mad´ri-gal
mael´strom
mae´stro
mag´a-zine´
ma-gen´ta
mag´got
ma´gi
mag´ic
mag´i-cal
mag´i-cal-ly
ma-gi´cian
mag-is-te´ri-al
mag´is-trate
mag´ma
mag-na-nim´i-ty
mag-nan´i-mous
mag´nate

mag´net
mag-net´ic
mag´net-ism
mag´net-ize
mag-ne´to
mag-nif´i-cence
mag-nif´i-cent
mag-nif´i-co
mag´ni-fied
mag´ni-fi-er
mag´ni-fy
mag´ni-tude
ma-hog´a-ny
maid´en-hood
maid´en-ly
mail´a·ble
mail´bag
mail´box
mail´er
main´land
main´ly
main´stay
main-tain´
main´te-nance
ma-jes´tic
ma-jes´ti-cal
ma-jes´ti-cal-ly
maj´es-ty
ma´jor
ma-jor-do´mo
ma-jor´i-ties
ma-jor´i-ty
make´–be-lieve

mak´er
make´shift
mak´ing
mal´ad-just´ed
mal´ad-just´ment
mal´a-droit´
mal´a-dy
mal-aise´
mal´a-prop-ism
ma-lar´ia
ma-lar´i-al
mal´con-tent
mal´e-dic´tion
mal´e-fac´tor
ma-lev´o-lence
ma-lev´o-lent
mal-fea´sance
mal´formed´
mal´ice
ma-li´cious-ly
ma-lign´
ma-lig´nan-cy
ma-lig´nant
ma-lin´ger
ma-lin´ger-er
mal-le-a-bil´i-ty
mal´le-a-ble
mal´let
mal-nu-tri´tion
mal-o´dor-ous
mal´prac-tice
malt´ose
mal-treat´

mal-treat´ment
malt´y
mam´mal
mam-ma´li-an
mam´ma-ry
mam´mon
mam´moth
man´age
man´age-a·bil´i-ty
man´age-a·ble
man´age-ment
man´ag-er
man´a-ge´ri-al
man´ag-ing
man´akin
man´date
man´da-to-ry
man´do-lin´
man´-eat-er
ma-neu´ver
ma-neu´ver-a·bil´-
  i-ty
ma-neu´ver-er
man´ful-ly
man´ger
man´gi-er
nian´gi-ly
man´gi-ness
man´gle
man´gler
man´gling
man´gy
man´han-dle

man´hole
ma´nia
ma´ni-ac
ma-ni´a-cal
man´ic
man´ic–de-pres´-
  sive
man´i-cure
man´i-cur-ist
man´i-fest
man-i-fes-ta´tion
man´i-fest-ly
man-i-fes´to
man-i-fes´tos
man´i-fold
man´i-kin
ma-nil´la
ma-nip´u-late
ma-nip-u-la´tion
ma-nip´u-la-tive
ma-nip´u-la-to-ry
man´kind´
man´li-ness
man´ly
man´ne-quin
man´ner-ism
man´ner-ly
man´ni-kin
man´nish
man´or
ma-no´ri-al
man´pow-er
man´sard

man´ser-vant
man´sion
man´slaugh-ter
man´tel
man´tel-piece
man´tle
man´tling
man´tra
man´u-al-ly
man-u-fac´ture
man-u-fac´tur-er
man-u-fac´tur-ing
ma-nure´
man´u-script
man-y
mar´a-thon
ma-raud´er
ma-raud´ing
mar´ble
mar´bled
mar´ble-ize
mar´bling
march´er
mar´ga-rine
mar´gin-al
mar-i-jua´na
ma-rim´ba
ma-ri´na
mar´i-nade´
mar´i-nate
mar´i-nat-ing
mar-i-na´tion
ma-rine´

mar´i-ner
mar´i-o-nette´
mar´i-tal-ly
mar´i-time
mark´ed-ly
mark´er
mar´ket
mar-ket-a·bil´i-ty
mar´ket-a·ble
mar´ket-er
mar´ket-ing
mar´ket-place
marks´man-ship
mar´ma-lade
ma-roon´
mar-quee´
mar´riage
mar´riage-a·ble
mar´ried
mar´row
mar´ry
mar´shal
mar´shaled
mar´shal-er
marsh´i-ness
marsh´mal-low
marsh-y
mar-su´pi-al
mar´tial
mar´tial-ly
mar´ti-net´
mar-ti´ni
mar´tyr

mar´tyr-dom
mar´vel
mar´veled
mar´vel-ing
mar´vel-ous-ly
mas-car´a
mas´cot
mas´cu-line
mas-cu-lin´i-ty
ma´ser
mash´er
mas´och-ism
mas´och-ist
mas´och-is´tic
ma´son
ma-son´ic
ma´son-ry
mas´quer-ade´
mas´sa-cred
mas´sa-cring
mas-sage´
mas-sag´er
mas-sag´ing
mas-seur´
mas-seuse´
mas´sive
mas´ter-ful
mas´ter-ful-ly
mas´ter-piece
mas´ter·y
mas´ti-cate
mas-ti-ca´tion
mas-ti´tis

mas´to-don
mas´toid
mas-toid-i´tis
mat´a-dor
match´less
match´mak-er
match´mak-ing
ma-te´ri-al-ist
ma-te´ri-al-is´tic
ma-te´ri-al-ism
ma-te´ri-al-ly
ma-te-ri-el´
ma-ter´nal
ma-ter´nal-ly
ma-ter´ni-ty
math-e-mat´i-cal
math-e-ma-ti´cian
math-e-mat´ics
mat´i-nee´
mat´ing
ma´tri-arch
ma´tri-ar´chal
ma´tri-ar-chy
ma´tri-ci´dal
ma´tri-cide
ma-tric´u-late
ma-tric-u-la´tion
mat´ri-mo´ni-al
mat´ri-mo-ny
ma´trix
ma´tron
ma´tron-ly
mat´ted

mat´ter
mat´ting
mat´tress
mat´u-rate
mat-u-ra´tion
ma-ture´
ma-ture´ly
ma-ture´ness
ma-tur´i-ty
maud´lin
maul´er
mau-so-le´um
mauve
mav´er-ick
mawk´ish
max´im
max´i-mal
max´i-mize
max´i-miz-er
max´i-mum
may´be
may´hem
may´on-naise
may´or
may´or-al-ty
may´pole
maze
ma-zur´ka
mead´ow
mea´gre (Br.)
meal´time
meal´y
meal´y-mouthed

mean
me-an´der
mean´ing
mean´ing-ful
mean´ing-less
mean´ly
mean´ness
meant
mean´time
mean´while
mea´sles
mea´sly
mea´sur-a·ble
mea´sure
mea´sured
mea´sure-less
mea´sure-ment
mea´sur-er
me-chan´ic
me-chan´i-cal
me-chan´i-cal-ly
mech´a-nism
mech´a-nize
med´al
med´aled
med´al-ist
me-dal´lion
med´dle
med´dler
med´dle-some
me´dia
me´di-an
me´di-ate

me-di-a´tion
me´di-a-tor
med´ic
med´i-cal
med´i-cal-ly
me-dic´a-ment
med´i-cate
med-i-ca´tion
med´i-ca-tive
me-dic´i-nal
med´i-cine
me-di-e´val
me´di-o´cre
me-di-oc´ri-ty
med´i-tate
med-i-ta´tion
med´i-ta-tive
med´i-tat-or
me´di-um
med´ley
me-du´sa
meek´ly
meek´ness
meer´schaum
meet´ing
meg´a-cy-cle
meg´a-phone
meg´a-ton
mel´an-choly
me-lange´
meld´er
me´lee
mel´io-rate

mel-io-ra´tion
mel´io-ra-tive
mel-lif´er-ous
mel-lif´lu-ence
mel-lif´lu-ent
mel-lif´lu-ous
mel´low-ness
me-lo´de-on
me-lod´ic
me-lod´i-cal-ly
me-lo´di-ous
mel´o-dra-ma
mel´o-dra-mat´ic
mel´o-dy
melt´a·ble
melt´er
mem´ber-ship
mem´brane
mem´bra-nous
me-men´to
me-men´tos
mem´oir
mem-o-ra-bil´ia
mem´o-ra-ble
mem-o-ran´da
mem-o-ran´dum
me-mo´ri-al
me-mo´ri-al-ize
mem´o-ries
mem-o-ri-za´tion
mem´o-rize
mem´o-riz-er
mem´o-riz-ing

mem´o-ry
men´ace
men´ac-ing
men´ac-ing-ly
me-nag´er-ie
men-da´cious
men-dac´i-ty
mend´er
men´di-cant
me´nial
men-in-gi´tis
men´o-pause
men´ses
men´stru-al
men´stru-ate
men-stru-a´tion
men´tal
men-tal´i-ty
men´tal-ly
men´thol
men´thyl
men´tion-a·ble
men´tion-er
men´tor
men´u
mer´can-tile
mer´ce-nary
mer´chan-dise
mer´chan-dis-er
mer´chan-dis-ing
mer´chant
mer´cies
mer´ci-ful-ly

mer´ci-ful-ness
mer´ci-less
mer-cu´ri-al
mer´cy
mere´ly
me-ren´gue
mer´est
mer-e-tri´cious
mer-gan´ser
merge
mer´gence
merg´er
me-rid´i-an
me-ringue´
mer´it
mer´it-ed
mer-i-to´ri-ous
mer´maid
mer´man
mer´ri-ly
mer´ri-ment
mer´ri-ness
mer´ry
mer´ry-mak-ing
me´sa
mesh´work
mesh´y
mes´mer-ism
mes´mer-ize
mes´mer-iz-ing
mes-quite´
mes´sage
mes´sen-ger

mess´i-ness
mess´mate
mess´y
met´a-bol´ic
me-tab´o-lism
me-tab´o-lize
met´al
me-tal´lic
met´al-lur´gic
met´al-lur´gi-cal
met´al-lur-gist
met´al-lur-gy
met´al-work
met´al-work-ing
met·a-mor´phic
met·a-mor´pho-sis
met´a-phor
met-a-phor´i-cal
meta-phys´i-cal
met´a-phys´ics
me´te-or
me-te-or´ic
me´te-or-ite
me-te-o-rol´o-gist
me-te-o-rol´o-gy
me´ter
meth´a-done
meth´ane
meth´a-nol
meth´od
me-thod´i-cal
me-thod´i-cal-ly
meth-od-ol´o-gy

me-tic´u-lous
met´ric
met´ri-cal
met´ro-nome
me-trop´o-lis
met´ro-pol´i-tan
met´tle
mez´za-nine´
mi´crobe
mi´cro-bi-ol´o-gist
mi´cro-bi-ol´o-gy
mi´cro-cosm
mi´cro-fiche
mi´cro-film
mi-crom´e-ter
mi´cron
mi-cro-or´ga-nism
ml´cro-phone
mi´cro-scope
mi´cro-scop´ic
mi´cro-wave
mid´dle
mid´dle–aged´
mid´dle-man
mid´dle-of–the
    road´
midg´et
mid´night
mid´riff
mid´stream´
mid´sum´mer
mid´way
mid´wife

mid´wife-ry

might´i-er

might´i-ly

might´i-ness

might´y

mi´graine

mi´grant

mi´grate

mi´grat-ing

mi-gra´tion

mi´gra-to-ry

mil´dew

mild´ly

mild´ness

mile´age

mile´post

mile´stone

mi-lieu´

mil´i-tan-cy

mil´i-tant-ly

mi -i-tar´ily

mil´i-ta-rism

mil´i-ta-ris´tic

mil´i-tary

mi-li´tia

milk´i-ness

milk shake

milk´y

mil´le-nary

mill´er

mil´li-gram

mil´li-me-ter

mil´li-ner

mil´li-ner·y

mill´ing

mil´lion

mi´lion-aire´

mil´lionth

mill´pond

mill´stream

mim´e-o-graph

mim´er

mim´ic

mim´icked

mim´ick-er

mim´ick-ing

mim´ic-ry

mim´ing

min´a-ret´

mince´meat

minc´er

minc´ing

mind´er

mind´ful

mind´less

min´er

min´er-al

min´er-al-ize

min´er-al-og´i-cal

min-er-al´o-gist

min-er-al´o-gy

min´gle

min´gling

min´i-a-ture

min´i-a-tur-ist

min´i-cam

min´i-mal

min´i-mize

min´i-miz-er

min´i-mum

min´ing

min´is-ter

min´is-te´ri-al

min´is-try

min´now

mi´nor

mi-nor´i-ty

min´strel

mint´er

min-u-et´

mi´nus

min´us-cule

min´ute *(time)*

mi-nute´ *(tiny)*

min´ute hand

min´ute-ly *(time)*

min´ute-man

mi-nute´ness *(tiny)*

mi-nu´tia

mi-nu´ti-ae

mir´a-cle

mi-rac´u-lous

mi-rac´u-lous-ly

mi-rage´

mired

mir´ing

mir´ror

mirth´ful

mirth´less

mis-ad-ven´ture
mis-al-li´ance
mis´an-thrope
mis´an-throp´ic
mis´ap-pre-hend´
mis-ap-pre-hen´-
  sion
mis-be-got´ten
mis-be-have´
mis-be-hav´ing
mis-be-hav´ior
mis-cal´cu-late
mis-cal-cu-la´tion
mis-car´riage
mis-car´ried
mis-car´ry
mis-car´ry-ing
mis-cel-la´neous
mis´cel-la-ny
mis´chief–mak´er
mis´chie-vous
mis´ci-ble
mis-con-ceive´
mis-con-cep´tion
mis-con´duct
mis´con-strue´
mis´cre-ance
mis´cre-an-cy
mis´cre-ant
mis-deed´
mis´de-mean´or
mis-di-rec´tion
mis-do´er

mi´ser
mis´er-a-ble
mis´er-a-bly
mi´ser-li-ness
mi´ser-ly
mis´ery
mis-fire´
mis´fit´
mis-for´tune
mis-giv´ing
mis-guide´
mis-guid´ed
mis-han´dle
mis´hap
mis´in-form´
mis´in-for-ma´-
  tion
mis-in-ter´pret
mis´in-ter-pre-ta´-
  tion
mis-judge´
mis-laid´
mis-lay´
mis-lead´ing
mis-man´age
mis-man´age-
  ment
mis-match´
mis-no´mer
mi-sog´a-mist
mi-sog´a-my
mi-sog´y-nist
mi-sog´y-ny

mis-place´
mis´print
mis´pro-nounce´
mis´quote´
mis´quot´ing
mis´rep-re-sent´
mis´sal
mis-shape´
mis-shap´en
mis´sile
miss´ing
mis´sion
mis´sion-ar-ies
mis´sion-ary
mis´sive
mis-spell´
mis-spelled´
mis-spell´ing
mis-spent´
mis-step´
mis-tak´able
mis-take´
mis-tak´en
mis-tak´en-ly
mis-tak´ing
mis´ter
mist´i-ness
mis-took´
mis-treat´ment
mis´tress
mist´y
mis-un-der-stand´
mis-un-der-stood´

mis-use´
mi´ter
mit´i-gate
mit´i-gat-ing
mit-i-ga´tion
mit´i-ga-tive
mit´i-ga-to-ry
mit´ten
mix´er
mix´ture
mix´–up
mne-mon´ic
moan´ing
mobbed
mob´bing
mo´bile
mo-bil´i-ty
mo-bi-li-za´tion
mo´bi-lize
mock´er
mock´er·y
mock´ing
mock´ing-ly
mo-dal´i-ty
mod´el
mod´eled
mod´el-ing
mo´dem
mod´er-ate-ly
mod´er-at-ing
mod-er-a´tion
mod´er-a-tor
mod´ern-ist

mo-der´ni-ty
mod-ern-i·za´tion
mod´ern-ize
mod´ern-iz-ing
mod´est-ly
mod´es-ty
mod´i-cum
mod´i-fi´able
mod-i-fi-ca´tion
mod´i-fied
mod´i-fi-er
mod´i-fy-ing
mod´ish
mod´u-lar
mod´u-late
mod-u-la´tion
mod´u-la-tor
mod´ule
mod´u-lus
mo´gul
mo´hair
moi´e-ty
moi-ré´
moist´en
moist´en-er
moist´ly
moist´ness
mois´ture
mois´ture-proof
mo´lar
mo-las´ses
mold´able
mold´er

mold´i-ness
mold´ing
mold´y
mo-lec´u-lar
mol´e-cule
mole´hill
mo-lest´
mo-les-ta´tion
mo-lest´er
mol´li-fied
mol´li-fy
mol´li-fy-ing
mol´lusk
mol´ten
mo´ment
mo´men-tar´i-ly
mo´men-tar·y
mo-men´tous
mo-men´tum
mon´arch
mon´ar-chist
mon´ar-chy
mon´as-te´ri-al
mon´as-tery
mo-nas´tic
mo-nas´ti-cism
mon-e-tar´i-ly
mon´e-tar·y
mon´ey
mon´eyed
mon´ey-mak-er
mon´ey-mak-ing
mon´ger

143

mon´grel
mon´i-ker
mon´i-tor
monk´ery
mon´key-shine
monk´ish
monks´hood
mon´o-chro-mat´-
  ic
mon´o-cle
mo-nog´a-mist
mo-nog´a-mous
mo-nog´a-my
mon´o-gram
mon´o-grammed
mon´o-lith
mon´o-lith´ic
mon´o-log
mon´o-logue
mon´o-ma´nia
mon´o-nu-cle-o´sis
mo-nop´o-lis´tic
mo-nop´o-lize
mo-nop´o-ly
mon´o-rail
mon´o-syl-lab´ic
mon´o-syl´la-ble
mon´o-the-ism
mon´o-the-ist
mon´o-the-is´tic
mon´o-tone
mo-not´o-nous
mo-not´o-ny

mon-sieur´
mon-soon´
mon´ster
mon-stros´i-ty
mon´strous
mon-tage´
month´ly
mon´u-ment
mon-u-men´tal
mood´i-ly
mood´i-ness
mood´y
moon´beam
moon´less
moon´light
moon´lit
moon´shine
moon´struck
moor´age
moor´ing
moped
mop´ing
mop´pet
mop´ping
mor´al
mo-rale´
mor´al-ism
mor´al-ist
mo-ral´i-ty
mor´al-ize
mor´al-ly
mo-rass´
mor-a-to´ri-um

mor´bid
mor-bid´i-ty
mor´bid-ly
mor-bif´ic
more-o-ver
morgue
mor´i-bund
morn´ing
mo´ron
mo-ron´ic
mo-rose´
mo-rose´ly
mor´phine
mor´sel
mor´tal
mor-tal´i-ty
mor´tal-ly
mor´tar
mor´tar-board
mort´gage
mort´ga-gee´
mort´gag-ing
mor-ti´cian
mor-ti-fi-ca´tion
mor´ti-fied
mor´ti-fy
mor´ti-fy-ing
mor´tise
mor´tis-ing
mor´tu-ary
mo-sa´ic
mosque
mos-qui´to

mos-qui´toes
moss´i-er
moss´i-ness
moss´y
most´ly
mo-tel´
moth´er
moth´er-land
moth´er-li-ness
moth´er-ly
mo-tif´
mo´tile
mo-til´i-ty
mo´tion
mo´tion-less
mo´ti-vate
mo´ti-vat-ing
mo-ti-va´tion
mo-tive
mot´ley
mo´tor-boat
mo´tor-cade
mo´tor-cy-cle
mo´tor-cy-clist
mo´tor-ist
mo´tor-ize
mot´tle
mot´tled
mot´tling
mot´to
mot´toes
moun´tain
moun´tain-eer´

moun´tain-ous
mount´ed
mount´er
mount´ing
mourn´er
mourn´ful
mourn´ing
mouse´trap
mous´tache
mous´y
mouth´ful
mouth´piece
mov´able
move´ment
mov´er
mov´ie
mov´ies
mov´ing
mowed
mow´er
mow´ing
mown
mu´ci-lage
muck´er
muck´rake
muck´y
mud´di-ness
mud´dle
mud´dled
mud´dy
mud´guard
muf´fin
muf´fle

muf´fler
muf´fling
muf´ti
mug´ger
mug´gi-ness
mug´ging
mug´gy
mul´ber-ry
mulch´er
mul´ish
mul´ti-col´ored
mul´ti-far´i-ous
mul´ti-lat´er-al
mul´ti-lay-er
mul-ti-lev´el
mul´ti-lin´gual
mul´ti-me´dia
mul´ti-na´tion-al
mul´ti-ple
mul´ti-plex
mul-ti-pli-ca´tion
mul-ti-plic´i-ty
mul´ti-plied
mul´ti-pli-er
mul´ti-ply
mul´ti-ply-ing
mul´ti-tude
mul-ti-tu´di-nous
mum´ble
mum´bling
mun-dane´
mu-nic´i-pal
mu-nic-i-pal´i-ty

mu-nif´i-cence
mu-nif´i-cent
mu-ni´tion
mu´ral
mur´der-er
mur´der-ess
mur´der-ous
murk´i-er
murk´i-ly
murk´y
mur´mur
mur´mur-ing
mus´cle–bound
mus´cu-lar
mus-cu-lar´i-ty
mus´cu-la-ture
mu-se´um
mush´room
mush´y
mu´sic
mu´si-cal
mu´si-cale´
mu´si-cal-ly
mu-si´cian
mu-si-col´o-gy
mus´ing
mus´ket
mus´ket-ry
musk´y
mus´lin
muss´y
mus´ter
must´i-ness

must´y
mu´tant
mu´tate
mu´tat-ing
mu-ta´tion
mut´ed
mute´ly
mute´ness
mu´ti-late
mu-ti-la´tion
mu´ti-la-tor
mu´ti-neer´
mut´ing
mu´ti-nied
mu´ti-nous
mu´tiny
mut´ter
mut´ter-ing
mu´tu-al
mu´tu-al-ly
mu´tu-el
muz´zle
muz´zling
my-o´pia
my-op´ic
myr´i-ad
myrrh
my-self´
mys´ter-ies
mys-te´ri-ous
mys-te´ri-ous-ly
mys´tery
mys´tic

mys´ti-cal
mys´ti-cism
mys´ti-fied
mys´ti-fy
mys´ti-fy-ing
mys-tique´
myth´ic
myth´i-cal
myth´i-cal-ly
myth´i-cist
myth´i-cize
myth-o-log´i-cal
my-thol´o-gy

N

nabbed
nab´bing
na´bob
na´dir
nag´ging
na´iad
nail´er
na-ive´
na-ive-té´
na´ked
na´ked-ness
nam´by–pam´by
name´less
name´ly
nam´er
name´sake
nam´ing
na´per·y

naph´tha
nap´kin
nap´per
nap´ping
nar´cis-sism
nar´cis-sist
nar-cis´sus
nar´co-lep-sy
nar-co-lep´tic
nar-co´sis
nar-cot´ic
nar´rate
nar-ra´tion
nar´ra-tive
nar´ra-tor
nar´row
nar´row-ly
nar´row–mind´ed
nar´row-ness
na´sal
na´sal-ly
nas´cent
nas´ti-ly
nas´ti-ness
nas´ty
na´tal
na´tion
na´tion-al
na´tion-al-ism
na´tion-al-ist
na´tion-al-is´tic
na-tion-al´i-ty
na´tion-al-ize

na´tion-al-ly
na´tion-wide´
na´tive
na´tive–born´
na-tiv´i-ty
nat´ti-ly
nat´ty
nat´u-ral
nat´u-ral-ist
nat´u-ral-is´tic
nat-u-ral-i·za´tion
nat´u-ral-ize
nat´u-ral-ly
nat´u-ral-ness
na´ture
naught
naugh´ti-ly
naugh´ti-ness
naugh´ty
nau´sea
nau´se-ate
nau´se-at-ed
nau´seous
nau´ti-cal
nau´ti-cal-ly
na´val *(marine)*
na´vel *(mark)*
na´vies
nav´i-ga-ble
nav´i-gate
nav-i-ga´tion
nav´i-ga-tor
na´vy

near´by´
near´est
near´ly
near´ness
near´sight-ed
neat´ly
neat´ness
neb´u-la
neb´u-lae
neb´u-lar
neb´u-lous
nec´es-sar´i-ly
nec´es-sar·y
ne-ces´si-tate
ne-ces´si-ties
ne-ces´si-ty
neck´lace
neck´tie
nec´ro-man-cer
nec´ro-man-cy
nec´tar
need´ful
need´i-er
need´i-est
nee´dle
nee´dler
need´less
need´less-ly
nee´dle-work
need´y
ne'er´–do–well
ne-far´i-ous
ne-gate´

ne-ga´tion
neg´a-tive
neg´a-tive-ly
neg´a-tiv-ism
neg-a-tiv´i-ty
ne-glect
ne-glect´er
ne-glect´ful
neg-li-gee´
neg´li-gence
neg´li-gent
neg´li-gent-ly
neg´li-gi-ble
ne-go´tia-ble
ne-go´ti-ate
ne-go´ti-at-ing
ne-go-ti-a´tion
ne-go´ti-a-tor
neigh´bor
neigh´bor-hood
neigh´bor-li-ness
neigh´bor-ly
neigh´bour (Br.)
nei´ther
nem´e-sis
ne´on
ne´o-phyte
neph´ew
nep´o-tism
nerve´less
ner´vous
ner´vous-ly
ner´vous-ness

nerv´y
nest´er
nes´tle
nes´tling (snuggle)
nest´ling (bird)
neth´er-most
net´ting
net´tle
net´tled
net´work
neu´ral
neu-ral´gia
neu-ral´gic
neu-ri´tis
neu-rol´o-gist
neu-rol´o-gy
neu-rol´y-sis
neu-ro´ses
neu-ro´sis
neu-rot´ic
neu´tral
neu-tral´i-ty
neu´tral-ize
neu´tral-iz-er
neu´tral-ly
neu-tri´no
neu´tron
nev´er
nev´er-the-less´
new´born
new´com-er
new´el
new´fan´gled

new´ly
new´–mown
new´ness
news´boy
news´cast-er
news´let-ter
news´pa-per
news´print
news´reel
news´room
news´stand
news´y
ni´a-cin
nib´ble
nib´bling
nice´ly
nice´ness
nic´est
ni´ce-ty
niche
nick´el
nick-el-o´de-on
nick´name
nic´o-tine
niece
nif´ty
nig´gle
nig´gling
night´club
night´fall
night´gown
night´ly
night´mare

night´time
ni´hi-lism
ni´hi-list
ni´hi-lis´tic
nim´ble
nim´ble-ness
nim´bly
nim´bus
nin´com-poop
nine´fold
nine´teen´
nine´teenth´
nine´ti-eth
nine´ty
nin´ny
ninth
nip´per
nip´ping
nip´ple
nip´py
ni´trate
ni´tric
ni´tride
ni´trite
ni´tro-gen
ni´trous
no-bil´i-ty
no´ble
no´ble-man
no´ble-wom-an
no´bly
no´body
noc-tur´nal

noc´turne
nod´ding
nod´u-lar
nod´ule
noise´less
noise´less-ly
nois´i-ly
nois´i-ness
nois´ing
noi´some
nois´y
no´mad
no-mad´ic
no´men-cla-ture
nom´i-nal
nom´i-nal-ly
nom´i-nal-ism
nom´i-nal-ist
nom´i-nal-ize
nom´i-nate
nom´i-nat-ed
nom-i-na´tion
nom´i-na-tive
nom´i-nee´
non·a-ge-nar´i-an
non-ag-gres´sion
non´cha-lance´
non´cha-lant´
non´cha-lant-ly
non-com-bat´ant
non-com-mis´-
    sioned
non-com-mit´tal

non-con-duc´tor
non-con-form´ist
non-con-form´i-ty
non´de-script
non-en´ti-ty
non-ex-is´tént
non´fic´tion
non-in-ter-ven´-
    tion
non-par´ti-san
non´pay´ment
non-plussed´
non-pro-duc´tive
non-prof´it
non-pro-li-fer-
    a´tion
non-sec-tar´i-an
non´sense
non-sen´si-cal
non se´qui-tur
non´stop´
noo´dle
noon´time
nor´mal
nor-mal´i-ty
nor´mal-ize
nor´mal-ly
nor´ma-tive
north´east´
north-east´er-ly
north-east´ern
north´er-ly
north´ern

north´ern-er
north´ern-most
north´ward
north´west´
north´west´er-ly
north-west´ern
nose´bleed
nose´—dive
nos-tal´gia
nos-tal´gic
nos´tril
nos´y
no´ta-ble
no´ta-bly
no´ta-ries
no´ta-rize
no´ta-ry
no-ta´tion
notched
notch´er
note´book
not´ed
note´pa-per
note´wor-thy
noth´ing
no´tice-able
no´tice-ably
no´tic-ing
no´ti-fi-ca´tion
no´ti-fied
no´ti-fi-er
no´ti-fy
no´ti-fy-ing

not´ing
no-to-ri´e-ty
no-to´ri-ous
no-to´ri-ous-ly
not-with-stand´-
   ing
nou´gat
nour´ish
nour´ish-ing
nour´ish-ment
nov´el
nov-el-ette´
nov´el-ist
nov´el-ize
no-vel´la
nov´el-ties
nov´el-ty
no-ve´na
nov´ice
no-vi´tiate
no´where
nox´ious
noz´zle
nu´ance
nu´bile
nu´cle-ar
nu´clei
nu-cle´ic
nu´cle-us
nude´ness
nudged
nudg´er
nudg´ing

nud´ism
nud´ist
nu´di-ty
nug´get
nui´sance
nul-li-fi-ca´tion
nul´li-fied
nul´li-fi-er
nul´li-fy
nul´li-fy-ing
num´ber
num´bered
num´ber-er
num´ber-less
numb´ing
numb´ly
numb´ness
nu´mer-al
nu-mer´i-cal
nu-mer´i-cal-ly
nu-mer-ol´o-gy
nu´mer-ous
nu-mis-mat´ics
nu-mis´ma-tist
num´skull
nun´nery
nup´tial
nurse´maid
nur´sery
nurs´ing
nur´ture
nur´tur-ing
nu´tri-ent

nu´tri-ment
nu-tri´tion
nu-tri´tion-al
nu-tri´tion-ist
nu-tri´tious
nu´tri-tive
nut´ti-er
nut´ti-ness
nut´ty
nuz´zle
ny´lon
nymph

O

oak´en
oar´lock
oars´man
oa´ses
oa´sis
oat´meal
ob´du-ra-cy
ob´du-rate
o-be´di-ence
o-be´di-ent
o-be´di-ent-ly
o-bei´sance
o-bei´sant
ob´e-lisk
o-bese´
o-be´si-ty
o-bey´
o-bey´ing
ob-fus´cate

ob-fus-ca´tion
o-bit´u-ar-ies
o-bit´u-ary
ob´ject *(n.)*
ob-ject´ *(v.)*
ob-ject´ing
ob-jec´tion
ob-jec´tion-able
ob-jec´tive
ob-jec´tive-ly
ob-jec´tive-ness
ob-jec-tiv´i-ty
ob´late
ob´li-gate
ob´li-gat-ing
ob-li-ga´tion
ob´li-ga-tor
o-blig´a-to-ry
o-blige´
o-blig´er
o-blig´ing
o-blig´ing-ly
o-blique´
o-blique´ly
ob-lit´er-ate
ob-lit-er-a´tion
ob-liv´i-on
ob-liv´i-ous
ob´long
ob-nox´ious
o´boe
o´bo-ist
ob-scene´

ob-scene´ly
ob-scen´i-ty
ob-scure´
ob-scure´ness
ob-scur´ing
ob-scu´ri-ty
ob-se´qui-ous
ob-se´qui-ous-ness
ob-serv´able
ob-serv´ance
ob-serv´ant
ob-ser-va´tion
ob-serv´a-to-ry
ob-serve´
ob-serv´er
ob-serv´ing
ob-sess´
ob-ses´sion
ob-ses´sive
ob-so-les´cence
ob-so-les´cent
ob-so-lete´
ob´sta-cle
ob-stet´rics
ob´sti-na-cy
ob´sti-nance
ob´sti-nate
ob´sti-nate-ly
ob-strep´er-ous
ob-struct´
ob-struct´er
ob-struc´tion
ob-struc´tion-ist

ob-struc´tive
.ob-tain´able
ob-trude´
ob-trud´er
ob-trud´ing
ob-tru´sion
ob-tru´sive
ob-tru´sive-ly
ob-tuse´
ob´vi-ate
ob´vi-at-ing
ob-vi-a´tion
ob´vi-ous
ob´vi-ous-ly
ob´vi-ous-ness
oc-ca´sion
oc-ca´sion-al
oc-ca´sion-al-ly
oc´ci-den´tal
oc-clu´sion
oc-cult´
oc-cul-ta´tion
oc-cult´ism
oc´cupan-cy
oc´cu-pant
oc-cu-pa´tion
oc-cu-pa´tion-al
oc´cu-pied
oc´cu-pi-er
oc´cu-py
oc´cu-py-ing
oc-cur´
oc-curred´

oc-cur´rence
oc-cur´rent
oc-cur´ring
o´cean
o·ce-an´ic
o·cean-og´ra-phy
oc´ta-gon
oc-tag´o-nal
oc´tal
oc´tane
oc´tave
oc-tet´
Oc-to´ber
oc-to-ge-nar´i·an
oc´u-list
odd´i-ty
odd´ly
odd´ment
odd´ness
od´ic
o´di-ous
od´ist
o´di-um
odom´e-ter
o´dor
o´dor-ant
o·dor-if´er-ous
o´dor-less
o´dor-ous
o´dour (Br.)
of´fal
off´beat
off´–cen´ter

off´–col´or
of-fend´
of-fend´er
of-fend´ing
of-fense´
of-fen´sive
of-fen´sive-ness
of´fer
of´fer-ing
of-fer-to´ri-al
of´fer-to-ry
of´fice
of´fice-hold-er
of´fi-cer
of-fi´cial
of-fi´cial-ly
of-fi´ci-ate
of-fi´cious
of-fi´cious-ly
off´shoot
off´spring
of´ten
of´ten-times
o´gle
o´gling
o´gre
oil´cloth
oil´er
oil´i-ness
oil´stone
oil´y
oint´ment
o·kay´

old´en
old–fash´ioned
old´–line´
old´ster
old´–time´
old–tim´er
o´leo
o´le-o-mar´ga-rine
ol-fac´tive
ol-fac´to-ry
ol´i-gar-chy
o·meg´a
o´men
om´i-nous
om´i-nous-ly
o·mis´sion
o·mit´
o·mit´ted
o·mit´ting
om´ni-bus
om-nip´o-tence
om-nip´o-tent
om-ni-pres´ent
om-niv´o-rous
once–o´ver
on´com-ing
one´ness
one´–piece´
on´er-ous
one-self´
one´–sid´ed
one´time
one´–way´

on´ion-skin
on´look-er
on´ly
on-o-mat-o-poe´ia
on´rush
on´set
on´slaught
on´to
o´nus
on´ward
on´yx
oozed
ooz´ing
o·pac´i-ty
o´pal
o·pal-esce´
o·pal-es´cence
o·pal-es´cent
o·paque´
o·paque´ly
o·paqu´er
o·paqu´ing
o´pen
o´pen–air´
o´pen–door´
o´pen-er
o´pen–faced
o´pen-hand´ed
o´pen-ing
o´pen-ly
o´pen–mind´ed
o´pen-ness
o´pen-work

op´er-a-ble
op´er-ate
op-er-a´tion
op-er-a´tion-al
op´er-a-tive
op´er-a-tor
op-er-et´ta
oph-thal-mol´o-
  gist
oph-thal-mol´o-gy
o´pi-ate
opin´ion
opin´ion-at-ed
o´pi-um
op-po´nent
op´por-tune´
op´por-tune´ly
op-por-tune´ness
op-por-tun´ism
op-por-tun´ist
op-por-tu´ni-ty
op-pos´a·ble
op-pose´
op-pos´ing
op´po-site
op-po-si´tion
op-press´
op-pres´sion
op-pres´sive
op-pres´sor
op-pro´bri-ate
op-pro´bri-ous
op-pro´bri-um

op´tic
op´ti-cal
op-ti´cian
op´tics
op´ti-mal
op´ti-mism
op´ti-mist
op-ti-mis´tic
op-ti-mis´ti-cal-ly
op´ti-mum
op´tion
op´tion-al
op-tom´e-trist
op-tom´e-try
op´u-lence
op´u-len-cy
op´u-lent
o´pus
or´a-cle
o´ral
o´ral-ly
o-rate´
o-ra´tion
or´a-tor
or-a-tor´i-cal
or-a-tor´i-cal-ly
or-a-to´rio
or´a-to-ry
or´bit
or´bit-al
or´bit-ed
or´bit-er
or´bit-ing

or´chard
or´ches-tra
or-ches´tral
or´ches-trate
or-ches-tra´tion
or-dain´
or´deal
or´der
or´dered
or´der-li-ness
or´der-ly
or´di-nal
or´di-nance
or-di-nar´i-ly
or´di-nary
or´di-nate
or-di-na´tion
ord´nance
or´gan
or´gan-dy
or-gan´ic
or-gan´i-cal-ly
or´ga-nism
or´gan-ist
or´ga-niz´a·ble
or-ga-ni-za´tion
or´ga-nize
or´ga-niz-er
or´ga-niz-ing
or´gy
o´ri-ent
o´ri-en´tal
o´ri-en-tate

o·ri-en-ta´tion
or´i-fice
or´i-gin
o·rig´i-nal
o·rig´i-nal´i-ty
o·rig´i-nal-ly
o·rig´i-nate
o·rig´i-nat-ing
o·rig-i-na´tion
o·rig´i-na-tor
or´na-ment
or´na-men´tal
or-na-men-ta´tion
or´nate´
or-nate´ness
or´nery
or-ni-thol´o-gist
or-ni-thol´o-gy
or´ni-thop-ter
or´phan
or´phan-age
or-tho-don´tia
or´tho-don´tics
or´tho-don´tist
or´tho-dox
or´tho-dox·y
or´tho-pae´dic
or´tho-pae´dist
os´cil-late
os-cil-la´tion
os-cil´lo-scope
os-si-fi-ca´tion
os´si-fied

154

os´si-fy
os-ten´si-ble
os-ten´si-bly
os-ten-ta´tion
os-ten-ta´tious
os-ten-ta´tious-ly
os´te o-my-e-li´tis
os´te-o-path
os´te-o-path´ic
os-te-op´a-thy
os´tra-cism
os´tra-cize
os´tra-ciz-ing
oth´er
oth´er-wise
ought
ounce
our-selves´
oust´er
out´break
out´burst
out´cast
out´class´
out´come
out´crop-ping
out´cry
out-do´
out-doors´
out´er-most
out´fit
out´fit-ter
out´go´ing
out´grew´

out´grow´
out´growth
out-ing
out-land´ish
out´law
out´let
out´line
out´look
out´mod´ed
out–of–date
out´post
out´pour-ing
out´put
out´rage
out-ra´geous
out-ra´geous-ly
out´reach
out´right
out´set
out-side´
out-sid´er
out´skirts
out´spo´ken
out-stand´ing
out-stretched´
out´ward-ly
out´wit´
o´va
o´val
o-va´tion
ov´en
o-ver-bear´ing
o-ver-came´

o´ver-cast
o´ver-coat
o-ver-come´
o´ver-draft
o´ver-drive´
o-ver-es´ti-mate
o´ver-flow
o´ver-hang´
o´ver-head
o´ver-joyed
o´ver-lap´
o-ver-lap´ping
o´ver-look´
o´ver-ly
o-ver-night´
o-ver-rate´
o-ver-rule´
o-ver-see´
o´ver-seer
o-ver-shad´ow
o´ver-sight
o-ver-slept´
o-vert´
o-ver-tak´en
o-ver-throw´
o´ver-time
o-vert´ly
o´ver-tone
o´ver-ture
o´ver-weight
o-ver-whelm´ing
o-ver-worked´
o´ver-wrought´

o´vu-late

o·vu-la´tion

o´vule

ow´ing

own´er

own´er-ship

ox´en

ox´i-da´tion

ox´ide

ox´i-dize

ox´y-gen

ox´y-gen-ate

ox-y-gen-a´tion

o´zone

P

paced

pace´mak-er

pac´er

pa-cif´ic

pac-i-fi-ca´tion

pac´i-fied

pac´i-fi-er

pac´i-fism

pac´i-fist

pac´i-fy

pac´i-fy-ing

pac´ing

pack´age

pack´ag-er

pack´ag-ing

pack´er

pack´et

pack´ing

pack´ing-house

pad´ding

pad´dle

pad´dler

pad´dling

pad´lock

pa´gan

pa´gan-ism

pag´eant

pag´eant-ry

paged

pag´er

pag´i-nate

pag-i-na´tion

pag´ing

pa-go´da

pail´ful

pain´ful

pain´ful´ly

pain´less

pain´less-ly

pains´tak-ing

pains´tak-ing-ly

paint´brush

paint´er

paint´ing

pa-ja´ma

pal´ace

pal´at-able

pal´ate

pa-la´tial

pale´ness

pal´ette

pal´i-mo-ny

pal´in-drome

pal´ing

pal-i-sade´

pall´bear-er

pal´li-ate

pal´li·a-tive

pal´lid

pal´lor

palm´ist

palm´is-try

pal-pa-bil´i-ty

pal´pa-ble

pal´pa-bly

pal´pate

pal-pa´tion

pal´pi-tate

pal´pi-tat-ing

pa´pi-ta´tion

pal´sied

pal´sy

pal´tri-ness

pal´try

pam´per

pamph´let

pam´phle-teer

pan-a-ce´a

pan-chro-mat´ic

pan-de-mo´ni-um

pan´el

pan´eled

pan´el-ing

pan´el-ist	par´a-lyse (Br.)	park´way
pan´ic	pa-ral´y-sis	par´lance
pan´icked	par´a-lyt´ic	par´lay (a bet)
pan´ick-ing	par´a-lyze	par´ley (a talk)
pan´icky	par´a-lyz-ing	par´lia-ment
pan´ic–strick-en	par´a-mount	par-lia-men´ta-ry
pan´o-ply	par´a·mour	par´lor
pan-o-ram´a	par-a-noi´a	pa-ro´chial
pan´o-ram´ic	par´a-noid	par´o-dy
pant´ing	par´a-ple´gic	par´o-dy-ing
pan´to-mime	par´a-site	pa-role´
pan´to-mimist	par´a-sit´ic	pa-roled´
pan´tries	par´a-sol	pa-rol-ee´
pan´try	par´boil	pa-rol´ing
pa´pa-cy	par´cel	par-quet´
pa´pal	par´celed	par´ried
pa´per-back	par´cel-ing	par´ry
pa´per-board	parch´ment	par´ry-ing
pa´per-hang-er	par´don	parse
pa´per-weight	par´don-able	par-si-mo´nious
par´a-ble	par´don-er	par´si-mo-ny
par´a-chute	pared	pars´ing
pa-rade´	par´ent-age	par´son
pa-rad´er	pa-ren´tal	par´son-age
pa-rad´ing	pa-ren´the-ses	par-take´
par´a-digm	pa-ren´the-sis	par-tak´en
par´a-dise	pa-ren´the-size	par-tak´er
par´a-dox	par´en-thet´ic	part´ed
par´a-gon	par´en-thet´i-cal	par´tial
par´a-graph	par´ing	par-ti·al´i-ty
par´al-lax	par´ish	par´tial-ly
par´al-lel	pa-rish´ion-er	par-tic´i-pant
par´al-leled	par´i-ty	par-tic´i-pate

par-tic-i-pa´tion	pass´port	path´way
par-tic´u-lar	pass´word	pa´tience
par-tic´u-lar-ly	paste´board	pa´tient
par´ties	past´ed	pa´tient-ly
part´ing	pas-tel´	pat´io
par´ti-san	past´er	pa-tis´se-rie
par-ti´tion	pas-teur-i·za´tion	pa´tois
par-ti´tion-er	pas´teur-ize	pa´tri-arch
par-ti´tion-ing	pas´time	pa´tri-ar´chal
part´ly	past´ing	pa´tri-archy
part´ner	pas´tor	pa-tri´cian
part´ner-ship	pas´to-ral	pa´tri-ot
par-took´	pas-to-rale´	pa´tri-ot´ic
part´–time´	pas´try	pa´tri-ot´i-cal-ly
par´ty	pas´ture	pa´tri-ot-ism
pass´able	patch´er	pa-trol´
pass´ably	patch´i-ness	pa-trolled´
pas´sage	patch´ing	pa-trol´ler
pas´sage-way	patch´work	pa-trol´ling
pass´book	patch´y	pa´tron
pas-sé´	pat´ent	pa´tron-age
pas´sen-ger	pat´ent-able	pa´tron-ize
pass´er	pat´ent-ly	pa´tron-iz-ing
pass´er-by	pa-ter´nal	pat´ter
pass´ing	pa-ter´nal-ism	pat´tern
pas´sion	pa-ter´nal-is´tic	pat´terned
pas´sion-ate	pa-ter´nal-ly	pat´tern-mak-er
pas´sion-ate-ly	pa-ter´ni-ty	pat´ting
pas´sive	pa-thet´ic	pat´ty
pas´sive-ly	pa-thet´i-cal-ly	pau´ci-ty
pas´sive-ness	pa-thol´o-gist	paunch´i-ness
pas´siv-ism	pa-thol´o-gy	paunch´y
pas´siv-ist	pa´thos	pau´per

pau´per-ism
paus´ing
pave´ment
pav´er
pa-vil´ion
pav´ing
pawn´bro-ker
pawn´shop
pay´able
pay´day
pay-ee´
pay´er
pay´ing
pay´ment
pay-o´la
pay´roll
peace´able
peace´ably
peace´ful
peace´ful-ly
peace´ful-ness
peace´mak-er
peace´time
peach´y
peaked (crested)
peak´ed (sickly)
peas´ant
peas´ant-ry
peb´ble
peb´bled
peb´bling
peb´bly
pec´cant

peck´ing
pec´u-late
pec´u-lat-ing
pec-u-la´tion
pe-cu´liar
pe-cu-li-ar´i-ty
pe-cu´ni-ar-y
ped´a-gog´ic
ped´a-gogue
ped´a-gogy
ped´al
ped´aled
pe-dan´tic
ped´ant-ry
ped´dle
ped´dler
ped´dling
ped´es-tal
pe-des´tri-an
pe-di-a-tri´cian
pe-di-at´rics
ped´i-gree
peel´er
peel´ing
peep´er
peep´hole
peer´age
peer´less
pee´vish
pee´vish-ness
peign-oir´
pel-la´gra
pel´let

pel´vic
pel´vis
pe´nal
pe´nal-ize
pe´nal-iz-ing
pen´al-ties
pen´al-ty
pen´ance
pench´ant
pen´cil
pen´ciled
pen´cil-ing
pend´ing
pen´du-lous
pen´du-lum
pen´e-tra-ble
pen´e-trate
pen´e-trat-ing
pen-e-tra´tion
pen-i-cil´lin
pe-nin´su-la
pe-nin´su-lar
pen´i-tence
pen´i-tent
pen-i-ten´tia-ry
pen´i-tent-ly
pen´man-ship
pen´nant
pen´nies
pen´ni-less
pen´ning
pen´ny
pe-nol´o-gist

pe-nol´o-gy
pen´sion
pen´sion-er
pen´sive
pen´sive-ly
pen´ta-gon
pent´house
pent´–up´
pe´on
peo´ple
pep´per·y
pep´py
pep´sin
pep´tic
per-cale´
per-ceiv´a·ble
per-ceiv´a·bly
per-ceive´
per-cent´
per-cent´age
per-cent´ile
per-cep´ti-ble
per-cep´ti-bly
per-cep´tion
per-cep´tive
per´co-late
per´co-la´tion
per´co-la-tor
per-cus´sion
per-cus´sive
pe-remp´tive
pe-remp´to-ri-ly
pe-remp´to-ry

pe-ren´nial
per´fect (adj.)
per-fect´ (v.)
per-fect´er
per-fec´tion
per´fect-ly
per-fec´tor
per-fid´i-ous
per-fid´i-ous-ly
per-fid´i-ous-ness
per´fi-dy
per´fo-rate
per´fo-rat-ed
per´fo-ra´tion
per´fo-ra-tor
per-form´
per-form´ance
per-form´er
per´fume
per-fum´er
per-fum´er·y
per-func´to-ry
per-haps´
per´il
per´il-ous
per´il-ous-ly
pe-rim´e-ter
pe´ri-od
pe-ri-od´ic
pe·ri-od´i-cal
pe-ri-od´i-cal-ly
per·i-pa-tet´ic
pe-riph´er-al

pe-riph´er-al-ly
pe-riph´er·y
per´i-phrase
per´i-scope
per´ish
per´ish-a·ble
per´jure
per´jur-er
per´jur-ing
per-ju´ri-ous
per´jur·y
perk´i-ness
perk´y
per´ma-nence
per´ma-nen-cy
per´ma-nent
per´ma-nent-ly
per´me-a·ble
per´me-ate
per-mis´si-ble
per-mis´sion
per-mis´sive
per-mit´ (v., n.)
per´mit (n.)
per-mit´ted
per-mit´ting
per-mu-ta´tion
per-ni´cious
per-ox´ide
per-pen-dic´u-lar
per´pe-trate
per´pe-tra-tor
per-pet´u-al

per-pet´u-ate
per-pe-tu´it·y
per-plex´
per-plexed´
per-plex´ing
per´qui-site
per´se-cute
per´se-cu´tion
per´se-cu-tor
per-se-ver´ance
per´se-vere´
per´se-ver´ing
per´si-flage
per-sist´
per-sist´ence
per-sist´ent
per-sist´ent-ly
per-snick´e-ty
per´son
per´son-al
per´son-al´i-ty
per´son-al-ize
per´son-al-ly
per-son-i-fi-ca´-
  tion
per-son´i-fy
per-son´i-fy-ing
per´son-nel´
per-spec´tive
per-spi-ca´cious
per-spi-cac´i-ty
per-spic´u-ous

per-spi-ra´tion
per-spire´
per-spir´ing
per-suad´a·ble
per-suade´
per-suad´er
per-suad´ing
per-sua´si·ble
per-sua´sion
per-sua´sive
per-sua´sive-ly
per-tain´
per´ti-nence
per´ti-nent
per-turb´
per-turb´a·ble
pe-rus´al
pe-ruse´
pe-rus´er
pe-rus´ing
per-vade´
per-vad´ing
per-va´sive
per-va´sive-ly
per-verse´
per-verse´ly
per-verse´ness
per-ver´sion
per-ver´sity
per-vert´ *(v.)*
per´vert *(n.)*
per-vert´ed
per´vi-ous

pes´ky
pes´si-mism
pes´si-mist
pes-si-mis´tic
pes-si-mis´ti-cal-ly
pes´ter
pes´tered
pes´ti-lence
pes´tle
pe-tite´
pe-ti´tion
pe-ti´tion-er
pet´ri-fied
pet´ri-fy
pet´ti-ly
pet´ti-ness
pet´ty
pet´u-lance
pet´u-lant
pew´ter
pha´lanx
phal´lic
phal´lus
phan´tasm
phan´tom
phar´aoh
phar´ma-ceu´ti-
  cal
phar-ma-ceu´tics
phar´ma-cist
phar-ma-col´o-gy
phar-ma-co-pe´ia
phar´ma-cy

phase

phas´er

phe´no-bar´bi-tal

phi´al

phi-lan´der

phi-lan´der-er

phil´an-throp´ic

phi-lan´thro-pist

phi-lan´thro-py

phil´a-tel´ic

phi-lat´e-list

phil´har-mon´ic

phi-los´o-pher

phil´o-soph´i-cal

phi-los´o-phize

phi-los´o-phy

phil´ter

phle-bi´tis

phlegm

pho´bia

pho´bic

pho-net´ic

pho-net´i-cal-ly

phon´ic

pho´no-graph

pho´ny

phos´phate

phos´phor

phos-pho-resce´

phos-pho-res´cent

pho´to

pho´to-gen´ic

pho´to-graph

pho-tog´ra-pher

pho´to-graph´ic

pho-tog´ra-phy

pho´ton

pho´to-stat

pho-to-syn´the-sis

phras´al

phrase

phras´ing

phre-nol´o-gist

phre-nol´o-gy

phy´lum

phys´i-cal

phys´i-cal-ly

phy-si´cian

phys´i-cist

phys´ics

phy-sique´

pi-an´ist

pi-a´no *(softly)*

pi-an´o
  (instrument)

pi-an´o-forte

pic´a-resque´

pic´co-lo

pic´co-lo-ist

pick´ax

pick´er

pick´et

pick´et-er

pick´et-ing

pick´ing

pick´le

pick´led

pick´ling

pick´pock-et

pic´nic

pic´nicked

pic´nick-er

pic´nick-ing

pic-to´ri-al

pic´ture

pic-tur-esque´

pic´tur-ing

pieced

piece´meal

piece´work

piec´ing

pie´crust

pierced

pierc´er

pierc´ing

pi´e-tism

pi´e-ty

pif´fle

pi´geon

pi´geon-hole

pi´geon–toed

pig´head-ed

pig´ment

pig-men-ta´tion

pig´pen

pig´skin

pik´er

pi-las´ter

pil´fer

pil′fer-age
pil′grim-age
pil′ing
pil′lage
pil′lag-er
pil′low
pil′low-case
pil′low-slip
pi′lot
pim′ple
pim′pled
pim′ply
pin′a-fore
pince′–nez′
pin′cers
pinch′–hit
pin′hole
pin′na-cle
pin′ning
pin′point
pin′up
pin′y
pi′o-neer′
pi′o-neered′
pi′ous
pi′ous-ly
pipe′line
pip′er
pip′ing
pi′quan-cy
pi′quant
pique
piqued

pi′ra-cy
pi′rate
pir′ou-ette′
pir′ou-ett′ed
pir′ou-ett′ing
pis′ca-to′ri-al
pis′ca-to-ry
pis′tol
pis′ton
pitch′er
pitch′ing
pit′e-ous
pit′e-ous-ly
pit′fall
pith′i-ness
pith′y
pit′i-a-ble
pit′ied
pit′i-er
pit′ies
pit′i-ful
pit′i-ful-ly
pit′i-less
pit′tance
pit′ted
pit′ter–pat′ter
pit′ting
pit′y
pit′y-ing
piv′ot
piv′ot-al
piv′ot-er
pix′ie

pix′y
piz-ze-ri′a
plac′a-ble
plac′ard
pla′cate
pla′cat-er
pla′cat-ing
pla-ce′bo
place′–kick
place′ment
plac′er
plac′id
plac′id-ly
plac′ing
pla′gia-rist
pla′gia-rize
pla′gia-riz-ing
pla′gia-ry
plague
plagu′ed
plagu′ing
plaid
plain′ly
plain′ness
plain′tiff
plain′tive
plain′tive-ly
plait
plan′et
plan-e-tar′i-um
plan′e-tar·y
plank′ing
plank′ton

planned
plan'ner
plan'ning
plan'tain
plan-ta'tion
plant'er
plant'ing
plaque
plas'ma
plas'ter
plas'tered
plas'ter-er
plas'ter-ing
plas'tic
pla-teau'
plat'ed
plate'ful
plat'en
plat'form
plat'ing
plat'i-num
plat'i-tude
pla-ton'ic
pla-toon'
plat'ter
plau'dit
plau'si·ble
plau'sive
play'bill
play'boy
play'er
play'ful
play'ful-ly

play'ful-ness
play'go-er
play'ground
play'house
play'ing card
play'mate
play'–off (n.)
play'thing
plaz'a
plea
plead'er
plead'ing
plead'ing-ly
pleas'ant
pleas'ant-ly
pleas'ant-ness
pleas'ant-ry
pleas'ing
plea'sur-a·ble
plea'sure
pleat
pleat'ed
ple-be'ian
pleb'i-scite
plec'trum
pledged
pledg'er
pledg'ing
ple'na-ry
plen'te-ous
plen'ti-ful
plen'ti-ful-ly
plen'ty

pleu'ri-sy
pli'a·ble
pli'an-cy
pli'ant
plied
pli'ers
plight
plod'ded
plod'der
plod'ding
plot'ter
plot'ting
plow
plow'er
plow'–hand
plow'ing
plow'share
pluck'i-er
pluck'y
plu'mage
plumb
plumb'er
plumb'ing
plum'met
plump'er
plump'ness
plun'der
plun'der-er
plun'der-ous
plunge'r
plung'ing
plu'ral
plu-ral'i-ty

plu-toc´ra-cy	po´lar	pol´y-chrome
ply´ing	po-lar´i-ty	pol´y-es-ter
pneu-mat´ic	po-lar-i-za´tion	poly-eth´yl-ene
pneu-mo´nia	po´lar-ize	po-lyg´a-mist
poach´er	po´lar-iz-er	po-lyg´a-mous
pock´et	po´lar-iz-ing	po-lyg´a-my
pock´et-book	po-lice´	pol´y-graph
pock´et-ful	po-lic´ing	pol´y-mer
po-di´a-trist	pol´i-cy	pol´y-no´mi-al
po-di´a-try	pol´ish	pol´yp
po´di-um	pol´ish-er	pol´y-syl-lab´ic
po´em	po-lite´	pol´y-the-ism
po´e-sy	po-lite´ly	pol´y-the-ist
po´et	po-lite´ness	pol´y-the-is´tic
po-et´ic	pol´i-tic	poly-vi´nyl
po-et´i-cal	po-lit´i-cal	pom´mel
po´et-ry	po-lit´i-cal-ly	pom´meled
po-grom´	pol-i-ti´cian	pom´pa-dour
poi´gnan-cy	po-lit´i-cize	pom-pos´i-ty
poi´gnant	pol´ka	pomp´ous
point´ed	pol´len	pon´cho
point´ed-ly	pol´len-ize	pon´der
point´er	pol´li-nate	pon´der-a·ble
poin´til-lism	pol´li-nat-ing	pon´der-ous
point´less	po´li-na´tion	po´nies
poised	poll´ster	pon´tiff
pois´ing	pol-lu´tant	pon-tif´i-cate
poi´son	pol-lute´	pon-tif´i-ca-tor
poi´son-er	pol-lut´er	pon-toon´
poi´son-ous	pol-lut´ing	po´ny
pok´er	pol-lu´tion	poo´dle
pok´ing	pol´o-naise´	poor´ly
pok´y	poly-chro-mat´ic	pop´gun

pop´lar

port´li-ness

pos-ter´i-ty

pop´lin

port´ly

post´hu-mous

pop´over

por´trait

post´hu-mous-ly

pop´pies

por´trai-ture

post -hyp-not´ic

pop´ping

por-tray´

post´mark

pop´py

posed

post´mas-ter

pop´py-cock

pos´er

post´mis-tress

pop´u-lace

pos´ing

post´—mor´tem

pop´u-lar

po-si´tion

post´paid´

pop-u-lar´i-ty

po-si´tion-er

post-pone´

pop-u-lar-i·za´tion

pos´i-tive

post-pone´ment

pop´u-lar-ize

pos´i-tive-ly

post´script

pop´u-lar-ly

pos´i-tiv-ism

pos´tu-late

pop´u-late

pos´i-tiv-is´tic

pos´tu-lat-ing

pop-u-la´tion

pos´i-tron

pos´ture

pop´u-lous

pos´se

pos´tur-ing

por´ce-lain

pos-sess´

po´ta-ble

por-nog´ra-pher

pos-sessed´

pot´bel-lied

por-no-graph´ic

pos-sess´es

pot´bel-ly

por-nog´ra-phy

pos-ses´sion

pot´boil-er

po-ros´i-ty

pos-ses´sive

po´ten-cy

po´rous

pos-ses´sive-ly

po´tent

por´ridge

pos-ses´sive-ness

po-ten´tial

por´ta-ble

pos-ses´sor

po-ten-ti-al´i-ty

por´tal

pos-si-bil´i-ty

po-ten´tial-ly

por-tend´

pos´si-ble

po´tent-ly

por´ter

pos´si-bly

pot´hole

port-fo´lio

post´age

po´tion

port´hole

post´al

pot´luck´

por´ti-co

post´card

pot-pour-ri´

por´ti-coes

post´date´

pot´shot

por´tion

post´er

pot´ted

port´li-er

pos-te´ri-or

pot´ter

pot'ter·y
poul'tice
poul'try
pounc'ing
pound'age
pound'er
pound'–fool'ish
poured
pour'er
pour'ing
pout'er
pout'ing
pout'ing-ly
pout'y
pov'er-ty
pov'er-ty–strick'-
  en
pow'der
pow'dered
pow'der·y
pow'er
pow'ered
pow'er-ful
pow'er-ful-ly
pow'er-house
pow'er-less
pow'wow
prac'ti-cal
prac-ti-cal'i-ty
prac'ti-cal-ly
prac'tice
prac'ticed
prac'tic-er

prac'tic-ing
prac-ti'tion-er
prag-mat'ic
prag-mat'i-cal-ly
prag'ma-tism
prag'ma-tist
prai'rie
praise'wor-thy
prais'ing
pranced
pranc'er
pranc'ing
prank'ster
prat'tle
prat'tler
prayed
prayer (plea)
pray'er (asker)
prayer'ful
preached
preach'er
preach'ing
preach'ment
preach'y
pre'am-ble
pre'ar-range'
pre-car'i-ous
pre-cau'tion
pre-cau'tion-ar·y
pre-cau'tious
pre-cede'
prec'e-dence
prec'e-dent

pre-ced'ing
pre'cept
pre-ces'sion
pre'cinct
pre'cious
prec'i-pice
pre-cip'i-tate
pre-cip'i-tate-ly
pre-cip-i-ta'tion
pre-cip'i-tous
pre-cip'i-tous-ly
pre-cise'
pre-cise'ly
pre-cise'ness
pre-ci'sion
pre-clude'
pre-clud'ing
pre-clu'sion
pre-co'cious
pre-coc'i-ty
pre'con-ceive'
pre-con-cep'tion
pre-cur'sor
pre-cur'so-ry
pred'a-tor
pred'a-to-ry
pred'e-ces-sor
pre-des-ti-na'tion
pre-des'tine
pre-de-ter'mine
pre-dic'a-ment
pre-dict'
pre-dict'a·ble

pre-dic´tion
pre-dic´tor
pred´i-lec´tion
pre´dis-pose´
pre-dis-pos´ing
pre-dis-po-si´tion
pre-dom´i-nant
pre-dom´i-nate
pre-em´i-nence
pre-em´i-nent
pre-em´i-nent-ly
pre-empt´
pre-emp´tion
pre-emp´tive
pre-emp´to-ry
preened
pre-fab´ri-cate
pref´ace
pref´ac-ing
pref´a-to-ry
pre-fer´
pref´er-a·ble
pref´er-a·bly
pref´er-ence
pref´er-en´tial
pre-ferred´
pre-fer´ring
pre´fix
preg´na-ble
preg´nan-cy
preg´nant
pre-hen´sile
pre-his-tor´ic

prej´u-dice
prej-u-di´cial
prel´ate
pre-lim´i-nar·y
prel´ude
pre-ma-ture´
pre-ma-ture´ly
pre-med´i-tate
pre-med-i-ta´tion
pre-med´i-ta-tive
pre-med´i-ta-tor
pre-mier´
pre-miere´
prem´ise
pre´mi-um
pre-mo-ni´tion
pre-oc-cu-pa´tion
pre-oc´cu-pied
pre-oc´cu-py
pre-or-dain´
pre-paid´
prep-a-ra´tion
pre-par´a-tive
pre-par´a-to-ry
pre-pare´
pre-pared´
pre-par´ed-ness
pre-par´er
pre-pay´ment
pre-pon´der-ance
pre-pos´ter-ous
pre-pos´ter-ous-ly
pre-req´ui-site

pre-rog´a-tive
pre´school´
pre´scient
pre-scribe´
pre-scrip´tion
pres´ence
pres´ent (now, gift)
pre-sent´ (give)
pre-sent´able
pre-sen-ta´tion
pre-sent´er
pres´ent-ly
pres-er-va´tion
pre-serv´a-tive
pre-serve´
pre-serv´er
pre-side´
pres´i-den-cy
pres´i-dent
pres´i-den´tial
pre-sid´er
pre-sid´ing
press´er
press´ing
press´man
pres´sure
pres´sur-ize
pres-ti-dig-i-ta´-
  tion
pres-tige´
pres-tig´i-ous
pre-sum´a·ble
pre-sum´a·bly

pre-sume′

pre-sumed′

pre-sum′er

pre-sump′tion

pre-sump′tive

pre-sump′tu-ous

pre-sup-pose′

pre-tend′

pre-tend′ed

pre-tend′er

pre′tense

pre-ten′tious

pre′text

pret′ti-ly

pret′ti-ness

pret′ty

pret′zel

pre-vail′

pre-vail′ing

prev′a-lence

prev′a-lent

pre-var′i-cate

pre-vent′

pre-vent′a·ble

pre-vent′a·tive

pre-ven′tion

pre-ven′tive

pre′view

pre′vi-ous

pre′vi-ous-ly

price′less

pric′ing

prick′le

prick′ly

priest′hood

priest′ly

prig′gish

pri′ma-cy

pri′mal

pri-mar′i-ly

pri′mar·y

pri-me′val

prim′i-tive

prim′ness

pri-mor′di-al

prince-ly

prin′cess

prin′ci-pal

prin-ci-pal′i-ty

prin′ci-pal-ly

prin′ci-ple

print′er

print′ing

pri′or

pri-or′i·tize

pri-or′i-ty

prism

pris′on-er

pris′sy

pris′tine

pri′va-cy

pri′vate

pri′vate-ly

pri-va′tion

pri′vat-ize

priv′i-lege

priv′i-leged

prob-a-bil′i-ty

prob′a·ble

prob′a·bly

pro′bate

pro-ba′tion

pro-ba′tion-al

pro-ba′tion-ar·y

prob′ing

prob′lem

prob′lem-at′ic

prob′lem-at′i-cal

pro-ce′dur-al

pro-ce′dure

pro-ceed′

pro-ceed′ing

proc′ess

proc′ess-ing

pro-ces′sion

pro-ces′sion-al

pro-claim′

proc-la-ma′tion

pro-cliv′i-ty

pro-cras′ti-nate

proc-tol′o-gy

proc′tor

pro-cure′

pro-cured′

pro-cure′ment

pro-cur′er

pro-cur′ing

prod′ding

prod′i-gal

pro-di´gious
prod´i-gy
pro-duce´ *(make)*
prod´uce *(product)*
pro-duc´ing
prod´uct
pro-duc´tion
pro-duc´tive
pro-duc-tiv´i-ty
pro-fane´
pro-fane´ly
pro-fan´er
pro-fan´ing
pro-fan´i-ty
pro-fess´
pro-fessed´
pro-fes´sion
pro-fes´sion-al
pro-fes´sion-al-ly
pro-fes´sor
pro´fes-so´ri-al
prof´fer
pro-fi´cien-cy
pro-fi´cient
pro´file
prof´it
prof´it-able
prof´it-ably
prof´it-less
prof´li-ga-cy
prof´li-gate
pro-found´
pro-found´ly

pro-fuse´
pro-fuse´ly
pro-fu´sion
prog´e-ny
prog-no´sis
prog-nos´ti-cate
prog-nos´ti-ca-tor
pro´gram
pro´gramed
pro´gram-er
pro´gram-ing
pro´grammed
pro´gram-mer
pro´gram-ming
prog´ress *(n.)*
pro-gress´ *(v.)*
pro-gres´sion
pro-gres´sive
pro-gres´sive-ly
pro-hib´it
pro-hi-bi´tion
pro-hi-bi´tion-ist
pro-hib´i-tive
proj´ect *(n.)*
pro-ject´ *(v.)*
pro-ject´ed
pro-jec´tile
pro-jec´tion
pro-lif´er-ate
pro-lif´ic
pro´log
pro´logue
pro-long´

pro-longed´
prom´e-nade´
prom´i-nence
prom´i-nent
prom´i-nent-ly
prom-is-cu´i-ty
pro-mis´cu-ous
prom´ise
prom´is-er
prom´is-ing
prom´is-so-ry
prom´on-to-ry
pro-mote´
pro-mot´er
pro-mot´ing
pro-mo´tion
pro-mo´tion-al
prompt
prompt´er
prompt´ly
prompt´ness
prom´ul-gate
prom-ul-ga´tion
pro´noun
pro-nounce´
pro-nounce´able
pro-nounced´
pro-nounce´ment
pro-nounc´ing
pro-nun-ci·a´tion
proof´read-er
prop-a-gan´da
prop´a-gate

prop-a-ga´tion
prop´a-ga-tive
pro-pelled´
pro-pel´ler
pro-pel´ling
pro-pen´si-ty
prop´er
prop´er-ly
prop´er-ties
prop´er-ty
proph´e-cies
proph´e-cy
  (prediction)
proph´e-sied
proph´e-si-er
proph´e-sy
  (predict)
proph´et
pro-phet´ic
pro-phet´i-cal
pro´phy-lac´tic
pro-pi´ti-ate
pro-pi´tious
pro-po´nent
pro-por´tion
pro-por´tion-al
pro-por´tion-ate
pro-por´tioned
pro-pos´al
pro-pose´
pro-pos´er
pro-pos´ing
prop-o-si´tion

pro-pri´e-tar·y
pro-pri´e-tor
pro-pri´e-ty
pro-pul´sion
pro-ra´ta
pro-rate´
pro-sa´ic
pro-scribe´
prose
pros´e-cute
pros´e-cu´tion
pros´e-cu-tor
pros´e-cu-to-ry
pros´e-lyte
pros´e-ly-tize
pros´pect
pro-spec´tive
pro-spec´tive-ly
pro-spec´tus
pros´per
pros-per´i-ty
pros´per-ous
pros´per-ous-ly
pros´the-sis
pros-thet´ic
pros´trate
pros´trat-ing
pros-tra´tion
pro-tect´
pro-tect´ing
pro-tect´ing-ly
pro-tec´tion
pro-tec´tive

pro-tec´tive-ly
pro-tec´tor
pro´té-gé´
pro´té-gée´
pro´tein
pro´test (n.)
pro-test´ (v.)
prot-es-ta´tion
pro-test´er
pro-test´ing
pro´to-col
pro´ton
pro-tract´ed
pro-trude´
pro-tru´sion
proud´ly
prov´a·ble
proved
prov´en
prov´en-der
prov´erb
pro-ver´bi·al
pro-vide´
pro-vid´ed
prov´i-dence
prov´i-dent
prov´i-den´tial
pro-vid´er
pro-vid´ing
pro-vin´cial
prov´ing
pro-vi´sion
prov-o-ca´tion

pro-voke´   psy-cho´sis   pul´pit
pro-vok´ing   psy-chot´ic   pulp´y
prow´ess   pto-maine´   pul-sa´tion
prowl´er   pu´ber-ty   pu´ver-i-za´tion
prox´ies   pu-bes´cence   pul´ver-ize
prox´y   pu-bes´cent   pum´mel
prude   pub´lic   punc´tu-al
pru´dence   pub-li-ca´tion   punc-tu-al´i-ty
pru´dent   pub´li-cist   punc´tu-ate
prud´er·y   pub-lic´i-ty   punc-tu-a´tion
prud´ish   pub´li-cize   punc´ture
prun´er   pub´lic-ly   punc´tured
prun´ing   pub´lic–spir´it-ed   punc´tur-ing
pru´ri-ence   pub´lish   pun´dit
pru´ri-ent   pub´lish-er   pun´gen-cy
pried   puck´er   pun´gent
pry´ing   puck´ered   pu´ni-ness
psalm´ist   puck´ish   pun´ish
psal´ter   pud´dle   pun´ish-a·ble
pseu´do   pud´dling   pun´ish-ment
pso-ri´a-sis   pudg´i-ness   pu´ni-tive
pso-ro´sis   pudg´y   punned
psy´che   puff´i-ness   pun´ning
psy-chi-at´ric   puff´y   pun´ster
psy-chi´a-trist   pu´gi-lism   pu´ny
psy-chi´a-try   pu´gi-list   pu´pil
psy´chic   pug-na´cious   pup´pet
psy-cho-anal´y-sis pug-na´cious-ly   pup´pe-teer´
psy-cho-an´a-lyze   pul´chri-tude   pup´py
psy´cho-log´i-cal   pul´ley   pur´chase
psy-chol´o-gist   pull´ing   pur´chased
psy-chol´o-gy   pul´mo-nary   pur´chas-er
psy´cho-path´ic   pulp´i-ness   pur´chas-ing

pure´ly
pur´ga-to-ry
purge
purg´er
purg´ing
pu-ri-fi-ca´tion
pu´ri-fi-er
pu´ri-fy
pur´ist
pu-ri-tan´i-cal
pu´ri-ty
pur-loin´
pur-port´
pur´pose
pur´pose-ful
pur´pose-ly
pur-su´ant
pur-sue´
pur-sued´
pur-su´er
pur-su´ing
pur-suit´
push´er
push´ing
push´over
pu´sil-lan´i-mous
puz´zle
puz´zle-ment
puz´zler
puz´zling
pyr´a-mid

Q

quack´ery
quack´ish
quack´ish-ly
quack´ish-ness
quad
quad´ded
quad´ran-gle
quad-ran´gu-lar
quad´rant
quad-ra-phon´ic
quad-ra-phon´ics
qua-draph´o-ny
qua-drat´ic
qua-dren´ni-al
qua-dren´ni-al-ly
qua-dren´ni-um
quad´ric
quad-ri-cen-
  ten´ni-al
quad´ri-ceps
quad´ri-cip´i-tal
quad´ri-lat´er-al
quad´ri-lat´er-al-
  ly
quad´ri-lin´gual
qua-drille´
qua-dril´lion
qua-dril´lionth
quad-ri-phon´ic
quad-ri-phon´ics
quad´ru-ped
quad´ru-pe-dal

quad-ru´ple
quad-ru´ple-ness
quad-ru´ply
quad-rup´let
quad´ru-plex
qua-dru´pli-cate
quad-ru´pling
quads
quaff
quaffed
quag´gy
quag´mire
quag´mir-y
qua´hog
quail
quaint
quaint´ly
quaint´ness
quake
quaked
quake´proof
quak´i-ly
quak´i-ness
quak´ing
quak´ing-ly
quak´y
qua´le
qual-i-fi-ca´tion
qual´i-fi-ca-to-ry
qual´i-fied
qual´i-fied-ly
qual´i-fied-ness
qual´i-fi-er

qual´i-fy
qual´i-fy-ing
qual´i-fy-ing-ly
qual´i-ta-tive
qual´i-ta-tive-ly
qual´i-ty
qualm
qualm´ish
qualm´ish-ly
qualm´ish-ness
quan´da-ry
quan´tic
quan´ti-fi-a-ble
quan´ti-fi-a-bly
quan-ti-fi-ca´tion
quan´ti-fi-er
quan´ti-fy
quan´tile
quan-tim´e-ter
quan´ti-tate
quan´ti-ta-tive
quan´ti-ta-tive-ly
quan´ti-ta-tive-
  ness
quan´ti-ty
quan-ti-za´tion
quan´tum
quar´an-tin-a-ble
quar´an-tine
quar´an-tin-er
quark
quar´rel
quar´reled

quar´rel-ing
quar´rel-ing-ly
quar´rel-some
quar´rel-some-ly
quar´rel-some-
  ness
quar´ri-er
quar´ry
quart
quar´tan
quar´ter
quar´ter-age
quar´ter-back
quar´ter-deck
quar´tered
quar-ter-fi´nal
quar´ter–hour´
quar´ter-ing
quar´ter-ly
quar´ter-mas-ter
quar´tern
quar´ter-staff
quar-tet´
quar´tic
quar´tile
quar´to
quar´tos
quarts
quartz
quartz-if´er-ous
quartz´ite
quartz-it´ic
quartz´ose

qua´sar
quash
qua´si
qua-si-crys´tal
qua-si–ju-di´cial
qua-si-par´ti-cle
quas´sia
qua´train
qua´tre
qua´ver
qua´vered
qua´ver-er
qua´ver-ing
qua´ver-ing-ly
qua´ver-y
quay
quay´age
quea´si-ly
quea´si-ness
quea´sy
queen´dom
queen´hood
queen´like
queen´li-ness
queen´ly
queen´–size
queer´ly
queer´ness
quell
quelled
quell´er
quench
quench´a·ble

quenched
quench´er
quench´less
que-nelle´
que´ried
que´rist
quer´u-lous
quer´u-lous-ly
quer´u-lous-ness
que´ri-er
que´ry
que´ry-ing
que´ry-ing-ly
que-sa-dil´la
quest
quest´er
quest´ing-ly
ques´tion
ques-tion-a-bil´i-
  ty
ques´tion-a-ble
ques´tion-a-ble-
  ness
ques´tion-a-bly
ques´tion-ar-y
ques´tion-er
ques´tion-ing
ques´tion-ing-ly
ques´tion-less
ques´tion-less-ly
ques´tion-naire´
quet-zal´
queue

queu´ing
quib´ble
quib´bled
quib´bler
quib´bling
quiche
quick
quick´en
quick´en-er
quick´en-ing
quick´–freeze´
quick´ie
quick´lime
quick´ly
quick´ness
quick´sand
quick´sand-y
quick´–set´ting
quick´sil-ver
quick´sil-ver-y
quick´step
quick´–tem´pered
quick´–wit´ted
quick´–wit´ted-ly
quick´–wit´ted-
  ness
quid
quid´di-ty
quid´nunc
qui-es´cence
qui-es´cen-cy
qui-es´cent
qui-es´cent-ly

qui´et
qui´et-ism
qui´et-ist
qui-et-is´tic
qui´et-ly
qui´et-ness
qui´e-tude
qui-e´tus
quill
quilt
quilt´ed
quilt´ing
quince
qui-nel´la
qui´nine
qui-nin´ic
quin´sy
quin´tain
quin´tal
quin´tant
quin-tes´sence
quin-tes-sen´tial
quin-tes-sen´tial-
  ly
quin-tet´
quint-tile
quin-til´lion
quin-til´lionth
quin-tu´ple
quin-tup´let
quip
quipped
quip´ping

quip´ster
quirk
quirk´i-ly
quirk´i-ness
quirk´y
quirt
quit
quit´claim
quite
quit´tance
quits
quit´ted
quit´ter
quit´ting
quit´tor
quiv´er
quiv´ered
quiv´er-er
quiv´er-ing
quiv´er-ing-ly
quiv´er-y
quix-ot´ic
quix-ot´i-cal-ly
quix´o-tism
quiz
quiz´mas-ter
quizzed
quiz´zi-cal
quiz-zi-cal´i-ty
quiz´zi-cal-ly
quiz´zing
quoin
quoit

quon´dam
quo´rum
quo´ta
quot-a-bil´i-ty
quot´a-ble
quot´a-bly
quo-ta´tion
quote
quot´ed
quot´er
quoth
quo-tid´i-an
quo´tient
quot´ing

R

rab´bet
rab´bet-ed
rab´bi
rab´bin-ate
rab-bin´ic
rab-bin´i-cal
rab´bin-ism
rab´bit
rab´bit-ry
rab´ble
rab´ble-ment
rab´bler
rab´ble–rous-er
rab´ble–rous-ing
rab´id
ra-bid´i-ty
rab´id-ly

rab´id-ness
ra´bies
rac-coon´
race
race´course
race´horse
rac´er
race´track
race´way
ra´cial
ra´cial-ism
ra´cial-ly
rac´i-ly
rac´ing
rac´ism
rac´ist
rack
rack´er
rack´et
rack´e-teer´
rack´ety
rack´ing-ly
rack´–rent
rac´i-ly
rac´i-ness
ra´con
rac´on-teur
rac´quet
rac´y
rad
ra´dar
ra´dar-scope
ra´di-al

ra´di-al-ly
ra´di-an
ra´di-ance
ra´di-an-cy
ra´di-ant
ra´di-ant-ly
ra´di-ate
ra-di-a´tion
ra-di-a´tion-al
ra´di-a-tive
ra´di-a-tor
rad´i-cal
rad´i-cal-ism
rad-i-cal-i-za´tion
rad´i-cal-ize
rad´i-cal-ly
ra´di·i
ra´di·o
ra-di·o-ac´tive
ra-di·o-ac´tive-ly
ra´di·o-ac-tiv´i-ty
ra´di·o-broad-cast
ra-di·o-car´bon
ra´di·o-cast
ra´dio-gram
ra´dio-graph
ra-di·og´ra-pher
ra-di·o-graph´ic
ra-di·o-graph´i-
   cal-ly
ra-di·og´ra-phy
ra´di·o-i´so-tope
ra-di·o-lo-ca´tion

ra-di·o-log´i-cal
ra-di-ol´o-gist
ra-di-ol´o-gy
ra-di·o-lu´cent
ra-di-om´e-ter
ra-di-o´paque´
ra´di·o-phone
ra-di·o-scop´ic
ra-di·o-scop´i-cal
ra-di-os´co-py
ra-di·o-sen´si-tive
ra-di·o-sen-si-
   tiv´i-ty
ra´di·o-tel´e-gram
ra´di·o-tel´e-
   graph
ra-di·o-te-leg´ra-
   phy
ra-di·o-tel´e-
   phone
ra-di·o-te-leph´o-
   ny
ra-di·o-ther´a-pist
ra-di·o-ther´a-py
ra´di-um
ra´di-us
ra´don
raf´fia
raff´ish
raff´ish-ly
raff´ish-ness
raf´fle
raf´fled

raf´fling
raft
raf´ter (timber)
raft´er (boatman)
rafts´man
rag
rag´a-muf-fin
rag´ged
rag´ged-ly
rag´ged-ness
rag´ged-y
rag´ing
rag´gle–tag´gle
rag´man
ra-gout´
rag´pick-er
rag´time
raid
raid´er
rail
rail´er
rail´head
rail´ing
rail´lery
rail´road
rail´road-ing
rail´–split-ter
rail´way
rai´ment
rain´bow
rain´coat
rain´drop
rain´fall

rain´i-er
rain´mak-er
rain´mak-ing
rain´proof
rain´squall
rain´storm
rain´wa´ter
rain´wear
rain´y
raise
raised
rais´er
rai´sin
rais´ing
rai-son´
rake
raked
rake´–off
rak´er
rak´ing
rak´ish
rak´ish-ly
rak´ish-ness
ral´lied
ral´ly
ram
ram´ble
ram´bler
ram´bling
ram´bling-ly
ram´bling-ness
ram-bunc´tious
ram-bunc´tious-ly

ram-bunc´tious-
  ness
ram´e-kin
ra´men
ram-i-fi-ca´tion
ram´i-fied
ram´i-form
ram´i-fy
ram´i-fy-ing
ram´jet
rammed
ram´ming
ramp
ram´page
ram-pa´geous
ram-pa´geous-ly
ram-pa´geous-
  ness
ram´pag-er
ram´pag-ing
ramp´an-cy
ram´pant
ram´pant-ly
ram´part
ram´rod
ram´shack-le
ram´shack-le-ness
ranch
ranch´er
ran-che´ro
ranch´man
ran´cid
ran-cid´i-ty

ran´cid-ly
ran´cid-ness
ran´cor
ran´cor-ous
ran´cor-ous-ly
ran´cor-ous-ness
rand´i-ness
ran´dom
ran´dom–ac´cess
ran-dom-i-za´tion
ran´dom-ize
ran´dom-iz-er
ran´dom-ly
ran´dom-ness
rand´y
range
ranged
rang´er
rang´i-ness
rang´ing
rang´y
rank
rank´er
rank´ing
rank´ish
ran´kle
ran´kled
ran´kling
ran´kling-ly
rank´ly
rank´ness
ran´sack
ran´som

ran´som-er
rant
rant´er
rant´ing
rant´ing-ly
ra-pa´cious
ra-pa´cious-ly
ra-pa´cious-ness
ra-pac´i-ty
rape
rap´id
rap´id–fire
ra-pid´i-ty
rap´id-ly
ra´pier
rap´ine
rap´ist
rapped
rap-pel´
rap´per
rap´ping
rap-port´
rap-proche-ment´
rap-scal´lion
rapt
rapt´ly
rapt´ness
rap-to´ri-al
rap´ture
rap´tur-ous
rap´tur-ous-ly
rap´tur-ous-ness
rare

rare´bit
rar´e-fied
rar´e-fy
rare´ly
rare´ness
rar´ing
rar´i-ty
ras´cal
ras-cal´i-ty
ras´cal-ly
rash
rash´er
rash´like
rash´ly
rash´ness
rasp
rasp´ber-ry
rasp´er
rasp´i-ness
rasp´ing
rasp´ing-ly
rasp´ing-ness
rasp´ish
rasp´y
ras´ter
rat´a-ble
rat´a-bly
ra-ta-touille´
ratch´et
rate
rat´er
rath´er
raths´kel-ler

rat-i-fi-ca´tion
rat´i-fied
rat´i-fy
rat´i-fy-ing
rat´ing
ra´tio
ra´tion
ra´tion-al
ra´tion-al-ly
ra´tion-al-ness
ra´tio-nale´
ra´tio-nal-ism
ra´tio-nal-ist
ra-tio-nal-is´tic
ra-tio-nal´i-ty
ra-tio-nal-i-za´tion
ra´tio-nal-ize
ra´tio-nal-ly
rat´ite
rat´line
rat-tan´
rat´tle
rat´tle-brained
rat´tler
rat´tle-trap
rat´tling
rat´tly
rat´ty
rau´cous
rau´cous-ly
rau´cous-ness
raunch
raun´chi-ly

raun´chi-ness	reach´a-ble	read´y–mix
raun´chy	reach´er	read´y-to-wear´
rav´age	re-act´	re-af-firm´
rav´age-ment	re-ac´tance	re-a´gent
rav´ag-er	re-ac´tant	re´al-ism
rav´ag-ing	re-ac´tion	re´al-ist
rave	re-ac´tion-al	re´al-is´tic
rav´el	re-ac´tion-ar-y	re-al-is´ti-cal-ly
rav´eled	re-ac´ti-vate	re-al´i-ty
rav´el-er	re-ac-ti-va´tion	re´al-iza´tion
rav´el-ment	re-ac´tive	re´al-ize
rav´el-ing	re-ac´tive-ly	re´al–life
rav´en-ous	re-ac´tive-ness	re´al-ly
rav´en-ous-ly	re-ac´tor	realm
rav´en-ous-ness	read	re´al-ness
ra-vine´	read-a-bil´i-ty	re-al´po-li-tik
rav´ing	read´a-ble	re´al-tor
rav´ing-ly	read´a-ble-ness	re´al-ty
rav-i-o´li	read´a-bly	ream´er
rav´ish	re-ad-dress´	re-an´i-mate
rav´ish-er	read´er	re-an-i-ma´tion
rav´ish-ing	read´er-ship	reap
rav´ish-ing-ly	read´i-ly	reap´er
raw´boned´	read´i-ness	re-ap-pear´
raw´hide	read´ing	re-ap-pear´ance
raw´ly	re-ad-just´	re-ap-point´
raw´ness	re-ad-just´a-ble	re-ap-por´tion
ray	re-ad-just´er	re-ap-por´tion-
ray´on	re-ad-just´ment	ment
raze	read´–on´ly	rear
ra´zor	read´out	rear´–end´
ra´zor-back	read´y	re-arm´
raz´zle–daz-zle	read´y–made	re-ar´ma-ment

rear′most
re-ar-range′
re-ar-range′ment
re-ar-rang′ing
rear′ward
rea′son
rea′son-a-ble
rea′son-a-ble-ness
rea′son-a-bly
rea′son-er
rea′son-ing
re-as-sem′ble
re-as-sert′
re-as-sume′
re-as-sur′ance
re′as-sure′
re-as-sur′ing
re-as-sur′ing-ly
re-awak′en
re′bar
re′bate
re′bat-er
reb′el (n., adj.)
re-bel′ (v.)
re-belled′
re-bel′ling
re-bel′lion
re-bel′lious
re-bel′lious-ly
re-bel′lious-ness
re′birth′
re′born′
re-bound′

re-broad′cast
re-buff′
re-build′
re-built′
re-buke′
re-buk′ing
re′bus
re-but′
re-but′ta-ble
re-but′tal
re-but′ted
re-but′ter
re-but′ting
re-cal′ci-tran-cy
re-cal′ci-trance
re-cal′ci-trant
re-call′ (v., n.)
re′call (n.)
re-call′a-ble
re-cant′
re′cap
re-cap-i-tal-i-za′-
    tion
re-cap′i-tal-ize
re-ca-pit′u-late
re-ca-pit-u-la′tion
re-ca-pit′u-la-tive
re-ca-pit′u-la-to-
    ry
re-cap′pa-ble
re′capped′
re′cap′ping
re′cap′ture

re-cast′
re-cede′
re-ced′ed
re-ced′er
re-ced′ing
re-ceipt′
re-ceiv′a-ble
re-ceive′
re-ceived′
re-ceiv′er
re-ceiv′er-ship
re-ceiv′ing
re′cent
re′cent-ly
re′cent-ness
re-cep′ta-cle
re-cep′tion
re-cep′tion-ist
re-cep′tive
re-cep′tive-ly
re-cep′tive-ness
re-cep-tiv′i-ty
re-cep′tor
re′cess
re′cess′er
re-ces′sion
re-ces′sion-al
re-ces′sion-ar-y
re-ces′sive
re-ces′sive-ly
re-ces′sive-ness
re-charge′
re-charge′a-ble

re-charge´er
re-cid´i-vism
re-cid´i-vist
re-cid-i-vis´tic
re-cid´i-vous
rec´i-pe
re-cip´i-ence
re-cip´i-ent
re-cip´ro-cal
re-cip-ro-cal´i-ty
re-cip´ro-cal-ly
re-cip´ro-cal-ness
re-cip´ro-cate
re-cip-ro-ca´tion
re-cip´ro-ca-tive
re-cip´ro-ca-tor
re-cip´ro-ca-to-ry
rec-i-proc´i-ty
re-ci´sion
re-cit´a-ble
re-cit´al
rec-i-ta´tion
rec´i-ta-tive´
re-cite´
re-cit´er
re-cit´ing
reck´less
reck´less-ly
reck´less-ness
reck´on
reck´on-a-ble
reck´on-er
reck´on-ing

re-claim
re-claim´able
rec-la-ma´tion
re-clas-si-fi-ca´-
   tion
re-clas´si-fy
re-clin´able
re-cline´
re-clin´er
re-clin´ing
re-clos´a-ble
rec´luse
re-clu´sive
rec-og-ni´tion
re-cog´ni-tive
re-cog´ni-to-ry
rec´og-niz-a-ble
rec´og-niz-a-bly
re-cog´ni-zance
rec´og-nize
rec´og-niz-er
re-coil´ *(react)*
re–coil´ *(to wind)*
re-coil´ing-ly
re-coil´less
rec-ol-lect´ *(recall)*
re–col-lect´
   (amass)
rec-ol-lect´ed
rec-ol-lect´ed-ly
rec-ol-lect´ed-ness
rec-ol-lec´tion
re´com-bine´

re-com-mence´
rec-om-mend´
rec-om-mend´a-
   ble
rec-om-men-da´-
   tion
rec-om-mend´er
re-com-mit´
re-com-mit´tal
re-com-mit´ment
rec´om-pen-sa·ble
rec´om-pense
rec´om-pens-er
rec´om-pens-ing
re-con´
re-con´cen-trate
rec-on-cil-a-bil´i-
   ty
rec´on-cil-a-ble
rec´on-cil-a-ble-
   ness
rec´on-cil-a-bly
rec´on-cile
rec´on-cile-ment
rec´on-cil-er
rec-on-cil-i-a´tion
rec´on-cil´ia-to-ry
rec´on-cil-ing
rec´on-dite
rec´on-dite-ly
rec´on-dite-ness
re-con-di´tion
re-con´nais-sance

re-con-noi´ter
re-con-sid´er
re-con-sid´er-a´-
 tion
re-con´sti-tute
re-con´sti-tut-
 a·ble
re-con´sti-tut-i·ble
re-con-sti-tu´tion
re-con-struct´
re-con-struct´er
re-con-struct´i·ble
re-con-struc´tion
re-con-struc´tion-
 al
re-con-struc´tor
re-cord´ *(v.)*
rec´ord *(n., adj.)*
re-cord´able
re-cord´er
rec´ord–hold-er
re-cord´ing
re-count´
re-coup´
re-coup´a·ble
re-coup´ment
re´course
re-cov´er
re-cov´er-a·ble
re-cov´ery
rec´re-ance
rec´re-an·cy
rec´re-ant

rec´re-ant-ly
rec´re-ate *(to play)*
re–cre-ate´ *(to do
 over)*
rec-re-a´tion
rec-re-a´tion-al
re–cre-a´tive
rec´re-a-tive
re-crim´i-nate
re-crim´i-nat-ing
re-crim-i-na´tion
re-crim´i-na-tive
re-crim´i-na-tor
re-crim´i-na-to-ry
re-cru-desce´
re-cru-des´cence
re-cru-des´cent
re-cruit´
re-cruit´a-ble
re-cruit´er
re-cruit´ment
rec´tal-ly
rec´tan-gle
rec-tan´gu-lar
rec-tan-gu-lar´i-ty
rec´ti-fi-a·ble
rec-ti-fi-ca´tion
rec´ti-fied
rec´ti-fi-er
rec´ti-fy
rec´ti-tude
rec´to
rec´tor

rec´tor-ate
rec-to´ri-al
rec´to-ry
re-cum´bence
re-cum´ben-cy
re-cum´bent
re-cum´bent-ly
re-cu´per-ate
re-cu-per-a´tion
re-cu´per-a-tive
re-cur´
re-curred´
re-cur´rence
re-cur´rent
re-cur´rent-ly
re-cur´ring
re-cuse´
re-cy´cla·ble
re-cy´cle
re-dact´
re-dac´tion
re-dac´tor
red´–blood´ed
red´cap
red´den
red´dish
red´dish-ness
re-dec´o-rate
re-dec-o-ra´tion
re-deem´
re-deem´a-ble
re-deem´er
re-demp´ti-ble

re-demp´tion
re-demp´tion-al
re-demp´tive
re-demp´tor
re-demp´to-ry
re-de-ploy´
re-de-ploy´ment
red´–faced
red´–hand´ed
red´head
red´head-ed
red´–hot´
re-di-rect´
re-dis-cov´er
re-dis-cov´er-y
re-dis-trib´ute
re-dis-tri-bu´tion
re-dis´trict
red´–let´ter
red´ness
re-do´
red´o-lence
red´o-len-cy
red´o-lent
red´o-lent-ly
re-dou´ble
re-dou´bling
re-doubt´
re-doubt´a-ble
red´–pen´cil
re-draw´
re-dress´
re-dress´able

re-dress´er
re-duce´
re-duc´er
re-duc-i-bil´i-ty
re-duc´i-ble
re-duc´i-bly
re-duc´ing
re-duc´tion
re-duc´tion-al
re-duc´tion-ist
re-duc´tion-is´tic
re-duc´tive
re-duc´tive-ly
re-dun´dan-cy
re-dun´dant
re-dun´dant-ly
re-du´pli-cate
re-du-pli-ca´tion
re-du´pli-ca-tive
reed´i-ness
reed´ing
re-ed´u-cate
re-ed´u-ca-tive
reed´y
reef
reek
reel´a-ble
re-elect´
re-elec´tion
reel´er
reel´–to-reel´
re-em-bark´
re-en-act´

re-en-force´
re-en-force´ment
re-en-gage´
re´en-list´
re-en´ter
re-en´trant
re-en´try
re-es-tab´lish
re-es-tab´lish-
 ment
re-ex-am-i-na´tion
re-ex-am´ine
re-fas´ten
re-fer´
ref´er-ee´
ref´er-ence
ref-er-en´dum
ref-er´ent
ref-er-en´tial
re-fer´ral
re-ferred´
re-fer´ring
re´fill (n.)
re-fill´ (v.)
re-fill´a-ble
re-fi-nance´
re-fine´
re-fined´
re-fine-ment
re-fin´er
re-fin´ery
re-fin´ing
re-fin´ish

re-fit´
re-flect´
re-flec´tance
re-flect´i·ble
re-flec´tion
re-flec´tion-al
re-flec´tive
re-flec´tive-ly
re-flec´tive-ness
re-flec-tiv´i-ty
re-flec´tor
re´flex
re-flex´ive
re-flex´ive·ly
re-flex´ive-ness
re-flex-iv´i-ty
re-flex-ol´o-gist
re-flex-ol´o-gy
ref´lu-ent
re´flux
re-for-est-a´tion
re-form´ (amend)
re–form (remold)
re-form´a-ble
ref-or-ma´tion
  (improvement)
re–for-ma´tion
  (new mold)
re-for´ma-to-ry
re-formed´
re-form´er
re-form´ism
re-form´ist

re-for´mu-late
re-for-mu-la´tion
re-fract´
re-frac´tion
re-frac´tion-al
re-frac´tive
re-frac´tive·ly
re-frac´tive-ness
re-frac´tor
re-frac´to-ri-ness
re-frac´to-ry
re-frain´
re-fran-gi-bil´i·ty
re-fran´gi-ble
re-fran´gi-ble-ness
re-fresh´
re-fresh´ing
re-fresh´ing-ly
re-fresh´ment
re-frig´er-ant
re-frig´er-ate
re-frig´er-at-ing
re-frig-er-a´tion
re-frig´er-a-tor
re-fu´el
ref´uge
ref-u-gee´
re-ful´gence
re-ful´gen-cy
re-ful´gent
re-ful´gent-ly
re´fund (n.)
re-fund´ (v.)

re-fund´a-ble
re-fur´bish
re-fur´bish-ment
re-fur´nish
re-fus´a-ble
re-fus´al
re-fuse´ (decline)
ref´use (trash)
re–fuse´ (join)
re-fus´ing
re-fut´able
re-fut´ably
re-fute´
re-fut´er
re-fut´ing
re-gain´
re-gain´a-ble
re´gal
re-gale´
re-gale´ment
re-ga´lia
re´gal´ing
re´gal-ly
re´gal-ness
re-gard´
re-gard´ful
re-gard´ful-ly
re-gard´ing
re-gard´less
re-gard´less-ly
re´gen-cy
re-gen´er-a-ble
re-gen´er-a-cy

re-gen´er-ate
re-gen-er-a´tion
re-gen´er-a-tive
re-gen´er-a-tive-ly
re-gen´er-a-tor
re´gent
reg´gae
re-gime´
reg´i-men
reg´i-ment
reg´i-men´tal
reg´i-men´tal-ly
reg-i-men´ta-ry
reg-i-men-ta´tion
re´gion
re´gion-al
re´gion-al-ism
re-gion-al-is´tic
re´gion-al-ize
re´gion-al-ly
reg´is-ter
reg´is-tered
reg´is-tra-ble
reg´is-trant
reg´is-trar
reg´is-trate
reg-is-tra´tion
reg´is-try
re-gress´
re-gres´sion
re-gres´sive
re-gres´sive-ly
re-gres´sor

re-gret´
re-gret´ful
re-gret´ful-ly
re-gret´ful-ness
re-gret´ta-ble
re-gret´ta-ble-ness
re-gret´ta-bly
re-gret´ted
re-gret´ter
re-gret´ting
re-group´
reg´u-lar
reg-u-lar´i-ty
reg-u-lar-i-za´tion
reg´u-lar-ize
reg´u-lar-ly
reg´u-lat-able
reg´u-late
reg-u-la´tion
reg´u-la-tive
reg´u-la-tive-ly
reg´u-la-tor
reg´u-la-to-ry
re-gur´gi-tate
re-gur-gi-ta´tion
re´hab
re-ha-bil´i-tant
re-ha-bil´i-tate
re-ha-bi´i-ta´tion
re-ha-bil´i-ta-tive
re-ha-bil´i-ta-tor
re´hash´
re-hear´

re-hear´ing
re-hears´a·ble
re-hears´al
re-hearse´
re-hears´er
re-hears´ing
re-heat´
re-house´
re-hy´drate
re-hy-dra´tion
re-i-fi-ca´tion
re´i-fy
reign
re-im-burs´able
re-im-burse´
re-im-burse´ment
re-im-port´
re-im-por-ta´tion
re-in-car´nate
re-in-car-na´tion
re-in-dus-tri-al-i-
   za´tion
re-in-dus´tri-al-ize
re-in-force´
re-in-forced´
re-in-force´ment
reins
re-in-sert´
re-in-stall´
re-in-stal-la´tion
re-in-state´
re-in-state´ment
re-in-sur´ance

re-in-sure´
re-in´te-grate
re-in-te-gra´tion
re-in-vent´
re-in-vest´
re-in-vig´o-rate
re-is´su-a-ble
re-is´sue
re-it´er-a-ble
re-it´er-ate
re-it-er-a´tion
re-it´er-a-tive
re-it´er-a-tive-ly
re-ject´ (v.)
re´ject (n.)
re-ject´able
re-ject´er
re-jec´tion
re-jec´tive
re-jec´tor
re-joice´
re-joic´ing
re-joic´ing-ly
re-join´
re-join´der
re-ju´ve-nate
re-ju-ve-na´tion
re-ju´ve-na-tive
re-ju´ve-na-tor
re-ju-ve-nes´cence
re-kin´dle
re-lapse´
re-lapsed´

re-laps´ing
re-lat´a-ble
re-late´
re-lat´ed
re-lat´ed-ness
re-lat´er
re-lat´ing
re-la´tion
re-la´tion-al
re-la´tion-ship
rel´a-tive
rel´a-tive-ly
rel´a-tive-ness
rel´a-tiv-ism
rel´a-tiv-ist
rel-a-tiv-is´tic
rel-a-tiv´i-ty
re-la´tor
re-lax´
re-lax´ant
re-lax-a´tion
re-laxed´
re´lay (send on)
re–lay´ (lay again)
re´layed
re-lease´ (liberate)
re´–lease´ (rent
    anew)
re-leased´
re-leas´er
re-leas´ing
rel´e-gate
rel´e-gat-ed

rel-e-ga´tion
re-lent´
re-lent´ing
re-lent´ing-ly
re-lent´less
re-lent´less-ly
re-lent´less-ness
rel´e-vance
rel´e-van·cy
rel´e-vant
rel´e-vant·ly
re-li-a-bil´i·ty
re-li´a-ble
re-li´a-ble-ness
re-li´a-bly
re-li´ance
re-li´ant
re-li´ant·ly
rel´ic
re-lied´
re-lief´
re-liev´a·ble
re-lieve´
re-lieved´
re-liev´er
re-liev´ing
re-li´gion
re-li´gion-ism
re-li´gion-ist
re-li-gi-ose´
re-li-gi-os´i-ty
re-li´gious
re-li´gious-ly

re-li´gious-ness
re-lin´quish
re-lin´quish-er
re-lin´quish-ment
rel´ish-ing
re-live´
re-load´
re-lo´cat-a·ble
re-lo´cate
re-lo-ca´tion
re-lu´cent
re-luc´tance
re-luc´tant
re-luc´tant·ly
rel-uc-tiv´i·ty
re-lume´
re-ly´
re-ly´ing
re-made´
re-main´
re-main´der
re-main´ing
re-make´
re-mand´
re-mand´ment
re-mark´
re-mark´a·ble
re-mark´a·ble-
  ness
re-mark´a·bly
re-mar´riage
re-mar´ry
re´match

re-me´di-a-ble
re-me´di-a-ble-
  ness
re-me´di-a-bly
re-me´di-al
re-me´di-al-ly
re-me-di-a´tion
rem´e-died
rem´e-dies
rem´e-dy
re-mem´ber
re-mem´ber-a·ble
re-mem´brance
re-mem´branc-er
re-mind´
re-mind´er
rem-i-nisce´
rem-i-nis´cence
rem-i-nis´cent
rem-i-nis´cent-ly
rem-i-nis´cer
rem-i-nis´cing
re-miss´
re-miss-i-bil´i-ty
re-miss´i-ble
re-miss´i-ble-ness
re-mis´sion
re-mis´sive
re-mit´
re-mit´ta·ble
re-mit´tal
re-mit´tance
re-mit´ted

re-mit´tence
re-mit´ten-cy
re-mit´tent
re-mit´tent-ly
re-mit´ter
re-mit´ting
re-mix´
rem´nant
re-mod´el
re-mod´eled
re-mon-e-ti-za´-
  tion
re-mon´e-tize
re-mon´strance
re-mon´strant
re-mon´strate
re-mon´strat-ing-
  ly
re-mon-stra´tion
re-mon´stra-tive
re-mon´stra-tive-
  ly
re-mon´stra-tor
re-morse´
re-morse´ful
re-morse´ful-ly
re-morse´ful-ness
re-morse´less
re-morse´less-ly
re-morse´less-ness
re-mote´
re-mote´ly
re-mote´ness

re-mot´est
ré-mou-lade´
re-mount´
re-mov´a-ble
re-mov´a-ble-ness
re-mov´a-bly
re-mov´al
re-move´
re-moved´
re-mov´ed-ly
re-mov´ed-ness
re-mov´er
re-mov´ing
re-mu´da
re-mu-ner-a-bil´i-
 ty
re-mu´ner-a-ble
re-mu´ner-a-bly
re-mu´ner-ate
re-mu-ner-a´tion
re-mu´ner-a-tive
re-mu´ner-a-tive-
 ly
re-mu´ner-a-tive-
 ness
re-mu´ner-a-tor
ren´ais-sance´
re-name´
rend
ren´der
ren´der-a-ble
ren´dez-vous
ren-di´tion

ren´e-gade
re-nege´
re-neg´er
re-neg´ing
re-ne-go´ti-ate
re-ne-go-ti-a´tion
re-new´
re-new-a-bil´i-ty
re-new´a-ble
re-new´al
re-newed´
ren´net
ren´nin
re-nom´i-nate
re-nom-i-na´tion
re-nounce´
re-nounce´a-ble
re-nounce´ment
re-nounc´ing
ren´o-vat-a-ble
ren´o-vate
ren´o-vat-ing
ren-o-va´tion
ren´o-va-tor
re-nown´
re-nowned´
rent´a-ble
rent´–a–car
rent´al
rent´er
rent´–free´
rent´ing
re-nun-ci-a´tion

re-nun´ci-a-tive
re-nun´ci-a-to·ry
re-oc´cu-py
re-o´pen
re-or-ga-ni-za´-
 tion
re-or´ga-nize
re-pack´age
re-paid´
re-paint´
re-pair´
re-pair-a-bil´i-ty
re-pair´a-ble
re-pair´er
re-pair´man
rep´a-ra·ble
rep´a-ra·bly
rep-a-ra´tion
re-par´a-tive
re-par´a-to·ry
re-par-ti´tion
re-past´
re-pa´tri-ate
re-pa-tri-a´tion
re-pay´
re-pay´a·ble
re-pay´ing
re-pay´ment
re-peal´
re-peal´a·ble
re-peal´er
re-peat´
re-peat-a-bil´i·ty

re-peat´a·ble
re-peat´ed
re-peat´ed-ly
re-peat´er
re-pel´
re-pelled´
re-pel´lence
re-pel´len·cy
re-pel´lent
re-pel´lent·ly
re-pel´ling
re-pent´
re-pent´ance
re-pent´ant
re-pent´ant-ly
re-pent´ing-ly
re-peo´ple
re-per-cus´sion
re-per-cus´sive
rep´er-toire
rep-er-to´ri-al
rep´er-to-ry
rep-e-ti´tion
rep´e-ti´tious
rep-e-ti´tious-ly
rep´e-ti´tious-ness
re-pet´i-tive
re-pet´i-tive-ly
re-pet´i-tive-ness
re-phrase´
re-place´
re-place´able
re-place´ment

re-plac´ing
re-plant´
re´play (n.)
re-play´ (v.)
re-plen´ish
re-plen´ish-er
re-plen´ish-ment
re-plete´
re-plete´ness
re-ple´tion
rep´li-ca
rep´li-cate
rep-li-ca´tion
rep´li-ca-tive
re-plied´
re-ply´
re-ply´ing
re´po
re-port´
re-port´a·ble
re-port´age
re-port´ed·ly
re-port´er
rep-or-to´ri-al
rep-or-to´ri-al-ly
re-pose´
re-pos´er
re-pose´ful
re-pose´ful-ly
re-pose´ful-ness
re-pos´ing
re-pos´it
re-po-si´tion

re-pos´i-to·ry
re-pos-sess´
re-pos-sess´a·ble
re-pos-ses´sion
rep-re-hend´
rep-re-hend´a·ble
rep-re-hend´er
rep-re-hen-si-bil´-
  i·ty
rep-re-hen´si·ble
rep-re-hen´si·ble-
  ness
rep-re-hen´si·bly
rep-re-hen´sion
rep-re-sent´
rep-re-sent-a-bil´-
  i·ty
rep-re-sent´a·ble
rep-re-sen-ta´tion
rep-re-sen-ta´tion-
  al
rep-re-sen-ta´tion-
  al-ism
rep-re-sent´a-tive
rep-re-sent´a-tive-
  ly
rep-re-sent´a-tive-
  ness
rep-re-sent´er
re-press´
re-pressed´
re-press´er
re-press´i·ble

re·pres´sion
re·pres´sive
re·pres´sive-ly
re·pres´sive-ness
re·pres´sor
re·prieve´
rep´ri-mand
rep´ri-mand-er
rep´ri-mand-ing-
  ly
re·print´ *(v.)*
re´print *(n.)*
re·pri´sal
re·prise´
re·proach´
re·proach´a·ble
re·proach´a·ble-
  ness
re·proach´a·bly
re·proach´ful
re·proach´ful-ly
re·proach´ful-ness
re·proach´ing
re·proach´ing-ly
rep´ro-bate
rep-ro-ba´tion
re´pro-duce´
re´pro-duc´er
re·pro-duc´i·ble
re·pro-duc-i-bil´-
  i·ty
re´pro-duc´ing
re-pro-duc´tion

re-pro-duc´tive
re-pro-duc´tive-ly
re-pro-duc´tive-
  ness
re·proof´
re·prov´a·ble
re·prov´a·ble-ness
re·prov´al
re·prove´
re·prov´ing
re·prov´ing-ly
rep´tile
rep-til´i·an
re·pub´lic
re·pub´li-can
re·pub´li-can-ism
re·pub-li-can-i-
  za´tion
re·pub´li-can-ize
re-pub-li-ca´tion
re·pub´lish
re·pu´di-ate
re·pu-di-a´tion
re·pu´di·a-tive
re·pu´di·a-tor
re·pu´di·a-to·ry
re·pugn´
re·pug´nance
re·pug´nan-cy
re·pug´nant
re·pug´nant-ly
re·pulse´
re·puls´ing

re·pul´sion
re·pul´sive
re·pul´sive-ly
re·pul´sive-ness
re·pur´chase
rep-u-ta-bil´i·ty
rep´u-ta·ble
rep´u-ta·ble-ness
rep´u-ta·bly
rep-u-ta´tion
re·pute´
re·put´ed
re·put´ed-ly
re·put´ing
re·quest´
re·quest´er
req´ui-em
re·quir´a·ble
re·quire´
re·quire´ment
re·quir´er
re·quir´ing
req´ui-site
req´ui-site-ly
req´ui-site-ness
req-ui-si´tion
req-ui-si´tion-ar·y
req-ui-si´tion-er
re·quit´a·ble
re·quit´al
re·quite´
re·quit´ed
re·quite´ment

re-quit´ing
re-read´
re´–re-cord´
re-re-lease´
re-run´
re-sal´a·ble
re´sale
re-scale´
re-sched´ule
re-scind´
re-scind´a·ble
re-scind´ment
re-scis´si-ble
re-scis´sion
re-scis´so·ry
re´script
res´cu-a·ble
res´cue
rea´cued
res´cu-er
res´cu-ing
re-search´
re-search´a·ble
re-search´er
re-search´ist
re-seat´
re-sect´
re-sect-a-bil´i·ty
re-sect´a·ble
re-sec´tion
re-sell´
re-sem´blance
re-sem´blant

re-sem´ble
re-sem´bler
re-sem´bling
re-sem´bling-ly
re-sent´
re-sent´ful
re-sent´ful-ly
re-sent´ful-ness
re-sent´ing-ly
re-sent´ment
re-serv´a·ble
res-er-va´tion
re-serve´
re-served
re-serv´ed-ly
re-serv´ed-ness
re-serv´ist
res´er-voir
re-set´
re-set´ting
re-set´tle-ment
re-ship´
re-ship´ment
re-side´
res´i-dence
res´i-den-cy
res´i-dent
res´i-den´tial
res-i-den´ti-ar·y
re-sid´ing
re-sid´u-al
re-sid´u-al-ly
re-sid´u-ar·y

res´i-due
re-sid´u-um
re-sign´
res-ig-na´tion
re-signed´
re-sign´ed-ly
re-sign´ed-ness
re-sil´ience
re-sil´ien-cy
re-sil´ient
re-sil´ient-ly
res´in
res´in-ous
re-sist´
re-sist´ance
re-sist´ant
re-sist´ant-ly
re-sist´er
re-sist-i-bil´i·ty
re-sist´i·ble
re-sist´i-ble-ness
re-sist´i·bly
re-sist´ing-ly
re-sis´tive
re-sis´tive-ly
re-sis´tive-ness
re-sis-tiv´i·ty
re-sis´tor
re-sold´
re-sole´
re-sol-u-bil´i·ty
re-sol´u·ble
re-sol´u·ble-ness

res´o-lute
res´o-lute-ly
res´o-lute-ness
res-o-lu´tion
re-solv´a·ble
re-solve´
re-solved´
re-solv´ed-ly
re-solv´ed-ness
re-solv´er
re-solv´ing
res´o-nance
res´o-nant
res´o-nant-ly
res´o-nate
res-o-na´tion
res´o-na-tor
re-sorb´
re-sorb´ent
re-sorp´tive
re-sort´
re-sound´
re-sound´ed
re-sound´ing
re-sound´ing-ly
re´source
re-source´ful
re-source´ful-ly
re-source´ful-ness
re-spect´
re-spect-a·bil´i·ty
re-spect´a·ble
re-spect´a·ble-ness

re-spect´a·bly
re-spect´er
re-spect´ful
re-spect´ful-ly
re-spect´ful-ness
re-spect´ing
re-spec´tive
re-spec´tive-ness
re-spell´
res´pi-ra·ble
res-pi-ra´tion
res-pi-ra´tion-al
res´pi-ra-tor
res´pi-ra-to·ry
re-spire´
re-spir´ing
res´pite
re-splen´dence
re-splen´den·cy
re-splen´dent
re-splen´dent-ly
re-spond´
re-spon´dence
re-spon´den-cy
re-spon´dent
re-spond´er
re-sponse´
re-spon-si-bil´i·ty
re-spon´si·ble
re-spon´si·ble-ness
re-spon´si·bly
re-spon´sive
re-spon´sive·ly

re-spon´sive-ness
re-spon-siv´i·ty
re-spon´sor
re-spon´so·ry
re´state´
res´tau-rant
res´tau-ra-teur´
rest´ful
rest´ful-ly
rest´ful-ness
rest´ing
res´ti-tute
res-ti-tu´tion
res´tive
res´tive-ly
res´tive-ness
rest´less
rest´less-ly
rest´less-ness
re´stock´
re-stor´a·ble
re-stor´a·ble-ness
re-stor´al
res-to-ra´tion
re-stor´a·tive
re-store´
re-stor´er
re-stor´ing
re-strain´
re-strain´a·ble
re-strained´
re-straint´
re-strict´

re-strict´ed
re-stric´tion
re-stric´tive
re-stric´tive-ly
re-stric´tive-ness
re-strike´
re-struc´ture
re-sult´
re-sult´ant
re-sum´a·ble
re-sume´ *(go on)*
ré´su-mé´
  (summary)
re-sum´ing
re-sump´tion
re-sur´face
re-surge´
re-sur´gence
re-sur´gent
res-ur-rect´
res-ur-rec´tion
res-ur-rec´tion-al
res-ur-rec´tion-ist
res-ur-rec´tor
re-sus´ci-ta·ble
re-sus´ci-tate
re-sus´ci-ta´tion
re-sus´ci-ta-tive
re-sus´ci-ta-tor
re´tail
re´tail-er
re-tain´
re-tain´a·ble

re-tain´er
re-tain´ing
re-take´
re-tal´i-ate
re-tal-i-a´tion
re-tal´i-a-tive
re-tal´i-a-tor
re-tal´i·a-to·ry
re-tard´
re-tard´ant
re-tar-da´tion
re-tard´ed
retch
re-tell´
re-ten´tion
re-ten´tive
re-ten´tive-ly
re-ten´tive-ness
re-ten-tiv´i-ty
re-ten´tor
re-think´
ret´i-cence
ret´i-cen-cy
ret´i-cent
ret´i-cent-ly
ret´i-na
ret´i-nal
ret-i-ni´tis
ret´i-nue
re-tire´
re-tired´
re-tir´ee´
re-tire´ment

re-tir´ing
re-tir´ing-ly
re-told´
re-tool´
re-tort´
re-touch´
re-trace´
re-trace´a·ble
re-trac´ing
re-tract´
re-tract-a-bil´i-ty
re-tract´a·ble
re-trac´tile
re-trac´tion
re-trac´tive
re-trac´tive-ly
re-trac´tive-ness
re-trac´tor
re´tread´
re-treat´
re-trench´
re-trench´ment
ret-ri-bu´tion
re-trib´u-tive
re-trib´u-tive-ly
re-trib´u-to-ry
re-triev-a-bil´i-ty
re-triev´a·ble
re-triev´al
re-trieve´
re-triev´er
re-triev´ing
ret-ro-ac´tive

ret-ro-ac′tive-ly
ret-ro-ac-tiv′i-ty
ret′ro-fit
ret′ro-grade
ret′ro-gress
ret-ro-gres′sion
ret-ro-gres′sive
ret-ro-gres′sive-ly
ret′ro-rock-et
ret′ro-spect
ret-ro-spec′tion
ret-ro-spec′tive
ret-ro-spec′tive-ly
re-turn′
re-turn′a·ble
re-turn·ee′
re-un′ion
re-u-nit′a·ble
re-u·nite′
re-u-nit′ing
re-used′
re-val′u-ate
re-val-u-a′tion
re-val′ue
re-vamp′
re-vamp′er
re-vamp′ment
re-veal′
re-veal′a·ble
re-veal′ing
re-veal′ing-ly
re-veal′ment
re-veg′e-tate

re-veg-e-ta′tion
rev′eil-le
rev′el
rev-e-la′tion
rev-e-la′tion-al
re-vel′a-to-ry
rev′eled
rev′el-er
rev′el-ing
rev′el-ment
rev′el-ry
re-venge′
re-venge′ful
re-venge′ful-ly
re-venge′ful-ness
re-veng′er
re-veng′ing
re-veng′ing-ly
rev′e-nue
re-ver′ber-ant
re-ver′ber-ant-ly
re-ver′ber-ate
re-ver-ber-a′tion
re-ver′ber-a-tive
re-ver′ber-a-tor
re-ver′ber-a-to-ry
re-vere′
rev′er-ence
rev′er-end
rev′er-ent
rev′er-en′tial
rev′er-ent-ly
rev′er-ie

re-ver′ing
re-ver′sal
re-verse′
re-verse′ly
re-vers′er
re-vers-i-bil′i-ty
re-vers′i·ble
re-vers′i·ble-ness
re-vers′i·bly
re-vers′ing
re-ver′sion
re-ver′sion-al
re-ver′sion-ar·y
re-vert′
re-vert′er
re-vert-i-bil′i-ty
re-vert′i·ble
re-vert′ment
re-view′
re-view′a·ble
re-view′er
re-vile′
re-vile′ment
re-vil′er
re-vil′ing
re-vil′ing-ly
re-vin′di-cate
re-vis′a·ble
re-vis′al
re-vise′
re-vised′
re-vis′er
re-vi′sion

re-vi´sion-al
re-vi´sion-ar-y
re-vi´sion-ism
re-vi´sion-ist
re-vis´it
re-vis-i-ta´tion
re-vis´er
re-vi´so-ry
re-vi-tal-i-za´tion
re-vi´tal-ize
re-viv-a·bil´i-ty
re-viv´a·ble
re-viv´a·bly
re-viv´al
re-viv´al-ism
re-viv´al-ist
re-viv-al-is´tic
re-vive´
re-viv´i-fy
re-viv´ing
rev-o-ca-bil´i-ty
rev´o-ca·ble
rev´o-ca·ble-ness
rev´o-ca·bly
rev-o-ca´tion
rev´o-ca-tive
rev´o-ca-to·ry
re-voice´
re-vok´a·ble
re-voke´
re-vok´er
re-vok´ing
re-volt´

re-volt´ing
re-volt´ing-ly
rev-o-lu´tion
rev´o-lu´tion-ar·y
rev-o-lu´tion-ist
rev-o-lu´tion-ize
re-volv´a·ble
re-volv´a·bly
re-volve´
re-volv´er
re-volv´ing
re-volv´ing–door´
re-vue´
re-vul´sion
re-vul´sion-ar·y
re-vul´sive
re-ward´
re-ward´a·ble
re-ward´ing
re-ward´ing-ly
re-wind´
re-wind´er
re-wir´a·ble
re-wire´
re-word´
re-write´ *(v.)*
re´write *(n.)*
re-zone´
rhap-sod´ic
rhap-sod´i-cal
rhap-sod´i-cal-ly
rhap´so-dize
rhap´so-diz-ing

rhap´so-dy
rhe´o-stat
rhet´o-ric
rhe-tor´i-cal
rhe-tor´i-cal-ly
rhe-tor´i-cal-ness
rhet-o-ri´cian
rheu-mat´ic
rheu´ma-tism
rhine´stone
rhi-ni´tis
rhi´no
rhi-noc´er-os
rhi-nol´o-gist
rhi-nol´o-gy
rhi´no-plas-ty
rhom´boid
rhom´bus
rhu´barb
rhyme
rhyme´ster
rhym´ing
rhythm
rhyth´mic
rhyth´mi-cal
rhyth´mi-cal-ly
rhyth´mics
rhyth´mist
rib´ald
rib´ald-ly
rib´al-dry
rib´and
ribbed

rib´bing
rib´bon
rib´boned
rib´bon-y
ri-bo-fla´vin
ri-bo-nu´cle-ase
ri´bo-nu-cle´ic
ri´bo-some
ric´er
rich´en
rich´es
rich´ly
rich´ness
rick
rick´et-i-ness
rick´ets
rick-ett´si-al
rick´et·y
rick´ey
ric´o-chet
ric´o-cheted
ri-cot´ta
rid´dance
rid´den
rid´der
rid´ding
rid´dle
rid´dled
ride´a·ble
rid´er
rid´er-less
rid´er-ship
ridge

ridge´pole
ridg´ing
ridg´y
rid´i-cule
ri-dic´u-lous
ri-dic´u-lous-ly
ri-dic´u-lous-ness
rid´ing
rife´ly
rife´ness
riff
rif´fle
rif´fling
riff´raff
ri´fle
ri´fle-man
ri´fle-ry
ri´fling
rig-a-to´ni
rigged
rig´ger
rig´ging
right´–an´gled
righ´teous
righ´teous-ly
righ´teous-ness
right´ful
right´ful-ly
right´ful-ness
right´–hand-ed
right´–hand-ed-ly
right´–hand-ed-
   ness

right´–hand-er
right´ist
right´ly
right´–mind-ed
right´ness
right´–of-way
right´–think´ing
right´–to–die´
right´–to–life´
right´–to–work´
right´ward
rig´id
ri-gid´i-ty
rig´id-ly
rig´id-ness
rig´ma-role
rig´or
rig´or-ism
rig´or-ist
rig-or-is´tic
rig´or-ous
rig´or-ous-ly
rig´or-ous-ness
rig´our (Br.)
rime
rim´fire
rim´less
rimmed
rim´ming
rim´y
rind
ring
ringed

ring´er
ring´ing
ring´ing-ly
ring´lead-er
ring´let
ring´mas-ter
ring´–necked
ring´side
ring´–tailed
ring´toss
rink´y–dink
rins´a·ble
rinse
rinsed
rins´er
rins´ing
ri´ot
ri´ot-er
ri´ot-ous
ri´ot-ous-ly
ri´ot-ous-ness
ripe´ly
rip´en
ripe´ness
rip´off
ripped
rip´per
rip´ping
rip´ple
rip´pled
rip´plet
rip´pling
rip´pling-ly

rip´ply
rip´–roar-ing
rip´saw
rip´snort´er
rise
ris´en
ris´er
ris´i·ble
ris´ing
risk
risk´i-ly
risk´i-ness
risk´less
risk´y
ri-sot´to
ris-qué´
rite
rit´u-al
rit´u-al-ism
rit´u-al-ist
rit´u-al-is´tic
rit´u-al-is´ti-cal-ly
rit´u-al-ize
rit-u-al-i-za´tion
rit´u-al-ly
ritz´i-ness
ritz´y
ri´val
ri´valed
ri´valing
ri´val-ly
ri´val-rous
ri´val-ry

rive
riv´en
riv´er
riv´er-bank
riv´er-bed
riv´er-boat
riv´er-side
riv´et
riv´et-er
riv´et-ing
riv´u-let
road´bed
road´block
road´house
road´ie
road´run-ner
road´side
road´ster
road´way
road´work
roam´er
roar´ing
roar´ing-ly
roast´a·ble
roast´ed
roast´er
rob
robbed
rob´ber
rob´ber·y
rob´bing
robe
rob´in

rob´ing
ro´bot
ro-bot´ics
ro´bot-ize
ro-bust´
ro-bus´tious
ro-bus´tious-ly
ro-bust´ly
ro-bust´ness
rock´–bot´tom
rock´er
rock´et
rock´e-teer´
rock´et-er
rock´et-ry
rock´ing
rock´ing-ly
rock´y
ro-co´co
ro´dent
ro´de-o
roe
roent´gen
roent-gen-og´ra-
  phy
roent-gen-ol´o-gy
rogue
rogu´er-y
rogu´ish
rogu´ish-ly
rogu´ish-ness
roil
rois´ter

rois´ter-er
rois´ter-ous
rois´ter-ous-ly
role´–play-ing
roll´a-way
roll´back
rolled
roll´er
rol´lick
rol´lick-ing
rol´lick-ing-ly
rol´lick-some
roll´ing
roll´mops
roll´–on
ro´ly–po´ly
ro-maine´
ro-mance´
ro-manc´er
ro-manc´ing
ro-man´tic
ro-man´ti-cal-ly
ro-man´ti-cism
ro-man´ti-cist
ro-man-ti-ci-za´-
  tion
ro-man´ti-cize
romp´er
romp´ing-ly
romp´ish
ron´do
roof´er
roof´ing

roof´less
roof´line
roof´top
rook´er·y
rook´ie
room´er
room-ette´
room´ful
room´ie
room´i-ly
room´i-ness
room´mate
room´y
roost´er
root´age
root´ed
root´ed-ness
root´er
root´less
root´less-ness
root´let
root´stock
root´y
rope
roped
rope´dance
rope´danc-er
rope´danc-ing
rope´mak-er
rope´mak-ing
rop´er
rop´i-ness
rop´y

ro´sa-ry
rose´bud
rose´bush
rose´–col-ored
rose´mar·y
ro-se´o-la
ro-sette´
rose´wood
ros´in
ros´i-ness
ros´ter
ros´trum
ros´y
ro´ta-ry
ro´tat-a·ble
ro´tate
ro-ta´tion
ro-ta´tion-al
ro´ta-tive
ro´ta-tive-ly
ro´ta-tor
rote
ro-tis´ser-ie
ro´to-gra-vure´
ro´to-till-er
rot´ten-ly
rot´ten-ness
rot´ter
rot´ting
ro-tund´
ro-tun´da
ro-tun´di-ty
ro-tund´ly

ro-tund´ness
rou·é´
rouge
rouged
rough
rough´age
rough´–and–
  read´y
rough´–and–
  tum´ble
rough´en
rough´en-er
rough´er
rough´house
rough´ish
rough´ly
rough´neck
rough´ness
rough´shod
roug´ing
rou-lade´
rou-lette´
round´a·bout
round´ed
round´ed-ly
round´ed-ness
round´er
round´house
round´ish
round´ly
round´ness
round´–shoul-
  dered

round´up (n.)
rouse
roused
rous´er
rous´ing
roust´a·bout
rout
route
rout´ed
rout´er
rou-tine´
rou-tine´ly
rou-tine´ness
rou-tin´ize
rout´ing
roux
rove
rov´er
rov´ing
row´boat
row´dies
row´di-ly
row´di-ness
row´dy
row´dy-ish
row´dy-ism
row´er
roy´al
roy´al-ist
roy´al-ly
roy´al-ty
rubbed
rub´ber

rub´ber-ize
rub´ber-neck
rub´ber-y
rub´bing
rub´bish
rub´bish-y
rub´ble
rub´bly
rub´down
rube
ru-be´o-la
ru´bric
ru´bri-cal
ru´bri-cate
ru-bri-ca´tion
ru´bri-ca-tor
ru´by
ruck´sack
ruck´us
rud´der
rud´di-ness
rud´dy
rude
rude´ly
rude´ness
rud´est
ru´di-ment
ru-di-men-ta´ri-ly
ru-di-men´ta-ri-
  ness
ru-di-men´ta-ry
rue´ful
rue´ful-ly

rue´ful-ness
ru-fes´cence
ru-fes´cent
ruff
ruffed
ruf´fi-an
ruf´fi-an-ly
ruf´fi-an-ism
ruf´fle
ruf´fled
ruf´fler
ruf´fling
rug
rug´ged
rug´ged-ly
rug´ged-ness
ru´in
ru´in-a·ble
ru´in-ate
ru-in-a´tion
ru´ined
ru´in-ing
ru´in-ous
ru´in-ous-ly
ru´in-ous-ness
rul´a·ble
rule
ruled
rul´er
rul´er-ship
rul´ing
rum
ru-ma´ki

rum´ble
rum´bler
rum´bling
rum´bling-ly
rum´bly
ru´mi-nant
ru´mi-nate
ru-mi-na´tion
ru´mi-na-tive
ru´mi-na-tive-ly
ru´mi-na-tor
rum´mage
rum´mag-er
rum´mag-ing
rum´my
ru´mor
ru´mor-mon-ger
rump
rump´er
rum´ple
rum´pled
rum´pling
rum´ply
rum´pus
rum´run-ner
run´a·bout
run´a·round
run´a·way
run´dle
run´–down´
rung
run´–in
run´ner

run´ner–up´
run´ning
run´ny
run´off
run´–of–the–mili´
runt
run´–through
runt´ish
runt´y
run´way
rup´tur-a·ble
rup´ture
rup´tured
rup´tur-ing
ru´ral
ru´ral-ism
ru´ral-ist
ru´ral-ite
ru-ral-i-za´tion
ru´ral-ize
ru´ral-ly
ru´ral-ness
rush´ing
rus´set
rust
rus´tic
rus´ti-cal-ly
rus´ti-cate
rus-ti-ca´tion
rus´ti-ca-tor
rus-tic´i·ty
rust´i-ness
rus´tle

rus´tler
rust-tling
rust´proof
rust´y
ru´ta-ba´ga
ruth´ful
ruth´ful-ly
ruth´ful-ness
ruth´less
ruth´less-ly
ruth´less-ness
rut´ted
rut´tish
rut´tish-ly
rut´tish-ness
rut´ty

S

sab-bat´i-cal
sa´ber
sa´ber–rat-tling
sa´ber-tooth
sa´ber–toothed
sa´ble
sa·bot´
sab´o-tage
sab´o-teur´
sac´cha-rate
sac´cha-ride
sac´cha-rin
  (swetener)
sac´cha-rine
  (sweet)

sa-chet´
sack´cloth
sack´ful
sack´ing
sac´ra-ment
sac-ra-men´tal
sac-ra-men´tal-
  ism
sac-ra-men´tal-ist
sac-ra-men´tal-ly
sa´cred
sa´cred-ly
sa´cred-ness
sac´ri-fice
sac´ri-fice-a·ble
sac´ri-fi´cial
sac´ri-fic-ing
sac´ri-lege
sac´ri-le´gious
sac´ri-le´gious-ly
sac´ri-le´gious-
  ness
sac´ris-ty
sac´ro-il´i·ac
sac´ro-sanct
sac´ro-sanc´ti-ty
sac´ro-sanct-ness
sad
sad´den
sad´den-ing
sad´der
sad´dle
sad´dle-bag

sad´dler
sad´dler·y
sad´dle-sore
sad´dle-tree
sa´dism
sa´dist
sa-dis´tic
sa-dis´ti-cal-ly
sad´ly
sad´ness
sa-fa´ri
safe–con´duct
safe´crack-er
safe´–de-pos-it
safe´guard
safe´keep-ing
safe´ly
saf´est
safe´ty
saf´fron
sa´ga
sa-ga´cious
sa-ga´cious-ly
sa-ga´cious-ness
sa-gac´i-ty
sage´ly
sage´ness
sagged
sag´ger
sag´ging
sag´gy
sail´boat
sail´cloth

sailed
sail´er
sail´fish
sail´ing
sail´or
sail´or-ing
sail´plane
saint´ed
saint´hood
saint´li-ness
saint´ly
sa´ke *(wine)*
sa-laam´
sal-a·bil´i-ty
sal´a·ble
sal´a·bly
sa-la´cious
sa-la´cious-ly
sa-la´cious-ness
sa-lac´i-ty
sal´ad
sal´a-man-der
sa-la´mi
sal´a-ried
sal´a-ry
sales´clerk
sales´peo-ple
sales´per-son
sa´lience
sa´li-ent
sal-i-na´tion
sa´line
sa-lin´i-ty

sa-li´va
sal´i-var-y
sal´i-vate
sal-i-va´tion
sal´lied
sal´low
sal´ly
sal´ly-ing
sal-mo-nel´la
sa-lon´
sa-loon´
sal´sa
sal´si-fy
salt´box
salt´cel-lar
salt´ed
salt´er
salt´i-er
salt´i-ly
sal-tim-boc´ca
sal-tine´
salt´i-ness
salt´ish
salt´ish-ness
salt´less
salt´ness
salt´shak-er
salt´wa-ter
salt´y
sa-lu´bri-ous
sa-lu´bri-ous-ly
sa-lu´bri-ous-ness
sa-lu´bri-ty

sal-u-tar´i·ly
sal´u-tar-i-ness
sal´u-tar·y
sal-u-ta´tion
sal-u-ta´tion-al
sa-lu´ta-to·ry
sa-lute´
sa-lut´ing
sal´va·ble
sal´vage
sal´vage-a·ble
sal´vag-er
sal-va´tion
sal-va´tion-al
salve
salved
sal´ver
sal´vo
same´ness
sam´o-var
sam´pan
sam´ple
sam´pler
sam´pling
sa´mu-rai
san´a-tive
san-a-to´ri-um
san´a-to·ry
sanc´ti-fi-a-ble
sanc-ti-fi-ca´tion
sanc´ti-fied
sanc´ti-fi-er
sanc´ti-fy

sanc´ti-fy-ing
sanc-ti-mo´ni-ous
sanc-ti-mo´ni-ous-
  ly
sanc-ti-mo´ni-ous-
  ness
sanc´ti-mo-ny
sanc´tion
sanc´tion-a-ble
sanc´tion-er
sanc´ti-ty
sanc´tu-ar·y
sanc´tum
sanc´tus
sand
san´dal
san´daled
san´dal-wood
sand´bag
sand´bank
sand´blast
sand´box
sand´er
sand´i-er
sand´i-ness
sand´lot
sand´man
sand´pa-per
sand´stone
sand´storm
sand´wich
sand´y
sane

san-er
sane´ly
sane´ness
san´for-ize
san-grí´a
san´guine
san´guine-ly
san´guine-ness
san-guin´e-ous
san-guin´e-ous-
  ness
san-i-tar´i-an
san´i-tar-i-ly
san´i-tar-i-ness
san´i-tar·i·um
san´i-tar·y
san-i-ta´tion
san-i-ti-za´tion
san´i-tize
san´i-tiz-er
san´i-ty
sap´id
sa-pid´i-ty
sap´id-ness
sap´i-ence
sa´pi-ens
sap´i-ent
sap´i-ent-ly
sap´ling
sa´por
sap´o-rif´ic
sap´per
sap´phire

sap´ping
sap´py
sap-sa´go
sap´suck-er
sar´casm
sar-cas´tic
sar-cas´ti-cal-ly
sar-co´ma
sar-coph´a-gi
sar-coph´a-gus
sar-dine´
sar-don´ic
sar-don´i-cal-ly
sar-don´i-cism
sa´ri
sa-rong´
sar-sa-pa-ril´la
sar-to´ri-al
sar-to´ri-al-ly
sash
sa-shay´
sa-shi´mi
sas´sa-fras
sas´sy
sa-tan´ic
sa-tan´i-cal
sa-tan´i-cal-ly
satch´el
sat´ed
sa-teen´
sat´el-lite
sa-tia-bil´i-ty
sa´tia-ble

sa´tia-bly
sa´ti-ate
sa-ti-a´tion
sa-ti´e-ty
sat´in
sat´in-y
sat´ire
sa-tir´ic
sa-tir´i-cal
sa-tir´i-cal-ly
sat´i-rist
sat´i-riz-a-ble
sat-i-ri-za´tion
sat´i-rize
sat´i-riz-er
sat´i-riz-ing
sat-is-fac´tion
sat-is-fac´to-ri-ly
sat-is-fac´to-ri-
   ness
sat´is-fac´to-ry
sat´is-fied
sat´is-fi-er
sat´is-fy
sat´is-fy-ing
sat´is-fy-ing-ly
sa-to´ri
sa´trap
sa´tra-py
sat´u-ra-ble
sat´u-rant
sat´u-rate
sat´u-rat-ed

sat´u-rat-er
sat´u-rat-ing
sat-u-ra´tion
sat´u-ra-tor
sat-ur-na´lia
sa´tyr
sauced
sauce´pan
sau´cer
sau´ci-ly
sau´ci-ness
sau´cy
sau´er-bra-ten
sau´er-kraut
sau´na
saun´ter
saun´ter-ing
sau´sage
sau-té´
sau-téed´
sau-té´ing
sau-terne´
sav´able
sav´age
sav´age-ly
sav´age-ness
sav´age-ry
sa-van´na
sa-vant´
saved
sav´er
sav´ing
sav´ior

sa´vor
sa´vor-ous
sa´vory
sa´vour (Br.)
sav´vi-ness
sav´vy
saw´buck
saw´dust
sawed´–off´
saw´horse
saw´mill
saw´tooth
saw´–toothed
saw´yer
sax´o-phone
sax´o-phon-ist
say´a-ble
say´ing
say´–so
scab´bard
scabbed
scab´bi-ly
scab´bi-ness
scab´bing
sca´bi-ous
scab´ble
scab´bler
scab´by
sca´bies
scab´rous-ly
scaf´fold
scaf´fold-ing
scag

scal´a-ble
scal´a-wag
scald´ed
scald´er
scale
scaled
scale´down
scal´er
scal´ing
scal´lion
scal´lop
scal´loped
sca-lop-pi´ni
scalp
scal´pel
scalp´er
scal´y
scam
scamp
scam´per
scam´pi
scamp´ish
scan´dal
scan´dal-ize
scan´dal-monger
scan´dal-ous
scan´dal-ous-ly
scan´dal-ous-ness
scanned
scan´ner
scan´ning
scant´i-ly
scant´i-ness

scant´ling
scant´ly
scant´ness
scant´y
scape´goat
scarce
scarce´ly
scarce´ness
scar´city
scare´crow
scared
scarf
scar´i-ly
scar´ing
scar´let
scarred
scar´ring
scary
scathe
scath´ing
scat´ter
scat´ter-brain
scat´tered
scat´ter-er
scat´ter-ing
scat´ter-shot
scav´enge
scav´eng-er
scav´eng-ing
sce-nar´io
scene
sce´ner·y
sce´nic

sce´ni-cal
scent´ed
scep´ter
scep´tic
scep´ti-cal
scep´ti-cism
sched´ule
sched´uled
sched´ul-ing
sche-mat´ic
sche-mat´i-cal-ly
scheme
schem´er
schem´ing
schem´ing-ly
schism
schiz´oid
schiz-o-phre´ni-a
schiz-o-phren´ic
schlep
schlock
schmaltz
schmaltz´y
schmear
schmooze
schmuck
schnook
schol´ar
schol´ar-li-ness
schol´ar-ly
schol´ar-ship
scho-las´tic
scho-las´ti-cal-ly

school´book
school´boy
school´child
school´girl
school´house
school´ing
school´marm
school´mas-ter
school´mate
school´room
school´teach-er
school´work
school´yard
schoo´ner
schuss
sci-at´ic
sci-at´i-ca
sci´ence
sci-en-tif´ic
sci-en-tif´i-cal-ly
sci´en-tism
sci´en-tist
scim´i-tar
scin-til´la
scin´til-late
scin´til-lat-ing
scin-til-la´tion
scin´til-la-tor
sci´on
scis´sors
scle-ro´sis
scoff´er
scoff´ing-ly

scoff´law
scold´er
scold´ing
scold´ing-ly
sco-li-o´sis
sconce
scone
scoop´er
scoop´ful
scoot´er
scope
scorch´er
scorch´ing
score´board
score´card
scored
score´keep-er
scor´ing
scorn´er
scorn´ful
scorn´ful-ly
scorn´ful-ness
scor´pi-on
scot´-free´
scoun´drel
scour
scourge
scourg´er
scourg´ing
scour´ings
scout
scout´ing
scowl´er

scowl´ing-ly
scrab´ble
scrab´bler
scrab´bling
scrab´bly
scrag´gi-ly
scrag´gi-ness
scrag´gly
scrag´gy
scram´ble
scram´bler
scram´bling
scrap´book
scrape
scraped
scrap´er
scrap´ing
scrapped
scrap´per
scrap´pi-ly
scrap´pi-ness
scrap´ping
scrap´ple
scrap´py
scratch´board
scratch´er
scratch´i-ly
scratch´i-ness
scratch´proof
scratch´y
scrawl´er
scrawl´y
scrawn´i-ness

scrawn´y
screak
screak´y
scream
scream´er
scream´ing
screech
screech´y
screed
screen´a-ble
screen´er
screen´ing
screen´play
screen´writ-er
screw´ball
screw´driv-er
screw´up
screw´y
scrib´ble
scrib´bler
scrib´bling
scribe
scrib´er
scrim´mage
scrim´mag-er
scrimp
scrimp´i-ly
scrimp´i-ness
scrimp´y
scrim´shaw
scrip
script´er
scrip´tur-al

scrip´tur-al-ly
scrip´ture
script´writ-er
script´writ-ing
scriv´en-er
scrof´u-lous
scrof´u-lous-ly
scrof´u-lous-ness
scroll
scroll´work
scro´tum
scrounge
scroung´er
scroung´ing
scrub´ba-ble
scrub´ber
scrub´bi-ness
scrub´bing
scrub´by
scruff´y
scrump´tious
scrump´tious-ly
scrump´tious-ness
scrunch
scru´ple
scru-pu-los´i-ty
scru´pu-lous
scru´pu-lous-ly
scru´pu-lous-ness
scru-ta-bil´i-ty
scru´ta·ble
scru-ti-ni-za´tion
scru´ti-nize

scru´ti-niz-er
scru´ti-niz-ing-ly
scru´ti-ny
scu´ba–dive
scud´ded
scuff
scuf´fle
scuf´fling
scuf´fling-ly
scull
scul´ler·y
sculpt
sculp´tor
sculp´tur-al
sculp´tur-al-ly
sculp´ture
sculp´tured
scum
scum´ble
scum´bled
scum´my
scurf
scurf´y
scur-ril´i-ty
scur´ril-ous
scur´ril-ous-ly
scur´ril-ous-ness
scur´ried
scur´ry
scur´ry-ing
scur´vy
scut
scutch´eon

scut´tle
scut´tle-butt
scut´tling
scuzz´y
scythe
scyth´ing
sea´bed
sea´bird
sea´borne
sea´coast
sea´far-er
sea´far-ing
sea´floor
sea´food
sea´go-ing
seal´able
seal´ant
sealed´–beam´
seal´er
sea´lift
seal´ing
seal´skin
sea´man
sea´man-like
sea´man-ship
sea´men
seam´i-ness
seam´less
seam´less-ly
seam´less-ness
seam´ster
seam´stress
seam´y

sé´ance
sea´plane
sea´port
search´a-ble
search´er
search´ing
search´ing-ly
search´light
sea´scape
sea´shell
sea´shore
sea´sick
sea´sick-ness
sea´side
sea´son
sea´son-a-ble
sea´son-a-bly
sea´son-al
sea´son-al-ly
sea´son-ing
seat´ed
seat´er
seat´ing
seat´mate
seat´–of–the–
  pants´
sea´wall
sea´ward
sea´way
sea´weed
sea´wor-thi-ness
sea´wor-thy
se-ba´ceous

se´bum
se´cant
se-cede´
se-ced´ed
se-ced´er
se-ced´ing
se-ces´sion
se-ces´sion-al
se-ces´sion-ism
se-ces´sion-ist
se-clude´
se-clud´ed
se-clud´ed-ness
se-clud´ing
se-clu´sion
se-clu´sive
se-clu´sive-ly
se-clu´sive-ness
sec´ond
sec´ond-ar-i-ly
sec´ond-ar-i-ness
sec´ond-ar-y
sec´ond-er
sec´ond–guess´
sec´ond-hand´
sec´ond-ly
sec´ond–rate´
se´cre-cy
se´cret
sec´re-tar´i-al
sec-re-tar´i-at
sec´re-tary
se-crete´

se-cret´ed
se-cre´tion
se-cre´tion-ar-y
se´cre-tive
se´cre-tive-ly
se´cre-tive-ness
se´cret-ly
se´cret-ness
sect
sec-tar´i-an
sec-tar´i-an-ism
sec´tion-al
sec´tion-al-ism
sec´tion-al-ist
sec´tion-al-ly
sec-tion-al-i-za´-
   tion
sec´tion-al-ize
sec´tor
sec-to´ri-al
sec´u-lar
sec´u-lar-ism
sec´u-lar-ist
sec-u-lar´i-ty
sec-u-lar-i·za´tion
sec´u-lar-ize
sec´u-lar-ly
se-cur´a·ble
se-cure´
se-cure´ly
se-cure´ness
se-cur´ity
se-dan´

se-date´
se-date´ly
se-date´ness
se-da´tion
sed´a-tive
sed´en-tar´i-ly
sed´en-tar´i-ness
sed´en-tar·y
sed´i-ment
sed-i-men´tal
sed´i-men-tar´i-ly
sed´i-men´ta-ry
sed-i-men-ta´tion
sed-i-men-tol´o-gy
sed-i-men-to-log´-
   ic
sed-i-men-to-log´i-
   cal
sed-i-men-tol´o-
   gist
se-di´tion
se-di´tious
se-di´tious-ly
se-di´tious-ness
se-duce´
se-duc´er
se-duc´i-ble
se-duc´ing
se-duc´tion
se-duc´tive
se-duc´tive-ly
se-duc´tive-ness
se-duc´tress

se-du´li-ty
sed´u-lous
sed´u-lous-ly
sed´u-lous-ness
seed´bed
seed´cake
seed´case
seed´er
seed´i-ness
seed´ing
seed´less
seed´ling
seed´pod
seed´y
see´ing
seek´er
seem´ing
seem´ing-ly
seem´li-ness
seem´ly
seep´age
seer´suck-er
see´saw
seethe
seeth´ing
seeth´ing-ly
see´–through
seg´ment
seg-men´tal
seg-men´tal-ly
seg´men-tar-y
seg-men-ta´tion
seg´re-ga·ble

seg´re-gate
seg´re-gat-ed
seg-re-ga´tion
seg-re-ga´tion-ist
se´gue
sei-gneur´
seine
seis´mic
seis´mi-cal-ly
seis-mic´i-ty
seis´mism
seis´mo-gram
seis´mo-graph
seis-mog´ra-pher
seis-mo-graph´ic
seis-mog´ra-phy
seis-mo-log´ic
seis-mo-log´i-cal
seis-mol´o-gist
seis-mol´o-gy
seis-mom´e-ter
seis-mom´et-ry
seiz´a·ble
seize
seiz´er
seiz´ing
sei´zure
sel´dom
se-lect´
se-lec´tion
se-lec´tive
se-lec´tive-ly
se-lec´tive-ness

se-lec-tiv´i-ty
se-lect´man
se-lec´tor
self´–a-base´ment
self´–ab-sorbed´
self´–ab-sorp´tion
self´–act´ing
self´–ap-point´ed
self´–as-sur´ance
self´–as-sured´
self´–cen´tered
self´–cen´tered-
 ness
self´–com-posed´
self´–con-fessed´
self´–con´fi-dence
self´–con´fi-dent
self´–con´fi-dent-ly
self´–con-grat´u·la-
 to·ry
self´–con´scious
self´–con´scious-ly
self´–con´scious-
 ness
self´–con-tained´
self´–con-tra-dic´-
 ting
self´–con-tra-dic´-
 tion
self´–con-tra-dic´-
 tor-y
self´–con-trol´
self´–con-trol´led

self–de-ceit´
self–de-cep´tion
self–de-fense´
self–de-lud´ed
self–de-lu´sion
self–de-ni´al
self–de-ny´ing
self´–de-struct´
self´–de-struc´tion
self´–de-struc´tive
self–de-ter-mi-na´-
    tion
self–de-vo´tion
self–dis´ci-pline
self–dis´ci-plined
self´–doubt´
self´–doubt´ing
self´–ef-face´ment
self´–ef-fac´ing
self´–em-ployed´
self–es-teem´
self–ev´i-dent
self–ev´i-dent·ly
self´–ex-plan´a-
    to·ry
self´–ex-pres´sion
self–ful-fill´ing
self–ful-fill´ment
self–gov´erned
self–gov´ern-ing
self–gov´ern-ment
self´–grat-i-fi-ca´-
    tion

self–help´
self´–hyp-no´sis
self´–im´age
self–im-por´tance
self–im-por´tant
self–im-por´tant·ly
self–im-posed´
self´–im-prove´-
    ment
self´–in-crim´-
    i·nat-ing
self´–in-crim-in-
    a´tion
self´–in-duced´
self´–in-dul´gence
self´–in-dul´gent
self–in´ter-est
self´ish
self´ish-ly
self´ish-ness
self–know´ledge
self´less
self´less-ly
self´less-ness
self´–lim´it-ing
self–liq´ui-dat-ing
self´–load´er
self´–load´ing
self´–love´
self´–made´
self´–mail´er
self´–per-pet´u·at-
    ing

self–pit´y
self–por´trait
self–pos-sessed´
self–pres-er-va´-
    tion
self´–pro-pelled´
self´–pro-pul´sion
self–pro-tec´tion
self–re-gard´
self–reg´ulating
self–re-li´ance
self–re-li´ant
self–re-spect´
self–re-spect´ing
self´–re-straint´
self–right´eous
self–right´eous·ly
self–right´eous-
    ness
self–sac´ri-fice
self–sac´ri-fic-ing
self´same
self–sat´is-fied
self´–serv´ing
self´–start-er
self´–start-ing
self–suf-fi´cien-cy
self–suf-fi´cient
self–sup-port´ing
self´–taught´
self´–will´
self´–wind´ing
self´–worth´

sell´a·ble
sell´er
sell´ing
sell´–off
sell´out
selt´zer
sel´vage
selves
se-man´tic
se-man´ti-cal´ly
se-man´tics
sem´a-phore
sem-a-phor´ic
sem´blance
se-mes´ter
sem-i-ab´stract
sem-i-ab-strac´-
   tion
sem-i-an´nu-al
sem-i-an´nu-al-ly
sem-i-ar´id
sem-i-au-to-mat´ic
sem-i-au-ton´o-
   mous
sem´i-cir-cle
sem-i-cir´cu-lar
sem-i-clas´si-cal
sem´i-co-lon
sem-i-con-duc-tor
sem-i-con´scious
sem-i-con´scious-
   ness
sem-i-dark´ness

sem´i-de-tached´
sem´i-fi-nal
sem-i-fi´nal-ist
sem-i-for´mal
sem´i-gloss
sem´i-lit´er-a-cy
sem´i-lit´er-ate
sem´i-month´ly
sem´i-nal
sem´i-nal-ly
sem´i-nar
sem-i-nar´i-an
sem´i-nary
sem-i-of-fi´cial
sem-i-per´me-
   a·ble
sem´i-pre´cious
sem´i-pri´vate
sem´i-pro-fes´-
   sion-al
sem´i-pro-fes´-
   sion-al-ly
sem-i-pub´lic
sem-i-skilled´
sem-i-soft´
sem-i-sol´id
sem-i-sweet´
sem-i-week´ly
sem-i-year´ly
sem-o-li´na
sen´ate
sen´a-tor
sen-a-to´ri-al

send´a-ble
send´er
send´ing
send´–off
se´nile
se-nil´i-ty
sen´ior
se-nior´i-ty
sen´na
se-ñor´
se-ño´ra
se-ño-ri´ta
sen´sate
sen-sa´tion
sen-sa´tion-al
sen-sa´tion-al-ism
sen-sa´tion-al-ist
sen-sa-tion-al-is´-
   tic
sen-sa´tion-al-ize
sen-sa´tion-al-ly
sensed
sense´less
sense´less-ly
sense´less-ness
sen-si-bil´i-ty
sen´si-ble
sen´si-ble-ness
sen´si-bly
sens´ing
sen´si-tive
sen´si-tive-ly
sen´si-tive-ness

sen-si-tiv´i·ty
sen-si-ti·za´tion
sen´si-tize
sen´si-tiz-er
sen´sor
sen-so´ri-al
sen´so-ry
sen´su-al
sen´su-al-ism
sen´su-al-ist
sen-su-al-is´tic
sen-su-al-i-za´tion
sen´su-al-ize
sen-su-al´i-ty
sen´su-al-ly
sen´su-ous
sen´su-ous-ly
sen´su-ous-ness
sen´tence
sen-ten´tial
sen-ten´tial-ly
sen´tience
sen´tient
sen´tient-ly
sen´ti-ment
sen-ti-men´tal
sen-ti-men´tal-ism
sen-ti-men´tal-ist
sen-ti-men-tal´i-ty
sen-ti-men-tal-i-
  za´tion
sen-ti-men´tal-ize
sen-ti-men´tal-ly

sen´ti-nel
sen´try
sep-a-ra-bil´i-ty
sep´a-ra·ble
sep´a-ra·bly
sep´a-rate
sep´a-rate-ly
sep´a-rate-ness
sep-a-ra´tion
sep´a-rat-ism
sep´a-rat-ist
sep´a-ra-tive
sep´a-ra-tor
se´pia
sep´sis
sep-ten´ni-al
sep-ten´ni-al-ly
sep-tet´
sep´tic
sep-ti-ce´mia
sep-tic´i-ty
sep-til´lion
sep-tu´age-nar´i-
  an
sep´tu-ple
sep´ul-cher
se-pul´chral
se-pul´chral-ly
se-qua´cious
se-qua´cious-ly
se-quac´i-ty
se´quel
se´quence

se´quenc-er
se´quenc-ing
se´quent
se-quen´tial
se-quen-ti-al´i-ty
se-quen´tial-ly
se-ques´ter
se-ques´tered
se´quin
se´quined
se-quoi´a
se-ra´glio
se-ra´pe
ser´a-phim
ser´e-nade´
ser´e-nad´er
ser´e-nad´ing
ser-en-dip´i-tous
ser-en-dip´i-tous-
  ly
ser-en-dip´i-ty
se-rene´
se-rene´ly
se-rene´ness
se-ren´i-ty
serf´dom
serge
ser´geant
se´ri-al
se´ri-al-ism
se´ri-al-ist
se´ri-al-ize
se´ri-al-ly

se´ri-ate
se´ri-ate-ly
se´ries
ser´if
se-ri-o-com´ic
se´ri-ous
se´ri-ous-ly
se´ri-ous–mind´ed
se´ri-ous–mind´-
  ed-ly
se´ri-ous–mind´-
  ed-ness
se´ri-ous-ness
ser´mon
ser-mon´ic
ser-mon´i-cal
ser´mon-ize
ser´mon-less
se´rous-ness
ser´pent
ser´pen-tine
ser´rate
ser´rat-ed
ser-ra´tion
ser´ried
ser´ried-ly
se´rum
serv´a-ble
ser´vant
served
serv´er
serv´ice
serv-ice-a-bil´i-ty

serv´ice-a-ble
serv´ice-a-ble-ness
serv´ice-a-bly
ser-vi-ette´
ser´vile
ser´vile-ly
ser´vile-ness
ser-vil´i-ty
serv´ing
ser´vi-tor
ser´vi-tude
ses´a-me
ses´qui-cen-ten´ni-
  al
ses´sion
ses´tet
set´back
set´off
set´screw
set-tee´
set´ter
set´ting
set´tle
set´tle-a-ble
set´tle-ment
set´tler
set´tling
set´–to
set´up
sev´en
sev´en-fold
sev´en-teen´
sev´en-teenth´

sev´enth
sev´en-ti-eth
sev´en-ty
sev´en-ty–six´
sev´er
sev-er-a-bil´i-ty
sev´er-a-ble
sev´er-al
sev´er-al-ly
sev´er-al-ty
sev´er-ance
se-vere´
sev´ered
se-vere´ly
se-vere´ness
se-ver´i-ty
sew´a-ble
sew´age
sew´er
sew´er-age
sew´ing
sex-a-ge-nar´i-an
sex-ag´e-nary
sex´i-ly
sex´i-ness
sex´ism
sex´ist
sex´less
sex-ol´o-gist
sex-ol´o-gy
sex´tant
sex-tet´
sex-til´lion

sex´ton	shak´i-ly	shape´less-ly
sex-tup´let	shak´ing	shape´less-ness
sex´u-al	shak´y	shape´li-ness
sex-u-al´i-ty	shal-lot´	shape´ly
sex´u-al-ly	shal´low-ly	shap´er
sex´y	shal´low-ness	shape´–up
shab´bi-ly	sha´man	shap´ing
shab´bi-ness	sham´ble	shar´able
shab´by	shame	shard
shack´le	shamed	share
shack´led	shame´faced	share´crop-per
shack´ling	shame´ful	share´hold-er
shade	shame´ful-ly	shar´er
shad´ed	shame´ful-ness	share´ware
shad´i-er	shame´less	shar´ing
shad´i-ly	shame´less-ly	shark´skin
shad´i-ness	shame´less-ness	sharp´–eared´
shad´ing	sham´ing	sharp´–edged´
shad´ow	shammed	sharp´en
shad´ow-box	sham´mer	sharp´en-er
shad´ow-i-ness	sham´ming	sharp´en-ing
shad´ow-ing	sham-poo´	sharp´er
shad´ow·y	sham-pooed´	sharp´–eyed´
shad´y	sham´rock	sharp´ly
shaft	shan´dy	sharp´ness
shag´gi-ly	shan´dy-gaff	sharp´shoot-er
shag´gi-ness	shank	sharp´shoot-ing
shag´gy	shan´ty	sharp´–sight-ed
shak´a·ble	shan´ty-town	sharp´–tongued
shake´down	shap´a-ble	sharp´–wit´ted
shak´en	shape	shat´ter
shak´er	shaped	shat´tered
shake´–up	shape´less	shat´ter-er

shat'ter-proof
shaved
shave'ling
shave'tail
shav'en
shav'er
shav'ing
shawl
sheaf
shear
shear'er
shear'ing
sheath
sheathe
sheathed
sheath'ing
sheave
shed'der
she'–dev-il
shed'ding
sheen
sheep'cote
sheep dog
sheep'fold
sheep'herd-er
sheep'ish
sheep'ish-ly
sheep'ish-ness
sheep'shank
sheep'shear-ing
sheep'skin
sheep'walk
sheer

sheer'ness
sheet'ing
sheik'dom
shelf
shel-lac'
shel-lacked'
she'lack'ing
shelled
shell'er
shell'fish
shell'–shocked
shel'ter
shel'tered
shel'ter-ing
shel'ter-less
shelves
shelv'ing
she-nan'i-gan
shep'herd
shep'herd-ess
sher'bet
sher'iff
sher'ry
shi-at'su
shib'bo-leth
shield
shift'er
shift'i-er
shift'i-ly
shift'i-ness
shift'ing
shift'less
shift'less-ly

shift'less-ness
shift'y
shil'ling
shil'ly–shal-ly
shim'mer
shim'mer-ing-ly
shim'mery
shim'ming
shim'my
shin'bone
shin'dig
shine
shin'er
shin'gle
shin'gled
shin'i-er
shin'i-ly
shin'ing
shin'i-ness
shin'ing
shin'ny
shin'plas-ter
shin'y
ship'board
ship'build-er
ship'build-ing
ship'fit-ter
ship'load
ship'mate
ship'ment
ship'own-er
shipped
ship'per

ship´ping
ship´shape
ship´wreck
ship´wright
ship´yard
shire
shirk´er
shirr
shirred
shirr´ing
shirt´ing
shirt´mak-er
shirt´mak-ing
shirt´sleeve
shirt´tail
shirt´waist
shiv´ery
shoal
shoat
shock
shock´a-ble
shock´er
shock´ing
shock´ing-ly
shock´proof
shock´–re-sist´ant
shod´di-ly
shod´di-ness
shod´dy
shoe´horn
shoe´ing
shoe´lace
shoe´mak-er

shoe pol´ish
shoe´shine
shoe´string
sho´gun
shoo´–in
shoot´er
shoot´ing
shoot´out
shop´keep-er
shop´keep-ing
shop´lift
shop´lift-er
shopped
shop´per
shop´ping
shop´talk
shop´worn
shore´line
shor´ing
short´age
short´bread
short´cake
short´change
short´com-ing
short´cut
short´en
short´en-er
short´en-ing
short´fall
short´haired
short´hand´ed
short´–haul
short´–lived´

short´ly
short´ness
short´–range´
short´sight-ed
short´sight-ed-ly
short´sight-ed-
   ness
short´stop
short´–tem´pered
short´wave´
short´–wind´ed
short´y
shot´gun
should
shoul´der
shoul´dered
shout´ed
shout´er
shove
shoved
shov´el
shov´eled
shov´el-er
shov´el-ful
shov´el-ing
shov´er
shov´ing
show´boat
show´case
show´down
showed
show´er
show´i-ness

show'ing
show'man
show'man-ship
shown
show'–off
show'room
show'–stop-per
show'y
shrap'nel
shred'der
shred'ding
shrew
shrewd'ly
shrewd'ness
shrew'ish
shrieked
shriek'ing
shrill
shril'ly
shrill'ness
shril'ly
shrimp'er
shrine
shrined
shrin'er
shrink'a·ble
shrink'age
shrink'–wrap
shrive
shriv'el
shriv'eled
shriv'el-ing
shroud'ed

shrub'ber-y
shrub'by
shrug
shrugged
shrug'ging
shrunk'en
shtick
shuck'ing
shud'der
shuf'fle
shuf'fle-board
shuf'fled
shut'fling
shunned
shun'ning
shun'pike
shunt'ing
shut'down (n.)
shut'eye
shut'–in
shut'off
shut'out
shut'ter
shut'ting
shut'tle
shut'tle-cock
shy'ly
shy'ness
shy'ster
sib'ling
sick'bed
sick'en
sick'en-ing

sick'en-ing-ly
sick'ie
sick'le
sick'led
sick'li-er
sick'li-ness
sick'ly
sick'ness
sick'room
side'bar
side'board
side'burns
side'car
sid'ed
side'kick
side'line
si-de're-al
side'sad-dle
side'show
side'split-ter
side'split-ting
side'swipe
side'track
side'walk
side'wall
side'ways
side'wind-er
si'dle
si'dled
si'dling
siege
si-es'ta
sieve

sift´er
sift´ings
sigh´ing
sight´ed
sight´er
sight´less
sight´less-ly
sight´less-ness
sight´ly
sight´–read
sight´–read-er
sight´see
sight´see-ing
sight´seer
sig´ma
sig´moid
sign
sig´nal
sig´naled
sig´nal-ing
sig-nal-i-za´tion
sig´nal-ize
sig´nal-ly
sig´nal-man
sig´na-to-ry
sig´na-ture
sign´board
sig´net
sig-nif´i-cance
sig-nif´i-cant
sig-nif´i-cant-ly
sig-ni-fi-ca´tion
sig-nif´i-ca-tive

sig-nif´i-ca-tive-
  ness
sig´ni-fi-a·ble
sig´ni-fied
sig´ni-fier
sig´ni-fy
sig´ni-fy-ing
sign´post
si´lence
si´lenc-er
si´lenc-ing
si´lent
si´lent-ly
sil-hou-ette´
sil-hou-et´ted
sil´i-con
silk´en
silk´i-er
silk´i-ly
silk´i-ness
silk´screen
silk´worm
silk´y
sil´li-ly
sil´li-ness
sil´ly
si´lo
si´los
silt´y
sil´van
sil´ver
sil´ver–plat´ed
sil´ver-smith

sil´ver–tongued´
sil´ver-ware
sil´very
sim´i-lar
sim-i-lar´i-ty
sim´i-lar-ly
sim´i-le
si-mil´i-tude
sim´mer
sim-pat´i-co
sim´per
sim´pered
sim´per-er
sim´per-ing
sim´per-ing-ly
sim´ple
sim´ple–mind´ed
sim´ple–mind´ed-
  ly
sim´ple–mind´ed-
  ness
sim´ple-ness
sim´pler
sim´plest
sim´ple-ton
sim´plex
sim-plic´i-ty
sim-pli-fi-ca´tion
sim´pli-fied
sim´pli-fi-er
sim´pli-fy
sim´pli-fy-ing
sim-plis´tic

sim-plis´ti-cal-ly
sim´ply
sim´u-late
sim´u-lat-ing
sim-u-la´tion
sim´u-la-tive
sim´u-la-tor
si´mul-cast
si-mul-ta-ne´i-ty
si-mul-ta´ne-ous
si-mul-ta´ne-ous-
  ly
si-mul-ta´ne-ous-
  ness
since
sin-cere´
sin-cere´ly
sin-cere´ness
sin-cer´est
sin-cer´i-ty
sin´e-cure
sin´e-cur-ist
sin´ew
sin´ew-y
sin´ful
sin´ful-ly
sin´ful-ness
sing´a·ble
singe
singed
singe´ing
sing´er
sing´ing

sin´gle
sin´gle–act´ing
sin´gle–ac´tion
sin´gle–breast´ed
sin´gle–dig´it
sin´gle–hand´ed
sin´gle–hand´ed-ly
sin´gle–knit
sin´gle–mind´ed
sin´gle–mind´ed-
  ness
sin´gle-ness
sin´gle–phase
sin´gle–space´
sin´gling
sin´gly
sing´song
sin´gu-lar
sin-gu-lar´i-ty
sin´gu-lar-ize
sin´gu-lar-ly
sin´is-ter
sin´is-ter-ly
sin´is-ter-ness
sin´is-tral
sin´is-tral-ly
sink´a·ble
sink´age
sink´er
sink´hole
sink´ing
sin´less
sinned

sin´ner
sin´ning
sin´u-ate
sin´u-ate-ly
sin-u-a´tion
sin-u-os´i-ty
sin´u-ous
sin´u-ous-ly
sin´u-ous-ness
si´nus
si-nus-i´tis
si´phon
sipped
sip´per
sip´ping
sired
si´ren
sir´ing
sir´loin
sis´si-ness
sis´sy
sis´sy-ish
sis´ter
sis´ter-hood
sis´ter–in–law
sis´ter-li-ness
sis´ter-ly
si-tar´
si-tar´ist
sit´com
sit´–in
sit´ter
sit´ting

sit´u-ate	skel´e-tal	skim´mer
sit´u-at-ed	skel´e-tal-ly	skim´ming
sit-u-a´tion	skel´e-ton	skimp´i-est
sit-u-a´tion-al	skel´e-ton-ize	skimp´i-ly
sit-u-a´tion-al-ly	skep´tic	skimp´i-ness
sit´–up	skep´ti-cal	skimp´ing
six´fold	skep´ti-cal-ly	skimp´ing-ly
six´–foot´	skep´ti-cism	skimp´y
six´–pack	sketch	skin–deep´
six´pence	sketch´book	skin´–dive
six´–shoot-er	sketched	skin´flint
six´teen´	sketch´i-est	skin´ful
six´teenth´	sketch´i-ly	skin´head
sixth	sketch´i-ness	skin´less
six´ti-eth	sketch´y	skinned
six´ty	skew´er	skin´ner
six´ty–nine´	skew´ness	skin´ni-est
siz´a-ble	skid´ded	skin´ni-ness
siz´a-ble-ness	skid´der	skin´ning
siz´a-bly	skid´ding	skin´ny
sized	skid´dy	skin´ny–dip
siz´ing	skid´proof	skin´tight´
siz´zle	skied	skip´pa-ble
siz´zled	skies	skip´per
siz´zling	skiff	skip´ping
siz´zling-ly	ski´ing	skip´ping-ly
skate´board	skilled	skir´mish
skat´ed	skil´let	skir´mish-er
skat´er	skill´ful	skirt´ing
skat´ing	skill´ful-ly	skit´ter
ske-dad´dle	skill´ful-ness	skit´ter-y
skeet	skim	skit´tish
skein	skimmed	skit´tish-ly

skit´tish-ness
skit´tles
skive
skiv´er
skoal
skul´dug´ger-y
skulk´er
skulk´ing
skull´cap
sky´–blue´
sky´box
sky´cap
sky´dive
sky´div-er
sky´div-ing
sky´–high
sky´hook
sky´jack
sky´lark
sky´light
sky´line
sky´rock-et
sky´scrap-er
sky´writ-ing
slack´en
slack´ened
slack´er
slack´ness
slacks
slag´gy
slain
slake
slaked

slak´ing
sla´lom
slam´–bang´
slammed
slam´mer
slam´ming
slan´der
slan´der-er
slan´der-ing-ly
slan´der-ous
slan´der-ous-ly
slang´i-ness
slang´y
slant´ing
slant´ing-ly
slant´wise
slap´dash
slap´hap-py
slap´jack
slapped
slap´ping
slap´stick
slash´er
slash´ing
slat´–back
slate
slat´ed
slat´ing
slat´ted
slat´tern
slat´tern-li-ness
slat´tern-ly
slat´ting

slat´y
slaugh´ter
slaugh´ter-er
slaugh´ter-house
slaugh´ter-ous
slave
slav´ery
slav´ish
slav´ish-ly
slav´ish-ness
slay´er
slay´ing
sleaze
slea´zi-er
slea´zi-ly
slea´zi-ness
slea´zy
sled´der
sled´ding
sledge
sledge´ham-mer
sleek´ly
sleek´ness
sleep
sleep´er
sleep´i-ly
sleep´i-ness
sleep´ing
sleep´less
sleep´less-ly
sleep´less-ness
sleep´walk-er
sleep´walk-ing

sleep´wear
sleep´y
sleep´y-head
sleet
sleet´y
sleeve´less
sleigh´ing
sleight
slen´der
slen´der-ize
slen´der-ness
slept
sleuth
slew
slice´a-ble
sliced
slic´er
slic´ing
slick
slick´er
slick´ly
slick´ness
slid´able
slide
slid´er
slid´ing
slight
slight´ing
slight´ing-ly
slight´ly
slight´ness
slime
slim´i-er

slim´i-ly
slim´i-ness
slim´ly
slim´ness
slim´y
sling´–back
sling´er
sling´shot
slink´i-ly
slink´i-ness
slink´ing
slink´y
slip´case
slip´cov-er
slip´knot
slip´–on
slip´page
slipped
slip´per
slip´per-i-ness
slip´pery
slip´ping
slip´shod
slip´stream
slip´–up
slip´way
slith´er
slith´ery
slit´ting
sliv´er
sliv´o-vitz
slob´ber
slob´ber-ing

sloe´berry
sloe´–eyed
slo´gan
slo-gan-eer´
slog´ging
sloped
slop´ing
slopped
slop´pi-ly
slop´pi-ness
slop´ping
slop´py
sloshed
slosh´y
slot
sloth
sloth´ful
sloth´ful-ly
sloth´ful-ness
slot´ted
slouch
slouch´i-ly
slouch´i-ness
slouch´ing
slouch´y
slough
slough´y
slov´en
slov´en-li-ness
slov´en-ly
slow´down
slow´–foot´ed
slow´–foot´ed-ness

slow´ly
slow´ness
slow´poke
slow´–release
slow´–wit´ted
slow´–wit´ted-ly
slow´–wit´ted-ness
sludge
sludg´er
sludg´y
slug´fest
slug´gard
slug´gard-li-ness
slug´gard-ly
slug´ger
slug´gish
slug´gish-ly
slug´gish-ness
sluice´way
sluic´ing
slum´ber
slum´ber-ous
slum´ber-ous-ly
slum´ber-ous-ness
slum´lord
slum´ming
slum´my
slump
slurp
slurred
slur´ring
slur´ry
slush´i-ness

slush´y
slut´tish
slut´tish-ly
slut´tish-ness
sly´ly
sly´ness
smack´er
smack´ing
smack´ing-ly
small´–claims´
small´ish
small´–mind´ed
small´–mind´ed-ly
small´–mind´ed-
  ness
small´ness
small´pox
small´–time´
smarm´i-ness
smarm´y
smart´en
smart´ly
smart´ness
smart´y
smart´y–pants
smashed
smash´er
smash´ing
smash´ing-ly
smash´up
smat´ter-ing
smear
smeared

smear´i-ness
smear´y
smell´er
smell´i-ness
smell´ing
smell´y
smelt´er
smid´gen
smiled
smil´ing
smil´ing-ly
smirk´er
smirk´ing
smirk´ing-ly
smith-er-eens´
smith´y
smit´ten
smock
smock´ing
smog´gy
smok´able
smoke´house
smoke´less
smok´er
smoke´stack
smok´i-er
smok´ing
smok´i-ness
smok´y
smol´der
smol´dered
smol´der-ing
smooch

smooth´bore
smooth´en
smooth´ie
smooth´ly
smooth´ness
smooth´–tongued
smor´gas-bord
smoth´er
smoth´ered
smoth´er-y
smudge
smudg´er
smudg´i-ly
smudg´i-ness
smudg´ing
smudg´y
smug
smug´gle
smug´gler
smug´ly
smug´ness
smut
smut´ti-ly
smut´ti-ness
smut´ty
sna´fu´
snag
snagged
snag´ging
snag´gle-tooth
snag´gle-toothed
snail´like
snake´bite

snake´skin
snak´i-ly
snak´i-ness
snak´y
snap´per
snap´pi-ly
snap´pi-ness
snap´pish
snap´pish-ly
snap´pish-ness
snap´py
snap´shot
snared
snar´ing
snarled
snarl´ing
snarl´ing-ly
snarl´ish
snatch´er
snatch´y
snaz´zy
sneaked
sneak´er
sneak´i-ly
sneak´i-ness
sneak´ing
sneak´y
sneer´ing
sneer´ing-ly
sneezed
sneeze´guard
sneez´er
sneez´ing

snick´er
snick´er-ing
snide´ness
sniff´er
sniff´ing
snif´fle
snif´fler
snif´fly
snif´ter
snig´ger
snipe
snip´er
snip´ing
snipped
snip´pet
snip´pi-er
snip´pi-ly
snip´pi-ness
snip´ping
snip´py
snit
snitch
sniv´el
sniv´el-er
sniv´el-ing
snob´ber-y
snob´bish
snob´by
snook´er
snoop´er
snoop´y
snoot´i-ly
snoot´i-ness

snoot´y

snooze

snored

snor´er

snor´ing

snor´kel-er

snort´er

snort´ing

snout

snow´ball

snow´bank

snow´bird

snow´–blind

snow´bound

snow´drift

snow´fall

snow´flake

snow´i-er

snow´i-ly

snow´i-ness

snow´man

snow´mo-bile

snow´pea

snow´plow

snow´shoe

snow´slide

snow´storm

snow´suit

snow´tire

snow´y

snub

snubbed

snub´ber

snub´bing

snub´–nosed

snuff´box

snuff´er

snuf´fle

snuf´fled

snuf´fler

snuf´fly

snug´ger-y

snug´gle

snug´gled

snug´gling

snug´ly

snug´ness

soak´ing

soap´box

soap´i-er

soap´i-ly

soap´i-ness

soap op´era

soap´stone

soap´suds

soap´y

soar´ing

soar´ing-ly

so´a-ve

sob´bing

so´ber

so´ber-ly

so´ber–mind´ed

so´ber-ness

so´ber-sides

so-bri´e-ty

so´bri-quet

so´–called´

soc´cer

so-cia-bil´i-ty

so´cia-ble

so´cia-ble-ness

so´cia-bly

so´cial

so´cial-ism

so´cial-ist

so-cial-is´tic

so´cial-ite

so-ci-al´i-ty

so-cial-i-za´tion

so´cial-ize

so´cial-iz-er

so´cial-ly

so´cial–mind´ed

so´cial-ness

so-ci´e-tal

so-ci´e-tal-ly

so-ci´e-ty

so-ci-o-ec-o-

    nom´ic

so-ci-o-ec-o-

    nom´i-cal-ly

so´ci-o-log´ic

so´ci-o-log´i-cal

so´ci-o-log´i-cal-ly

so-ci-ol´o-gist

so-ci-ol´o-gy

so´ci-o-path

so-ci-o-path´ic

sock´et
so´da
sod´bust-er
sod´den
sod´den-ly
sod´den-ness
sod´ding
so´di-um
sod´om-ite
sod´omy
so´fa
sof´fit
soft´–boiled´
soft´bound
soft´–core
soft´–cov-er
soft´en
soft´en-er
soft´en-ing
soft´head
soft´head´ed
soft´head´ed-ness
soft´heart-ed
soft´heart-ed-ly
soft´heart-ed-ness
soft´ly
soft´ness
soft´–shell
soft´–shoe
soft´–soap
soft´–spo´ken
soft´ware
soft´y

sog´gi-ly
sog´gi-ness
sog´gy
soil´age
soiled
soil´ure
soi-rée´
so´journ
so´journ-er
sol´ace
sol´aced
sol´ac-er
sol´ac-ing
so´lar
so-lar´i-um
so-lar-iza´tion
so´lar-ize
sol´der
sol´der-a-ble
sol´dered
sol´der-er
sol´dier
sol´dier-li-ness
sol´dier-ly
sold´–out´
sol´e-cism
sol´e-cist
sol´e-cis´tic
soled
sole´ly
sol´emn
so-lem´ni-fy
so-lem´ni-ty

sol-em-ni-za´tion
sol´em-nize
sol´emn-ly
sol´emn-ness
so´le-noid
sole´plate
so-lic´it
so-lic-i-ta´tion
so-lic´i-tor
so-lic´i-tous
so-lic´i-tous-ly
so-lic´i-tous-ness
so-lic´i-tude
sol´id
so´i-dar´i-ty
so-lid-i-fi-ca´tion
so-lid´i-fied
so-lid´i-fi-er
so-lid´i-fy
so-lid´i-ty
sol´id–look-ing
sol´id-ly
sol´id-ness
sol´id–state´
so-lil´o-quist
so-lil´o-quize
so-lil´o-quy
sol´ip-sism
sol´ip-sist
sol-ip-sis´tic
sol´i-taire
sol´i-tar-i-ly
sol´i-tar-i-ness

sol´i-tar-y
sol´i-tude
sol-i-tu-di-nar´i-
   an
so´lo
so´lo-ist
sol´stice
sol-sti´tial
sol-u-bil´i-ty
sol´u-ble
sol´u-ble-ness
sol´u-bly
sol´ute
so-lu´tion
solv-a-bil´i-ty
solv´a·ble
solve
solved
sol´ven-cy
sol´vent
solv´ing
so-mat´ic
so-mat´i-cal-ly
so´ma-to-gen´ic
so-ma-tol´o-gy
som´ber-ly
som´ber-ness
som-bre´ro
some´body
some´day
some´how
some´one
some´place

som´er-sault
some´thing
some´time
some´times
some´way
some´what
some´where
som-me-lier´
som-nam´bu-lant
som-nam´bu-late
som-nam-bu-
   la´tion
som-nam´bu-lism
som-nam´bu-list
som-nam´bu-
   lis´tic
som-ni-fa´cient
som-nif´er-ous
som-nif´ic
som-nil´o-quist
som-nil´o-quy
som´no-lence
som´no-lent
som´no-lent-ly
so´nance
so´nant
so´nar
so-na´ta
song´bird
song´book
song´fest
song´ster
song´stress

song´writ-er
son´ic
son´-in-law
son´net
son´ne-teer´
son´ny
son´o-gram
so-nom´e-ter
so-nor´i-ty
so-no´rous
so-no´rous-ly
so-no´rous-ness
soon´er
soon´est
soothe
soothed
sooth´er
sooth´ing
sooth´ing-ly
sooth´say
sooth´say-er
sooth´say-ing
soot´i-ly
soot´i-ness
soot´y
soph´ism
soph´ist
soph´is-ter
so-phis´tic
so-phis´ti-cal-ly
so-phis´ti-cate
so-phis´ti-cat-ed
so-phis-ti-ca´tion

soph´is-try
soph´o-more
soph-o-mor´ic
soph-o-mor´i-cal-
  ly
so´por
sop-o-rif´er-ous
sop-o-rif´ic
sop´ping
sop´py
so-pra´no
sorb-a·bil´i-ty
sorb´a·ble
sor´be-fa´cient
sor´bet
sor´cer-er
sor´cer-ess
sor´cer-ous
sor´cery
sor´did
sor´did-ly
sor´did-ness
sore´head
sore´head-ed-ness
sore´ly
sore´ness
sor´ghum
so-ror´i-ty
sorp´tion
sorp´tive
sor´rel
sor´ri-ly
sor´ri-ness

sor´row-ful
sor´row-ful-ly
sor´row-ful-ness
sor´ry
sort
sort´a-ble
sort´ed
sor´ter
sor´tie
sort´ing
sot´ted
sot´tish
sot´tish-ly
sot´tish-ness
souf-flé´
sought´–af-ter
soul´ful
soul´ful-ly
soul´ful-ness
soul´less
soul´less-ly
soul´less-ness
soul´–search-ing
sound´a·ble
sound´a-like
sound´board
sound´er
sound´ing
sound´less
sound´less-ly
sound´less-ness
sound´ly
sound´ness

sound´proof
sound´proof-ing
sound´track
soup-çon´
soup´i-er
soup´spoon
soup´y
sour´ball
source´book
source´ful
source´ful-ness
source language
source´less
sour´dough
sour´ish
sour´ly
sour´ness
sour´puss
sou´sa-phone
souse
soused
south´bound
south-east´
south-east´er
south-east´er-ly
south-east´ern
south´er-ly
south´ern
south´ern-er
south´ern-ly
south´ern-most
south´land
south´ward

south-west´
south-west´er
south-west´er-ly
south-west´ern
sou-ve-nir´
souv-la´ki
sov´er-eign
sov´er-eign-ty
so´vi-et
soy´a
soy´bean
space´–age
space´borne
space´craft
spaced´–out
space´flight
space´less
space´man
space´port
space´ship
space´shot
space´suit
space´walk
spac´ey
spa´cial
spac´ing
spa´cious
spa´cious-ly
spa´cious-ness
spack´le
spade
spad´ed
spade´ful

spade´work
spad´er
spad´ing
spa-ghet´ti
span
span´dex
span´gle
span´gled
span´gly
span´iel
spank´er
spank´ing
spanned
span´ner
span´ning
spare´a-ble
spared
spare´ly
spare´ness
spare´rib
spar´ing
spar´ing-ly
spar´ing-ness
spark´i-ly
spark´ish
spar´kle
spar´kler
spark´let
spark´like
spar´kling
spar´kling-ly
spar´kly
spark´y

sparred
spar´ring
spar´row
sparse´ly
sparse´ness
spar´si-ty
spasm
spas-mod´ic
spas-mod´i-cal-ly
spas´tic
spas´ti-cal-ly
spate
spa´tial
spa-ti-al´i-ty
spat´ter
spat´ter-ing
spat´ting
spat´u-la
spat´u-late
spawn
spawned
spawn´er
speak´able
speak´easy
speak´er
speak´er-phone
speak´ing
spear´fish
spear´head
spear´mint
spec
spe´cial-ism
spe´cial-ist

spe-ci-al´i-ty
spe-cial-i-za´tion
spe´cial-ize
spe´cial-ly
spe´cial-ty
spe´cie *(money)*
spe´cies *(class)*
spec´i-fi-a·ble
spe-cif´ic
spe-cif´i-cal-ly
spec-i-fi-ca´tion
spec-i-fic´i-ty
spec´i-fied
spec´i-fi-er
spec´i-fy
spec´i-fy-ing
spec´i-men
spe´cious
spe´cious-ly
spe´cious-ness
speck´le
speck´led
speck´ling
specs
spec´ta-cle
spec´ta-cled
spec-tac´u-lar
spec-tac´u-lar-ly
spec´tate
spec´ta-tor
spec´ter
spec´tral
spec-tral´i-ty

spec´tral-ly
spec´tral-ness
spec´tro-gram
spec´tro-graph
spec-tro-graph´ic
spec-trol´o-gy
spec´tro-scope
spec-tro-scop´ic
spec´trum
spec´u-late
spec´u-lat-ing
spec-u-la´tion
spec´u-la-tive
spec´u-la-tive-ly
spec´u-la-tive-ly
spec´u-la-tive-ness
spec´u-la-tor
speech´i-fi-er
speech´i-fy
speech´less
speech´less-ly
speech´less-ness
speed´boat
speed´boat-ing
speed´er
speed´i-ly
speed´i-ness
speed´ing
speed-om´e-ter
speed´–read
speed´ster
speed´–up
speed´way

speed´writ-ing
speed´y
spe´le-ol´o-gist
spe-le-o-log´i-cal
spe-le-ol´o-gist
spe-le-ol´o-gy
spell´bind-er
spell´bind-ing-ly
spell´bound
spell´er
spell´ing
spe-lunk´er
spe-lunk´ing
spend´a-ble
spend´er
spend´ing
spend´thrift
spent
sperm
sphere
spher´i-cal
spher´i-cal-ly
sphe´roid
sphinx
spiced
spic´i-ly
spic´i-ness
spic´ing
spic´y
spi´der
spi´dery
spiel´er
spiff´i-ly

spiff´i-ness
spiff´y
spig´ot
spiked
spik´i-ly
spik´i-ness
spik´ing
spik´y
spill´a-ble
spill´age
spilled
spill´er
spill´ing
spill´–o-ver
spill´proof
spill´way
spin
spin´ach
spi´nal
spin´dle
spin´dling
spin´dly
spin´–dry´
spine´less
spine´less-ly
spine´less-ness
spin´et
spin´ner
spin´ning
spin´–off
spin´ster
spin´ster-ish
spin´y

spi´ral
spi´raled
spi´ral-ing
spi´ral-ly
spire
spir´it
spir´it-ed
spir´it-ed-ly
spir´it-ed-ness
spir´it-ism
spir´it-less
spir´it-less-ly
spir´it-less-ness
spi-ri-to´so
spir´i-tu-al
spir´i-tu-al-ism
spir´i-tu-al-ist
spir-i-tu-al-is´tic
spir-i-tu-al´i-ty
spir´i-tu-al-ize
spir´i-tu-al-ly
spit´ball
spite´ful
spite´ful-ly
spite´ful-ness
spit´ing
spit´ting
spit´tle
splash´down
splash guard
splash´i-ly
splash´i-ness
splash´ing

splash´y
splat´ter
splay
splen´dent-ly
splen´did
splen´did-ly
splen´did-ness
splen-dif´er-ous
splen-dif´er-ous-ly
splen-dif´er-ous-
   ness
splen´dor
splen´dor-ous
splen´drous
spliced
splic´er
splic´ing
splint
splin´ter
splin´tered
split´–lev´el
split´ting
split´–up
splotch´y
splurge
splurged
spoil´age
spoiled
spoil´er
spoil´ing
spoil´sport
spoke
spo´ken

spokes'per-son
sponge
sponged
spong'er
spon'gi-ness
spong'ing
spong'y
spon'sor
spon'sor-ship
spon-ta-ne'i-ty
spon-ta'ne-ous
spon-ta'ne-ous-ly
spon-ta'ne-ous-
  ness
spook'i-ness
spook'ish
spook'y
spool'er
spoon'–feed
spoon'ful
spoon'y
spo-rad'ic
spo-rad'i-cal-ly
sport'fish-ing
sport'i-ly
sport'i-ness
sport'ing
sport'ing-ly
spor'tive
spor'tive-ly
spor'tive-ness
sports'cast-er
sports'cast-ing

sports'man
sports'man-like
sports'man-ship
sports'wear
sports'woman
sports'writ-er
sports'writ-ing
sport'y
spot'less
spot'less-ly
spot'less-ness
spot'light
spot'ted
spot'ter
spot'ti-er
spot'ti-ness
spot'ting
spot'ty
spot'–weld
spous'al
spouse
spout'er
sprained
sprang
sprawl'er
sprawl'ing
sprayed
spray'er
spread'er
spread'ing
spright'ful
spright'ful-ly
spright'li-ness

spright'ly
spring'board
spring'er
spring'i-ly
spring'i-ness
spring'ing
spring'–load'ed
spring'time
spring'y
sprin'kle
sprin'kler
sprin'kling
sprint'er
spritz'er
sprock'et
spruced
spruc'ing
spruce'ly
spry'ly
spry'ness
spu-mo'ni
spunk
spunk'i-ly
spunk'i-ness
spunk'y
spu'ri-ous
spu'ri-ous-ness
spurn'ing
spurred
spur'ring
spurt'ed
sput'ter
sput'ter-ing

spy´ing
squab´ble
squab´bled
squab´bler
squab´bling
squad´ron
squal´id
squal´id-ly
squal´id-ness
squall
squal´or
squan´der
squan´dered
squan´der-er
squan´der-ing
square
squared
square´ly
squar´ing
squar´ish
squash´i-ness
squash´ing
squash´y
squat´ly
squat´ness
squat´ted
squat´ter
squat´ting
squat´ty
squawked
squawk´er
squawk´y
squeak´er

squeak´i-ly
squeak´i-ness
squeak´ing
squeak´y
squeak´y–clean´
squeal´er
squeal´ing
squea´mish
squeam´ish-ly
squeam´ish-ness
squee´gee
squeez´a-ble
squeez´a-bly
squeeze´box
squeezed
squeez´er
squeez´ing
squelch
squelched
squelch´er
squig´gle
squig´gly
squint´ed
squint´er
squint´ing
squint´y
squirm
squirm´er
squirm´ing
squirm´y
squirt´ed
squirt´ing
squish´y

stabbed
stab´bing
sta-bil´i-ty
sta-bi-li-za´tion
sta´bi-lize
sta´bi-liz-er
sta´ble
sta´bled
sta´ble-ness
sta´bly
sta´bling
stack´a-ble
stacked
stack´er
sta´di-um
staffed
staff´er
stage´coach
stage´hand
stag´er
stage´struck
stage´y
stag´ger
stag´ger-ing
stag´i-ness
stag´ing
stag´nance
stag´nant
stag´nant-ly
stag´nate
stag´nat-ing
stag-na´tion
stag´y

stain´a-ble

sta´ple

star-va´tion

stain´er

sta´pled

starve

stain´ing

sta´pler

starved

stain´less

sta´pling

starve´ling

stair´case

star´board

starv´er

stair´way

starch´i-ness

starv´ing

stair´well

starch´y

stat´ed

stake´out

star´–crossed

state´hood

stak´ing

star´dom

state´li-ness

stalac´tite

stared

state´ly

stalag´mite

star´er

state´ment

stale´mate

star´gaze

state´room

stale´ness

star´gaz-er

states´man

stalked

star´gaz-ing

states´man-like

stalk´er

star´ing

state´wide

stalk´ing

stark´ly

stat´ic

stal´wart

stark´ness

sta´tion

stam´i-na

star´less

sta´tion-ary

stam´mer

star´let

sta´tio-ner

stam´mer-er

star´light

sta´tio-nery

stam´mer-ing

starred

sta´tion-mas-ter

stamped

star´ri-ness

sta-tis´tic

stam-pede´

star´ring

sta-tis´ti-cal

stamp´er

star´ry

sta-tis´ti-cal-ly

stance

star´ry–eyed

stat-is-ti´cian

stand´a-lone

star´–shaped

sta-tis´tics

stan´dard–bear-er

star´ship

stat´u-ary

stan-dard-i-za´-
  tion

star´–stud-ded

stat´ue

start´er

stat-u-esque´

stan´dard-ize

star´tle

stat´u-ette´

stand´ing

star´tling

stat´ure

stand´off´ish

star´tling-ly

sta´tus

stand´out

start´–up

stat´ute

stat´u-to-ry
staunch´ly
staunch´ness
stay´ing
stead´fast
stead´fast-ly
stead´fast-ness
stead´i-ly
stead´i-ness
stead´y
stealth´ful
stealth´ful-ly
stealth´i-ly
stealth´i-ness
stealth´y
steam´bath
steam´boat
steam´er
steam´i-ness
steam´roll-er
steam´ship
steam´y
steel´i-ness
steel´work-er
steel´y
steep´en
steep´er
stee´ple
stee´ple-chase
stee´pled
stee´ple-jack
stee´ple-less
steep´ly

steep´ness
steer´age
steer´ing
stein
stel´lar
stemmed
stem´ming
stem´ware
sten´cil
sten´ciled
sten´cil-ing
sten´o
ste-nog´ra-pher
sten´o-graph´ic
sten-to´ri-an
step´broth-er
step´child
step´daugh-ter
step´fa-ther
step´lad-der
step´moth-er
step´par-ent
stepped´–up´
step´per
step´ping
step´sis-ter
ster-e-o-phon´ic
ster´e-o-type
ster-e-o-typ´i-cal
ster´ile
ster´ile-ness
ste-ril´i-ty
ster-i-li-za´tion

ster´i-lize
ster´i-liz-er
stern´ly
stern´most
stern´ness
ster´oid
steth´o-scope
ste´ve-dore
stew´ard
stew´ard-ess
stew´ard-ship
stick´ball
stick´er
stick´i-er
stick´i-ness
stick´ing
stick´–in–the–
  mud
stick´ler
stick´pin
stick´y
stiff´en
stiff´en-er
stiff´en-ing
stiff´ly
stiff´–necked´
stiff´ness
sti´fle
sti´fling
sti´fling-ly
stig´ma
stig´ma-tize
sti-let´to

still´born
still´ness
stilt´ed
stim´u-lant
stim´u-late
stim-u-la´tion
stim´u-la-tor
stim´u-li
stim´u-lus
sting´er
stin´gi-er
stin´gi-ly
stin´gi-ness
sting´ing
stin´gy
stink´er
stink´ing
stink´y
stint´ing
sti´pend
stip´ple
stip´pled
stip´pling
stip´u-la-ble
stip´u-late
stip´u-lat-ing
stip-u-la´tion
stip´u-la-tor
stip´u-la-to-ry
stir´-fry
stirred
stir´ring
stitch´er

stitch´ing
stock-ade´
stock´bro-ker
stock´hold-er
stock´ing
stock´pile
stock´room
stock´y
stodg´i-ness
stodg´y
sto´gie
sto´gy
sto´ic
sto´i-cal
sto´i-cism
stoke
stoked
stok´er
stok´ing
stole
sto´len
stol´id
stol´id-ly
stom´ach
stom´ach-ache
stone´-broke
stone china
stone crush´er
stone´cut-ter
stone´-deaf
ston´i-ly
ston´i-ness
ston´ing

ston´y
stop´gap
stop´light
stop´-off
stop´o-ver
stopped
stop´per
stop´ping
stop´watch
stor´age
stored
store´front
store´house
store´keep-er
store´room
sto´ried
stor´ing
storm´i-ly
storm´i-ness
storm´proof
storm´y
sto´ry-board
sto´ry-book
sto´ry-tell-er
stout´-heart´ed
stout´-heart´ed-ly
stout´-heart´ed-
   ness
stout´ish
stout´ly
stout´ness
stove´pipe
stow´age

strad´dle
strad´dler
strad´dling
strag´gle
strag´gler
strag´gling
strag´gly
straight´–ahead
straight´away
straight´en-er
straight´–faced
straight-for´ward
straight´ness
straight´–out´
strained
strain´er
strait´jacket
strait´–laced
strange´ly
strange´ness
strang´er
stran´gle
stran´gler
stran´gling
stran´gu-late
stran-gu-la´tion
strap´less
strapped
strap´ping
stra´ta
stra-te´gic
stra-te´gi-cal
stra-te´gi-cal-ly

strat´e-gist
strat´e-gy
strat-i-fi-ca´tion
strat´i-fied
strat´i-form
strat´i-fy
strat´i-fy-ing
strat´o-sphere
straw´ber-ry
stray´er
stray´ing
streak´i-ness
streak´y
stream
stream´bed
stream´er
stream´ing
stream´let
stream´lined
street´car
street´light
street´–smart
strength´en
strength´en-er
strength´en-ing
stren´u-ous
stren´u-ous-ly
stren´u-ous-ness
stressed´–out´
stress´ful
stress´ful-ly
stress´less
stretch´a-ble

stretch´er
stretch´er–bear-er
stretch´i-ness
strewn
stri´ate
stri´at´ed
stri-a´tion
strick´en
strict´ly
strict´ness
stric´ture
stride
stri´dence
stri´den-cy
stri´dent
stri´dent-ly
strid´er
strid´ing
strike´break-er
strike´break-ing
strike´out
strik´er
strik´ing
strik´ing-ly
strin´gen-cy
strin´gent
strin´gent-ly
string´er
string´i-ness
string´ing
string´y
striped
strip´er

strip´ing

strip´ling

stripped

stripped´–down´

strip´per

strip´ping

strive

striv´en

striv´ing

stroke

stroked

strok´er

strok´ing

stroll´er

strong

strong´box

strong´hold

strong´–mind´ed

strong´–willed´

struc´tur-al

struc´tur-al-ize

struc´tur-al-ly

struc´ture

strug´gle

strug´gled

strug´gler

strug´gling

strum´mer

strum´ming

strum´pet

strung´–out´

strut´ted

strut´ter

strut´ting

stub´ble

stub´born-ly

stub´born-ness

stuc´co

stuck´–up

stu´dent

stud´ied

stu´dio

stu´di-ous

stu´di-ous-ly

stu´di-ous-ness

stud´y

stud´y-ing

stuffed

stuff´i-ly

stuff´i-ness

stuff´ing

stuff´y

stul´ti-fied

stul´ti-fy

stul´ti-fy-ing

stum´ble

stum´bler

stum´bling

stunned

stun´ning

stun´ning-ly

stunt´ed

stu´pe-fied

stu´pe-fy

stu´pe-fy-ing

stu-pen´dous

stu-pen´dous-ly

stu´pid

stu-pid´i-ty

stu´pid-ly

stu´pid-ness

stu´por

stur´di-ness

stur´dy

stur´geon

stut´ter

stut´ter-er

stut´ter-ing

style

styled

style´less

styl´ing

styl´ish

styl´ish-ly

styl´ish-ness

styl´ist

styl´ize

sty´lus

sty´mie

sty´mied

suave´ly

suave´ness

suav´i-ty

sub´com-mit-tee

sub-con´scious

sub-con´scious-ly

sub-con´scious-
ness

sub-con´tract

sub´con-trac-tor
sub´cul-ture
sub´di-vide
sub´di-vid-er
sub´di-vid-ing
sub´di-vi-sion
sub-due´
sub-dued´
sub-du´er
sub-du´ing
sub´ject (n., adj.)
sub-ject´ (v.)
sub-jec´tion
sub-jec´tive
sub-jec´tive-ly
sub-jec´tive-ness
sub-jec-tiv´i-ty
sub´ju-gate
sub´ju-gat-ing
sub´ju-ga´tion
sub´lease´
sub-let´
sub´let´ting
sub-lime´
sub-lime´ly
sub-lim´in-al
sub-lim´in-al-ly
sub´ma-rine
sub-ma-rin´er
sub-merge´
sub-merged´
sub-merse´
sub-mersed´

sub-mers´i-ble
sub-mer´sion
sub-min´i-a-ture
sub-mis´sion
sub-mis´sive
sub-mis´sive-ly
sub-mis´sive-ness
sub-mit´ted
sub-mit´ter
sub-mit´ting
sub-or´di-nate
sub-or´di-nate-ly
sub-or-di-na´tion
sub-poe´na
sub-poe´naed
sub´rou-tine
sub-scribe´
sub-scrib´er
sub-scrib´ing
sub-script
sub´sec´tion
sub´se-quent
sub´se-quent-ly
sub-ser´vi-ence
sub-ser´vi-ent
sub-ser´vi-ent-ly
sub-side´
sub-sid´ence
sub-sid´i-ar-y
sub-sid´ing
sub´si-dize
sub´si-dy
sub-sist´

sub-sist´ence
sub-sist´ent
sub´stance
sub-stand´ard
sub-stan´tial
sub-stan´tial-ly
sub-stan´ti-ate
sub-stan-ti-a´tion
sub´stan-tive
sub´sta-tion
sub´sti-tute
sub´sti-tut-ed
sub´sti-tut-ing
sub´sti-tu´tion
sub´strate
sub´ter-fuge
sub-ter-ra´ne-an
sub-ter-ra´ne-ous
sub´ti-tle
sub´tle
sub´tle-ness
sub´tle-ty
sub´tly
sub´to-tal
sub-tract´
sub-trac´tion
sub-trac´tive
sub-trop´ics
sub´urb
sub-ur´ban
sub-ur´ban-ite
sub-ur´bi-a
sub-ver´sive

sub-vert´
sub´way
sub–ze´ro
suc-cess´ful
suc-cess´ful-ly
suc-ces´sion
suc-ces´sive-ly
suc-ces´sor
suc-cinct´
suc-cinct´ly
suc-cinct´ness
suc´cor
suc´co-ry
suc´cu-lence
suc´cu-lent
suc-cumb´
suck´er
suck´le
suck´ling
suc´tion
sud´den-ly
sud´den-ness
suds-y
sued
suede
su´et
suf´fer
suf´fer-ance
suf´fer-er
suf´fer-ing
suf-fice´
suf-ficed´
suf-fi´cien-cy

suf-fi´cient
suf-fi´cient-ly
suf-fic´ing
suf´fix
suf´fo-cate
suf´fo-cat-ing
suf-fo-ca´tion
suf´frage
suf´frag-ette´
suf´frag-ist
suf-fuse´
suf-fus´ing
suf-fu´sion
suf-fu´sive
sug´ar-free
sug´ar-i-ness
sug´ar-less
sug´ar-plum
sug´ar-y
sug-gest´
sug-gest´i-ble
sug-gest´i-bly
sug-ges´tion
sug-ges´tive
sug-ges´tive-ly
su´i-ci´dal
su´i-cide
suit´a-ble
suit´a-bly
suit´case
suite
suit´ing
suit´or

sul´fate
sul´fide
sul´fite
sul´fur
sul-fu´ric
sul´fu-rous
sulk´i-ly
sulk´i-ness
sulk´y
sul´len-ly
sul´len-ness
sul´lied
sul´ly
sul´tri-er
sul´tri-ness
sul´try
sum´mable
sum-mar´i-ly
sum´ma-rize
sum´ma-ry
sum-ma´tion
sum´mer
sum´mer-house
sum´mer-sault
sum´mer-time
sum´mery
sum´ming-up
sum´mit
sum´mon
sum´moned
sum´mon-er
sum´mon-ing
sum´mons

242

sump´tu-ous
sump´tu-ous-ly
sump´tu-ous-ness
sun´beam
sun´burn
sun´burned
sun´dae
sun´der
sun´di-al
sun´down
sun´dried
sun´dry
sun´glass-es
sunk´en
sun´lamp
sun´light
sun´lit
sun´ni-er
sun´ning
sun´ny
sun´rise
sun´room
sun´screen
sun´set
sun´shine
sun´stroke
sun´tan
su´per
su-per-
   abun´dance
su-per-abun´dant
su-perb´
su-perb´ly

su-per-cil´i-ous
su´per-com-put-er
su´per-con-duc´-
   tor
su-per-e-go
su-per-fi´cial
su-per-fi-ci-al´i-ty
su-per-fi´cial-ly
su-per´flu-ous
su-per´flu-ous-ly
su´per-he-ro
su´per-high-way
su-per-hu´man
su-per-hu´man-ly
su´per-im-pose´
su-per-in-tend´
su-per-in-tend´ent
su-pe´ri-or
su-pe-ri-or´i-ty
su-per´la-tive
su-per´la-tive-ly
su´per-mar-ket
su-per-nat´u-ral
su-per-no´va
su´per-nu´mer-
   ary
su-per-sede´
su´per-sed´ing
su-per-son´ic
su´per-star
su-per-sti´tion
su-per-sti´tious
su-per-sti´tious-ly

su´per-struc-ture
su´per-vise
su´per-vis-ing
su´per-vi´sion
su´per-vi-sor
su´per-vi´so-ry
sup´per
sup´per-time
sup-plant´
sup-plant´er
sup´ple
sup´ple-ment
sup-ple-men´tal
sup-ple-men´tal-ly
sup´ple-men´tary
sup´ple-ness
sup´pli-cant
sup´pli-cate
sup´pli-cat-ing
sup-pli-ca´tion
sup-plied´
sup-pli´er
sup-ply´
sup-ply´ing
sup-port´a-ble
sup-port´er
sup-port´ing
sup-port´ive
sup-pos´a-bly
sup-pose´
sup-posed´
sup-pos-ed´ly
sup-pos´ing

sup-po-si´tion
sup-pos´i-to-ry
sup-press´
sup-pres´sant
sup-pres´sion
sup-pres´sor
su-prem´a-cy
su-preme´
su-preme´ly
sur-cease´
sur´charge
sure´fire´
sure ´foot-ed
sure´ly
sur´e-ty
sur´face
sur´faced
sur´fac-er
sur´fac-ing
surf´board
sur´feit
surf´er
surf´ing
surge
sur´geon
sur´gery
sur´gi-cal
sur´gi-cal-ly
surg´ing
sur´li-ness
sur´ly
sur-mise´
sur-mis´ing

sur-mount´
sur-mount´a-ble
sur-mount´ed
sur´name
sur-pass´
sur-pass´ing
sur´plice
sur´plus
sur-pris´able
sur-prise´
sur-prised´
sur-pris´ing
sur-pris´ing-ly
sur-re´al
sur-re´al-ist
sur-ren´der
sur-ren´der-er
sur-rep-ti´tious
sur-rep-ti´tious-ly
sur´rey
sur´ro-gate
sur-round´ed
sur-round´ing
sur´tax
sur-veil´lance
sur-vey´ (v.)
sur´vey (n.)
sur-vey´ing
sur-vey´or
sur-viv´a-ble
sur-viv´al
sur-viv´al-ist
sur-vive´

sur-vi´vor
sus-cep-ti-bil´i-ty
sus-cep´ti-ble
sus-cep´tive
sus´pect (n.)
sus-pect´ (v.)
sus-pend´ed
sus-pend´er
sus-pend´i-ble
sus-pense´
sus-pense´ful
sus-pen´sion
sus-pi´cion
sus-pi´cious
sus-pi´cious-ly
sus-pi´cious-ness
sus-tain´
sus-tain´a-ble
sus-tained´
sus-tain´ing
sus´te-nance
su´ture
su´tur-ing
svelte
swabbed
swab´ber
swab´bing
swad´dle
swad´dled
swad´dling
swag´ger
swag´ger-ing
swag´ger-ing-ly

swal´low
swal´low-er
swamp
swamp´i-ness
swamp´land
swamp´y
swank´i-ness
swank´y
swarmed
swarm´ing
swarth´i-ness
swarth´y
swash´buck-ler
swash´buck-ling
swathe
swat´ter
sway´back
sway´backed
sway´ing
swear´ing
sweat´band
sweat´i-ness
sweat´pants
sweat´shirt
sweat´shop
sweat´y
sweep´er
sweep´ing
sweep´stakes
sweet´-and-sour´
sweet´bread
sweet´en
sweet´en-er

sweet´en-ing
sweet´heart
sweet´ie
sweet´ish
sweet´ly
sweet´meats
sweet´ness
sweet´shop
swelled
swell´ing
swel´ter
swel´ter-ing
swept´back
swerved
swerv´ing
swift´ly
swift´-foot´ed
swift´ness
swim´mer
swim´ming
swin´dle
swin´dler
swin´dling
swing´er
swing´ing
swiped
swip´ing
swirl´ing
swirl´y
switch´board
switch´er
switch´man
switch´yard

swiv´el
swiv´eled
swiv´el-ing
swiz´zle
swol´len
swoon´ing
sword´fish
sword´play
swords´man
syc´o-phant
sy-co´sis
syl-lab´ic
syl-lab-i-ca´tion
syl-lab´i-fy
syl´la-ble
syl´la-bub
sylph´like
syl´van
sym-bi´o-sis
sym-bi-ot´ic
sym´bol
sym-bol´ic
sym-bol´i-cal-ly
sym´bol-ism
sym´bol-ize
sym-met´ri-cal
sym´me-try
sym-pa-thet´ic
sym´pa-thize
sym´pa-thiz-er
sym´pa-thiz-ing
sym´pa-thy
sym-phon´ic

sym-phon´i-cal-ly
sym´pho-ny
sym-po´si-um
symp´tom
symp-to-mat´ic
syn´a-gogue
syn´chro-nize
syn´chro-niz-ing
syn´co-pate
syn´co-pat-ed
syn´co-pat-ing
syn-co-pa´tion
syn´di-cate
syn´di-cat-ing
syn-di-ca´tion
syn´di-ca-tor
syn´drome
syn´er-gy
syn´od
syn´o-nym
syn-on´y-mous
syn-on´y-mous-ly
syn-op´sis
syn´tax
syn´the-sis
syn´the-size
syn´the-siz-er
syn´the-siz-ing
syn-thet´ic
syn-thet´i-cal-ly
sy´phon
sy-ringe´
syr´up

syr´up-y
sys´tem
sys-tem-at´ic
sys-tem-at´i-cal-ly
sys´tem-a-tize
sys-tem´ic
sys-tol´ic

T

tabbed
tab´bing
tab´by
tab´er-na-cle
ta´ble
tab´leau
tab´leaux
ta´ble-cloth
ta´ble-ful
ta´ble–hop
ta´ble-land
tab´let
ta´ble-top
ta´ble-ware
ta´bling
tab´loid
ta-boo´
tab´u-lar
tab´u-late
tab´u-lat-ing
tab-u-la´tion
ta-chom´e-ter
tac´it
tac´it-ly

tac´i-turn
tac-i-tur´ni-ty
tac´i-turn-ly
tack´i-ness
tack´le
tack´ler
tack´less
tack´ling
tack´y
tact´ful
tact´ful-ly
tact´ful-ness
tac´tic
tac´ti-cal
tac´ti-cal-ly
tac-ti´cian
tac´tics
tac´tile
tac-til´i-ty
tact´less
tact´less-ly
tad´pole
taf´fe-ta
taf´fy
tag´a-long
tagged
tag´ging
tail´board
tailed
tail´gate
tail´ing
tail´less
tail´light

tai´lor
tai´lored
tai´lor-ing
tai´lor–made´
tail´pipe
tail´spin
tail´wind
taint
take´a-way
tak´en
take´out
take´o-ver
tak´er
tak´ing
talc
tal´cum
tale´bear-er
tal´ent-ed
tale´tell-er
tale´tell-ing
tal´is-man
talk´a-thon
talk´a-tive
talk´a-tive-ly
talk´a-tive-ness
talk´er
talk´i-ness
talk´ing-to
tal´lied
tall´ness
tal´low
tal´ly
ta´lus

tam´able
tam´bou-rine´
tam´a-ble
tame´a-ble
tamed
tame´ly
tame´ness
tam´er
tam´ing
tamp
tam´per
tan´dem
tan´ge-lo
tan´gent
tan-gen´tial
tan-gen´tial-ly
tan´ger-ine´
tan-gi-bil´i-ty
tan´gi-ble
tan´gi-ble-ness
tan´gi-bly
tang´i-ness
tan´gle
tan´gled
tan´gle-ment
tan´gler
tan´gling
tan´gly
tan´go
tan´goed
tang´y
tan´kard
tank´er

tank´ful
tanned
tan´ner
tan´nery
tan´nic
tan´nin
tan´ning
tan´nish
tan´ta-lize
tan´ta-liz-er
tan´ta-liz-ing-ly
tant´amount
tan´trum
taped
tape´line
ta´per
tap´er
ta´per-ing
ta´per-ing-ly
tap´es-tried
tap´es-try
tape´worm
tap-i-o´ca
tapped
tap´per
tap´ping
tap´room
tap´root
tar-an-tel´la
ta-ran´tu-la
tar´di-ly
tar´di-ness
tar´dy

tar´get
tar´get-a-ble
tar´iff
tar-na´tion
tar´nish
tar´nish-able
ta´rot
tar´pa-per
tar-pau´lin
tar´pon
tar´ra-gon
tarred
tar´ried
tar´ring
tar´ry
tar´ry-ing
tar´sus
tar´tan
tar´tar
tart´ish
tart´ly
tart´ness
tart´y
task´mas-ter
tas´sel
tas´seled
tas´sel-ing
taste
taste´ful
taste´ful-ly
taste´ful-ness
taste´less
taste´less-ly

taste´less-ness
taste´mak-er
tast´er
tast´i-ness
tast´ing
tast´y
tat´ter
tat´tered
tat´ter-sall
tat´ting
tat´tle
tat´tler
tat´tle-tale
tat-too´
tat-too´er
taught
taunt´er
taunt´ing
taunt´ing-ly
taupe
taut´en
taut´ly
taut´ness
tau-to-log´ic
tau-to-log´i-cal
tau-to-log´i-cal-ly
tau-tol´o-gy
tav´ern
ta-ver´na
taw´dri-ly
taw´dri-ness
taw´dry
tawn´i-er

taw´ni-ness
tawn´y
tax-a-bil´i-ty
tax´a-ble
tax´a-ble-ness
tax-a´tion
tax´–ex-empt´
tax´–free
tax´i
tax´i-cab
tax´i-der-mist
tax´i-der-my
tax´ied
tax´ing
tax´pay-er
tax´pay-ing
tea´cake
teach´a-ble
teach´a-bly
teach´er
teach´–in
teach´ing
tea´cup
tea´cup-ful
tea´house
tea´ket-tle
team´mate
team´ster
team´work
tea´pot
tear´a-ble
tear´a-way
tear´drop

tear´ful
tear´ful-ly
tear´ful-ness
tear´i-ly
tear´i-ness
tear´ing
tear´ing-ly
tear´jerk-er
tear´less
tea´room
tear´–stained
tear´y
teas´a-ble
teased
teas´er
teas´ing
teas´ing-ly
tea´spoon
tea´spoon-ful
tea´time
tech
tech´ie
tech´ni-cal
tech-ni-cal´i-ty
tech´ni-cal-ly
tech-ni´cian
tech´nics
tech-nique´
tech´no-crat
tech-nol´o-gy
tech´y
tec-ton´ic
tec-ton´i-cal-ly

tec-ton´ics
ted´dy
te´di-ous
te´di-ous-ly
te´di-ous-ness
te´di-um
teem´ing
teen´age
teen´–ag´er
teen´sy
teen´y-bop-per
tee´ny–wee´ny
tee´ter-board
teethe
teethed
teeth´ing
tee-to´tal
tee´to-tal-er
teg´u-ment
teg-u-men´tal
tel´e-cast
tel´e-cast-er
tel-e-com-mu´ni-
  cate
tel-e-com-mu-ni-
  ca´tions
tel´e-com-mut-ing
tel´e-con-fer-ence
tel´e-gram
tel´e-graph
te-leg´ra-pher
tel-e-graph´ic
te-leg´ra-phy

tel-e-ki-ne´sis
tel-e-ki-net´ic
tel´e-mar-ket-er
tel´e-mar-ket-ing
te-lem´e-try
tel-e-path´ic
tel-e-path´i-cal-ly
te-lep´a-thy
tel´e-phone
tel-e-phon´ic
tel´e-pho´to
tel´e-port
tel-e-por-ta´tion
tel´e-scope
tel´e-scop´ic
tel´e-scop´i-cal-ly
tel´e-thon
tel´e-vise
tel´e-vi-sion
tel´ex
tell´a-ble
tell´er
tell´ing
tell´ing-ly
tell´tale
te-mer´i-ty
tem´peh
tem´per
tem´per-a
tem´per-a-ment
tem´per-a-men´tal
tem´per-a-men´-
  tal-ly

249

tem´per-ance
tem´per-ate
tem´per-ate-ly
tem´per-ate-ness
tem´per-a-ture
tem´pered
tem´per-er
tem´pest
tem-pes´tu-ous
tem-pes´tu-ous-ly
tem-pes´tu-ous-
  ness
tem´plar
tem´plate
tem´ple
tem´plet
tem´po
tem´po-ral
tem´po-ral-ly
tem-po-rar´i-ly
tem´po-rar-i-ness
tem´po-rar-y
tem´po-rize
tempt´a-ble
temp-ta´tion
tempt´er
tempt´ing
tempt´ing-ly
tempt´ing-ness
tempt´ress
tem-pu´ra
ten´a-ble
ten´a-ble-ness

ten´a-bly
te-na´cious
te-na´cious-ly
te-na´cious-ness
te-nac´i-ty
ten´an-cy
ten´ant
tend´en-cy
ten-den´tious
ten-den´tious-ly
ten-den´tious-ness
tend´er
ten´der
ten-der-a-bil´i-ty
ten´der-a-ble
ten´der-foot
ten´der-heart-ed
ten´der-ize
ten´der-iz-er
ten´der-loin
ten´der-ly
ten´der-ness
ten-di-ni´tis
ten´don
ten´dril
ten´e-ment
ten´et
ten´fold
ten´nis
ten´on
ten´or
ten´pins
tense

tense´ly
tense´ness
ten´si-ble
ten´sile
ten´sile-ly
ten´sile-ness
ten´sion
ten´sion-less
ten´sor
ten´–speed
ten´–spot
ten´ta-cle
ten´ta-cled
tent´age
ten´ta-tive
ten´ta-tive-ly
ten´ta-tive-ness
tent´ed
tent´er
ten´ter-hook
tent´mak-er
ten´u-ous
ten´u-ous-ly
ten´u-ous-ness
ten´ure
tep´id
tep´id-ly
tep´id-ness
te-qui´la
ter-i-ya´ki
term´er
ter´mi-na-ble
ter´mi-na-bly

ter´mi-nal
ter´mi-nal-ly
ter´mi-nate
ter-mi-na´tion
ter´mi-na-tive
ter´mi-na-tive-ly
ter´mi-na-tor
ter-mi-nol´o-gy
ter´mi-nus
ter´mite
ter´ra
ter´race
ter´ra–cot´ta
ter-rain´
ter´ra-pin
ter-raz´zo
ter´ri-ble
ter´ri-ble-ness
ter´ri-bly
ter´ri-er
ter-rif´ic
ter-rif´i-cal-ly
ter´ri-fied
ter´ri-fy
ter´ri-fy-ing-ly
ter-rine´
ter-ri-to´ri-al
ter-ri-to´ri-al-ize
ter-ri-to´ri-al-ly
ter´ri-to-ry
ter´ror
ter´ror-ism
ter´ror-ist

ter´ror-ize
ter´ror-iz-er
ter´ry-cloth
terse´ly
terse´ness
ter´ti-ar-y
test´a-ble
tes´ta-ment
tes´tate
test´–drive
test´er
tes´ti-fi-er
tes´ti-fy
tes´ti-ly
tes-ti-mo´ni-al
tes´ti-mo-ny
tes´ti-ness
tes-tos´ter-one
test´–tube
tes´ty
tet´a-nus
tet´a-ny
tête–à–tête
teth´er
teth´ered
te´trarch
text´book
tex´tile
tex´tu-al
tex´ture
thank´ful
thank´ful-ly
thank´ful-ness

thank´less
thanks´giv´ing
thank´–you
that
thatch
thatch´er
the´a-ter
the´a-ter-go-er
the´a-ter–in–the–
  round´
the´a-tre (Br.)
the-at´ri-cal
the-at-ri-cal´i-ty
the-at´ri-cal-ly
the-at´rics
their
the-mat´ic
the-mat´i-cal-ly
theme
them-selves´
thence´forth
the-oc´ra-cy
the-o-crat´ic
the-o-crat´i-cal
the-o-lo´gian
the-o-log´i-cal
the-ol´o-gize
the-ol´o-giz-er
the-ol´o-gy
the´o-rem
the-o-ret´i-cal
the-o-ret´ics
the´o-rist

the´o-rize
the´o-ry
the-os´o-phy
ther´a-peu´tic
ther´a-peu´ti-cal-
  ly
ther´a-pist
ther´a-py
there´abouts
there´af´ter
there´by´
there´fore´
there-in´
there-in-af´ter
there-of´
there-to´
there-to-fore´
there´upon´
there-with´
ther´mal
ther´mo-cou-ple
ther-mo-dy-nam´-
  ics
ther-mog´ra-phy
ther-mom´e-ter
ther´mo-nu´cle-ar
ther´mo-stat
ther´mo-stat´ic
the-sau´rus
the´sis
thi-am´ine
thick´en
thick´en-ing

thick´et
thick´–head-ed
thick´ish
thick´ness
thick´set´
thick´–skinned´
thief
thieve
thiev´ery
thieves
thiev´ing
thiev´ish
thiev´ish-ly
thiev´ish-ness
thigh´bone
thim´ble
thim´ble-ful
think´a-ble
think´a-bly
think´er
think´ing
thin´ly
thin´ner
thin´ness
thin´–skinned´
third´–class
third´–degree´
third´ly
third´–rate´
thirst´i-ly
thirst´i-ness
thirst´y
thir´teen´

thir´teenth´
thir´ti-eth
thir´ty
this´tle
thith´er
thong
tho´rax
thorn´bush
thorn´i-ly
thorn´i-ness
thorn´less
thorn´like
thorn´y
thor´ough
thor´ough-bred
thor´ough-fare
thor´ough-go-ing
thor´ough-ly
thor´ough-ness
thought´ful
thought´ful-ly
thought´ful-ness
thought´less
thought´less-ly
thought´less-ness
thought´–out´
thou´sand
thou´sandth
thrash´er
thrash´ing
thread´bare
thread´er
thread´worm

thread´y
threat´en
threat´en-ing
threat´en-ing-ly
three´–cor´nered
three´–di-men´-
  sion-al
three´fold
three´–leg´ged
three´pence
three´pen-ny
three´–phase
three´–piece´
three´–ply´
three´–quar´ter
three´–ring
three´some
three´–speed
three´–wheel´er
thresh´er
thresh´ing
thresh´old
threw
thrice
thrift´i-er
thrift´i-ly
thrift´i-ness
thrift´shop
thrift´y
thrill´er
thrill´ing
thrill´ing-ly
thrive

thriv´ing
throat´i-ly
throat´i-ness
throat´y
throb´bing
throb´bing-ly
throe
throm-bo´sis
throne
throng
throt´tle
throt´tled
through-out´
throw´a-way
throw´back
thrust´er
thrust´ing
thru´way
thug´ger-y
thug´gish
thumb´hole
thumb´nail
thumb´print
thumb´screw
thumbs´–down
thumbs´–up
thumb´tack
thump´er
thump´ing
thun´der
thun´der-a-tion
thun´der-bolt
thun´der-clap

thun´der-cloud
thun´der-head
thun´der-ing
thun´der-ing-ly
thun´der-ous
thun´der-ous-ly
thun´der-show-er
thun´der-storm
thun´der-struck
thus´ly
thwart
thyme
thy´roid
thy-roid-ec´to-my
ti-ar´a
tick´er
tick´et
tick´et-er
tick´ing
tick´le
tick´ler
tick´lish
tick´lish-ly
tick´lish-ness
tid´al
tid´bit
tide´land
tide´wa-ter
ti´di-ly
ti´di-ness
ti´dings
ti´dy
tie´back

tie´break-er
tie´–dye
tie´–dye-ing
tie´pin
tiered
tight´en
tight´en-er
tight´en-ing
tight´–fist´ed
tight´–fist´ed-ness
tight´–knit´
tight´–lipped
tight´ly
tight´ness
tight´rope
tight´wad
ti´gress
tiled
til´ing
till´age
till´er
tilt´a-ble
tilt´er
tim´ber
tim´bered
tim´ber-land
tim´ber-line
tim´bre
time´card
time´–con-sum´-
  ing
time´–hon´ored
time´keep-er

time´less
time´less-ly
time´less-ness
time´li-er
time´li-ness
time´ly
time´–out
time´piece
tim´er
time´sav-ing
time´–share
time´ta-ble
time´–test-ed
time´worn
tim´id
ti-mid´i-ty
tim´id-ly
tim´id-ness
tim´ing
tim´o-rous
tim´o-rous-ly
tim´o-rous-ness
tinc´ture
tin´der-box
tin´foil
tinge´ing
tin´gle
tin´gled
tin´gler
tin´gly
tin´gling
ti´ni-er
ti´ni-ness

tin´ker
tin´ker-er
tin´ner
tin´ni-er
tin´ni-ly
tin´ni-ness
tin´ny
tin´sel
tin´seled
tin´sel-ly
tin´smith
tint´er
tin´type
tin´work
ti´ny
tip´off
tip´per
tip´ping
tip´ple
tip´si-ly
tip´si-ness
tip´ster
tip´sy
tip´toe
tip´–top
ti´rade
tired
tired´ly
tire´less
tire´less-ly
tire´less-ness
tire´some
tire´some-ly

tir´ing
tis´sue
ti´tan
ti-tan´ic
ti-ta´ni-um
tithe
tith´er
tith´ing
tit´il-late
tit´il-lat-ing
tit-il-la´tion
tit´il-la-tive
ti´tle
ti´tled
ti´tle-hold-er
tit´ter
tit´ter-ing
tit´u-lar
toad´ish
toad´stool
toad´y
to´–and–fro´
toast´er
toast´mas-ter
toast´mis-tress
toast´i-ness
toast´y
to-bac´co
to-bac´co-nist
to-bog´gan-er
to-bog´gan-ing
to-bog´gan-ist
to-day´

tod´dle
tod´dler
tod´dy
to–do´
toe´hold
toe´nail
toe´–to-toe´
tof´fee
to´fu
to´ga
to´gaed
to-geth´er
to-geth´er-ness
tog´ger-y
tog´gle
toil´er
toi´let
toi´let-ry
toi-lette´
toil´some
toil´some-ly
toil´some-ness
to´ken
to´ken-ism
tol´er-a-ble
tol´er-a-ble-ness
tol´er-a-bly
tol´er-ance
tol´er-ant
tol´er-ant-ly
tol´er-ate
tol-er-a´tion
toll´booth

toll´–free´
toll´gate
toll´house
to-ma-til´lo
to-ma´to
tom´boy
tomb´stone
tom´cat
tom-fool´er-y
to-mor´row
ton´al
to-nal´i-ty
tone´–deaf
tone´less
ton´er
tongs
tongue
tongue´–tied
ton´ic
to-night
ton´nage
ton-neau´
ton´sil
ton-sil-lec´to-my
ton-sil-li´tis
ton-so´ri-al
ton´y
tool´box
tool´mak-er
tool´mak-ing
tool´room
tool´shed
tooth´ache

tooth′brush
tooth′less
tooth′paste
tooth′some
tooth′y
top′coat
top′flight′
top′–heavy
top′ic
top′i-cal-ly
top′less
top′most
top′–notch′
to-pog′ra-pher
top-o-graph′ic
to-pog′ra-phy
top′per
top′ping
top′ple
top′pling
top′–se′cret
top′soil
torch′bear-er
torch′light
tor-ment′ *(v.)*
tor′ment *(n.)*
tor-ment′ing-ly
tor-men′tor
tor-na′do
tor-na′does
tor-pe′do
tor-pe′does
tor′pid

tor-pid′i-ty
tor′pid-ly
tor′por
tor′por-if′ic
torque
tor′rent
tor-ren′tial
tor′rid
tor′sion
tor′sion-al
tor′so
tor′toise
tor′toise-shell
tor′tu-ous
tor′ture
tor′tur-er
tor′tur-ous-ly
toss′ing
toss′pot
to′tal
to′taled
to′tal-ing
to′tal-ism
to-tal′i-tar′i-an
to-tal′i-ty
to′tal-ize
to′tal-ly
to′tem
tot′ing
tot′ter
tot′ter-ing
touch′a-ble
touch′down

tou-ché′
touched
touch′i-ness
touch′ing
touch′stone
touch′–type
touch′–typ′ist
touch′–up
touch′y
tough′en
tough′en-er
tough′ie
tough′ly
tough′–mind′ed
tough′ness
tou-pee′
tour′ism
tour′ist
tour′ist-y
tour′na-ment
tour′ney
tour′ni-quet
tou′sle
tou′sled
tow′a-ble
tow′age
to′ward
tow′el
tow-el-ette′
tow′el-ing
tow′er
tow′er-ing
tow′line

town´house
towns´folk
town´ship
towns´peo-ple
tow´rope
tox´ic
tox´i-cant
tox-ic´i-ty
tox-i-col´o-gist
tox-i-col´o-gy
tox´in
trace´a-ble
trace´a-bly
trac´er
tra´chea
tra´che-al
trac´ing
track´a-ble
track´er
track´ing
track´less
tract
trac-ta-bil´i-ty
trac´ta-ble
trac´ta-ble-ness
trac´ta-bly
trac´tion
trac´tor
trade´mark
trade´–off
trad´er
trad´ing
tra-di´tion

tra-di´tion-al
tra-di´tion-al-ism
tra-di´tion-al-ist
tra-di´tion-al-ly
tra-duce´
tra-duce´ment
tra-duc´er
tra-duc´ing-ly
traf´fic
traf´ficked
traf´fick-er
traf´fick-ing
tra-ge´di-an
trag´e-dy
trag´ic
trag´i-cal-ly
trag-i-com´e-dy
trail´blaz-er
trail´er
train´a-ble
train-ee´
train´er
train´ing
train´load
trai´tor
trai´tor-ous
trai´tor-ous-ly
trai´tor-ous-ness
tra-jec´to-ry
tramp´er
tram´ple
tram´pler
tram´pling

tram´po-line´
tram´way
trance´like
tran´quil
tran´quil-ize
tran´quil-iz-er
tran-quil´li-ty
tran´quil-ly
tran´quil-ness
trans-act´
trans-ac´tion
tran-scend´
tran-scen´den-cy
tran-scen´dent
tran-scen-den´tal
trans-con-ti-nen´-
　tal
tran-scribe´
tran-scrib´er
tran´script
tran-scrip´tion
trans´fer *(n., v.)*
trans-fer´ *(v.)*
trans-fer´a-ble
trans-fer´al
trans-fer´ence
trans-ferred´
trans-fer´ring
trans-fig-u-ra´tion
trans-fig´ure
trans-fix´
trans-form´
trans-for-ma´tion

trans-form´er
trans-fuse´
trans-fu´sion
trans-gress´
trans-gres´sion
trans-gres´sor
tran´sience
tran´sien-cy
tran´sient
tran´sient-ly
tran-sis´tor
tran-sis´tor-ize
tran´sit
tran-si´tion
tran-si´tion-al
tran-si´tion-al-ly
tran-si-to´ri-ly
tran´si-to-ri-ness
tran´si-to-ry
trans-lat´a-ble
trans-late´
trans-la´tion
trans-la´tion-al
trans-la´tive
trans-la´tor
trans-lit-er-a´tion
trans-lu´cence
trans-lu´cen-cy
trans-lu´cent
trans-lu´cent-ly
trans-mi´grate
trana-mi-gra´tion
trans-mis´si-ble

trans-mis´sion
trans-mit´
trans-mit´ta·ble
trans-mit´tal
trans-mit´ter
trans-mog´ri-fy
trans-oce-an´ic
tran´som
trans-par´en-cy
trans-par´ent
trans-par´ent-ly
trans-par´ent-ness
tran-spire´
trans-plant´
trans-plant´er
tran-spon´der
trans-port´ *(v.)*
trans´port *(n.)*
trans-port´a-ble
trans-por-ta´tion
trans-pose´
trans-po-si´tion
trans-ship´ment
tran-sub-stan´ti-
  ate
trans-verse´
tra-peze´
trap´per
trap´pings
trash´i-ness
trash´man
trash´y
trat-to-ri´a

trau´ma
trau-mat´ic
trau-mat´i-cal-ly
trau´ma-tism
trau´ma-tize
travail´
trav´el
trav´eled
trav´el-er
trav´el-ing
trav´el-ogue
tra-vers´able
trav´erse
tra-verse´
trav´es-ty
trawl´er
treach´er-ous
treach´er-ous-ly
treach´er-ous-ness
treach´ery
trea´cle
tread´ing
trea´dle
tread´mill
trea´son
trea´son-a-ble
trea´son-ous
trea´son-ous-ly
trea´sure
trea´sur-er
trea´sur·y
treat´a-ble
trea´ties

trea´tise

treat´ment

trea´ty

tre´ble

tree´less

tree´lined

tree´top

trek´king

trel´lis

trel´lis-work

trem´ble

trem´bler

trem´bling

trem´bling-ly

trem´bly

tre-men´dous

tre-men´dous-ly

tre-men´dous-ness

trem´e-tol

trem´or

trem´u-lous

trem´u-lous-ly

trem´u-lous-ness

tren´chant

trench´er-man

trend´i-ness

trend´set-ter

trend´y

tres´pass-er

tressed

tres´tle

tri´ad

tri´al

tri´an-gle

tri-an´gu-lar

tri-an´gu-late

tri-an-gu-la´tion

tri-ath´lon

trib´al

trib´al-ism

trib´al-ly

tribes´man

tri-bu´nal

trib´u-tar-y

trib´ute

trich-i-no´sis

tri´chro-mat´ic

tri-chro´ma-tism

tri´–cit´y

trick´er-y

trick´i-ly

trick´i-ness

trick´le

trick´ster

trick´y

tri´cy-cle

tried´–and–true´

tri-en´nial

tri-en´nial-ly

tri´fle

tri´fler

tri´fling

tri´fling-ly

tri-fo´cal

trig´ger

trig-o-nom´e-try

tri-lat´er-al

tri-lat´er-al-ly

tri-lin´gual

tri-lin´gual-ly

tril´lion

tril´lionth

tril´o-gy

tri-mes´ter

trim´ly

trim´mer

trim´ming

trin´ket

tri´o

tri´ple

tri´ple–deck´er

tri´ple–space

trip´let

trip´li-cate

tri´pod

trip´ping-ly

trip´tych

trip´wire

tri-sect´

tri-sec´tion

tris-kai-dek-a-
   pho´bi-a

tris-kai-dek-a-
   pho´bic

tri´state

trite´ly

trite´ness

tri´umph

tri-um´phal

tri-um´phant
tri-um´phant-ly
tri-um´vi-rate
triv´et
triv´ia
triv´i-al
triv-i-al´i-ty
triv´i-al-ize
triv´i-al-ly
tri-week´ly
tro´che
trod´den
trog´lo-dyte
troi´ka
troll´er
trol´ley
trol´lop
trom-bone´
trom-bon´ist
tromp
troop´er
troop´ship
tro´phy
trop´ic
trop´i-cal
trop´i-cal-ly
trot´ter
trot´ting
trou´ba-dour
trou´ble
trou´bled
trou´ble-mak-er
trou´ble-mak-ing

trou´ble-shoot
trou´ble-shoot-er
trou´ble-some
trough
trounce
troupe
troup´er
trou´sers
trous´seau
trow´el
trow´eled
tru´an-cy
tru´ant-ly
truck´driv-er
truck´er
truck´le
truck´ling
truck´load
truc´u-lence
truc´u-lent
trudge
trudg´ing
true´heart´ed
true´–life´
truf´fle
tru´ism
tru´ly
trumped´–up´
trum´pery
trum´pet
trum´pet-er
trun´cate
trun´cat-ed

trun-ca´tion
trun´cheon
trun´dle
trunk´ful
truss´ing
trust´bust-er
trust´bust-ing
trust´ee´
trust-ee´ship
trust´ful
trust´ful-ness
trust´i-ness
trust´ing
trust´wor-thi-ness
trust´wor-thy
trust´y
truth´ful-ly
truth´ful-ness
try´ing
try´ing-ly
tryst
tsu-nam´i
tub´by
tube´less
tu´ber
tu´ber-ous
tub´ing
tu´bu-lar
tuft´ed
tuft´ing
tug´–of–war´
tu-i´tion
tu´lip

tum´ble-down
tum´bler
tum´bling
tum´my
tu´mor
tu´mour (Br.)
tu´mult
tu-mul´tu-ous
tu-mul´tu-ous-ly
tun´dra
tune´ful
tune´less
tun´er
tune´-up
tu´nic
tun´ing
tun´nel
tun´neled
tun´nel-er
tun´nel-ing
tur´ban
tur´bine
tur´bo-charg-er
tur´bot
tur´bu-lence
tur´bu-lent
tu-reen´
tur´gid
tur-gid´i-ty
tur´gid-ly
tur´gid-ness
tur´key
tur´mer-ic

tur´moil
turn´a-bout
turn´a-round
turn´coat
turn´ing
tur´nip
turn´off
turn´on
turn´pike
turn´stile
turn´ta-ble
tur´pen-tine
tur´pi-tude
tur´quoise
tur´ret
tur´ret-ed
tur´tle
tus´sle
tu´te-lage
tu´tor
tu´tored
tu-to´ri-al
tux-e´do
twad´dle
twang´y
tweez´ers
twelfth
twelve
twen´ti-eth
twen´ty
twice´-told´
twi´light
twine

twinge
twin´ing
twin´kle
twin´kling
twist´a-ble
twist´er
twitch´er
twitch´ing
twitch´y
twit´ter-ing
twit´ter-y
two´-faced
two´fer
two´-fist´ed
two´-seat´er
two´-sid´ed
two´some
two´-step
two´-tone
ty-coon´
ty´ing
tyke
tym´pan
tym´pa-nist
type´cast
type´set
type´writ-er
type´writ-ten
ty´phoid
ty-phoon´
ty´phus
typ´i-cal-ly
typ-i-fi-ca´tion

typ´i-fy
typ´ist
ty´po
ty-pog´ra-pher
ty-po-graph´ic
ty-po-graph´i-cal
ty-pog´ra-phy
ty-pol´o-gist
ty-pol´o-gy
ty-ran´ni-cal
tyr´an-nize
tyr´an-nous
tyr´an-nous-ly
tyr´an-ny
ty´rant
ty´ro

U

ubiq´ui-tous
ubiq´ui-tous-ly
ubiq´ui-tous-ness
ubi´qui-ty
ud´der
ug´li-ness
ug´ly
uku-le´le
ul´cer
ul´cer-ate
ul-cer-a´tion
ul´cer-a-tive
ul´cer-ous
ul-te´ri-or
ul´ti-ma

ul´ti-ma-cy
ul´ti-mate
ul´ti-mate-ly
ul-ti-ma´tum
ul´tra
ul-tra-clean´
ul-tra-con-serv´a-
    tive
ul-tra-fine´
ul-tra-light´
ul´tra-ma-rine´
ul-tra-mod´ern
ul-tra-pure´
ul-tra-pu´ri-ty
ul-tra-son´ic
ul-tra-son´i-cal-ly
ul-tra-son´ics
ul-tra-sound´
ul-tra-vi´o-let
um´ber
um-bil´i-cal
um-bil´i-cal-ly
um´brage
um-bra´geous
um-bra´geous-ly
um´bral
um´laut
um´pire
un-abat´ed
un-a´ble
un-abridged´
un-ac-cept´a-ble
un-ac-cent´ed

un-ac-com´pa-
    nied
un-ac-count´a·ble
un-ac-count´a·ble-
    ness
un-ac-count´a·bly
un-ac-cus´tomed
un-ac-quaint´ed
un-adorned´
un-adul´ter-at-ed
un-ad-vised´
un-ad-vis´ed-ly
un-ad-vis´ed-ness
un-af-fect´ed
un-af-fect´ed-ly
un-af-fect´ed-ness
un-afraid´
un-aid´ed
un-al´ter-a·ble
un-al´ter-a·ble-
    ness
un-al´ter-a·bly
un-al´tered
un-am-bi´tious
un-am-biv´a-lent
una-nim´i-ty
u-nan´i-mous
u-nan´i-mous-ly
u-nan´i-mous-ness
un-an-nounced´
un-an´swer-a·ble
un-an´swer-a·bly
un-ap-peal´a·ble

un-ap-peal´a·bly
un-ap-proach´-
    a·ble
un-ap-proach´-
    a·ble-ness
un-ap-proach´-
    a·bly
un-ap-pro´pri-at-
    ed
un-apt´
un-apt´ly
un-apt´ness
un-arm´
un-armed´
un-a-shamed´
un-a-sham´ed-ly
un-a-sham´ed-
    ness
un-asked´
un-as-sail´a·ble
un-as-sail´a·ble-
    ness
un-as-sail´a·bly
un-as-sist´ed
un-as-sum´ing
un-at-tached´
un-at-tain´able
un-at-tend´ed
un-at-trac´tive
un-au´tho-rized
un-a-vail´ing
un-a-vail´ing-ly
un-avoid´a·ble

un-avoid´a·bly
un-a-ware´
un-a-ware´ly
un-a-ware´ness
un-a-wares´
un-bal´ance
un-bal´anced
un-barred´
un-bear´a·ble
un-bear´a·ble-ness
un-bear´a·bly
un-beat´a·ble
un-beat´a·bly
un-beat´en
un-be-com´ing
un-be-com´ing-ly
un-be-com´ing-
    ness
un-be-got´ten
un-be-known´
un-be-lief´
un-be-liev´a·ble
un-be-liev´a·bly
un-be-liev´er
un-be-liev´ing
un-bend´
un-bend´a·ble
un-bend´ing
un-bend´ing-ly
un-bent´
un-bi´ased
un-bi´ased-ly
un-bid´den

un-bind´
un-blam´able
un-bleached´
un-blem´ished
un-blink´ing
un-blink´ing-ly
un-block´
un-blush´ing
un-blush´ing-ly
un-blush´ing-ness
un-bolt´
un-bolt´ed
un-born´
un-bos´om
un-bound´
un-bound´ed
un-bound´ed-ly
un-bound´ed-ness
un-bowed´
un-brace´
un-braid´
un-brand´ed
un-break´able
un-bri´dle
un-bri´dled
un-bro´ken
un-bro´ken-ly
un-bro´ken-ness
un-buck´le
un-budge´a·ble
un-budge´a·ble-
    ness
un-budge´a·bly

un-bun´dle
un-bun´dled
un-bur´den
un-but´ton
un-but´toned
un-cage´
un-caged´
un-called—for
un-can´ni-ly
un-can´ni-ness
un-can´ny
un-cap´
un-cared´–for
un-ceas´ing
un-ceas´ing-ly
un-ceas´ing-ness
un-cer-e-mo´ni-
  ous
un-cer-e-mo´ni-
  ous-ly
un-cer-e-mo´ni-
  ous-ness
un-cer´tain
un-cer´tain-ly
un-cer´tain-ness
un-cer´tain-ty
un-chain´
un-chained´
un-chal´lenged
un-change´able
un-changed´
un-charged´
un-char´i-ta-ble

un-char´i-ta-ble-
  ness
un-char´i-ta-bly
un-chart´ed
un-char´tered
un-chaste´
un-checked´
un-chris´tian
un-chris´tian-ly
un´ci-al
un´ci-form
un-cir´cum-cised
un-civ´il
un-civ´il-ized
un-civ´il-ly
un-civ´il-ness
un-clad´
un-clasp´
un-clasped´
un-clas´si-fied
un´cle
un-clean´
un-clean´li-ness
un-clean´ly
un-clean´ness
un-cloak´
un-clog´
un-closed´
un-clothe´
un-cloud´ed
un-coil´
un-com´fort-a-ble
un-com´fort-a-bly

un-com-mer´cial
un-com-mit´ted
un-com´mon
un-com´mon-ly
un-com´mon-ness
un-com-mu´ni-ca-
  tive
un-com-plain´ing
un-com´pro-mis-
  ing
un-com´pro-mis-
  ing-ly
un-con-cern´
un-con-cerned´
un-con-cern´ed-ly
un-con-cern´ed-
  ness
un-con-di´tion-al
un-con-di´tion-al-
  ly
un-con-di´tioned
un-con-di´tioned-
  ness
un-con-form-
  a·bil´i-ty
un-con-form´a·ble
un-con-form´a·bly
un-con-form´i-ty
un-con-nec´ted
un-con-nect´ed-ly
un-con-nect´ed-
  ness
un-con´quered

un-con´scion-a·ble
un-con´scion-
  a·ble-ness
un-con´scion-a-
  bly
un-con´scious
un-con´scious-ly
un-con´scious-ness
un-con-sti-tu´tion-
  al
un-con-sti-tu-tion-
  al´i-ty
un-con-sti-tu´tion-
  al-ly
un-con-trol´la·ble
un-con-trolled´
un-con-struct´ed
un-con-ven´tion-al
un-con-ven´tion-
  al-ist
un-con-ven-tion-
  al´i-ty
un-con-ven´tion-
  al-ly
un-cork´
un-cor-rupt´ed
un-count´ed
un-cou´ple
un-couth´
un-couth´ly
un-couth´ness
un-cov´er
un-cov´ered

un-crit´i-cal
un-crit´i-cal-ly
un-cross´
unc´tion
unc´tu-ous
unc´tu-ous-ly
unc´tu-ous-ness
un-cul´ti-vat-ed
un-cul´tured
un-cured´
un-curl´
un-cut´
un-damped´
un-daunt´ed
un-daunt´ed-ly
un-daunt´ed-ness
un-de-ceiv´a·ble
un-de-ceive´
un-de-ceiv´er
un-de-cid´ed
un-de-cid´ed-y
un-de-cid´ed-ness
un-de-feat´ed
un-de-filed´
un-de-fined´
un-dem-o-crat´ic
un-de-mon´stra-
  ble
un-de-mon´stra-
  tive
un-de-mon´stra-
  tive-ly
un-de-ni´a·ble

un-de-ni´a·ble-
  ness
un-de-ni´a·bly
un´der
un-der-a-chieve´
un-der-a-
  chieve´ment
un-der-a-chiev´er
un-der-act´
un-der-ac´tive
un-der-age´
un´der-age
un´der-arm
un´der-bel-ly
un-der-bid´
un´der-bid-der
un´der-bite
un´der-bod-y
un´der-brush
un-der-cap-i-tal-i-
  za´tion
un-der-cap´i-tal-
  ize
un´der-car-riage
un-der-charge´
un´der-class
un-der-class´man
un´der-clothes
un´der-cloth´ing
un´der-coat
un´der-coat-ing
un-der-com´pen-
  sate

un-der-cov´er
un´der-croft
un´der-cur-rent
un´der-cut
un-der-de-vel´op
un-der-de-vel´oped
un-der-de-vel´op-ment
un´der-dog
un´der-done
un-der-em´pha-size
un-der-em-ployed´
un-der-em-ploy´ment
un-der-es´ti-mate
un-der-es-ti-ma´-tion
un-der-ex-pose´
un-der-ex-po´sure
un-der-feed´
un´der-foot´
un´der-fur
un´der-gar-ment
un-der-gird´
un´der-glaze
un-der-go´
un´der-gone´
un´der-grad
un-der-grad´u-ate
un´der-ground

un´der-growth
un´der-hand
un´der-hand-ed
un´der-hand-ed-ly
un´der-hand-ed-ness
un-der-in-sure´
un-der-in-sured´
un-der-lay´
un-der-lie´
un´der-line
un´der-lin-er
un´der-ling
un´der-ly-ing
un-der-mine´
un´der-most
un-der-neath´
un-der-nour´ished
un-der-nour´ish-ment
un´der-paid´
un´der-pants
un´der-pass
un´der-pay´
un-der-pay´ment
un-der-pin´
un´der-pin-ning
un-der-price´
un´der-priv´i-leged
un-der-pro-duc´tion
un-der-rate´

un-der-re-port´
un-der-run´
un´der-score
un´der-sea
un-der-seas´
un´der-sec´re-tary
un-der-sell´
un´der-shirt
un-der-shoot´
un´der-side
un´der-sign
un´der-signed
un´der-size
un´der-sized
un´der-skirt
un-der-staffed´
un-der-stand´
un-der-stand´a·ble
un-der-stand´-a·bly
un-der-stand´ing
un-der-stand´ing-ly
un-der-state´
un-der-stat´ed
un-der-stat´ed-ness
un´der-state-ment
un-der-stood´
un-der-strength´
un´der-study
un´der-sur-face
un´der-take

un´der-tak-er
un´der-tak´ing
un´der–the–
   coun´ter
un´der–the–ta´ble
un´der-things
un´der-tone
un-der-took´
un´der-tow
un´der-trick
un-der-val-u-a´-
   tion
un-der-val´ue
un´der-wa´ter
un´der-way
un´der-wear
un´der-weight
un´der-world
un-der-work´
un´der-write
un´der-writ-er
un´der-writ´ten
un-de-served´
un-de-sign´ing
un-de-sir-a-bil´i-
   ty
un-de-sir´a·ble
un-de-sir´a·ble-
   ness
un-de-sir´a·bly
un-de-vel´oped
un´dies
un-di-rect´ed

un-dis´ci-plined
un-dis-cov´ered
un-dis-mayed´
un-dis-posed´
un-dis-put´ed
un-dis-tin´guished
un-dis-turbed´
un-di-ver´si-fied
un-di-vid´ed
un-do´
un-dock´
un-do´ing
un-done´
un-doubt´ed
un-doubt´ed-ly
un-dress´
un-dressed´
un-due´
un´du-lant
un´du-late
un´du-lat-ed
un-du-la´tion
un´du-la-tor
un´du-la-to-ry
un-du´ly
un-dy´ing
un-earned´
un-earth´
un-earth´li-ness
un-earth´ly
un-eas´i-ly
un-eas´i-ness
un-eas´y

un-ed´u-cat-ed
un-em-ploy´a·ble
un-em-ployed´
un´em-ploy´ment
un-end´ing
un-en-dur´a·ble
un-e´qual
un-e´qual-ly
un-e´qual-ness
un-e´qualed
un-e-quiv´o-cal
un-e-quiv´o-cal-ly
un-e-quiv´o-cal-
   ness
un-err´ing
un-err´ing-ly
un-err´ing-ness
un-es-sen´tial
un-es-sen´tial-ly
un-e´ven
un-e´ven-ly
un-e´ven-ness
un-e-vent´ful
un-e-vent´ful-ly
un-e-vent´ful-ness
un-ex-cep´tion-
   a·ble
un-ex-cep´tion-
   a·ble-ness
un-ex-cep´tion-
   a·bly
un-ex-cep´tion-al
un-ex-pect´ed

un-ex-pect´ed-ly
un-ex-pect´ed-
  ness
un-ex-plained´
un-ex-plored´
un-ex-pres´sive
un-ex-pres´sive-
  ness
un-ex´pur-gat-ed
un-fail´ing
un-fail´ing-ly
un-fail´ing-ness
un-fair´
un-fair´ly
un-fair´ness
un-faith´ful
un-faith´ful-ly
un-faith´ful-ness
un-fa-mil´iar
un-fa-mil-i-ar´i-ty
un-fa-mil´iar-ly
un-fas´ten
un-fath´om-a-ble
un-fa´vor-a·ble
un-fa´vor-a·ble-
  ness
un-fa´vor-a·bly
un-feel´ing
un-feel´ing-ly
un-feel´ing-ness
un-feigned´
un-feign´ed-ly
un-fet´ter

un-fet´tered
un-fin´ished
un-fit´
un-fit´ting
un-flag´ging
un-flap-pa-bil´i-ty
un-flap´pa-ble
un-flap´pa-bly
un-fledged´
un-flinch´ing
un-flinch´ing-ly
un-fo´cused
un-fold´
un-fold´a-ble
un-fore-seen´
un-for-get´ta-ble
un-for-get´ta-ble-
  ness
un-for-get´ta-bly
un-for-giv´a-ble
un-for-giv´ing
un-for-giv´ing-
  ness
un-formed´
un-for´tu-nate
un-for´tu-nate-ly
un-for´tu-nate-
  ness
un-found´ed
un-found´ed-ly
un-found´ed-ness
un-freeze´
un-friend´li-ness

un-friend´ly
un-frock´
un-fruit´ful
un-fruit´ful-ly
un-fruit´ful-ness
un´ful-filled´
un-fund´ed
un-furl´
un-fur´nished
un-gain´li-ness
un-gain´ly
un-gen´er-ous
un-gen´er-ous-ly
un-gird´
un-girt´
un-glue´
un-glued´
un-god´li-ness
un-god´ly
un-gov-ern-a·bil´i-
  ty
un-gov´ern-a·ble
un-gov´ern-a·ble-
  ness
un-gov´ern-a·bly
un-gra´cious
un-gra´cious-ly
un-gra´cious-ness
un-gram-mat´i-cal
un-gram-mat-i-
  cal´i-ty
un-grate´ful
un-grate´ful-ly

un-grate´ful-ness
un-ground´ed
un-grudg´ing
un-grudg´ing-ly
un-guard´ed
un-guard´ed-ly
un-guard´ed-ness
un´guent
un´gu-late
un-ham´pered
un-hand´
un-hand´y
un-hap´pi-ly
un-hap´pi-ness
un-hap´py
un-harmed´
un-har´ness
un-health´ful
un-health´i-ly
un-health´i-ness
un-health´y
un-heard´
un-heard´–of
un-hes´i-tat-ing
un-hes´i-tat-ing-ly
un-heed´ed
un-heed´ing
un-hes´i-tat-ing-ly
un-hinge´
un-ho´ly
un-hook´
unhoped´–for
un-horse´

un-hur´ried
un-hur´ried-ly
un-hur´ried-ness
un-hurt´
u´ni-corn
u´ni-cy-cle
un-iden´ti-fied
u´ni-fi-a-ble
u-ni-fi-ca´tion
u´ni-fied
u´ni-form
uni-form´i-ty
u´ni-form-ly
u´ni-form-ness
u´ni-fy
u´ni-fy-ing
u-ni-lat´er-al
u-ni-lat´er-al-ly
un-imag´i-na-tive
un-im-paired´
un-im-peach-a-
   bil´i-ty
un-im-peach´a·ble
un-im-peach´-
   a·ble-ness
un-im-peach´a·bly
un-im-por´tance
un-im-por´tant
un-im-proved´
un-in-cor´po-rat-
   ed
un-in-formed´
un-in-hab´it-ed

un-in-hib´it-ed
un-in-i´ti-at-ed
un-in´jured
un-in-spired´
un-in-tel´li-gent
un-in-tel´li-gent-ly
un-in-tel-li-gi-bil´-
   i-ty
un-in-tel´li-gi-ble-
   ness
un-in-tel´li-gi-bly
un-in-ten´tion-al
un-in-ten´tion-al-
   ly
un-in´ter-est-ed
un-in´ter-est-ed-ly
un-in´ter-est-ed-
   ness
un-in-ter-rupt´ed
un-in-vit´ed
un´ion
un´ion-ist
un-ion-i-za´tion
un´ion-ize
u-ni-po´lar
u-nique´
u-nique´ly
u-nique´ness
u´ni-sex
u´ni-son
u´nit
u´ni-tary
u-nite´

u-nit´ed
u-nit´ing
u´nit-ize
u´nit-iz-er
u´ni-ty
u-ni-ver´sal
u-ni-ver´sal-ism
uni-ver-sal´i-ty
u-ni-ver-sal-i-za´-
  tion
u-ni-ver´sal-ize
u-ni-ver´sal-ly
u-ni-ver´sal-ness
u´ni-verse
u-ni-ver´si-ty
un-just´
un-jus´ti-fi-able
un-just´ly
un-just´ness
un-kempt´
un-kempt´ly
un-kempt´ness
un-kind´
un-kind´li-ness
un-kind´ly
un-kind´ness
un-know´a-ble
un-know´ing
un-know´ing-ly
un-known´
un-lace´
un-law´ful
un-law´ful-ly

un-law´ful-ness
un-lead´ed
un-learn´
un-learned´
un-learn´ed-ly
un-leash´
un-leav´ened
un-less´
un-let´tered
un-li´censed
un-like´
un-like´li-hood
un-like´ly
un-like´ness
un-lim´ber
un-lim´it-ed
un-link´
un-liq´ui-dat-ed
un-list´ed
un-live´
un-load´
un-lock´
un-looked´–for
un-loose´
un-loos´en
un-luck´i-ly
un-luck´i-ness
un-luck´y
un-made´
un-make´
un-man´
un-man´age-a·ble
un-man´li-ness

un-man´ly
un-manned´
un-man´nered
un-man´nered-ly
un-man´ner-li-
  ness
un-man´ner-ly
un-mar´ried
un-mask´
un-masked´
un-mean´ing
un-mean´ing-ly
un-meas´ur-a-ble
un-meas´ur-a·bly
un-meas´ured
un-meas´ured-ly
un-mel´lowed
un-mend´a·ble
un-men´tion-a·ble
un-men´tion-
  a·ble-ness
un-mer´ci-ful
un-mer´ci-ful-ly
un-mer´ci-ful-ness
un-mind´ful
un-mind´ful-ly
un-mind´ful-ness
un-mis-tak´a·ble
un-mit´i-gat-ed
un-mit´i-gat-ed-ly
un-mixed´
un-mix´ed-ly
un-moor´

un-mor´al
un-mo-ral´i-ty
un-mor´al-ly
un-mort´gaged
un-moved´
un-mov´ing
un-muz´zle
un-named´
un-nat´u-ral
un-nat´u-ral-ly
un-nat´u-ral-ness
un-nec-es-sar´i-ly
un-nec-es-sar´i-
    ness
un-nec´es-sar-y
un-nerve´
un-no´ticed
un-num´bered
un-ob-served´
un-ob-tru´sive
un-oc´cu-pied
un-of-fi´cial
un-o´pened
un-or´ga-nized
un-orig´i-nal
un-or´tho-dox
un-os´ten-ta´tious
un-pack´
un-paged´
un-paid´
un-pal-at-at-a-
    bil´i-ty
un-pal´at-a·ble

un-pal´at-a·bly
un-par´al-leled
un-par´don-a·ble
un-par-lia-men´-
    ta-ry
un-per´fo-rat-ed
un-per-turbed´
un-pile´
un-pin´
un-pleas´ant
un-pleas´ant-ly
un-pleas´ant-ness
un-plug´
un-plumbed´
un-pop´u-lar
un-pop-u-lar´i-ty
un-pop´u-lar-ly
un-prac´ti-cal
un-prac-ti-cal´i-ty
un-prac´ti-cal-ly
un-prac´ticed
un-prec´e-dent-ed
un-prec´e-dent-
    ed-ly
un-pre-dict-a·bil´-
    i-ty
un-pre-dict´a·ble
un-pre-dict´a·ble-
    ness
un-pre-dict´a·bly
un-prej´u-diced
un-pre-med´i-tat-
    ed

un-pre-pared´
un-pre-ten´tious
un-prin´ci-pled
un-print´a·ble
un-print´a·bly
un-proc´essed
un-pro-duc´tive
un-pro-fes´sion-al
un-pro-fes´sion-
    al-ly
un-prof-it-a·bil´i-
    ty
un-prof´it-a·ble
un-prof´it-a·ble-
    ness
un-prof´it-a·bly
un-prom´is-ing
un-prom´is-ing-ly
un-pro-pi´tious
un-pro-tect´ed
un-pro-voked´
un-pub´lished
un-pun´ished
un-qual´i-fi-a·ble
un-qual´i-fied
un-qual´i-fied-ly
un-quench´able
un-ques´tion-a·ble
un-ques´tion-a·bly
un-ques´tioned
un-qui´et
un-qui´et-ly
un-qui´et-ness

un-quote´

un-rav´el

un-rav´el-er

un-read´

un-read-a·bil´i-ty

un-read´a·ble

un-read´a·ble-ness

un-read´a·bly

un-read´y

un-re´al

un-re-al´i-ty

un-re´al-iz-a·ble

un-re´al-ized

un-re´al-ly

un-rea´son

un-rea´son-a·ble

un-rea´son-a·ble-
ness

un-rea´son-a·bly

un-rea´son-ing

un-rea´son-ing-ly

un-rec´og-niz-able

un-re-con-struct´-
ed

un-reel´

un-re-flect´ing

un-re-flect´ing-ly

un-re-flec´tive

un-re-flec´tive-ly

un-re-gen´er-a-cy

un-re-gen´er-ate

un-re-gen´er-ate-
ly

un-re-lent´ing

un-re-lent´ing-ly

un-re-lent´ing-
ness

un-re-li´able

un-re-li´gious

un-re-mit´ting

un-re-mit´ting-ly

un-re-quit´ed

un-re-serve´

un-re-served´

un-re-serv´ed-ly

un-re-serv´ed-ness

un-rest´

un-re-strained´

un-re-straint´

un-re-strict´ed

un-righ´teous

un-righ´teous-ly

un-righ´teous-ness

un-ripe´

un-ripe´ly

un-ripe´ness

un-ri´valed

un-roll´

un-root´

un-ruf´fled

un-ru´li-ness

un-ru´ly

un-sad´dle

un-safe´

un-said´

un-sal´able

un-san´i-tar·y

un-sat-is-fac´to-ri-
ly

un-sat-is-fac´to-ri-
ness

un-sat-is-fac´to-ry

un-sat´is-fied

un-sa´vor-i-ly

un-sa´vor-i-ness

un-sa´vor·y

un-scathed´

un-schol´ar-ly

un-schooled´

un-sci-en-tif´ic

un-sci-en-tif´i-cal-
ly

un-scram´ble

un-screw´

un-script´ed

un-scru´pu-lous

un-scru´pu-lous-ly

un-scru´pu-lous-
ness

un-seal´

un-sealed´

un-sea´son-a·ble

un-sea´son-a·ble-
ness

un-sea´son-a·bly

un-sea´soned

un-seat´

un-seem´li-ness

un-seem´ly

un-seen'
un-self'ish
un-self'ish-ly
un-self'ish-ness
un-set'tle
un-set'tled
un-shack'le
un-shak'a·ble
un-shak'en
un-shaped'
un-shap'en
un-shav'en
un-sheathe'
un-shell'
un-shod'
un-sight'ly
un-signed'
un-skilled'
un-skill'ful
un-skill'ful-ly
un-snap'
un-snarl'
un-so'cia-ble
un-so'cia-ble-ness
un-so'cia-bly
un-so-lic'it-ed
un-so-lic'i-tous
un-so-phis'ti-cat-
  ed
un-so-phis'ti-cat-
  ed-ly
un-so-phis'ti-cat-
  ed-ness

un-so-phis-ti-ca'-
  tion
un-sound'
un-sound'ly
un-sound'ness
un-spar'ing
un-spar'ing-ly
un-spar'ing-ness
un-speak'a·ble
un-speak'a·ble-
  ness
un-speak'a·bly
un-spe'cial-ized
un-spec'u-la-tive
un-spoiled'
un-spo'ken
un-spot'ted
un-sta'ble
un-sta'ble-ness
un-sta'bly
un-stained'
un-stead'i-ly
un-stead'i-ness
un-stead'y
un-stick'
un-stop'
un-stop'pa-ble
un-stop'pa-bly
un-strap'
un-stressed'
un-string'
un-struc'tured
un-strung'

un-stuck'
un-stud'ied
un-sub-stan'tial
un-sub-stan-ti-
  al'i-ty
un-sub-stan'tial-ly
un-suc-cess'ful
un-suit'a·ble
un-suit'ed
un-sul'lied
un-sung'
un-sup-port'ed
un-sur-passed'
un-sus-pect'ed
un-sus-pect'ed-ly
un-sym-pa-thet'ic
un-taint'ed
un-tam'a·ble
un-tamed'
un-tan'gle
un-tar'nished
un-taught'
un-teach'
un-ten-a-bil'i-ty
un-ten'a·ble
un-ten'a·ble-ness
un-think'
un-think'a·ble
un-think'a·bly
un-think'ing
un-think'ing-ly
un-ti'di-ly
un-ti'di-ness

un-ti´dy
un-tie´
un-til´
un-time´li-ness
un-time´ly
un-tir´ing
un-ti´tled
un´to
un-told´
un-touch-a·bil´i-ty
un-touch´a·ble
un-touched´
un-to´ward
un-trained´
un-tram´meled
un´trans-lat´a·ble
un-trav´eled
un-tra-vers´a·ble
un-tried´
un-trou´bled
un-true´
tin-truth´
un-truth´ful
un-truth´ful-ly
un-truth´ful-ness
un-tu´tored
un-used´
un-u´su-al
un-u´su-al-ly
un-ut´ter-a·ble
un-ut´ter-a·bly
un-var´nished
un-var´y-ing

un-veil´
un-veil´ing
un-ven´ti-lat-ed
un-ver´i-fied
un-vir´tu-ous-ly
un-voiced´
un-want´ed
un-war´i-ly
un-war´i-ness
un-war´rant-ed
un-war´y
un-washed´
un-wa´ver-ing
un-wel´come
un-well´
un-wept´
un-whole´some
un-whole´some-ly
un-whole´some-
　ness
un-wield´i-ness
un-wield´y
un-will´ing
un-will´ing-ly
un-will´ing-ness
un-wind´
un-wise´
un-wise´ly
un-wished´–for
un-wit´ting
un-work´able
un-world´ly
un-wor´thi-ly

un-wor´thi-ness
un-wor´thy
un-wrap´
un-writ´ten
un-yield´ing
un-yoke´
un-zip´
up´–and–com´ing
up´–and–down´
up´beat
up´braid´
up´bring-ing
up´com-ing
up´date
up´draft
up´end´
up´–front´
up´grade
up-heav´al
up-held´
up-hill´
up-hold´
up-hold´er
up-hol´ster
up-hol´ster-er
up-hol´ster·y
up´lift (n.)
up´lift´ (v.)
up´load
up´most
up-on´
up´per
up´per-class´man

up′per-cut
up′per-most
up′pish
up′pish-ly
up′pish-ness
up′pi-ty
up-raise′
up-rear′
up′right
up′right-ly
up′right-ness
up′ris-ing
up′roar
up-roar′i-ous
up-roar′i-ous-ly
up-roar′i-ous-ness
up′root
up′set (n.)
up-set′ (v., adj.)
up′shot
up′stage′
up′stairs′
up-stand′ing
up′start
up′stream′
up′stroke
up-surge′
up′swept
up′sy–dai′sy
up′thrust
up′tight′
up′—to—date′
up′town′

ura′ni-um
ur′ban
ur-bane′
ur-bane′ly
ur-bane′ness
ur′ban-ize
ur′chin
urge
ur′gen-cy
ur′gent-ly
urg′ing
u′ri-nary
u-rol′o-gist
u-rol′o-gy
us′a-ble
us′a-ble-ness
us′a-bly
us′age
use′a·ble
used
use′ful
use′ful-ly
use′ful-ness
use′less
use′less-ness
us′er
us′er–friend′ly
ush′er
u′su-al-ly
u′su-al-ness
u-surp′
u-sur-pa′tion
u-surp′er

u′su-ry
uten′sil
u′ter-ine
u′tile
u-til-i-tar′i-an
u-til-i-tar′i-an-ism
u-til′i-ty
u′ti-liz-a-ble
u′ti-li-za′tion
u′ti-lize
u′ti-liz-er
ut′most
u-to′pi-an
ut′ter-a-ble
ut′ter-ance
ut′ter-er
ut′ter-most

V

va′can-cy
va′cant
va′cant-ly
va′cant-ness
va′cat-a-ble
va′cate
va′cat-ing
va-ca′tion-er
va-ca′tion-land
vac′ci-nate
vac-ci-na′tion
vac-cine′
vac′il-lant
vac′il-late

vac´il-lat-ing
vac-il-la´tion
vac´il-la-tor
vac´il-la-to-ry
va-cu´i-ty
vac´u-ous
vac´u-ous-ly
vac´u-ous-ness
vac´u-um
vac´uum–packed
vag´a-bond
va´gary
va´gran-cy
va´grant
va´grant-ly
vague
vague´ly
vague-ness
vain-glo´ri-ous
vain-glo´ri-ous-ly
vain-glo´ri-ous-
ness
vain´glo-ry
vain´ly
vain´ness
val´ance
val-e-dic´tion
val-e-dic-to´ri-an
val´e-dic´to-ry
va´lence
val´en-tine
val´et
val´iance

val´ian-cy
val´iant
val´iant-ly
val´id
val´i-date
val-i-da´tion
va-lid´i-ty
val´id-ly
val´id-ness
va-lise´
val´ley
val´or
va´o-ri-za´tion
val´or-ous
val´or-ous-ly
val´our (Br.)
val´u-a·ble
val´u-a·ble-ness
val´u-a·bly
val´u-ate
val-u-a´tion
val-u-a´tion-al
val´u-a-tor
val´ue
val´ue–add´ed
val´ued
val´ue-less
val´u-ing
valve
val´vu-lar
val´vu-late
val´vule
val-vu-li´tis

va-moose´
vamp´er
vam´pire
vam-pir´ic
vam´pir-ish
vam´pir-ism
vamp´ish
van´dal
van´dal-ism
van-dal-is´tic
van´dal-ize
van-dyke´
vane
van´guard
van´guard-ism
van´guard-ist
va-nil´la
va-nil´lin
van´ish-er
van´ish-ing
van´i-ty
van´quish
van´quish-a·ble
van´quish-er
van´quish-ment
van´tage
vap´id
va-pid´i-ty
vap´id-ly
vap´id-ness
va´por
va-por-es´cence
va´por-if´ic

276

va´por-ish
va´por-ish-ness
va´por-iz-a·ble
va-por-i·za´tion
va´por-ize
va´por-iz-er
va´por-ous
va´por-ous-ly
va´por-ous-ness
va´por-ware
var-i-a·bil´i-ty
var´i-a·ble
var´i-a·ble-ness
var´i-a·ble–rate´
var´i-a·bly
var´i-ance
var´i-ant
var-i-a´tion
var-i-a´tion-al
var´i-col-ored
var´i-cose
var-i-cos´i-ty
var´ied
var´ied-ness
var´i-e-gate
var´i-e-gat-ed
var´i-e-ga´tion
var´i-e-ga-tor
va-ri´e-tal
va-ri´e-ty
var´i-ous
var´i-ous-ly
var´i-ous-ness

var´nish
var´nish-er
var´si-ty
var´y
var´y-ing-ly
vas´cu-lar
vase
va-sec´to-my
vast´ly
vast´ness
vaude´ville
vaude-vil´lian
vault´ing
vaunt
vaunt´ing
vaunt´ing-ly
vec´tor
veer
veer´ing
ve´gan
veg´e-ta-ble
veg-e-tar´i-an
veg-e-tar´i-an-ism
veg´e-tate
veg-e-ta´tion
veg´e-ta-tive
veg´e-ta-tive-ly
veg´gie
ve´he-mence
ve´he-ment
ve´he-ment-ly
ve´hi-cle
ve-hic´u-lar

veiled
veil´ing
veined
veldt
vel´lum
ve-loc´i-ty
ve-lour´
ve-lou-té´
vel´vet
vel´vet·y
ve´nal
ve-nal´i-ty
ve´nal-ly
vend´er
ven-det´ta
vend´i·ble
vend´i·bly
ven´dor
ve-neer´
ve-neer´ing
ven´er-a·ble
ven´er-a·ble-ness
ven´er-a·bly
ven´er-ate
ven-er-a´tion
ven´er-a-tor
ven´geance
venge´ful
venge´ful-ly
venge´ful-ness
ve´ni-al
ve-ni-al´i-ty
ve´ni-al-ly

ven´i-son
ven´om
ven´om-ous
ven´om-ous-ly
ve´nous
ve´nous-ly
ve´nous-ness
ven´ti-late
ven-ti-la´tion
ven´ti-la-tor
ven-tril´o-quism
ven-tril´o-quist
ven´ture
ven´tur-er
ven´ture-some
ven´tur-ing
ven´tur-ous
ven´tur-ous-ly
ven´tur-ous-ness
ven´ue
ve-ra´cious
ve-ra´cious-ly
ve-ra´cious-ness
ve-rac´i-ty
ve-ran´da
ver´bal *(adj.)*
verb´al *(n.)*
ver´bal-ist
ver-bal-i-za´tion
ver´bal-ize
ver´bal-iz-er
ver´bal-ly
ver-ba´tim

ver´bi-age
verb´i-fy
ver-bose´
ver-bose´ly
ver-bose´ness
ver-bos´i-ty
ver´dan-cy
ver´dant
ver´dant-ly
ver´dict
verge
verg´ing
ver´i-fi-a·ble
ver-i-fi-ca´tion
ver´i-fied
ver´i-fy
ver-i-si-mil´i-tude
ver´i-ta-ble
ver´i-ta-bly
ver´i-ty
ver-mi-cel´li
ver-mil´ion
ver´min
ver-mouth´
ver-nac´u-lar
ver-nac´u-lar-ism
ver-nac´u-lar-ly
ver´nal
ver´nal-ly
ver´sant
ver´sa-tile
ver´sa-tile-ly
ver-sa-til´i-ty

versed
ver-si-fi-ca´tion
ver´si-fied
ver´si-fi-er
ver´si-fy
ver´sion
ver´so
ver´sus
ver´te-bra
ver´te-brae
ver´te-bral
ver´te-brate
ver´ti-cal
ver´ti-cal-ly
ver´ti-go
verve
ver´y
ves´per
ves´sel
vest´ed
ves´tige
ves-tig´ial
ves-tig´ial-ly
vest´ing
ves´ti-ture
vest´ment
vest´–pock-et
ves´try
ves´try-man
vet´er-an
vet-er-i-nar´i-an
vet´er-i-nar·y
ve´to

ve´toed
ve´to-er
ve´toes
ve´to-ing
vex-a´tion
vex-a´tious
vex-a´tious-ly
vex´ed
vex´ed-ly
vi-a·bil´i-ty
vi´a-ble
vi´a-duct
vi´al
vi´and
vi´bran-cy
vi´brant
vi´brant-ly
vi´bra-phone
vi´bra-phon-ist
vi´brate
vi´brat-ing
vi-bra´tion
vi-bra´tion-al
vi-bra´to
vi´bra-tor
vi´bra-to-ry
vic´ar
vic´ar-age
vi-car´i-ous
vi-car´i-ous-ly
vi-car´i-ous-ness
vice—con´sul
vice—pres´i-dent

vice´roy
vi-chys-soise´
vi-cin´i-ty
vi´cious
vi´cious-ly
vi´cious-ness
vi-cis´si-tude
vi-cis-si-tu´di-nar-
y
vi-cis-si-tu´di-
nous
vic´tim
vic-tim-i-za´tion
vic´tim-ize
vic´tim-iz-er
vic-to´ri-ous
vic´to-ry
vict´ual
vict´ualed
vict´ual-er
vid´e-o-cas-sette
vid´e-o-con-fer-
ence
vid´e-o-disc
vid´e-o-re-cord-er
vid´e-o-tape
vid´e-o-tap-er
view´a·ble
view´er
view´er-ship
view´find-er
view´ing
view´point

view´y
vig´il
vig´i-lance
vig´i-lant
vig´i-lant-ly
vig-i-lan´te
vig-i-lan´tism
vi-gnette´
vig´or
vig´or-ous
vig´or-ous-ness
vig´our (Br.)
vile
vile´ly
vile´ness
vil-i-fi-ca´tion
vil´i-fi-er
vil´i-fy
vil´i-fy-ing
vil´la
vil´lage
vil´lag-er
vil´lain
vil´lain-ess
vil´lain-ous
vil´lain-y
vin-ai-grette´
vin-ci-bil´i-ty
vin´ci-ble
vin´di-ca-ble
vin´di-cate
vin-di-ca´tion
vin´di-ca-tive

vin´di-ca-tor
vin-dic´tive
vin-dic´tive-ly
vin-dic´tive-ness
vin´e-gar
vin´e-gar-y
vin´er·y
vine´yard
vin´tage
vint´ner
vi´nyl
vi-o´la
vi-o-la-bil´i-ty
vi´ol-a·ble
vi´ol-a·ble-ness
vi´ol-a·bly
vi´o-late
vi-o-la´tion
vi´o-la-tor
vi´o-lence
vi´o-lent-ly
vi´o-let
vi-o-lin´
vi-o-lin´ist
vi´per
vi´per-ish
vi´per-ous
vi´per-ous-ly
vi´ral
vir´gin
vir´gin-al
vir-gin´i-ty
vir´ile

vir´il-ism
vi-ril´i-ty
vi-rol´o-gist
vi-rol´o-gy
vir´tu-al
vir-tu-al´i-ty
vir´tu-al-ly
vir´tue
vir´tue-less
vir-tu-os´i-ty
vir-tu-o´so
vir´tu-ous-ly
vir´tu-ous-ness
vir´u-lence
vir´u-lent-ly
vi´rus
vis´age
vis´cose
vis-cos´i-ty
vis´cous
vis´cous-ly
vis´cous-ness
vis-i·bil´i-ty
vis´i·ble
vis´i·ble-ness
vis´i·bly
vi´sion
vi´sion-al
vi´sion-ar-i-ness
vi´sion-ar·y
vi´sioned
vi´sion-less
vis´it

vis´i-tant
vis-it-a´tion
vis´i-tor
vi´sor
vis´ta
vi´su-al
vis´u-al-ist
vis-u-al´i-ty
vis´u-al-iz-a·ble
vis-u-al-i-za´tion
vis´u-al-ize
vis´u-al-iz-er
vis´u-al-ly
vi´tal
vi-tal´i-ty
vi-tal-i-za´tion
vi´tal-ize
vi´tal-ly
vi´tal-ness
vi´ta-min
vi-ta-min´ic
vi´ti-ate
vi´ti-at-ed
vi-ti-a´tion
vi´ti-a-tor
vit´re-ous
vit´re-ous-ly
vit´re-ous-ness
vi-tres´cence
vi-tres´cent
vit´ric
vit´ri-fi-a·ble
vit-ri-fi-ca´tion

280

vit´ri-fy
vit´ri-ol
vit´ri-ol´ic
vi-tu´per-ate
vi-tu-per-a´tion
vi-tu´per-a-tive
vi-tu´per-a-tor
vi-va´cious
vi-va´cious-ly
vi-va´cious-ness
vi-vac´i-ty
viv´id
viv´id-ly
viv´id-ness
viv-i-fi-ca´tion
viv´i-fied
viv´i-fy
viv´i-sect
viv-i-sec´tion
viv-i-sec´tion-al
viv-i-sec´tion-ist
vix´en
vix´en-ish
vix´en-ly
vi-zier´
vo-cab´u-lar·y
vo´cal
vo´cal-ist
vo-cal-i-za´tion
vo´cal-ize
vo´cal-iz-er
vo´cal-ly
vo´cal-ness

vo-ca´tion
vo-ca´tion-al
vo-ca´tion-al-ism
vo-ca´tion-al-ist
vo-ca´tion-al-ly
voc´a-tive
voc´a-tive-ly
vo-cif´er-ant
vo-cif´er-ate
vo-cif-er-a´tion
vo-cif´er-a-tor
vo-cif´er-ous
vo-cif´er-ous-ly
vo-cif´er-ous-ness
vod´ka
vogue
vogu´ish
vogu´ish-ness
voice
voiced
voic´ed-ness
voice´ful
voice´ful-ness
voice´less
voice´less-ly
voice´–o-ver
voice´print
voic´ing
void´a·ble
void´ance
void´ed
void´ness
vol´a-tile

vol´a-tile-ness
vo-a-til´i-ty
vol´a-til-iz-a·ble
vo-a-til-i-za´tion
vol-can´ic
vol-can´i-cal-ly
vol-ca´no
vol-ca´noes
vol-can-ol´o-gist
vol-can-ol´o-gy
vo-li´tion
vo-li´tion-al
vo-li´tion-al-ly
vo-li´tion-ar·y
vol´i-tive
vol´ley
vol´ley-ball
volt´age
vo´u-bil´i-ty
vol´u-ble
vol´u-ble-ness
vol´u-bly
vol´ume
vo-lu-mi-nos´i-ty
vo-lu´mi-nous
vo-lu´mi-nous-ly
vo-lu´mi-nous-
　ness
vol´un-tar´i-ly
vol´un-ta-rism
vol´un-tar-y
vol-un-tar´i-ly
vol-un-teer´

vol´un-teered
vo-lup´tu-ar·y
vo-lup´tu-ous
vo-lup´tu-ous-ly
vo-lup´tu-ous-ness
vom´it
voo´doo
vo-ra´cious-ly
vo-ra´cious-ness
vo-rac´i-ty
vor´tex
vor´ti-ces
vot´a-ble
vote
vot´er
vot´ing
vo´tive
vo´tive-ly
vouch´er
vouch-safe´
vow
vow´el
voy´age
voy´ag-er
voy´a-geur´
vo-yeur´
vo-yeur´ism
voy-eur-is´tic
voy-eur-is´ti-cal-ly
vul-can-i·za´tion
vul´can-ize
vul´can-iz-er
vul´gar

vul-gar´i-an
vul´gar-ism
vu´gar´i-ty
vul´gar-ly
vul´gar-ness
vul-ner-a·bil´i-ty
vul´ner-a·ble
vul´ner-a·ble-ness
vul´ner-a·bly
vul´ture
vul´tur-ous
vy´ing

W

wack´i-ly
wack´i-ness
wack´o
wack´y
wad´ding
wad´dle
wad´dled
wad´dler
wad´dling
wad´dling-ly
wad´dly
wade
wad´er
wad´ing
wa´fer
waf´fle
waf´fler
waf´fling
waf´fly

waft
waft´er
wage´less
wa´ger
wag´es
wag´ger-y
wag´gish
wag´gish-ness
wag´gle
wag´gling
wag´gly
wag´ing
wag´on
wag´on-er
wag´on-load
wail´ing
wain´scot-ing
waist´band
waist´coat
waist´ed
waist´line
wait´er
wait´ing
wait´list
wait´per-son
wait´ress
waive
waiv´er
wake´ful
wake´ful-ness
wak´en
wak´en-er
wak´en-ing

wake´–up
walk´a·ble
walk´a-bout
walk´a-thon
walk´a-way
walk´er
walk´ie—talk´ie
walk´–in
walk´ing
walk´–on
walk´way
wall´board
wall´cov-er-ing
walled
wal´let
wall´flow-er
wal´lop
wal´lop-er
wal´lop-ing
wal´low
wall´paper
wall´–to–wall´
wal´nut
wal´rus
waltz´er
wan´der
wan´der-er
wan´der-ing
wan´der-ing-ly
wan´der-lust
wane´y
wan´gle
wan´gled

wan´gler
wan´gling
wan´ing
wan´ly
wan´na-be
wan´ness
want´ing
wan´ton
wan´ton-ly
wan´ton-ness
war´ble
war´bled
war´bler
war´bling
war´den
ward´er
ward´robe
ward´room
ware´house
war´fare
war´–horse
war´i-ly
war´i-ness
war´like
war´lord
warm´–blood´ed
warmed´–o´ver
warm´er
warm´heart-ed
warm´heart-ed-ly
warm´heart-ed-
   ness
warm´ish

warm´ly
war´mon-ger
warm´ness
warm´up
warn´er
warn´ing
warn´ing-ly
warp´age
war´path
warp´ing
war´rant
war´rant-a-ble
war´rant-ee´
war´rant-er
war´ran-tor´
war´ran-ty
war´ri-or
war´time
war´y
wash´a-ble
wash´–and–wear´
wash´ba-sin
wash´board
wash´bowl
wash´cloth
wash´day
washed´–out´
washed´–up´
wash´er
wash´er-wom-an
wash´ing
wash´room
wash´stand

wash´tub
wash´up
wash´y
wasp´i-ly
wasp´i-ness
wasp´ish
wasp´ish-ly
wasp´ish-ness
wasp´y
was´sail
was´sail-er
wast´age
waste´bas-ket
wast´ed
waste´ful
waste´ful-ly
waste´ful-ness
waste´land
wast´er
wast´ing
was´trel
watch´band
watch cap
watch´case
watch´dog
watch´er
watch´ful
watch´ful-ly
watch´ful-ness
watch´mak-er
watch´mak-ing
watch´tow-er
watch´word

wa´ter-bed
wa´ter-borne
wa´ter bug
wa´ter-col-or
wa´ter-course
wa´ter-craft
wa´tered
wa´ter-er
wa´ter-fall
wa´ter-fowl
wa´ter-front
wa´ter-i-ness
wa´ter-less
wa´ter-less-ly
wa´ter-less-ness
wa´ter-line
wa´ter-locked
wa´ter-logged
wa´ter-mark
wa´ter-mel-on
wa´ter-pick
wa´ter-pow-er
wa´ter-proof
wa´ter-proof-ing
wa´ter—re-pel-lent
wa´ter—ski
wa´ter-sport
wa´ter-spout
wa´ter-tight
wa´ter-way
wa´ter-wheel
wa´ter-works
wa´ter-y

watt´age
wave´length
wav´er (hailer)
wa´ver (vacillate)
wa´ver-er
wa´ver-ing
wav´i-ness
wav´ing
wav´y
wax´en
wax´i-ness
wax´ing
wax´works
wax´y
way´bill
way´far-er
way´far-ing
way´laid
way´lay
way´lay-er
way´—out´
way´ward
way´ward-ness
wa-zir´
weak´en
weak´ened
weak´en-er
weak´ling
weak´—kneed´
weak´ly
weak´—mind´ed
weak´—mind´ed-ly
weak´ness

wealth´i-er
wealth´i-ness
wealth´y
wean´ling
weap´on
weap´on-ry
wear-a·bil´i-ty
wear´a·ble
wear´er
wea´ri-ful
wea´ri-ful-ly
wea´ri-ful-ness
wea´ri-less
wea´ri-less-ly
wea´ri-ly
wea´ri-ness
wear´ing
wea´ri-some
wea´ry
wea´ry-ing
wea´seled
wea´sel-ly
weath´er
weath´er—beat-en
weath´er-cock
weath´ered
weath´er-ing
weath´er-ize
weath´er-proof
weath´er-strip-
  ping
weave
weav´er

weav´ing
web
webbed
web´bing
web´site
wed´ded
wed´ding
wedged
wedge—shaped
wedg´ing
wedg´y
wed´lock
weed´er
weed´i-ness
weed´kill-er
weed´y
week´day
week´end-er
week´ly
week´night
weep´er
weep´i-ness
weep´ing
weep´y
wee´vil
weigh
weight
weight´ed
weight´i-ly
weight´i-ness
weight´less
weight´less-ness
weight´lift-er

weight´lift-ing
weight´y
weird´ly
weird´ness
wel´come
wel´com-er
weld´a-ble
weld´er
wel´fare
well´–ad-vised´
well´–ap-point´ed
well—bal´anced
well—be-haved´
well´—be´ing
well´–belov´ed
well´born
well´bred´
well´–defined´
well´–fed´
well´–found´ed
well´–groomed´
well´–ground´ed
well´–han´dled
well´–heeled´
well´–in-formed´
well´–inten´tioned
well´—known´
well´–made´
well´–man´nered
well´–mean´ing
well´–off´
well´–read´
well´–round´ed

well´spring
well´-thought´-of
well´-timed´
well´—to—do´
well´—trained´
well´-wish-er
well´-worn´
wend´ing
west´er
west´er-ly
west´ern
west´ern-er
west´ern-ism
west´ern-most
west´ward
weth´er
wet´land
wet´ness
wet´ting
whacked
whal´er
whal´ing
what-ev´er
what´not
what-so-ev´er
whee´dle
whee´dled
whee´dler
wheel´bar-row
wheel´base
wheel´chair
wheel´er–deal´er
wheel´house

wheel´wright
wheeze
wheez´y
when-ev´er
when´so-ev´er
where´a-bouts
where´as´
where´by´
where´fore´
where´of´
where´so-ev´er
where´up-on´
wher-ev´er
where´with-al
wheth´er
whet´stone
which-ev´er
whim´per
whim´pered
whim´per-ing
whim´si-cal
whim´si-cal-ly
whim´sy
whined
whin´ing
whin´nied
whin´ny
whip´cord
whip´lash
whip´ping
whip´poor-will
whip´saw
whirl´pool

whirl´wind
whirl´y-bird
whir´ring
whisk´er
whisk´ered
whisk´er·y
whis´key
whis´ky
whis´per
whis´pered
whis´per-er
whis´per-ing
whis´per·y
whis´tle
whis´tle–blow-er
whis´tle–blow-ing
whis´tler
whis´tling
white´cap
white´—hot´
whit´en-ing
white´–tie
white´wall
white´wash
whith´er
whit´ish
whit´tle
whit´tled
whit´tler
whit´tling
who-ev´er
whole´–grain
whole´heart-ed-ly

286

whole´ness
whole´sale
whole´sal-er
whole´some
whole´some-ly
whole´some-ness
whol´ly
whom-so-ev´er
whoop´ee
whop´per
whorl
who-so-ev´er
wick´ed
wick´ed-ly
wick´ed-ness
wick´er
wick´er-work
wick´et
wick´ing
wide´–an´gle
wide´–awake´
wide´bod·y
wide´—eyed
wide´ly
wid´en
wide´–o´pen
wide´–rang´ing
wide´–screen´
wide´spread´
wid´get
wid´ow
wid´ow-er
width

wield
wield´er
wield´y
wie´ner-wurst
wife´less
wife´li-ness
wife´ly
wig´gle
wig´gler
wig´gling
wig´gly
wig´let
wild´–and–wool´ly
wild´cat
wil´der-ness
wild´fire
wild´life
wild´ly
wild´ness
willed
will´ful
will´ful-ly
will´ful-ness
will´ing
will´ing-ly
will´ing-ness
will—o'—the—
   wisp
wil´low-y
will´pow-er
wil´y
wimp´y
win

wince
winch
winc´ing
wind´age
wind´bag
wind´blown
wind´–borne
wind´break-er
wind´burn
wind´ed
wind´fall
wind´i-er
wind´i-ness
wind´ing
wind´ing-ness
wind´jam-mer
wind´lass
wind´less
wind´mill
win´dow
win´dow-less
win´dow-pane
win´dow–shop
win´dow–shop-er
win´dow—shop-
   ping
win´dow-sill
wind´pipe
wind´proof
wind´shield
wind´storm
wind´surf-er
wind´surf-ing

wind´–swept	wire´tap	with-hold´ing
wind´ward	wire´tap-per	with-in´
wind´y	wir´ing	with-out´
wine´glass	wir´y	with-stand´
wine´mak-ing	wis´dom	with-stand´ing
win´er-y	wise´a-cre	wit´less
wine´tast-ing	wise´crack	wit´less-ly
winged	wise´ly	wit´less-ness
wing´less	wis´est	wit´ness
wing´span	wish´bone	wit´ness–box
wing´spread	wish´ful	wit´ness-er
wing´tip	wish´ful-ly	wit´ted
wink´er	wish´ful-ness	wit´ti-cism
wink´ing	wish´y—wash·y	wit´ti-ly
win´na-ble	wisp´i-ness	wit´ti-ness
win´ner	wisp´y	wit´ting
win´ning	wist´ful	wit´ting-ly
win´ning-ly	wist´ful-ly	wit´ty
win´nings	wist´ful-ness	wiz´ard
win´now-er	witch´craft	wiz´ard-ry
win´some-ly	witch´y	wiz´ened
win´some-ness	with-al´	wob´ble
win´ter-green	with-draw´	wob´bler
win´ter-ish	with-draw´al	wob´bli-ness
win´ter-ize	with-drawn´	wob´bly
win´ter-time	with-drew´	woe´be-gone
win´try	with´er	woe´ful
wipe´out	with´ered	woe´ful-ly
wip´er	with´er-ing	woe´ful-ness
wip´ing	with´er-ing-ly	wom´an-hood
wired	with-held´	wom´an-ish
wire´less	with-hold´	wom´an-ize
wir´er	with-hold´er	wom´an-iz-er

wom´an-kind
wom´an-ly
wom´en
wom´en-folk
won´der
won´dered
won´der-er
won´der-ful
won´der-ful-ly
won´der-ful-ness
won´der-land
won´der-ment
won´der—work-er
won´drous
won´drous-ly
won´drous-ness
wont *(habit)*
won't *(will not)*
wood´block
wood´carv-ing
wood´craft
wood´cut
wood´cut-ter
wood´ed
wood´en
wood´en-ly
wood´en-ness
wood´grain
wood´i-er
wood´i-ness
wood´land
wood´pile
wood´shed

woods´y
wood´wind
wood´work
wood´work-er
wood´work-ing
wood´y
woo´er
wool´en
wool´li-ness
wool´ly
wooz´i-ly
wooz´i-ness
wooz´y
word
word´i-ly
word´i-ness
word´ing
word´less
word´less-ly
word´play
word´y
work
work´a·ble
work´a-day
work-a-hol´ic
work´bas-ket
work´bench
work´book
work´day
worked
worked´–up´
work´er
work´flow

work´horse
work´ing
work´man-ship
work´place
work´room
work´shop
work´ta-ble
work´week
world´beat-er
world´–class´
world´li-ness
world´ly–mind´ed
world´ly—wise
world´–shak-ing
world´–wea-ry
world´wide´
worm´—eat-en
worm´y
worn´—out´
wor´ried
wor´ried-ly
wor´ri-some
wor´ri-some-ly
wor´ry
wor´ry-ing
worse
wors´en
wor´ship
wor´shiped
wor´ship-er
wor´ship-ful
wor´ship-ing
worst´–case´

worth
wor´thi-ly
wor´thi-ness
worth´less
worth´less-ly
worth´less-ness
worth´while´
wor´thy
would´–be
wound´ed
wo´ven
wraith´like
wran´gle
wran´gler
wran´gling
wrap´a-round
wrap´per
wrap´ping
wrap´–up
wrath´ful
wrath´ful-ly
wrath´ful-ness
wreck´age
wreck´er
wreck´ing
wrench
wrest
wres´tle
wres´tler
wres´tling
wretch
wretch´ed
wretch´ed-ly

wretch´ed-ness
wrig´gle
wrig´gler
wrig´gly
wring´er
wring´ing
wrin´kle
wrin´kled
wrin´kling
wrin´kly
wrist´band
wrist´watch
write´–in
writ´er
writhe
writhed
writh´er
writh´ing
writh´ing-ly
writ´ing
writ´ten
wrong´do-er
wrong´do-ing
wrong´ful
wrong´ful-ly
wrong´ful-ness
wrong´head´ed
wrong´ly
wrong´ness
wroth
wrought
wrought´–up´
wry´ly

wry´ness

X

xen´o-phile
xen-o-phil´i-a
X—ray *(v.)*
xy´lo-graph
xy-log´ra-pher
xy-lo-graph´ic
xy-lo-graph´i-cal
xy-log´ra-phy
xy´lo-phone
xy´lo-phon-ist

Y

yacht
yacht´ing
yachts´man
yam´mer
yam´mer-er
yam´mer-ing-ly
yap´per
yap´ping
yap´ping-ly
yard´age
yard´stick
yawn´er
yawn´ing
year´book
year´–end´
year´ling
year´long
year´ly

yearn´ing

yearn´ing-ly

year´–round´

yeast´i-ness

yeast·y

yel´low

yel´low-ish

yel´low·y

yelp´er

yeo´man

yes´–man

yes´ter-day

yes´ter-year

yield´a-ble

yield´er

yield´ing

yo´del

yo´del-er

yo´del-ing

yo´ga

yo´gi

yo´gurt

yo´kel

yon´der

young´ish

young´ster

your-self´

youth´ful

youth´ful-ly

youth´ful-ness

yuck´y

yule

yum´my

yup´pie

Z

za´ni-ly

za´ni-ness

za´ny

zeal´ot

zeal´ot-ry

zeal´ous

zeal´ous-ly

zeal´ous-ness

ze´bra

ze´nith

zeph´yr

ze´ro

ze´roes

ze´ros

zest´ful

zest´ful-ly

zest´ful-ness

zest´y

zig´zag

zig´zag-ging

zing´er

zing´y

zin´ni-a

zip´per

zip´py

zith´er

zo´di-ac

zo-di´a-cal

zom´bie

zon´al

zon´al-ly

zo´na-ry

zoned

zon´ing

zo-o-graph´ic

zo-o-graph´i-cal

zo-og´ra-phy

zoo´keep-er

zo-o-log´i-cal

zo-o-log´i-cal-ly

zo-ol´o-gist

zo-ol´o-gy

CAPITALIZATION

There are no rules that cover every situation for capitalization, but with knowledge of certain principles and consideration of the purpose to be served, it is possible to attain a considerable degree of uniformity.

Proper names

Proper names are capitalized.

> Rome
> Brussels
> John Macadam
> the Macadam family
> Italy
> Anglo-Saxon

Derivatives of proper names

Derivatives of proper names are usually capitalized.

> **Roman** (*of Rome*)
> **Washingtonian**
> **New Yorker**
> **Italian**

Derivatives of proper names that have acquired independent common meaning or that are no longer identified with the source name are not capitalized. Generally, this depends on general and long-accepted usage.

> **roman** (*a type style, but* **Times Roman***, a particular typeface is a proper name and should be capitalized*)
> **macadam** (*crushed rock*)
> **italicize**
> **watt** (*electric unit*)
> **venetian blinds**
> **plaster of paris**
> **pasteurize**

Common nouns and adjectives in proper names

A common noun or adjective forming an essential part of a proper name is capitalized; the common noun used alone as a substitute for the name of a place or thing is not capitalized.

Massachusetts Avenue	the avenue
Washington Monument	the monument
Statue of Liberty	the statue
Hoover Dam	the dam
Boston Light	the light
Modoc National Forest	the national forest
Panama Canal	the canal
Soldiers' Home of Ohio	the soldiers' home
Johnson House *(hotel)*	Johnson house *(residence)*
Crow Reservation	the reservation
Cape of Good Hope	the cape
Jersey City	the city
also Washington City, *but* city of Washington	
Cook County	the county
Great Lakes	the lakes
Lake of the Woods	the lake
North Platte River	the river
Charles the First	Charles I
Seventeenth Census	the 1960 census

If a common noun or adjective forming an essential part of a name becomes separated from the rest of the name by an intervening common noun or adjective, the entire expression is no longer a proper noun and is therefore not capitalized.

Eastern States	eastern farming States
Western States	western farming States

Short forms of proper names

A common noun used alone as a well-known short form of a specific proper name is usually capitalized.

the **Capitol** *(at Washington),* **but State capitol** *(building)*
the **Channel** *(English Channel)*
the **District** *(District of Columbia)*

The plural form of a common noun

The plural form of a common noun that is normally capitalized as part of a proper name is also capitalized.

Seventh and I Streets
Lakes Erie and Ontario
Potomac and James Rivers
State and Treasury Departments
British and French Governments
Presidents Washington and Adams

Common noun as part of a reference

A common noun used with a date, number, or letter, merely to denote time or sequence, or for the purpose of reference does not usually form a proper name and is therefore not capitalized. There are, however, exceptions depending on common practice and usage, especially when the reference comes to characterize a specific item or set of items

act of 1928 *or* Act of 1928
amendment 5 *or* Amendment 5
article 1 *or* Article 1   book I *or* Book I
chapter 11 *or* Chapter 11   column 2
exhibit D   figure 7
interstate 95, *but usually* Interstate 95 or Route 66
page 2   paragraph 4
part I   plate IV
room A722   rule 8 *or* Rule 8

Common noun as part of a reference (cont.)
    schedule K *or* Schedule K   section 3
    spring 1926 *or* Spring 1926   table 4
    title IV *or* Title IV
    treaty of 1919 *or* Treaty of 1919
    volume X   war of 1914, *but* War of 1812

Definite article in proper place names

To achieve greater distinction or to adhere to the common form, the word *the* (or its equivalent in a foreign language) used as a part of an official name or title is capitalized. When such name or title is used adjectively, *the* is not capitalized.

    British Consul v. The Mermaid *(title of legal case)*
    The Dalles *(OR)*; The Weirs *(NH); but* the Dalles
      region; the Weirs' streets
    The Hague; *but* the Second Hague Conference
    El Salvador, Las Cruces, L'Esterel
    The Netherlands, *but* the Congo, the Sudan

In common practice, *the* is not capitalized in references to periodicals, vessels, airships, trains, firm names, etc.

    the *Times*   the *Mermaid*
    the Federal Express   the *Atlantic Monthly*
    the *Los Angeles Times*   the *Washington Post*

Particles in names of persons

In foreign names such particles as *d' da, de, della, den, du, van,* and *von* are generally capitalized unless preceded by a forename or title. Individual usage, if ascertainable, should be followed.

    Da Ponte, Cardinal da Ponte
    Du Pont, E.I. du Pont de Nemours & Co.
    Van Rensselaer, Stephen van Rensselaer
    Von Braun, Wernher von Braun

but d'Orbigny, Alcide d'Orbigny
de la Madrid, Miguel de la Madrid

In anglicized names such particles are usually capitalized, even if preceded by a forename or title, but individual usage, if ascertainable, should be followed.

Reginald De Koven
Thomas De Quincey
Henry van Dyke *(his usage)*
Samuel F. Du Pont

If copy is not clear as to the form of such a name (for example, *La Forge* or *Laforge*), the two-word form should be used.

De Kalb County *(AL, GA, IL, IN),*
but **DeKalb County** *(TN)*

In names set in capitals, *de, von,* etc., are also capitalized.

Names of organized bodies

The full names of organized bodies and their shortened names are capitalized; other substitutes most often regarded as common nouns are capitalized only in certain specified instances to indicate preeminence or distinction.

National governmental units:

U.S. Congress: **98th Congress, the Congress, Congress, the Senate, the House, Committee of the Whole, the Committee;** *but* **committee** *(nonspecific)*

Department of Agriculture: **the Department, Division of Publications, the Division,** *similarly* **all departmental units;** *but* **legislative, executive, and judicial departments**

Bureau of the Census: **the Census Bureau, the Bureau;** *but* **the agency**

Interstate Commerce Commission: **the Commission**

Government Printing Office: **the Printing Office, the Office**

American Embassy, British Embassy: **the Embassy;** *but* **the consulate, the consulate general**

Treasury of the United States: **General Treasury, National Treasury, Public Treasury, the Treasury, Treasury notes**

Department of Defense: **Military Establishment, Armed Forces, All-Volunteer Forces;** *but* **armed services**

Other: **French Ministry of Foreign Affairs, the Ministry; French Army, British Navy**

International organizations:

United Nations: **the Council, the Assembly, the Secretariat**

Hague Peace Conference of 1907: **the Hague Conference, the Peace Conference, the Conference**

Common-noun substitutes:

Virginia Assembly: **the assembly, the senate, the house of delegates**

California State Highway Commission: **Highway Commission of California, the highway commission**

Montgomery County Board of Health: **the Board of Health, Montgomery County, the board of health, the board**

Common Council of the City of Pittsburgh: **the common council, the council**

Buffalo Consumers' League: **the consumers' league, the league**

Republican Party: **the party**

Southern Railroad Co.: **the Southern Railroad, Southern Co., Southern Road, the railroad company, the company**

Riggs National Bank: **the Riggs Bank, the bank**

Yale School of Law: **Yale University School of Law; School of Law, Yale University; school of law**

Organized Bodies

The names of members and adherents of organized bodies are capitalized to distinguish them from the same words used merely in a descriptive sense.

a Representative (U.S. Congress)

a Socialist	a Democrat
an Odd Fellow	an Elk
a Communist	a Liberal
a Boy Scout	a Shriner

Names of countries, domains, etc.

The official designations of countries, national domains, and their principal administrative divisions are capitalized only if used as part of proper names, as proper names, or as proper adjectives.

United States: **the Republic, the Nation, the Union, the Government;** *also* **Federal, Federal Government;** *but* **republic** *(when not referring specifically to one entity),* **republican** *(in general sense),* **a nation devoted to peace**

New York State: **the State, a State** *(definite political subdivision of first rank),* **State of Veracruz, Balkan States, six States of Australia, State rights;** *but* **state** *(referring to a federal government, the body politic),* **foreign states, church and state, statehood, state's evidence**

Territory (Canada): **Yukon, Northwest Territories, the Territory(ies), Territorial;** *but* **territory of American Samoa, Guam, Virgin Islands**

Dominion of Canada: **the Dominion;** *but* **dominion** *(in general sense)*

Ontario Province, Province of Ontario: **the Province, Provincial;** *but* **province, provincial** *(in general sense)*

Crown Colony of Hong Kong, Cyprus: **the colony, crown colony**

The similar designations *commonwealth confederation (federal), government, nation (national), powers, republic,* etc., are capitalized only if used as part of proper names, as proper names, or as proper adjectives.

> British Commonwealth, Commonwealth of Virginia: **the Commonwealth;** *but* **a commonwealth government**
>
> Swiss Confederation: **the Confederation, the Federal Council, the Federal Government;** *but* **confederation**
>
> French Government: **the Government, French and Italian Governments, Soviet Government, the Governments;** *but* **government** *(in general sense),* **the Churchill government, European governments**
>
> Cherokee Nation: **the nation;** *but* **Greek nation, American nations**
>
> **National Government** *(of any specific nation);* but **national customs**
>
> Allied Powers, Allies *(in World Wars I and II); but* **our allies, weaker allies, Central Powers** *(in World War I); but* **the powers, European powers**
>
> Republic of South Africa: **the Republic,** *but* **republic** *(in general sense)*

Names of regions, localities, and geographic features

A descriptive term used to denote a definite region, locality, or geographic feature is a proper name and is therefore capitalized; also for temporary distinction a coined name of a region is capitalized.

> the North Atlantic States   the Gulf States
> the Central States   the Pacific Coast States
> the Lake States   East North Central States
> Eastern North Central States
> Far Western States   Eastern United States
> the West   the Midwest
> the Middle West   Far West

Names of regions, localities, etc. (cont.)
    the **Eastern Shore** *(Chesapeake Bay)*
    the **Badlands** *(SD and NE)*
    the **Continental Divide** *(Rocky Mountains)*
    Deep South   **Midsouth**
    the **Occident**   the **Orient**
    the **Far East**   **Far Eastern**   the **East**
    Middle East   **Middle Eastern** **Mideast**
    the **Promised Land** the **Continent** *(continental Europe)*
    the **Western Hemisphere**
    the **North Pole**   the **North and South Poles**
    the **Temperate Zone** the **Torrid Zone**
    the **East Side, Lower East Side** *(sections of a city)*
    Western Europe *(political entity)*
       but **lower 48** *(States)*, the **Northeast corridor**

A descriptive term used to denote mere direction or position is not a proper name and is therefore not capitalized.
    north   south   east   west
    northerly   northern   northward
    eastern   oriental   occidental
    east Pennsylvania   southern California
    northern Virginia
    west Florida *but* West Florida *(1763–1819)*
    eastern region   western region
    north–central region   east coast
    eastern seaboard   central Europe
    south Germany   southern France

Names of calendar divisions
The names of divisions are capitalized.
    January, February, March, etc.
    Monday, Tuesday, Wednesday, etc.
     but spring, summer, autumn, fall, winter

Names of historic events, etc.

The names of holidays, ecclesiastic feast and fast days, and historic events are capitalized.

Battle of Bunker Hill   Christian Era
Middle Ages. *but* 20th century
Feast of the Passover   the Passover
Fourth of July   the Fourth
Reformation   Renaissance   Veterans Day
War of 1812, World War I, *but* war of 1914, Korean war

Trade names

Trade names, variety names, and names of market grades and brands are capitalized. Common nouns following such names are not capitalized.

Foamite, Plexiglas, Snow Crop *(trade names)*
Choice lamb, Yellow Stained cotton *(market grade)*
Red Radiance rose *(variety)*

Scientific names

The name of a phylum, class, order, family, or genus is capitalized; the name of a species is not capitalized, even though derived from a proper name.

Arthropoda *(phylum)*   Crustacea *(class)*
Hypoparia *(order)*   Agnostidae *(family)*
Agnostus *(genus)* Agnostus canadensis; Aconitum
    wilsoni; Epigaea repens *(genus and species)*

In scientific descriptions coined terms derived from proper names are not capitalized.

aviculoid   menodontine

Capitalize the names of the celestial bodies Sun and Moon, as well as the planets Earth, Mercury, Venus, Mars, Jupiter, Saturn, Uranus, Neptune, and Pluto. Lowercase the word *moon* in such expressions as "the moons of Jupiter."

does not apply.

CAPITALIZATION

Fanciful appellations

A fanciful appellation used with or for a proper name is capitalized.

Big Four	Hub *(Boston)*	New Frontier
Dust Bowl	Keystone State	
Prohibition	Great Society	New Deal
Great Depression	Holocaust	Third World

Personification

A vivid personification is capitalized.

The Chair recognized the gentleman from New York.

For Nature wields her scepter mercilessly.

All are architects of Fate,

Working in these walls of Time.

Religious terms

Words denoting the Deity except *who, whose,* and *whom;* names for the Bible and other sacred writings and their parts; and names of confessions of faith and of religious bodies and their adherents and words specifically denoting Satan are all capitalized.

Heavenly Father, the Almighty, Lord, Thee, Thou, He, Him; *but* himself, God's fatherhood

Mass, red Mass, Communion

Divine Father; *but* divine providence, divine guidance, divine service

Son of Man, Jesus' sonship, the Messiah; *but* a messiah, messiahship, messianic, messianize, christology, christological

Bible, Holy Scriptures, Scriptures, Word, Koran; *also* Biblical, Scriptural, Koranic

New Testament, Ten Commandments

Gospel (memoir of Christ); *but* gospel truth

Apostles' Creed, Augsburg Confession

303

Episcopal Church, an Episcopalian, Catholicism, a
  Protestant
Christian; *also* Christendom, Christianity, Christianize
Black Friars, Brother(s); King's Daughters, Daughter(s);
  Ursuline Sisters, Sister(s)
Satan, His Satanic Majesty, Father of Lies, the Devil;
  but a devil, the devils, devil's advocate

Titles of persons

Civil, religious, military, and professional titles, as well as
those of nobility, immediately preceding a name are capitalized.

President Lincoln	King George
Ambassador Gibson	Lieutenant Fowler
Chairman Smith	Dr. Bellinger
Nurse Cavell	Professor Leverett

Vice-Presidential candidate White
  but baseball player Jones, maintenance man Smith

To indicate preeminence or distinction in certain specified
instances, a common-noun title immediately following the
name of a person or used alone as a substitute for it is capitalized.

Title of a head or assistant head of state:

George Washington, President of the United States:
  the President, the President-elect, the Executive, the
  Commander in Chief, former President Truman;
  similarly the Vice President, the Vice-President-elect
Charles Robb, Governor of Virginia: the Governor of
  Virginia, the Governor; *similarly* the Lieutenant Governor; *but* secretary of state of Idaho, attorney general
  of Maine

CAPITALIZATION

Title of a head or assistant head of a National governmental unit:

Secretary of State: the Secretary; *similarly* the Acting Secretary, the Under Secretary, the Director; the Chief or Assistant Chief; the Chief Clerk; etc.

Titles of the military:

General of the Army Supreme Allied Commander Chairman, Joint Chiefs of Staff; *but* the commanding general; general *(military title standing alone)*

Titles of members of diplomatic corps:

the American Ambassador	the British Ambassador
the Ambassador	the Senior Ambassador
His Excellency	the Envoy
the Minister	the Chargé d'Affaires
the Chargé	Ambassador at Large
Minister Without Portfolio	

but the consul general; the consul; the attaché; etc.

Title of a ruler or prince:

Elizabeth II, Queen of England: the Queen, the Crown, Her Most Gracious Majesty, Her Majesty; *similarly* the Emperor, the Sultan, etc.

Charles, Prince of Wales: His Royal Highness

In formal lists of delegates and representatives of governments, all titles and descriptive designations immediately following the names should be capitalized if any one is capitalized.

A title in the second person is capitalized.

Your Excellency	Your Highness
Your Honor	Mr. Chairman
Madam Chairman	Mr. Secretary

but not salutation:

my dear General	my dear sir

Titles of publications, documents, acts, laws, etc.

In the English titles of periodicals, series of publications, annual reports, historic documents, and works of art, the first word and all important words are capitalized.

Atlantic Charter, Balfour Declaration;
   but British white paper

Reader's Digest; *but* Newsweek magazine

Uniform Code of Military Justice, House Resolution 45, Presidential Proclamation No. 24, Executive Order No. 24, Royal Decree No. 24, Public Law 89–1;
   but Senate bill 416; House bill 61

Declaration of Independence; the Declaration

Constitution (of th e United States or other country);
   but New York State constitution: first amendment, 12th amendment (see rule 12.10).

Kellogg Pact, North Atlantic Pact, Treaty of Versailles;
   but treaty of peace, treaty of 1919

The Blue Boy, Excalibur, Whistler's Mother *(paintings)*

All principal words are capitalized in titles of addresses, articles, books, captions, chapter and part headings, editorials, essays, headings, headlines, motion pictures and plays (including television and radio programs), papers, short poems, reports, songs, subheadings, subjects, and themes.

In the short or popular titles of acts (Federal, State, or foreign) the first word and all important words are capitalized.

Revenue Act   Walsh–Healey Act

Freedom of Information Act;
   but the act, Harrison narcotic law, Harrison narcotic bill, interstate commerce law, sunset law

Capitalization of the titles of books, etc., written in a foreign language should conform to custom in that language.

First words

The first word of a sentence, of a direct quotation, or of a line of poetry, is capitalized.

> He asked, "And where are you going?"
>
> Lives of great men all remind us
> We can make our lives sublime.

The first word of a fragmentary quotation is not capitalized.

> He objected to "the phraseology, not to the ideas."

Headlines

Generally, centered heads are set in capitals, and sideheads are set in lowercase with only the first word and proper names capitalized, In heads making two lines, wordbreaks should be avoided.

In heads set in caps, a small-cap *c* or *ac* is usually used in such names as *McLean* or *MacLeod;* otherwise a lowercase *c* or *ac* is used.

In such names as *LeRoy, DeHostis, LaFollette,* etc. (one-word forms only), set in caps, the second letter of the particle is made a small cap, if available; otherwise lowercase is used.

In matter set in caps and small caps or caps and lowercase, capitalize all principal words, including parts of compounds which would be capitalized standing alone. The articles *a, an,* and *the;* the prepositions *at, by, for, in, of, on, to,* and *up;* the conjunctions *and, as, but, if, or,* and *nor;* and the second element of a compound numeral are not capitalized.

> **World en Route to All-Out War**
> **Man Hit With 2-Inch Pipe**
> **Yankees May Be Winners in Zig-Zag Race**
> **Ex-Senator Is To Be Admitted**
> **Building on Twenty-first Street**
> **One Hundred and Twenty-three Years**

If a normally lowercased short word is used in juxtaposition with a capitalized word of like significance, it should also be capitalized.

Buildings In and Near Minneapolis

In a heading set in caps and lowercase or in caps and small caps, a normally lowercased last word, if it is the only lowercased word in the heading, should also be capitalized.

All Returns Are In

The first element of an infinitive is capitalized.

Controls To Be Applied; *but* **Aid Sent to Disaster Area**

In matter set in caps and small caps, such abbreviations as *etc.*, *et al.*, and *p.m.* are set in small caps; in matter set in caps and lowercase, these abbreviations are set in lowercase.

PLANES, GUNS, SHIPS, ETC.
James Bros. et al. *(no comma)*
In re the 8 p.m. Meeting
Planes, Guns, Ships, etc.

Accents in cap lines are usually omitted even if the same words carry accents in text.

Addresses, salutations, and signatures

The first word and all principal words in addresses, salutations, and signatures are capitalized.

Interjections

The interjection *O* is always capitalized; within a sentence, other interjections are not capitalized.

Sail on, O Ship of State!
For lo! the days are hastening on.
But, oh, how fortunate!

Capitalization Examples

Academy: **Air Force Academy**
    Coast Guard Academy
    National Academy of Sciences
    Naval Academy *but* **service academies**

Act (Federal, State, or foreign), popular title:
    Appropriation Act   **Flood Control Act**
    Lend–Lease Act; *but* **lend–lease materials, etc.**
    Revenue Act   **River and Harbor Act**
    Tariff Act   **Trademark Act**
    Walsh–Healey Act; *but* **Walsh–Healey law (or bill)**

ACTION *(independent Federal agency)*

Adjutant General, the

Administration: **Farmers Home Administration**
    Food and Drug Administration
    Veterans' Administration
    but **Adams administration; administration bill, etc.**

Administrative Law Judge Davis;
    but **Judge Davis, an administrative law judge**

Ages: **Age of Discovery**   **Dark Ages**
    Elizabethan Age   **Golden Age** *(of Pericles)*
    Middle Ages
    but **atomic age, Cambrian age, ice age, space age, etc.**

Agreement:
    General Agreement on Tariffs and Trade (GATT)
    International Wheat Agreement, the wheat agreement
    but **the Geneva agreement, the Potsdam agreement,**
    Paris peace agreement

Airport: **La Guardia Airport, National Airport, the airport**

Alliance for Progress, Alliance for Progress program

alliances and coalitions: **Atlantic alliance**
   European Economic Community
   North Atlantic Treaty Organization

Ambassador: **British Ambassador, the Ambassador, the Senior Ambassador, Ambassador at Large**

amendment: **Social Security Amendments of 1954, 1954 amendments, the social security amendments**

American: **American Legion**
   American National Red Cross, the Red Cross

Amtrak *(National Railroad Passenger Corporation)*

Ancient Free and Accepted Masons, a Mason, a Freemason

Arab States, Arabic numerals

Archives: **National Archives, the Archives, Archivist of the United States, the Archivist**

Arctic: **Arctic Circle**   **Arctic Current**
   Arctic Ocean   **Arctic zone**
   arctic clothing   **arctic conditions**

Area: **Cape Hatteras Recreational Area, White Pass Recreation Area, etc.**
   but **free trade area, Metropolitan Washington area, bay area**

Articles of Confederation *(U.S.)*

Association:
   American Association for the Advancement of Science
   Federal National Mortgage Association (Fannie Mae)
   Young Women's Christian Association

Atlantic: **Atlantic Charter**   **Atlantic coast**
   Atlantic Coast States   **mid–Atlantic**
   Atlantic time, standard time *but* **transatlantic**

Authority: **Port of New York Authority, the port authority**
   Tennessee Valley Authority

Awards: **Academy Award, Distinguished Service Award,**
   Merit Award, Mother of the Year Award, etc.

Bank: **Export–Import Bank of Washington,**
   Export–Import Bank   **Farm Loan Bank of Dallas**
   Dallas Farm Loan Bank   **farm loan bank**
   farm loan bank at Dallas
   Federal Reserve Bank of New York
   Richmond Federal Reserve Bank;
      but **Reserve bank at Richmond**
   Federal Reserve bank,   **Reserve bank**
      but **blood bank, soil bank**

bay: **San Francisco Bay area, the bay area**

belt: **Bible Belt**   **Corn Belt**   **Cotton Belt**
         Dairy Belt   **Sun Belt**   **Wheat Belt**
   but **money belt**

Bible, Biblical, Scriptures, etc.

Bill of Rights *(historic document); but* **GI bill of rights**

board: **Civil Aeronautics Board**
   Federal Reserve Board
   Board of Health of Montgomery County, Montgomery
   County Board of Health, the board of health

bond: **Government bond**   **savings bond**
        series EE bond   **Treasury bond**

borough: **Borough of the Bronx, the borough**

Bowl: **Dust Bowl, Rose Bowl, the bowl**

Boy Scouts *(organization),* **a Boy Scout, a Scout, Scouting**

Brother(s) *(adherent of religious order)*

Calendar, if part of name, else **calendar**

311

Capital, Capital City, National Capital *(Washington, DC)*;
   but the capital (State)

Capitol Building *(with State name)*, the capitol:
   Halls of Congress   Capitol Hill; the Hill
   Capitol rotunda   Senate wing

caucus: Republican caucus;
   but Black Caucus *(incorporated name)*

center: Agricultural Research Center
   Kennedy Center for the Performing Arts, the Kennedy
   Center   Lincoln Center

Central America

Central States

central time

century: first century, 20th century, etc.

chairman: Chairman of the Board of Directors *(Federal)*;
   but chairman of the board of directors *(non-Federal)*

chamber: Chamber of Commerce of Ada, Ada Chamber of
   Commerce, the chamber of commerce

the Chamber *(Senate or House)*

Chargé d'Affaires, British, etc.; the Chargé d'Affaires;
   the Chargé

cheese: bleu cheese, Camembert cheese, Cheddar or cheddar cheese, cottage cheese, cream cheese, Parmesan
   cheese, provolone cheese, Roquefort cheese

Chief of Staff

Chief Judge, if referring to Federal unit

Christian, Christian name, Christendom, Christianity,
   Christianize, *but* christen

church calendar: Christmas   Easter
  Lent   Pentecost   Whitsuntide

city: East Side   French Quarter *(New Orleans)*
  Latin Quarter *(Paris)*   North End
  the Loop *(Chicago)*   City Hub *(Boston)*
  Twin Cities   Windy City *(Chicago)*
  New York City; *but* city of New York

coast: **Atlantic, east, gulf, west**

code: **Federal Criminal Code**
  Internal Revenue Code   Tax Code
  Penal Code   Criminal Code
  Television Code   Uniform Code of Military Justice
  ZIP Code (copyrighted)
  but civil code, flag code, Morse code

college: **Cornell College   College of Bishops**
  but electoral college

college degrees: **bachelor of arts, master's degree, etc.**

commission: **Commission of Fine Arts**
                  Commission on Civil Rights

commissioner:
  Commissioner of Immigration and Naturalization
  Commissioner of Patents
    but a U.S. commissioner

committee: **Appropriations Committee**
  Subcommittee on Appropriations
  **Democratic National Committee, Democratic national
  committeeman, Republican National Committee, Republican national committeeman, the national committee, the committee**
  but Baker committee, ad hoc committee

Common Cause

Common Market *(European Economic Community)*

Commonwealth of Australia, Virginia, etc.;
British Commonwealth, the Commonwealth

community: **European Economic Community, the Community;** *but* **the Atlantic community**

comptroller: **Comptroller of the Currency**

confederate: **Confederate** *(of the American Confederacy)*
Confederate Army   **Confederate Government**
Confederate soldier   **Confederate States**

congress: **National Congress of Parents and Teachers**
national legislature: **Congress, the Congress,**
Congress of the United States, Congress of Bolivia,
First Congress, Second Congress, 11th Congress

Congressional: **Congressional Directory**
First Congressional District, the First District,
the congressional district
Congressional Medal of Honor
but **congressional action, congressional committee**

constitution: Capitalized with the name of a country or
standing alone when referring to a specific constitution;
New York State Constitution; the Constitution

consul: **British consul, consul general, British consul general, consulate, British consulate**

Consumer Price Index *(official title)*
but **a consumers' price index** *(descriptive)*

continent: **American Continent, the continent**
but **the Continent** *(continental Europe)*

continental: **Continental Army, Continental Congress,**
Continental Divide, Continental Shelf,

a continental shelf, continental Europe, continental
United States

Corn Belt

corporation: Federal Deposit Insurance Corporation
Rand Corporation, Union Carbide Corporation,
the corporation

corps: Adjutant General's Corps
          Job Corps   Marine Corps
Corps of Engineers, Army Engineers, the Engineers;
   but Army engineer, the corps
Peace Corps, Peace Corpsman, the corpsman
Reserve Officers' Training Corps *(ROTC)*
Youth Corps
but diplomatic corps, corpsman, hospital corpsman

Cotton Belt

council: Boston City Council, the council
Her Majesty's Privy Council; the Privy Council;
the Council

county: Prince Georges County, county of Prince Georges,
the county

court (of law): Circuit Court of the United States for the
Tenth Circuit, Circuit Court for the Tenth Circuit, the
circuit court, the court, the tenth circuit
Court of Appeals for the State of North Carolina, the
court of appeals, the court

Crown, if referring to a ruler; but crown colony, lands, etc.

current: Arctic Current   Humboldt Current
         Japan Current   customhouse . customs official

Dairy Belt

Dark Ages

decorations, medals, etc., awarded by any national government: the medal, the cross, the ribbon
Commendation Ribbon, Congressional Medal of Honor, Distinguished Service Cross, Good Conduct Medal, Legion of Merit, Medal of Freedom, Medal of Honor, Purple Heart, Silver Star Medal; *also* Carnegie Medal, Olympic Gold Medal; *but* gold medal

department: Department of Agriculture
Yale University Department of Economics, the department of economics, the department

Diet (Japanese legislative body)

disease: acquired immune deficiency syndrome *(AIDS)*
German measles   Parkinson's

Dixie, Dixiecrat

Dust Bowl

Elizabethan Age

Emancipation Proclamation

Eurodollar

exchange: New York Stock Exchange, the stock exchange, the exchange

farm: Johnson Farm; *but* Johnson's farm

Father of his Country *(Washington)*

Federal *(sovereign power)*

Federal Government *(of any national government)*
but a federal form of government

First Family *(Presidential)*

First Lady *(wife of President)*

flags: Old Glory, Stars and Stripes, Tricolor *(French)*, Union Jack *(British)*

Foreign Office: Minister of Foreign Affairs, the Minister
  Ministry of Foreign Affairs, the Ministry

forest: Angeles National Forest, Black Forest;
  but State and National forests

Girl Scouts *(organization)*: a Girl Scout, a Scout, Scouting

G-man

Golden Rule

Gospel, if referring to the first four books of the
    New Testament; *but* gospel truth

great: Great Depression   Great Divide
         Great White Way (New York City)
         great circle (navigation)

gross national product *(GNP)*

High School *(if part of name)*; Western High School,
  the high school

Holy Scriptures; Holy Writ *(Bible)*

Hospital, if part of a name; else the hospital, hospital
  corpsman

international: International Court of Justice, the Court
    international banks   international dateline
    international boundary   international law

Interstate 95, I-95, the interstate

Irish potato

Ivory Coast

Jersey cattle

Job Corps

judge: chief judge, circuit judge, district judge; *but* Judge
  Bryan

lake: Lake Erie, Lake of the Woods, Salt Lake; the lake

line: **DEW** *(Distant Early Warning)* line   **State line**

Metropolitan New York; *but* **New York metropolitan area**

Middle Ages

Middle Atlantic States

mint: **Philadelphia Mint, the mint**

Monument: **Bunker Hill Monument**
          Washington Monument   **the monument**

Mr. Chairman; Mr. Secretary; etc.

national: **National Archives   National Forest**
     Yellowstone National Park, Yellowstone Park,
     the national park, the park
     national anthem   national customs
     national spirit   national defense

numbers: capitalized if spelled out as part of a name
     Air Force One *(Presidential plane)*   **Charles the First**

office: **Executive Office   Foreign Office**
     Office of Management and Budget   Patent Office
     but **New York regional office, the regional office**

Pope; *but* **papal, patriarch, pontiff, primate**

prize: **Nobel Prize   Pulitzer Prize**

project: **Project Vanguard;** *but* **Vanguard project**
     Project Head Start

Quad Cities

the Reformation

Sabbath; Sabbath Day

Sermon on the Mount

Third World

ZIP Code *(Postal)*